COMPARING MEDIA FROM AROUND THE WORLD

ROBERT MᶜKENZIE

East Stroudsburg University of Pennsylvania

with contributions by Ian Weber and Nabil Dajani

PEARSON

Boston ■ New York ■ San Francisco

Mexico City ■ Montreal ■ Toronto ■ London ■ Madrid ■ Munich

Paris ■ Hong Kong ■ Singapore ■ Tokyo ■ Cape Town ■ Sydney

Series Editor: *Molly Taylor*
Series Editorial Assistant: *Suzanne Stradley*
Marketing Manager: *Mandee Eckersley*
Senior Production Editor: *Beth Houston*
Editorial-Production Service: *Stratford Publishing Services, Inc.*
Composition Buyer: *Linda Cox*
Manufacturing Buyer: *JoAnne Sweeney*
Electronic Composition: *Stratford Publishing Services, Inc.*
Cover Administrator: *Joel Gendron*

For related titles and support materials, visit our online catalog at www.ablongman.com.

Copyright © 2006 Pearson Education, Inc.

Between the time website information is gathered and then published, it is not unusual for some sites to have closed. Also, the transcription of URLs can result in typographical errors. The publisher would appreciate notification where these errors occur.

ISBN 0-205-40242-9

Library of Congress Cataloging-in-Publication Data

TK

Printed in the United States of America

10 9 8 7 6 5 4 3 2 1   09 08 07 06 05

Photo Credits: Page 204, Sun (London), March 7, 2003, page 3; www.thesun.co.uk; reprinted by permission, ©NISyndication Limited, London.

Slainte, Willie. . . .
Luceo Non Uro

CONTENTS

CHAPTER EIGHT   Accessibility of Media   137

CHAPTER NINE   Media Content   185

CHAPTER TEN   News Reporting   249

CHAPTER ELEVEN   Media Imports and Exports   303

CHAPTER TWELVE   Media Audiences   327

CHAPTER THIRTEEN   Conclusion   357

References   363

Index   367

PREFACE

That the world continues to be affected by globalization is an overused but bluntly accurate cliché. And the role of media distribution and consumption in facilitating globalization has been monumental. Not only do media continuously spread content around the world to even the most remote areas, but media industries also have become a central component of the world economy. Accordingly, there is a growing need for universities to have access to books that support course offerings in the study of media from around the world to enhance a better understanding of the position of media in our lives and the ways in which media shape our overall consciousness of the world. Outside of the university setting, there is also a pressing need for people who are experts on the media as well as people who are naturally interested in the media to have access to factual information about how media differ across the world. *Comparing Media from Around the World* should prove to be a valuable contribution to the needs of both of these audiences. It is my hope that *Comparing Media from Around the World* offers a wealth of information and perspective on many of the exciting and profound ways in which mass media are both different and similar across the globe.

WHY I PUT TOGETHER THIS BOOK

I decided to put together this book because of various levels of enlightenment that I have seen people (including myself) go through when traveling to other countries and getting exposed to media in those countries. As people in a foreign country begin to look at or read foreign newspapers, watch foreign television shows, listen to foreign radio programs, and surf foreign web sites, they quickly learn that there are many fundamental differences between the media originating in their own country and the media in other countries. People who experience and study media from a variety of countries usually learn how the media available in a particular country shape idiosyncratic perceptions of both that country and of foreign countries. Such realizations constitute life-changing developments in peoples' awareness of both the limitations and the possibilities of media in shaping interpretations about the countries and the peoples of the world. What people who study media from another country usually realize is that in order to identify the boundaries of perceptions created by domestic media, they must be exposed to media from another country.

Much of the information presented in this book is the result of on-site research conducted specifically for this project. During the two and a half years it took me to write the book, I personally collected information on location in six of the countries: France, Ghana, México, Sweden, the UK, and the USA. While I was in these countries, I pursued three main research activities. One activity involved meeting with and interviewing officials who worked for government-related media regulators, professionals who worked for media organizations, scholars who had expertise on the media, and citizens who were knowledgeable about the media. I conducted the interviews according to a standard protocol of questions and topics, and recorded each interview on my laptop computer. In total, I recorded approximately eighty hours of interviews during my research. These interviews generated much of the information that is presented in Chapter 6 on Regulation of Media, Chapter 7 on Financing of Media, Chapter 8 on Accessibility of Media, and Chapter 12 on Media Audiences. The people I interviewed are listed in the acknowledgments. My second research activity was to access and collect media samples from each country: all national newspapers and selected regional and local newspapers; publications that listed television programs; a sampling of television programs, and public and private television newscasts (which I recorded on videotape); publications that listed radio programs; a sampling of radio programs, public and private radio newscasts (which I recorded on cassette and on my laptop computer); and internet web pages (which I consulted primarily in internet cafés). My third research activity was to take digital photographs of media outlets and samples of media content to illustrate concepts in this book.

Most of the writing and the ideas in this book are my own. However, for two of the countries discussed—China and Lebanon—the material is contributed by three scholars who have lived, traveled, and researched in those countries. Ian Weber, Ph.D., Assistant Professor of the Department of Communication at Texas A&M University in the USA, and his assistant Lu Jia, a Chinese graduate student at the School of Communication and Information at Nanyang Technological University in Singapore, contributed the material on China. Ian Weber's credentials include having worked for News Corporation as a freelance photojournalist in Europe and as a staff photographer and then as a journalist for the Australian Provincial Newspaper (APN) Group in Australia. Nabil Dajani, Ph.D., Professor of Communication at the American University of Beirut in Lebanon, contributed the material on Lebanon for this book. Nabil Dajani's credentials include having served as a member of UNESCO's International Panel of Experts on Communication Research and having helped to initiate the international debate for a new world communication and information order (which is discussed in this book in Chapter 2 on Climate of Globalization). These three contributors also provided digital photographs for the material on China and Lebanon.

I also had a lot of help for this book from two other colleagues, particularly the material in Chapter 9 on Media Content and Chapter 10 on News Reporting. For the material I wrote on French media in these chapters, I was generously assisted by Francois Taveneaux, an Instructor of English at the University of Nancy in Nancy, France. For the material I wrote on Swedish media in these two chapters, I was generously assisted by Peter Arvell, president of Akkafrakt, a transportation company in Sweden.

HOW THIS BOOK MIGHT BE USED

This book is targeted at four different audiences. The primary audience is students at universities across the world taking lower- or upper-division courses that go by many different titles, but in essence are focused on how media differ across the world. Some common titles of these courses include Comparative Media, Comparative Media Systems, International Media, International Telecommunications, Global Media, Global Media System, International Mass Communication, and Transnational Media. Another audience for this book is students taking courses in political science, rhetorical studies, and international management, who may find the book useful as a supplemental text. Another audience for this book is researchers seeking access to readings on the interplay between media and culture, regulation, and globalization. And a fourth audience is general-interest readers who want to know what kinds of media outlets and media content are available in some countries across the world.

This book can be used according to at least two methods. One method is to tackle the material in the longer chapters—particularly Chapter 6 on Regulation of Media, Chapter 9 on Media Content, and Chapter 10 on News Reporting—in more than one discussion session. It may be appropriate during these readings to include two to four countries per discussion session. A second method—especially for instructors and readers who find material on certain countries to be of less interest than material on other countries—is to exclude selected countries from discussions and/or reading assignments related to certain chapters. In either case, readers and instructors would benefit from accessing foreign media content during discussions of most chapters, because foreign media content should be used to illustrate concepts presented throughout the book.

ACKNOWLEDGMENTS

I would like to express my appreciation to people who helped me with this project, as well as the institutions that provided support for my research:

Senior Research Assistant Heather Metz, East Stroudsburg University of Pennsylvania, USA

Other Research Assistants Laurie Cubria, East Stroudsburg University of Pennsylvania, USA
Megan Drobniak, East Stroudsburg University of Pennsylvania, USA
Jillian Kane, East Stroudsburg University of Pennsylvania, USA

Production Assistants Frank Kutch, Kelly McKenzie

Translation Assistants Marcus Arnfeldt, Vanessa Diaz, Peter Arvell, Rolph Lucassen, Angela McKenzie, Rosben Olivera, Adria Perez, Jeff Ruth, Francois Taveneaux, Tanya Verba, and Ralph Vitello

Sources of Financial or Resource Support
Bonnie Lynch, Vice President of Academic Affairs, East Stroudsburg University of Pennsylvania, USA; Joe Cavanaugh, Interim Dean of Arts and Sciences, East Stroudsburg University of Pennsylvania, USA; Bonnie Neumann, Dean of Arts and Sciences, East Stroudsburg University of Pennsylvania, USA; Department of Communication Studies, East Stroudsburg University of Pennsylvania, USA; Faculty Development and Research Committee, East Stroudsburg University of Pennsylvania, USA; Pearson Publishing, USA; Summer Mini-Grant, East Stroudsburg University of Pennsylvania, USA; Summer Sessions, East Stroudsburg University of Pennsylvania, USA; US Embassy, México

Experts Who Were Interviewed or Consulted
Ivor Agyeman-Duah, Head of Public Affairs, Ghana Embassy, Washington DC, USA / Frank Asante, former Journalist, Ghana News Agency, Ghana / Edmond Sa'b of an-Nahar, Executive Editor-in-Chief of *an-Nahar* newspaper, Lebanon / Miguel Angel Sanchez de Armas, Director of RadioTelevision of Veracruz, México / Abdulai Awudu, Head of Production, Television Africa, Ghana / Angel Martinez Armengol, Website Coordinator, *Diario Xalapa* newspaper, México / Gösta Backlund, Assistant Producer, Swedish Television (SVT), Sweden / Susan Berg, Information Officer, Radio and Television Authority, Sweden / Lydia Boakye, Editor, Ghana Broadcasting Corporation, Ghana / Philip Candice, Senior Media and Public Relations Officer, Independent Television Commission (ITC), UK / James Dickmeyer, Press Attache, US Embassy, México / Nana Essilfie-Conduah, Head of Current Affairs, *TV Africa*, Ghana / Jon Henley, Paris Bureau Chief, *Guardian* newspaper, France / Milena Hurtado, Professor of Foreign Languages, East Stroudsburg University of Pennsylvania, USA / Ivonne Gutiérrez Carlin, Managing Editor for *La Politica* newspaper, México / Mario Lozano Carbonell, Coordinator of Information at Avan News, México / Lorna Carmichael, Public Relations Manager, the *Sun*, UK / Joseph E. T. Dottey, Deputy Executive Secretary, National Media Commission, Ghana / Waddick Doyle, Chair of the Department of International Communication, American University of Paris, France / Bernard Forson, Deputy Director-General, National Communications Authority, Ghana / Raymundo Jimenez Garcia, Columnist, *Image of Veracruz* newspaper, México / Mario Daniel Badillo Gonzalez, Media Analyst for the Office of the Governor of the State of Veracruz, México / Alvaro Luis Lozano Gonzalez, Legal Director for Radio, Television, Cinematography, Secretary of the Government, México / Miguel Valera Hernandez, Coordinator of Information, *Punta Yaparte* newspaper, México / Hack Kampmann, Senior Adviser, Broadcasting Commission (GRN), Sweden / Daniel Kenu, Senior Reporter, Sports, Ghana News Agency (GNA), Ghana / Ulrika Koling, Legal Advisor, Radio and Television Authority, Sweden / Carmen Landa, Cultural Affairs Specialist, US Embassy, México / Sven Linderoth, Channel Manager, Swedish Radio, Sweden / Messan Mawugbe, Director of Research and Monitoring, National Media

Commission, Ghana / Isabelle Mariani, Director of International Affairs, Conseil Superieur De L'Audiovi-suel (CSA); Maitre de Conferences a l'lnstitut d'Etnoles Politiques de Paris; Charges de Couter France à l'Universite de Paris I, France / Jån Martennson, Freelance Columnist for *Sydsvenska Dagbladet*, Sweden / Catherine Mathis, Vice President of Corporate Communications, *The New York Times* Company, New York / Julie McCatty, Chief Press Officer, The UK Radio Authority, UK / Jose Ortiz Medina, Columnist, Coordina-tor of Information, *The Local Milenio* newspaper, México / Yvonne Mignot-Lefevre, Researcher, Centre National de la Recherche Scientifique, University of PARIS VII, France / Andrea Millwood Hargrave, Research Director, Broadcasting Standards Commission (BSC), UK / Anna Mansson, Legal Adviser, Broad-casting Commission (GRN), Sweden / Mikael Nilsson, Head of Corporate Communication and International Relations, Swedish Radio (SR), Sweden / Felice Nudelman, College Marketing Manager, *New York Times* newspaper, New York, USA / Carlos Antonio Ortiz, Contacto Informativo, México / Sam Quainoo, Professor of Political Science, East Stroudsburg University of Pennsylvania, USA / Mike Perko, Chief of Office of Communications and Industry Information, Federal Communications Commission (FCC), USA / Ebo Quansah, Editor, *Evening News* newspaper, Ghana / Ekuba Quarmine, Producer, Ghana Television, Ghana / Seth Quarmine, Public Relations/Media Coordinator, ArtRack, Ghana / Bo Reimer, Professor of Media and Communication Science, Malmö University, Sweden / Arturo Montano Robles, Press Specialist, US Embassy, México / Nina Rosenkvist, Communications Officer, The Swedish Radio and Television Authority, Sweden / Tony Stoller, External Relations Director, Office of Communications (Ofcom), Britain, UK / Deepak Tripathi, former producer, BBC World Service, UK / Leonel Bellido Villa, Coordinator of Engineer-ing, Radiotelevision de Veracruz, México / Ernesto Villanueva, coordinator of the Area of Law and Informa-tion, National Autonomous University of México, México / Hans-Heinrich Vogel, Professor of Public Law, University of Lund, Sweden / Juan Carlos Prieto Williams, IT and Telecom Commercial Specialist, US Com-mercial Service, US Embassy México / Patricia Boakye Yiadom, editor, Ghana Broadcasting Corporation, Ghana / Samuel Yirenkyi, Radio Announcer, Joy FM, Ghana

Other Assistants
Alyssa Acken, Peter Arvell, Joe Ashcroft, Andre Aubertin, Chris Babcock, Judi Bevin, Lisa Bompartito, Bill Bretzger, Jessica Curtis, Andrea Devoto, Martina Doncheski, Jim Fagin, Foley, Kathy Glidden, Angela Grison, Keith Hering, Penny Hugger, John Jay, Jillian Kane, Michael Kish, Frank Kutch, Erin La Scala, Dan Lynch, Lois Lynch, Rolph Lucassen, Culley McGuire, Angela McKenzie, Cameron McKenzie, Fiona McKenzie, Gordon McKenzie, Patricia McKenzie, Willie McKenzie, Amparo Garrido Méndez, Odalys Metz, Patricia Miller, Mickey Moynihan, Brian Murphy, Kay O'Grady, Emily Paris, Reginald Perry, Katy Ritten-house, Kevin Ross, Mike Southwell, Greg Stolarik, Jennifer Stolarik, Florence Taveneaux, Molly Taylor, Guy Thomas, Luis Vidal, Wenjie Yan

Reviewers
Anthony B. Chan, University of Washington / Fernando P. Delgado, Arizona State University / Paul Gross-wiler, University of Maine / Harry W. Haines, Trinity University / William Hart, Old Dominion University / Fran Hassencahl, Old Dominion University / Martin P. LoMonaco, Nassau Community College / Norbert Mundorf, University of Rhode Island / Jyotika Ramaprasad, Southern Illinois University / Ted Schwalbe, State University of New York, Fredonia / John L. Sullivan, Muhlenberg College

Institutional Support
I am especially grateful to East Stroudsburg University of Pennsylvania, USA, for granting me a sabbatical to write this book, and for providing substantial resources and funding to help facilitate my research. I also want to express my appreciation to other institutions where I gained access to research data: the University of Brighton, England; the London School of Economics, England; the Seaford Public Library, England; Sussex University, England; the University of Veracruzana, México; and the University of the Virgin Islands, St. Croix.

ABOUT THE AUTHOR

Robert McKenzie, Ph.D., is a Professor in the Department of Communication Studies at East Stroudsburg University of Pennsylvania, USA. He also serves as the department's Internship Coordinator, and as the Advisor for the university's 1000-watt radio station, WESS (90.3 FM), at which he also hosts a talk show and a "Stones Hour" (an hour of the Rolling Stones). He served as an Ambassador for International Programs at East Stroudsburg University during a sabbatical he took in 2003. His publication record includes journal articles and book chapters on international media, college radio, radio and television news, obscenity and indecency regulations, and television talk shows. He was raised in the USA and has also lived in England (his father was raised in Scotland, and his mother was raised in England). He can be reached by e-mail (mckenzie@po-box.esu.edu) or visit his web site (http://www.esu.edu/~mckenzie).

■ ■ ■ ■ ■

CHAPTER 1

INTRODUCTION

PRIMER QUESTIONS

1. Where have you been in the world? What countries have you visited?
2. What countries or regions of the world do you feel that you have some familiarity with?
3. What countries or regions of the world do you feel that you know very little about?
4. What kinds of foreign newspapers, radio programs, television shows, and web sites from other countries have you been exposed to?
5. What are the main sources of information in your life (media sources and nonmedia sources) that have taught you about those countries and regions of the world that you have not visited?

The world is so big that trying to conceptualize its size, even in the most general of terms, is intimidating—to say the least. Try picturing in your head all the land on the surface of the world, an area that covers some 93 million square kilometers (about 58 million square miles). As large an area as this is, all that land covers a mere quarter of the world's total surface area. The other three quarters (some 280 million square kilometers—about 174 million square miles) is covered by water. These massive, abstract numbers can be made more tangible by considering that it would take the average passenger airplane two full days of nonstop flying to circle the equator all the way around the world. Along the way, the plane would pass through 22 different time zones.

The gargantuan size of the world is rivaled not only by the number of people who live on it, but also by the number of languages those people use to communicate. In 2004, the total population of the world was approximately 6.5 billion, collectively speaking some 7,000 languages. Because China has the largest population in the world, more people speak Chinese than any other language (about 885 million people). Next is Spanish, spoken by about 332 million people. Then comes English, spoken by about 322 million people. Even though there are more people in the world who speak Chinese than English, and more people who speak Spanish than English, in fact English is spoken in more places than either Chinese or Spanish. One reason for the worldwide reach of English is that it is the most frequently used language in media content circulating to more places around the world. For example, according to internetworldstats.com, in 2004 the English language comprised 35.9 percent of total internet use, followed by Chinese (13.2 percent), Japanese (8.3 percent), German (6.8 percent), and Spanish (6.7 percent).

The world has about 200 countries. Considering how many countries and how many people there are, plus all the means of transportation that are available, it is truly incredible that most people experience only a minuscule portion of the world. Consider these statements: The average person travels to just *a few* of the world's 200 countries in a lifetime. Most people do not even visit *most* of the world's countries. Hardly anyone visits *all* of the world's countries. And either by choice or circumstance, plenty of people never leave the *one* country where they live. When you put these statements together, it becomes astonishing that the vast majority of people see only a minuscule portion of the world in their lifetimes—even people who travel quite a bit.

So how do most people come to know what they think they know about the world's countries? Well, it should come as no great revelation that people learn about the majority of the world's countries not by experiencing them directly, but instead by gaining secondhand information from friends, family, teachers, coworkers, and of course the media. The term **media** can have a very broad definition, as in any technology that carries a message—ranging from a T-shirt to a telephone to a television. But the term *media* can also be divided into two more narrow definitions: *mass media* (e.g., newspapers, magazines, radio, and television) and *personal media* (e.g., mobile [cell] phones, pagers, fax machines, and personal digital assistants [PDAs]). **Mass media** tend to distribute standardized messages to mass audiences, whereas **personal media** tend to distribute customized messages to smaller audiences or to individuals. Mass media traditionally have been used for synchronous (at the same time), "point to mass" communication (e.g., a radio song heard by thousands of listeners driving cars). Personal media traditionally have been used to facilitate asynchronous (at different times), "point to point" communication (e.g., an email message from a sister read the next day by a brother).

However, the traditional distinction between these two media is breaking down because the internet is radically challenging previous paradigms of media distribution patterns. For a start, the internet is both an auxiliary outlet for content already created for newspaper, radio, and television media, as well as a primary outlet for web page content in its own right. The internet also allows for point-to-point communication that is both asynchronous (e.g., sending an email) and synchronous (e.g., instant messaging), plus it allows for point-to-mass communication that is both asynchronous (e.g., a mass email) and synchronous (e.g., a web blog).

At any rate, it is clear that what we think we know about the world is largely facilitated by a combination of newer and older media technologies constantly bringing information into our homes, our modes of transportation, our places of employment, our eating and drinking hangouts, and really just about anywhere we travel. When it comes right down to it, media are probably responsible for nurturing most of our ideas about unfamiliar locations across a world that is so gargantuan we hardly experience it directly.

MEDIA FROM AROUND THE WORLD

People experience media in radically different ways across the countries of the world because each country has a unique set of conditions that influence the accessible media content. Identifying and exploring these fascinating differences is what this book is all about. To take one example: Across different countries, are newspapers routinely purchased at shops or are they delivered to homes? Do people normally read newspapers in the morning or in the afternoon? How do governments, advertisers, audiences, and other entities influence the content that appears in newspapers? How and why do some influences serve to block certain kinds of content such as nudity, while permitting or even mandating other kinds of content such as truthful advertising? These questions reveal how interesting it is to compare the similarities and differences of newspapers across various countries of the world.

If enough of these kinds of questions are asked not just about newspapers, but about electronic media as well, a larger and more intriguing question soon emerges: What do we learn when we compare media from around the world? That is the central question pursued in this book. It is a question that produces a global perspective of the world's media rather than a local perspective from the vantage point of a single country. Thus, *Comparing Media from Around the World* attempts to provide insights into how the media that we access in a particular country help to shape perceptions of ourselves, of countries that we have never visited, and ultimately of the entity we call the world.

Four media in particular are compared in this book: newspapers, radio, television, and the internet. Individually, each of these media distributes content on a daily basis—unlike film or magazines. Collectively, newspapers, radio, television, and the internet distribute the bulk of media content around the world, and their combined impact on the daily lives of people across the world is colossal. Therefore, comparing these four media across various countries will provide a heady study of the interplay between people, governments, media companies, and media content around the world.

Yet, though these four media have much in common in terms of both worldwide reach and regular distribution of content, fundamentally the internet stands apart from the others—which to some extent presents an awkward fit for this book. What makes the internet so different from the other media is that it truly is a global medium, confined less by cultural or geographical factors than by audience accessibility. In other words, the internet is more about whether people can get to it, how long they have to access it, and how fast it is, than about what content it distributes. This fundamental difference between the internet and the other media is why, in several chapters of this book, the sections on the internet are shorter than the sections on newspapers, radio, and television. However, in the chapter that has to do with how audiences use media (Chapter 12), the material on the internet is much greater than the material on the other three media. Despite their fundamental differences, however, the four media of newspapers, radio, television and the internet can be studied as a group because they are pervasive across the sprawl of world media, and because they are continuously producing and distributing content to people all over the world.

Studying media content from around the world cannot be done in a vacuum. For example, examining a television show by itself does not tell us very much about how that television show came into being. This larger question is addressed only by studying elements of a larger media system that produced the television show. The elements of a media system that are studied in this book include the following: cultural characteristics of eight countries, philosophies for media systems, regulation of media, accessibility of media, media content, news reporting, imports/exports, financing of media, and media audiences. Taken together, these elements of a media system facilitate a process in which human beings generate ideas and then transform those ideas into media content that gets distributed to audiences across the world.

As you read this book and study how the elements of media systems compare across different countries, you probably will be exposed to new kinds of media content. This in itself can be exciting. However, even more appealing is the prospect that when you study foreign media, you have the chance to reach a higher level of understanding about the role of media in shaping your own perceptions of other countries and regions, of the world, and indeed of life. That is the raison d'être (reason to be) for *Comparing Media from Around the World*—to provide you with tools for examining media systems operating within and across different countries, which in turn will enable you to achieve a greater understanding of yourself, plus the country in which you live, plus a larger portion of the world.

EIGHT COUNTRIES SELECTED FOR *COMPARING MEDIA FROM AROUND THE WORLD*

The worth of this book in large part rests on the set of media systems that are compared. If too many media systems from too many countries are studied, the material can come across as a cacophony of disjointed facts rather than as a coherent whole, representing fair and equitable comparisons of the selected countries. On the other hand, if too few media systems are analyzed, the material will come across as a parochial case study with limited relevance to other media systems across the world. To avoid these pitfalls, three basic criteria were used to select the countries for this book. The first and most important criterion was to choose a group of countries that represents an interesting variety of languages, governmental structures, cultural attributes, socioeconomic conditions, histories, geographic locations, and ultimately media systems. The second criterion was to choose a manageable number of countries for generating interesting and primarily descriptive information about different media systems around the world. And the third criterion was to choose a group of countries that could be written about from the vantage point of firsthand experience. Using these criteria, eight countries were selected, which are previewed here in alphabetical order.

China (People's Republic of China)

China has a media system that is undergoing tremendous change in its political and economic structure as it incorporates free-market mechanisms into a communist governing structure. China continues to exercise tight control over content in newspapers, and on radio, television, and the internet. China has the world's largest population and therefore represents the largest potential domestic media audience. China is the only communist country studied in this book.

France

France has a media system in which the state is both a regulator of broadcast content and a competitor for broadcast audiences. The French government takes an active role in promoting culture in French media content. France has an extensive global media reach through its associations with former colonies and current territories. France has regulations that set quotas for how much foreign-language media can be imported, to preserve the stature of French culture and the French language.

Ghana (The Republic of Ghana)

Ghana has a media system that gained constitutional freedom from government control in 1992. As a result, democratic government and a private media sector are both in early stages of development. To a great extent, each relies on the other for legitimacy and continuing maturation. Compared to many other African countries, Ghana is politically stable, but continues to face challenges of poverty and poor public health. The Ghanaian government takes an active role in fostering the development of a private media sector and in educating journalists about professional ethics. Ghana is the only African country studied in this book.

Lebanon (The Republic of Lebanon)

Lebanon has a media system that is among the most advanced and free in the Middle East region. In the 1950s, the press developed into a pan-Arab media read by people all over the Arab world. This regional influence lasted until the civil war of 1975 to 1989, which drained human and material resources from the media in Lebanon. In post-civil-war Lebanon, the private sector plays a more active role in developing the country's media system than the government. The government, however, actively restricts content that arouses religious or ethnic conflicts. Lebanon is the only Arab country compared in this book.

México (Mexican United States)

México has a well-developed media system, even though México as a country continues to face challenges of poverty and hunger. México is a developing democracy, building on the elections of 2000 in which one political party's seventy-one-year hold on power was broken. The Mexican government takes an active and direct role in financing and regulating print media. The Mexican government has established a system in which government publicity is regularly distributed by print and broadcast media.

Sweden (Sverige)

Sweden has a media system that allows limited commercial competition in the broadcast marketplace. Sweden has a legal framework that provides citizens—including journalists— with unfettered access to public records. Because the Swedish language is not spoken very much outside of Scandinavia, there is little opportunity to export Swedish media content. Therefore, mass media in Sweden are often used to teach English as a second language to the population. The Swedish government takes an active role in restricting violent media content and protecting children from advertising.

The UK (United Kingdom)

The UK has a sophisticated media system that has a fairly equal balance between private commercial media and public noncommercial media. The publicly funded British Broadcasting Corporation (BBC) is one of the most recognizable media brands throughout the world. The UK has an extensive global reach in the distribution of media content because of the pervasive use of English around the world, and because of the UK's associations with Commonwealth and former colonial countries.

The USA (United States of America)

The USA's media system is the largest overall media exporter in the world. Television content originating from the USA occupies large portions of television broadcasts in other countries. Relative to other countries, imported media are not easy to find in the USA. The government in the USA for the most part prefers market forces to regulate media content, but takes an active role in restricting potentially obscene media content.

LIMITATIONS AND STRENGTHS OF THE EIGHT SELECTED COUNTRIES

In Map 1.1, the eight countries selected for comparison are shaded to show how they are spread out geographically across the world.

Of course, with approximately 200 countries in the world, it is natural to wonder about countries that could have or should have been included in this book, and to critique weaknesses of those selected. For example: Three of the countries have English as a first language (Ghana, the UK, and the USA). Three of the countries are located in Europe. Six of the countries are predominantly Christian (China is predominantly secular; Lebanon is 60 to 70 percent Muslim). And all of the countries are in the Northern Hemisphere. Readers concerned about these issues may also be concerned about other issues, such as whether China offers the best representation of Asia, or whether Ghana offers the best representation of Africa, or whether Lebanon is Muslim enough, and so on.

However, the countries selected for this book are not meant to be a representative sample of the media systems across the world. Rather, the prime directive of this book is to select countries that present a fascinating study of media systems around the world—media systems that happen to embody a considerable range of operations, policies, and content. Moreover, it is not necessary for this book to contain all the countries you would have selected, because its chapter structure is designed to allow you to extrapolate information so you can pursue your own comparisons and derive your own findings about additional countries or regions in which you have particular academic or personal interests.

BEYOND *COUNTRY* AS A UNIT OF ANALYSIS

Because media tend to spread across clusters of countries, the use of country as a unit of analysis in this book should serve only as a necessary starting point for revealing broader themes and trends in media systems that cross national boundaries into global regions. Accordingly, you should approach the material in *Comparing Media from Around the World* as a means of stimulating your own investigation and observation of themes and trends that exist in media systems from any or all countries across the world. Whatever the countries and regions are that you would like to examine, you should be able to inform your endeavor by applying the terms, concepts, theories, and analysis presented in this book. Especially in Chapters 4 through 12—which compare elements of the individual media systems that exist in these eight countries—the material should provide you with potent concepts that you can use to compare elements of media systems found in countries not discussed in this book. Therefore, by design, this book is not just about the media systems of eight countries. Rather, this book is written to enable you to apply the concepts discussed to any countries or regions in the world, including countries you have experienced, as well as countries with which you have little familiarity.

Obviously, a study of media across different countries cannot inventory and examine every newspaper, radio station, television channel, and web site that is distributed. That task is impossible not only because the universe of available media is so bountiful but also because the selection of media is in a constant state of flux. Therefore, the comparisons of media across the eight countries in this book are performed on examples of media that are understood to represent general and interesting themes of what is available. Above all else, the specific examples of media chosen for this book are intended to capture the spirit of a country's media system.

THE IMPORTANCE OF COMPARING

Comparing is an important word in the title of this book. Comparing is a fundamental tool of analytical thinking that enables distinctions to be drawn between two or more things. Moreover, comparing is a tool that we start using very early in life when we assess, for example, that some people are taller (or shorter) than others. A basic comparison of this sort is not about rendering a judgment as to which object is better or worse, but rather about evaluating how two or more objects are similar or different.

Yet, comparing can produce a more profound impact on our learning process than simply identifying similarities and differences. Comparing can produce a deeper understanding of the self. This understanding is made possible by discovering the **point of reference** by which we evaluate other objects and experiences. When we compare two or more objects, we often make assessments about those things that are different from what we have experienced; therefore, the process of comparing inadvertently helps us to identify the reference points that form conceptions of the self. In other words, when observing objects and experiences that are different, we also are defining ourselves by the things that are familiar rather than those that are unfamiliar. When it comes to comparing media systems, it is possible to define the points of reference that have been cultivated in you through your experiences with a particular set of media from particular countries or regions.

Furthermore, the use of comparing as a methodological tool to study media across the world is essential in overcoming the tendency to unfairly evaluate another country according to the values of your own country. In the book *Images of the U.S. Around the World* (1999) edited by Yayha Kamalipour, I describe the hasty affliction of **cultural myopia**, wherein people who are not exposed to another country through a range of media content are prone to evaluating that country with shortsighted negativity when they do come across basic information about that country. In essence, the shortsightedness makes unfamiliar objects in the foreground blurry (information about an unfamiliar convention in

MAP 1.1 *Map of World with Eight Selected Countries Shaded*
Source: DK Images.

another country, which lacks an evaluative context), but makes familiar objects in the background clear (information about a familiar convention in the "home" country, which includes an evaluative context). Because of the tendency to resolve the ambiguous foreign-country information using unambiguous home-country background information, misjudgments can occur. For example, have you ever heard someone ask whether it is true that the British drink warm beer? The underlying judgment in this question might really be: How can the British drink warm beer as it must taste really bad? In actual fact, the British commonly drink ales—a type of beer that is traditional in the UK—at 13°C/55°F. This temperature happens to be warmer than the usual temperature (7°C/45°F) at which lagers—a different kind of beer served in many other countries around the world—are commonly served. Therefore, on closer inspection the term *warm* is not as appropriate as the term *warmer,* a subtle mistake indicating that cultural myopia may be at play in evaluating ales by using familiar standards of the home country rather than standards of the UK. What does a beer description have to do with cultural myopia and the use of media? Well, it is a simple example of how cultural myopia can arise in the absence of basic background knowledge about habits of another country that otherwise could be obtained through media content. In the beer example, someone who has either visited the UK or who has watched certain television shows set in the UK (those with scenes taking place in pubs) would probably not use the term *warm* to describe beer served in the UK. Therefore, as a methodological tool, comparing media helps us to avoid cultural myopia in making shortsighted assessments about countries and cultures with which we are unfamiliar.

In this book, Chapter 3 introduces the variables (called elements) to be compared across media systems in France, Sweden, the UK, the USA, México, China, Ghana, and Lebanon. Though the concept of a media system is formally defined in Chapter 3, for now it can be understood as a collection of elements that interact with each other to produce media content. Beginning with Chapter 4 and continuing through Chapter 12, one element at a time is defined and then compared across the media systems of the eight countries. Identifying and defining elements of a media system helps to ensure that the comparisons of media systems in the eight countries are balanced and fair.

A RHETORICAL PERSPECTIVE

In the final analysis, this book would be of limited value if the discussions stopped at the level of comparison. To gain a fuller understanding of media from around the world, the analysis must lead to interpretations of the findings. Interpretation is derived from analyzing what a finding **means**. This book seeks to identify what the findings mean in terms of how the elements of a country's media system affect the content that is available, how that media system relates also to cultural characteristics that are unique to a country or common to a region, and how audiences within countries are led to interact with media.

This book uses a rhetorical perspective to help answer what the comparisons in this book might mean. As Martin Medhurst and Thomas Benson explain in *Rhetorical Dimensions of Media* (1984), a **rhetorical perspective** can offer an analysis of how media "invite" a particular audience to think, feel, or behave, given a particular context. For example, a rhetorical perspective can offer an analysis of how the overall selection of television channels that are accessible in a particular country invites an audience to watch some programs at the expense of other kinds of programs and, more important, to have a certain outlook as a result of, or in association with, the television viewing. A rhetorical perspective is particularly appropriate for a study of media around the world for two reasons. First, a rhetorical perspective does not conclude that there is one fixed meaning to a phenomenon; instead, it concentrates on reasonable meanings for a message, given the audience and the context. The key here is an underlying assumption that the audience plays an active role in making meaning from a message. In this book, **audience** has two definitions: (1) as readers of this book and (2) as the people who access the media content described in this book. The rhetorical perspective will be applied to both audiences to help interpret meanings from the comparisons of media across different countries.

Second, a rhetorical perspective provides a way to analyze what it is that we think we know through the media. Sometimes the outcomes of such an exercise are not so endearing. Part of this analysis involves identifying options for selecting media content that are available in some countries but not in others. Put another way, a rhetorical perspective analyzes how thoughts and opinions are shaped by routine sources of information and entertainment, which in turn are shaped by unique elements that make up a country's media system. Thus, when you see phrasing in this book such as the television show "invites" the audience to believe . . . or the newspaper "leads" the audience to think . . . , you are witnessing a rhetorical perspective being applied to the analysis. In other words, a rhetorical perspective is being used to indicate a reasonable meaning of an aspect of a media system that is being examined, given a context and an audience.

Because a rhetorical perspective can operate in the background of a study, it sometimes is difficult to spot when you are reading the results of the study. Therefore, it might satisfy your curiosity to know that a rhetorical perspective is at work in certain sections of all the chapters. The first rhetorical section is the Primer Questions at the beginning of each chapter. These questions are designed to involve you as the reader, as the audience for this book, in helping to make meaning from the material that is presented. In essence, the Primer Questions presented before the chapter's reading material begins should invite you to actively participate in the learning process. The second rhetorical section is the introduction to each chapter, wherein important conceptual material is provided as a setup for the ensuing comparisons of an element of media systems across the eight countries. Within this introductory material, you will find definitions of key terms to help tap into a common understanding of the categories of information that are being investigated. The third rhetorical section is the Comparative Summary at the ends of Chapters 4 through 12. In these three sections, rhetorical statements are made about the degrees of difference or similarity between the elements of media systems across the eight countries. These statements are designed to capture reasonable judgments about the major areas in which the media systems are different or similar. In addition to these three sections, you can spot a rhetorical perspective at work in most of Chapter 12 on media audiences and in Chapter 13, the conclusion. While Chapter 12 focuses on how audiences use media in the eight countries, Chapter 13 attempts to round up the findings from the previous chapters and then to speculate reasonable implications not only for the eight countries that were studied in this book but also for media systems across the world.

THE ORGANIZATION OF CHAPTERS IN THIS BOOK

Other books in this field are usually organized according to a vertical structure—that is, each chapter focuses on a specific country or region. But a vertical organization makes it difficult to compare media in countries that are discussed in the beginning with countries that are discussed way at the end of the book. Therefore, *Comparing Media from Around the World* has a horizontal structure: Each chapter focuses on an element of a media system that is compared across eight countries. The advantage of this organizational scheme is that comparisons between countries can be made within each chapter according to the particular element that has been isolated. To a great extent, this book is not primarily about the media systems of specific countries, but about the elements that make up a media system and the ways in which those elements have taken shape in some countries.

In each of the remaining chapters of this book, the order in which the eight countries are discussed will adhere to the following logic to create a natural flow to the information: The first three countries to be discussed are France, Sweden, and the UK, in that order, because they represent the most countries from a single geographical region (Europe). Because these three European countries are all well developed (as opposed to developing), the USA is discussed next because it too is a developed country. México follows because it shares a border with the USA in the region of North America. Then, China, Ghana, and Lebanon are discussed respectively, because—like México—they are developing countries. China follows México because, of the three remaining countries, it is closest in size and population to México; Ghana and Lebanon then follow China because they are both relatively small countries. The intention of presenting the countries in this particular order is to create a smooth and logical flow of the information presented in this book, not to imply that a media system in one country or media systems across a subgroup of countries are superior to a media system in another country or media systems across another subgroup of countries.

There are three special features in this book that are designed to enhance what can be learned. One special feature is the use of photos to show vivid examples of media. A second special feature of this book is the attempt to strike a productive balance between theory, criticism, and practice, especially in an academic field that goes by many names including global media, international media, world media, international telecommunications, global media systems, and many other variations. And a third special feature of *Comparing Media from Around the World* is the Primer Questions section mentioned earlier, which appears at the beginning of each chapter. Usually, discussion questions in textbooks are placed at the end of chapters, after the reader has already grappled with the information and is itching to move on to the next chapter. The result is that readers often skip over discussion questions because they are seen as unnecessarily redundant of the preceding material. Alternatively, Primer Questions placed at the beginning of a chapter can energize the baseline knowledge of the reader in such a way as to stimulate the reader's own discovery and understanding of ideas before they are subsequently explored in the rest of the chapter. As a consequence, the Primer Questions presented before each chapter's body of material should encourage the reader to participate more actively in the learning process, rather than passively accept the author's timeline for rendering information.

SUMMARY

The world is so large it is difficult to grasp as a whole, made up of individual countries. Media are instrumental in teaching people about most of the world's countries. Countries serve as a good starting point for comparing media across the world because each country possesses a set of unique characteristics that define the indigenous media system. A selection of eight very different countries—France, Sweden, the UK, the USA, México, China, Ghana, and Lebanon—provides a rich cross section of media systems to compare. Applying a rhetorical perspective to the comparisons helps to provide reasonable interpretations of observations about how media differ across the countries. Organizing book chapters by comparing elements that cut across the media systems of each of the eight countries helps us assess similarities and differences more clearly than organizing chapters by countries or regions.

■ ■ ■ ■ ■

CHAPTER 2

CLIMATE OF GLOBALIZATION

PRIMER QUESTIONS

1. What does *globalization* mean to you?

2. Do you think people, countries, and regions of the world are growing closer together or moving further apart? In what ways?

3. What factors are causing the world to come closer together or to move further apart?

4. What is the role of travel, communication technology, media companies, and audience media use in bringing the world closer together or moving it further apart?

5. What groups of people from which countries or regions might be dissatisfied with or concerned about the way in which media affect the world coming closer together or moving further apart? What do you think their concerns are?

Globalization is a kind of worldwide climate in which people, industries, governments, and countries across the world are being propelled into closer political, economic, and cultural unions. Though the globalization we are experiencing today appears to be in a period of intense acceleration, in future years the rate of globalization will make the current pace seem quite slow. Because globalization is happening all around us and is affecting the lives of everyone, we need to understand why it is taking place and how it relates to media circulating across the world. As Edward Herman and Robert McChesney chronicle in *The Global Media: The New Missionaries of Corporate Capitalism* (1997), the leading impetus for globalization is a corporate profit-making initiative that is reaching beyond domestic markets to fertile foreign markets in order to secure cheaper labor pools and raw materials, and new consumers for existing and yet-to-be-developed products and services. If you have ever called a help line for a product you have purchased and ended up talking to a customer service representative in another country—perhaps India—you have experienced a single instance of how globalization leads companies to outsource certain functions to cheaper labor markets located in foreign countries. The media industry is just one of many commercial industries worldwide that are contributing to the climate of globalization.

The promiscuity of corporate profit making is leading to increasing coordination among governments and global quasi-government institutions. Organizations such as the World Bank, the International Monetary Fund (IMF), the World Trade Organization (WTO), the World Health Organization (WHO), the International Telecommunications Union (ITU), the United Nations (UN), and the European Union (EU) are all international bodies to which national governments have ceded control over certain domestic economic and political activities. These international bodies increasingly influence the affairs of member countries.

Globalization is both a modern and a very old phenomenon. In ancient Greece, Plato wrote about a very early kind of globalization in *The Republic*. Though at that time the Greeks thought the entire world consisted of the region in close proximity to the Mediterranean Sea, Plato contemplated what an ideal nation-state would consist of within the known community of nation-states. Six thousand years after Plato, Marshall McLuhan, in *The Global Village: Transformations in World Life and Media in the 21st Century* (1992), wrote about a mind-set being created through advances in media technology wherein people all around the world feel connected to each other as if they lived in the same local community.

At the turn of the 2000 millennium, scholars from almost all university disciplines continue to study what globalization means, where we are in the globalization process, what the effects of globalization really are, and what the effects are likely to be. In the field of media, scholars have primarily studied globalization to understand the role of communication technologies both in facilitating globalization and in being facilitated by globalization. Much of the research has focused on the epistemological effects of globalization on human consciousness. Epistemology is essentially the study of how our knowledge is limited by the information to which we are exposed. Significant works that address the epistemology of globalization include Robert Stevenson's *Global Communication in the Twenty-First Century* (1994), Hamid Mowlana's *Global Communication in Transition: The End of Diversity?* (1996), Thomas McPhail's *Global Communication: Theories, Stakeholders, and Trends* (2002), and Yahya Kamalipour's *Images of the U.S. Around the World* (1999).

One area of communication research into epistemological effects of globalization involves a confinement of perceptions about foreign locations due to the particular selection and content of media that are accessed. Works such as Yahya Kamalipour's *Images of the U.S. Around the World* (1999) examine how the USA is perceived across selected countries through films, radio music, and television shows. This research has shown that the exported media tend to portray Americans as having unflattering qualities, such as being rich and boisterous. Ironically, these perceptions are often conveyed by media content exported from the USA. Epistemologically based research also examines this kind of theme from a reverse vantage point—for example, how people in the USA perceive other countries to be dangerous or backward on the basis of a limited range of media content that is generated primarily by USA media outlets. In essence, an epistemological line of inquiry can reveal how residents of a particular country are effectively held captive to a narrow perspective of other countries because of the limited selection of media that are accessed.

FOUR FACTORS STIMULATING GLOBALIZATION

Globalization is being stimulated by at least four factors that are converging through corporate commercialism into an aggressive pursuit of international markets. (See Figure 2.1.)

International Travel

The first factor affecting globalization is the exponential increase in international travel. Simply put, more people are traveling to more destinations than ever before. To fully appreciate the incredible expansion of the number of people traveling abroad, it is instructive to look at

FIGURE 2.1   *Four Factors Stimulating Globalization*
Source: Laurie Cubria.

data on "international tourist arrivals" from 1950 through 2000, as depicted in Figure 2.2. According to the World Tourism Organization (2002) in *Tourism Highlights* and *World Tourism in 2002: Better Than Expected,* the number of international tourists grew from around 200 million people in 1970 to more than 700 million people in 2002. It is estimated that by the year 2020, international travel will expand to over 1.5 billion people per year.

When people travel to other countries and regions of the world, they set into motion an exchange of information that helps give rise to a greater consciousness about countries and regions of the world. The exchange of information occurs at three levels. First, people who travel abroad gain knowledge about "foreign" countries. Second, people who travel abroad interact with people in other countries and thereby pass on information about their own country to the people in other cultures. Third, people who travel abroad bring back knowledge of foreign countries and spread information—however condensed it becomes— mainly through conversations with relatives, friends, and acquaintances.

Why are more people traveling abroad? Certainly television is helping to smooth the way for increased travel to foreign destinations. On satellite and cable channels in particular, travel shows provide audiences with a glimpse into the look and feel of foreign countries and cultures. These shows help to identify countries that might be interesting to visit because of their history, landscape, architecture, scenery, climate, foods, inexpensive goods, relaxed laws, and other attractive qualities. At a very basic level, travel shows help to demystify countries that previously might have been perceived as peculiar, or not perceived at all.

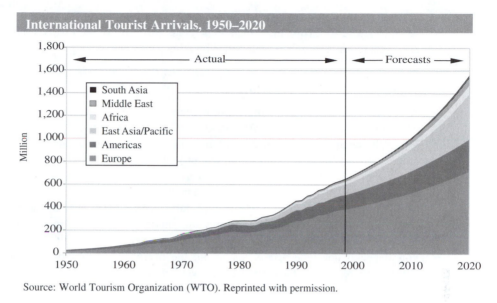

Source: World Tourism Organization (WTO). Reprinted with permission.

FIGURE 2.2   *International Tourist Arrivals, 1950–2020*

Source: World Tourism Organization (WTO). Reprinted with permission.

In addition, the growth in travel is due to an expansion in the number of airlines and airline routes. According to the Official Airline Guide (OAG), which operates the world's most comprehensive flight schedules database, the number of airlines in the world has increased dramatically. In 1929 there were thirty-five airlines. In 1993 there were 790 airlines. And in 2003 there were 930 airlines. The total number of passenger flights that took place throughout the world in 2002 was 25,652,223. The increase in airlines and airline routes has provided more options of destinations and airline carriers for travelers. In addition, the increase in airline routes has created more competition among airlines, causing a general drop in the prices of plane tickets. Increasingly, international travelers can schedule travel to more locations, and select from a wider range of departure and arrival times with fewer airplane connections.

Another reason that more people are traveling abroad is the internet. According to the Travel Industry Association of America, in 2003 close to 100 million people worldwide booked travel through the internet. Use of the internet for this task is advantageous to both airlines and travelers. Airlines use the internet to sell discount seats on flights that are underbooked. The internet makes it possible for airlines and brokers to sell discounted seats as last-minute trips. The internet also makes it possible for prospective travelers to conduct research into travel destinations by visiting chat rooms in which travel is commonly discussed. Prospective travelers can conduct keyword searches such as "biking travel," which brings up a range of web sites providing virtual tours of biking destinations. In essence, the internet provides travelers with more opportunities to customize their own trips by booking accommodations, transportation, and excursions themselves, rather than by booking a package through a travel company where these activities have been preselected. As a result, according to a Goldman Sachs study reported in the May 13, 2003, *London Evening Standard,* travelers are saving more than 50 percent of the cost of their trips if they book flights and hotel rooms themselves, rather than booking a package holiday.

Communication Technologies

A second factor that is playing a prominent role in globalization involves advances in communication technologies. At one level, the personal communication technologies—especially email and web-based interactive chat programs such as Instant Messenger, ICQ, and Windows Messenger—plus mobile (cell) phones, PDAs, and fax machines have made communication across national boundaries easier, cheaper, and faster. At another level, advances in television technologies are spurring corporate commercialism and globalization. Primarily because of satellite and cable distribution systems, television listings increasingly include channels and programs that either originate in foreign countries or make mention of people and events in foreign countries. As a result, depending on where you live and how you access television, the average selection of television programs includes more international content than ever before.

Global Media Conglomerates

A third factor affecting globalization is the rise of the global media conglomerate. A **global media conglomerate** is a giant parent corporation that presides over an amalgamation of wholly and partially owned subsidiaries, companies, and divisions that are scattered across the world, and that are afforded great local autonomy within individual countries in terms of product design and distribution. Global media conglomerates grow through mergers between companies, acquisitions of companies, and strategic alliances with other conglomerates. Sometimes it is difficult to trace media content back to a specific global media conglomerate because the company or division that produced the media content is jointly owned by more than one global media conglomerate. Therefore, global media conglomerates are not necessarily distinct entities, but instead are fragmented ownership alliances that sometimes intermingle with each other through joint ventures.

Global media conglomerates have largely replaced multinational companies as the predominant business model for overseas media distribution. As Richard Gershon explains in *Telecommunications Management* (2001), the old model of a multinational company places a central headquarters in a particular country and runs the subsidiary companies and the company divisions abroad according to a set of core values emanating from the central headquarters. In contrast, global media conglomerates have a decentralized value system that responds to local market conditions in individual countries and regions with content that may or may not be desired in home country or other foreign markets served by the conglomerate. For example, Viacom's *MTV* in the USA generally runs less risqué but more violent music videos than those aired by *MTV* in European countries. This example illustrates how media conglomerates have a decentralized value system that gears programming to the perceived unique market demands of individual countries and regions.

Global media conglomerates are greatly diversified, in that they attain revenue not only from a wide range of media products and services, but also from nonmedia products and services. For example, General Electric (GE) owns the National Broadcasting Company (NBC) television network, the GE Financial Network (which sells auto insurance, home mortgages, and stocks and bonds), and the General Electric Aircraft Engine corporation (which sells jet engines), as well as other properties. Table 2.1 lists the top seven global media conglomerates in the world in 2004. Consider how colossal their media holdings are, and consequently how many of their products and services touch your own life on a regular basis as you read newspapers, listen to the radio, watch television, and access the internet.

Yet, global media conglomerates can be difficult to conceptualize as distinct entities because they are incredibly complex organizations. Typically a giant parent company owns multiple subsidiary companies. For example, Viacom owns the Infinity Radio group, which in turns owns CBS Radio. Because the parent company is not usually in the forefront when media content is exhibited, the parent company can be largely invisible to the public. The subsidiary companies of global media conglomerates have greater name and identity recognition, though sometimes they also remain invisible when media content is exhibited if their branding is not present in the content.

Another complexity is the worldwide reach of global media conglomerates. Since it is impossible for us to be in all of the world's countries at the same time, it is difficult to understand a single instance of media content as one component in the worldwide organizational structure of a global media conglomerate. For example, when you watch a television show, most of the time you probably are not tracing the show back through the channel that carries it to the company that produced it, to the company that owns both the channel and the show, to the parent corporation that owns that company as well as other companies, to as many of the countries you can think of in which the show is distributed.

The rise of the global media conglomerate is challenging the conception of nationality as a primary defining influence on self-identity. Because the global media conglomerate is a decentralized and largely amorphous entity that stretches across country borders, audiences are targeted regardless of where they live. Such cross-border assembling of audiences has led to the conjecture that the role of national boundaries in helping to form individual identity and social cohesiveness is being greatly diminished. Some believe that the emerging conception of self is guided not as much by where a person lives, but rather by the media content that he or she accesses.

However, despite the diminishment of national boundaries, the country as a unit remains a central concept of globalization. That is, though media products are increasingly marketed across country borders, the products are shaped and consumed uniquely within individual countries, and influenced uniquely by regulations within individual countries that set the parameters of media content in response to countrywide perceptions of cultural values. For example, the children's television program *Blues Clues* is distributed in both the USA and in the UK. However, there are two essential differences that are a result of shaping *Blues Clues* as a product according to perceptions of production conventions and audience needs that differ between the countries. One difference is that the host of the program in the USA version is American, whereas the host of the program in the UK version is English. Another difference is that the UK version includes an educational song that the host sings about things children should do when they get ready for bed (e.g., brushing their teeth, and going potty so they "don't have to get up in the middle of the night"). In

TABLE 2.1   Global Media Conglomerates (GMC)

GMC	HOME COUNTRY	SELECTED PROPERTIES (FULL OR PARTIAL OWNERSHIP)	PRODUCTS/SERVICES
Time-Warner	USA	Time Life Books, Book of the Month Club, Warner Books, HBO, HBO en Espanol, HBO Hungary, Warner Brothers Studios, Hanna-Barbera Cartoons, Time Magazine, Fortune, Sports Illustrated, People, Atlantic Group Records, Warner Brothers music, AOL, CNN, New Line Cinema	Books, Cable, Direct Broadcast Satellite, Films, Film Production, TV Shows, TV Production, Magazines, Online Services, Music, Theme Parks, Retail Merchandise
Walt Disney	USA	Miramax Books, The Disney Channel, ESPN, A&E Television, History Channel, Tele-Munchen, Hamster Productions France, Scandinavian Broadcasting System, Eurosport England, Buena Vista Television, Touchstone Television, Walt Disney Pictures, Buenavista International, ABC Television Network, ABC Radio Network, ABC Internet Group, Nascar.com, Lyric Street Records, Mammoth Records, Disneyland, Disneyworid, MGM Studios	Books, Cable, Television Shows, Television Productions, Film Production, Magazines, Newspapers, Online Services, Music, Theater, Theme Parks and Resorts, Retail Merchandise
Bertelsmann	Germany	Random House, Ballantine, Fodor's, Book-of-the-Month Club, Bertelsmann Media, Circulo de Lectores, France Loisirs, Barnes&Noble, CLT-UFA television/radio, RTL TV, VOX television, Channel 5, UFA Film and Television Production, Holland Media House, Radio RTL, Fun Radio, Radio Hamburg, McCalls magazine, Femme magazine, Impulse Brigitte magazine, Nepszahadsa newspaper, Financial Times Deutschland newspaper, BMG, Arista Records, Lycos Fireball	Books, Television Shows, Television Stations, Television Production, Magazines, Newspapers, Music, Online Services
Viacom	USA	Simon and Schuster, The Free Press, CBS Television Network, MTV Networks, Nickelodeon, Paramount Television, Showtime, The Movie Channel, Infinity Radio, Infinity Outdoor, Paramount Pictures, United Cinemas International, Sonicnet.com, Blockbuster, Raging Waters theme park	Books, Cable, Television Shows, Television Production, Radio Shows, Radio Production, Billboard Advertising, Film Production, Online Services, Video Rental, Theme Parks
News Corporation	Australia	HarperCollins Publishing, Hearst Book Group, Zondervan Publishing House, Fox News, Fox Sports,	Books, Television Shows, Television Production, Cable, Direct Broadcast Satellite, Films,

TABLE 2.1   *(Continued)*

GMC	HOME COUNTRY	SELECTED PROPERTIES (FULL OR PARTIAL OWNERSHIP)	PRODUCTS/SERVICES
		Speedvision, Fox Family, BSkyB, National Geographic Channel, the History Channel, DirectTV, Sky Network Television, Sky Movies, TM3, Star TV, DirectTV, Twentieth Century Fox, TV Guide, The Weekly Standard, The Times Literary Supplement, The New York Post, the Sunday Times, The Sun, the News of the World, The Australian, The Sunday Tasmanian, Foxnews.com, Australian National Rugby League	Film Production, Magazines, Newspapers, Online Services, Sports Teams, Sports Leagues, Sports Complexes
NBC Universal	USA	Nathan, Bordas, les Presses-Solar-Belfond, Havas Poche, L'Express, Tempo Medico, Staywell, Knowledge Adventure, Larousse Multimedia, Bonjour.fr 01Net, Vizzavi, Flipside.com, Canal +, Spain Telepiu, Universal Pictures, SciFi Action and Suspense Channel, USA Network, Cineplex Odeon Corporation, MCA Records, Polygram, Decca, Interscope Music Publishing, Universal Concerts, Cegetel, Vivendi Telecomm, Universal City, Universal Studios Japan, Telemundo, Bravo, Trio, CNBC, ShopNBC, MSNBC, Mun2TV, NBC Universal Television, NBC Universal Distribution, Universal Production Studio	Books, Multimedia Publishing, Television Shows, Television Production, Cable, Films, Film Production, Movie Theaters, Magazines, Music, Telecomms, Online Services, Theme Parks, Spanish-Language Television Networks, Film Studios
Sony	Japan	Sony television equipment, Sony camera equipment, Sony audio equipment, Sony computers, 5500 Digital Media Incubator, Spinner.com, AXN Television, The Game Show Network, Bejing Television Arts Center, SkyPerfectTv, Sony Pictures, Sony Music, Columbia House, Epic Records, Duet, Post Pet, Music Choice Europe, PlayStation, Playstation.com, Columbia Tristar, Columbia Pictures, Sony/Loews Theatres, TheStation@sony.com	Electronics, Video Games, Broadband, Wireless, Television Shows, Television Production, Film Production, Film Theaters, Music, Music Publishing, Online Services

Source: Robert McKenzie.

the USA version, the time that would be filled by the educational-song segment is filled instead with advertisements or promotional messages for upcoming television shows.

Audience Curiosity

The final factor affecting globalization is an escalating curiosity by media audiences about other parts of the world. As we have already noted, satellite and cable television in particular is increasingly delivering shows originating from foreign countries, as well as domestic shows that portray foreign cultures. Across the globe, offerings in domestic television schedules and internet sites show an increase in content that is foreign based or centered on foreign countries.

However, for countries isolated by geography and with a limited history of importing media content, the taste for foreign material must be acquired. To the audience with minimal prior direct experience of foreign cultures, imported media content initially is often too "foreign" to be attractive. This is because the ability to understand, appreciate, and enjoy foreign programming is predicated to some extent on being familiar with the look of the foreign people, as well as the production conventions used to create the foreign content and the language that is spoken. In a way, the desire for foreign television programming is similar to drinking coffee or tea, which rarely tastes good to the first-time drinker because these drinks are so foreign—that is, so unlike anything encountered before. But once the taste for coffee or tea is "acquired" after more tries, then a person may seek these drinks out or even feel he or she needs them. Similarly, first-time audiences have little appetite for foreign media content because the taste has not been established yet for unusual styles, structure, and language. But after repeatedly accessing the foreign media content, the taste can become endemic to reading, listening, or viewing habits. This metaphor goes only so far in explaining the reaction to beginning experiences of foreign media content, but it does reveal how a critical stage of developing a taste for imported media content must be reached before foreign content is craved and actively pursued.

CRITICISMS OF GLOBALIZATION

Despite its potential to facilitate a greater understanding of the world, globalization receives three major criticisms advanced by various citizen groups, academics, governments, quasi-governmental bodies, and media professionals. Moreover, the criticisms have occurred at the highest levels of international debate, and have often pitted countries and regions against each other. For the most part, smaller, less developed, and economically poorer countries have been in conflict with larger, developed, and wealthier countries. The basic theme that ties all of these criticisms together is the idea that globalization is unfair or unjust to some countries and regions of the world.

Criticism 1: Homogenization of Media

Some economic scholars and media professionals have concluded that the increasing concentration of media ownership is leading to an incredible amount of "sameness," or **homogenization,** of products and services across the world. The sameness begins with smaller companies being bought by larger global media conglomerates, leading to a process of consolidation. For example, computer software companies such as Netscape have been bought and absorbed by global media conglomerates such as Time Warner; independent newspapers such as the *Sun* have been bought by conglomerates such as the News Corporation; television networks such as the Black Entertainment Network (BET) have been bought by conglomerates such as Viacom; and so on. These former companies were significant media companies in their own right, but as part of larger conglomerates, they largely serve as brands that take on a wider corporate strategy.

The increasing ownership of more media outlets by fewer companies has caused concern about whether the rise of the global media conglomerate represents a combination of too much power and world reach. Some scholars such as Ben Bagdikian in *The Media Monopoly* (1990) believe that an unhealthy paradox has emerged, in that the number of media choices continues to increase, but the number of ownership bodies behind the choices continues to decrease. In contrast, other scholars such as Benjamin Compaine in *Who Owns the Media?* (1979) counter that the power of global media conglomerates has been overstated because the revenue of the conglomerates today is actually comparable to the revenue of media companies in the 1950s. Regardless of where researchers stand in this debate, there is general agreement that the fundamental shake-up of the media industry has extended programs and publications to new parts of the world, which presents a new power structure that should be monitored.

Examples of formulas that can be used to illustrate how certain media products are homogenized across the world include:

- Newspaper layouts that divide the paper into "sections" placed in the following order: Current Events, Hard News, Feature, Local News, Sports, and Business.
- Radio formats that air only top-selling (pop) songs, and that feature fast-talking deejays often cracking predictable jokes.
- Television reality shows on which contestants are gradually eliminated, and on which some contestants engage in romance.
- Internet web pages with common links such as "about us," "home," and "contact us."

Behind a conglomerate's design and distribution of media products and services that end up being homogeneous is a conservative economic strategy that seeks to maximize profit through proven formulas in the design of content, rather than risk the failure of an unexpected smaller audience as a result of groundbreaking content. What is often difficult to recognize in a homogenized media environment is that that the idea for media content available domestically may have originated in a foreign country at a sister company that is owned by the same conglomerate, or a company that is owned by a separate conglomerate. For example, the reality-based talent show *Pop Idol*—on which viewers judge the contestants— was developed for a UK audience by the Bertelsmann production house Fremantle Media. Ironically, the show did not air on *Channel 5*, which is partly owned by Bertelsmann, but on competing *Channel 4*, because it had a bigger general audience than *Channel 5*. Then, after *Pop Idol*'s successful run in the UK, News Corporation's Fox Network bought a license to broadcast a similar formula of the show to the USA domestic audience under the modified title *American Idol*. Sometimes, the repackaging of media content so closely mirrors the original content that only the actors, some of the props, and a few colloquialisms are changed.

Criticism 2: Unfairness in Global Information Flow

A second criticism of globalization focuses on an inequality in the flow of information throughout the world's media. During the 1970s and the early 1980s, an agency of the United Nations called UNESCO (United Nations Educational, Scientific, and Cultural Organization) was the seat of an emotional debate about the flow of information through media around the world—particularly as it puts developing countries at a disadvantage, while putting Western countries at an advantage. The debate is summarized in *The Global Media Debate: Its Rise, Fall, and Renewal* (1993), edited by George Gerbner, Hamid Mowlana, and Kaarle Nordenstreng. Over the years, the debate has been labeled with various acronyms including the New International Information Order (NIIO), the New World Information Order (NWIO), and the New World Communication and Information Order (NWCIO). The debate lost momentum in 1984 when the USA withdrew from UNESCO, in part because of the criticisms of the information flow debate. Representatives from the USA argued that the First Amendment to the Constitution—guaranteeing the freedom of expression—prohibited any direct government interference in the flow of information into and out of the USA. Skeptics of the withdrawal by the USA argued that global media conglomerates were successful at lobbying US representatives to pull out of UNESCO in order to preserve the exclusive right of media executives to make the decisions about importing and exporting media.

Leading researchers in the area of global information flow include Al Hester in "Theoretical Considerations in Predicting Volume and Direction of International Information Flow" (1973), Robert Stevenson in *Global Communication in the Twenty-First Century* (1994), Mohammed Musa in *Beyond Cultural Imperialism* (1997), Howard Frederick in *Global Communication and International Relations* (1993), and Majid Tehranian in *Global Communication and World Politics* (1999). Essentially, global information flow is the study of how media content moves all around the world through newspapers, television programs, radio programs, web sites, and other media that people can access. Some questions that describe how global information flow is studied include: From which countries or regions of the world does media content going around the world often originate? Do some countries put out more media content to the rest of the world than other countries? To which countries or regions of the world does the media content go? Do people in some countries receive more foreign media content than in other countries? Do people in some countries receive more foreign media content than they do domestic media content? What is the nature of the content? Is the content old or new? Is the content positive or negative? Is the content in a foreign language or a language spoken widely within the home country? Global information flow is about identifying patterns in the movement of media content from and through countries and regions all around the world.

Criticisms about global information flow revolve around perceptions by representatives from developing countries that their countries receive sparse and unfair coverage in the flow of global information. One perception has to do with the use of the phrase *third world nations* to describe developing countries. This phrase has been rejected as being too demeaning to a given country. Historically speaking, the phrase *third world* was invented to describe countries that did not fit into a (first world) capitalist ideology or a (second world) communist ideology. However, though *third world* continues to be used in some discussions about developing countries, the phrase has largely gone out of favor not just because of its negative connotations but also because it has lost relevancy as countries have emerged that do not fit neatly into a capitalist or communist classification. A second perception has more to do with patterns of information flow around the world that produce inequities in the direction, volume, and representation of information flowing back and forth between weaker (impoverished, developing) countries and stronger (affluent, Western) countries. The criticism has singled out particular countries (the USA and the UK) and regional associations (Europe and North America; English-speaking countries) as being responsible for the unfair information flow. Howard Frederick pointedly refers to the USA in *Global Communication and International Relations* (1993) as "the world's most communicating nation."

Direction of Global Information Flow   The first criticized pattern is **direction,** or the way in which information moves around the world. The criticism is aimed at information flow that is mostly **unidirectional**—that is, when information flows mostly from one country or region to another country or region, but not vice versa. The five main situations cited by researchers as being unidirectional include the flow of information from Western countries into developing countries, from Northern Hemisphere countries into Southern Hemisphere countries, from English-speaking countries into non-English-speaking countries, from larger countries into smaller countries, and from wealthier countries into poorer countries.

Critics contend that countries with little information flowing out of them to the rest of the world are vulnerable to distorted perceptions about those countries being created in worldwide media content produced in foreign countries. We can draw a simply analogy here to help clarify this criticism. Think about a situation in which people have spoken negatively about you for whatever reasons to other people who did not know you. If you found out about this, you likely experienced frustration, the root of which was probably that someone other than yourself was creating perceptions of your identity. This same kind of feeling on a much grander scale corresponds to negative reactions that representatives of some countries have about what they see as problems in the direction of global information flow.

Disproportionate Volume of Global Information Flow   The second identified pattern is **volume,** or the amount of information that flows into or out of a country. Think of a country that exemplifies one of the following three scenarios having to do with the volume of information flow. In Scenario 1, a country's available media content is supplied mostly by domestic media sources. Critics of this scenario would argue that such a country is **ethnocentric** in its global information flow, in that it lacks a global perspective on life. In Scenario 2, a country's available media content is supplied mostly by foreign media sources. Critics of this scenario would argue that such a country is **exocentric** in its global information flow, in that it lacks a homegrown perspective on life. For many critics, Scenario 3 is the most desirable, wherein a country's available media content has a robust mixture of both domestic and foreign media sources. Such a country is said to be **worldcentric** in its global information flow, in that it offers a more global perspective on life.

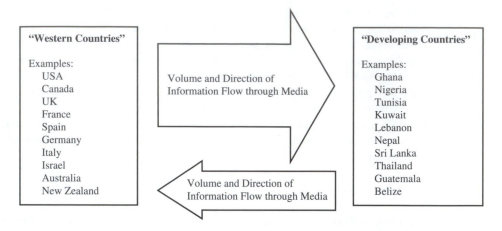

FIGURE 2.3   *Uneven Information Flow between "Western" and "Developing" Countries*
Source: Robert McKenzie.

One particular focus of the criticisms about the volume of global information flow is news flow. Critics argue that global news flow is dominated by Western **news wholesalers,** which sell information ("facts," news stories, audio sound bites, and video footage) to media organizations (primarily newspapers, television stations, and radio stations) around the world. These media organizations either redistribute the information they purchase or use it as a building block for constructing news reports. Global news wholesalers consist mainly of video news services (CNN, Reuters TV, and Worldwide Television News) as well as newswires. Much of the criticism in this area is directed at newswire content, because it provides the basic building blocks of hundreds and thousands of stories delivered by newspapers, radio, television, and the internet across the world. In *Global Communication in the Twenty-First Century* (1994), Robert Stevenson points out that approximately 50 percent of the news that circulates around the globe originates from the "big" newswire services: Associated Press and United Press International (both based in the USA), Reuters (based in the UK), and Agence France Press (based in France). All four newswires are based in Western countries. Facts such as these have led some critics to charge that too much of the global news flow is derived within the ideological framework of a Western-country orientation.

In Figure 2.3, the two main criticisms—direction and volume—about global information flow are depicted.

Country Misrepresentation in Global Information Flow   A third dimension of global information flow that has been criticized is the **misrepresentation** of countries—specifically, that developing countries are routinely portrayed in negative ways by foreign media. According to critics, what makes the impact of this pattern even worse is that information about foreign countries in the domestic media of some countries is meager from the start. As a result, any negative images of foreign countries in domestic media are amplified and tend to leave an especially indelible impression for audiences not yet familiar with basic background information about the countries in question. In addition, these negative images can become what people instinctively think about when certain developing countries are brought to their attention through the news media or through conversation with others.

To put this to the test, think of a developing country of your choice. What are the first images that come to your mind? Do you think of scenes of starvation, poverty, conflict, destruction, instability, and so on? If so, are these images balanced by any positive images that also readily come to your mind? The answers you come up with to these questions will clarify whether the criticism of misrepresentation is valid for certain countries according to your particular experiences.

Theories about Factors Influencing Global Information Flow   Those who participate in the debate about unequal global information flow commonly acknowledge that a major contributing factor is that some developing countries have difficulty supplying their own residents with domestically produced media content. Several circumstances have contributed to this problem. The first is that developing countries have lacked the technological resources needed to produce and distribute their own media content. Second, even if technology were available, developing countries also need to provide professional training for their would-be media practitioners. This means that a country must have an adequate and experienced supply of writers, on-air talent, directors, producers, engineers, and other personnel. Third, some developing countries have found it difficult to raise the investment capital needed to acquire technologies and to fund the many expenses involved in producing media content. Fourth, some developing countries have been destabilized by political or military conflicts that have affected continuous media operations. Fifth, some developing countries have a high rate of "reading illiteracy" (the percentage of people who cannot read easily), which interferes with the distribution of newspaper content, whereas other developing countries have a high rate of "electronic media illiteracy" (the percentage of people who cannot follow easily the narrative of a television show or the hyperlink structure of a web page—both of which are activities that must be learned).

Building on the work of Al Hester, theorists have proposed a number of factors to explain why information flows more readily between some countries, and more sparsely between other countries. Rather, this research points to the inequities in global information flow as being largely attributable to lateral relations between and among countries and regions. The theoretical factors for explaining information flow between two countries include:

> **Geography:** Are the countries close to each other? Do they border each other? Is one or both of the countries an island? Is one or both flanked by a border of steep mountains, open desert, dense jungle, or large bodies of water?
> **Language:** Do inhabitants of the countries speak similar languages and dialects? Do they have similar vocabularies?
> **Cultural/Historical Ties:** Do the countries have a shared cultural or historical tradition? Has there been emigration from one country to another? Do the countries celebrate the same or similar holidays?

Trade: Are goods bought and sold between the countries? Are goods made in one country sold in another country?

Military Cooperation: Do the countries have military alliances? Have the countries fought together or against each other in a war or conflict? Do the countries supply or receive military equipment and resources from each other?

Religion: Are the populations of the countries religious? Do the countries have similar or different religions?

You can apply these factors to the country you are in right now. Think of a foreign country, and apply some of these factors to the relationship between that foreign country and the country in which you are living. According to your analysis, do any of these factors seem to explain the volume, direction, and representation of information that flows between the country you are in, and another country?

UNESCO's Recommended Changes   The information order debate that occurred in the 1970s within UNESCO and the United Nations produced a line of thinking that the structure of global information flow possibly needed to be reconfigured and focused on three major changes:

1. Money should be provided by the United Nations to finance new regional newswire services, which would be indigenous to the developing countries on which the news would report. One such example, which grew out of the UNESCO recommendations, is the Caribbean News Corporation (CNC), formerly the Caribbean News Association (CANA), an online and wire service that provides news to island media in the Caribbean.
2. Indigenous news reporters—those who live in the foreign country—should be used by news organizations to report on foreign countries.
3. Editors, directors, producers, reporters, and other news personnel should make a conscientious effort to balance negative news stories with positive news stories when covering developing countries.

Criticism 3: Spread of Cultural Imperialism

A third criticism of globalization is **cultural imperialism** (sometimes referred to also as cultural hegemony), which has been advanced in varying degrees of severity by a host of scholars including Herbert Schiller in *Communication and Cultural Domination* (1976), Jeremy Tunstall in *The Media Are American* (1977), Nicholas Garnham in *Capitalism and Communication* (1990), and Peter Golding and Phil Harris in *Beyond Cultural Imperialism* (1977). Such scholars argue that culture in less media-savvy countries is being diluted by culture represented in the media content imported from more media-savvy countries. The term *culture* is used here to mean rituals, styles, and language that have historical longevity in a country.

Scholars who take a hard-line view of cultural imperialism criticize what they see as a replacement of the domestic culture of a country by a culture in the media from a foreign country. Aspects of a domestic culture are said to succumb to an imported culture if the imported media represents an inappropriate volume in relation to domestically produced media. The main forces behind the media invasion are said to be foreign governments and global conglomerates seeking to expand markets for their products and ideas to foreign audiences and to government leaders. To do this, they export media that cultivates values that promote an acceptance of the products and ideas they wish to market.

Some scholars have discussed cultural imperialism as a kind of **electronic colonialism,** a phrase that plays off classic colonialism. The old (classic) kind of colonialism involved a combination of military, political, and business strategies deployed by European countries—mainly Britain, Spain, Holland, and Portugal—in the eighteenth and nineteenth centuries to build empires out of conquered countries. Rulers in these countries commissioned ships to explore parts of the world in search of raw materials and exotic goods such as plants, spices, and minerals. In the process, the European countries colonized countries in Africa and in Central and South America, as well as islands in the Caribbean. The European countries set up extracting or manufacturing facilities in the colonies to bring raw materials or finished products back to the mother country. In many African countries such as Ghana, South Africa, and Madagascar, slaves were captured, bartered for, or purchased and then sold to sugar plantations located on Caribbean islands such as St. Croix and St. Lucia. These plantations produced not only sugar but also by-products like molasses and rum, which were then shipped back to Europe. As a result of colonization, much of the culture of the colonized countries and islands was replaced by the culture of the European countries. In contrast to that kind of colonization, the new kind of electronic colonialism is said to be less destructive but also less conspicuous. It begins with the combination of a desire by developing countries to stimulate their domestic media offerings, and a desire by media conglomerates and advertisers to sell products and services to foreign markets. These two factors lead to activities that facilitate electronic colonialism. One activity has been the gifting or discounting of equipment and old program content. As television and radio networks in the wealthier nations have updated their technology, they have sought to sell their old equipment or give it away to broadcasters in developing countries, as a tax write-off. Often, the program content has long since aired as a new series in the originating country and has been in syndication (sold as a rerun) for several years and maybe even decades. Thus, the argument runs that until a developing country begins to foster its own media content, certain cultural traditions are being diluted by traditions of the foreign culture represented by the imported and outdated media content.

A second level of cultural imperialism has to do with what is seen as an invasion of current media content. The criticism is aimed mostly but not entirely at Western media. The main invaders are said to be the television genres of sitcoms, dramas, movies, reality shows, and music television; the music genre of the pop format; and Hollywood films. The argument runs that people living in heavy media-importing countries are naturally curious about how people live in countries that have high visibility in global information flow. Naturally, these audiences satisfy their curiosities by accessing imported media imported from the high-profile countries. However, in so doing, an incremental but steady process takes place—particularly among younger audience members who are more open to change— whereby people in the importing country begin to dress, talk, and act like those portrayed in the foreign media. In other words, domestic audiences gradually discard their own cultural traditions—often subconsciously—as they emulate attributes of foreign cultures.

A few examples that illustrate the phenomenon of a culture being invaded by imported media are:

- Use of the term *l'hamburger* by French people speaking French, when there is no direct translation for that word in French.
- The widespread wearing of hip-hop clothing (baggy pants, backwards baseball caps, etc.) in countries and regions where mainly traditional clothing has been worn.
- The location of McDonald's, Burger King, Pizza Hut, and other fast-food restaurants in almost every major city, where previously take-out food was sold only by local vendors.

Proponents of cultural imperialism argue that these examples are indicative of an overall trend in the world toward a monolithic, Westernized culture, which is being promoted primarily by Western media exports.

A third level of cultural imperialism has to do with the **conventions used in the production of media content.** The argument here is that some countries import not only the content of media produced in foreign countries, but also ways in which content is produced and shaped. Production and distribution conventions include the financing of media operations (e.g., advertising revenue), the scheduling of television programs (e.g., television shows beginning exactly at :00 or :30 on the hour), the layout of newspaper copy (e.g., hard news followed by soft news followed by sports), the length of a radio song (e.g., less than five minutes), and so on. Critics warn that importing foreign media content leaves domestic media operators vulnerable to importing production conventions—such as plot development, camera angles, and advertising breaks—that automatically accompany the imported media.

Cultural imperialism critics focus much of their criticism on the USA and the UK. The USA receives the bulk of the criticism because it exports more media content than any other country in the world. However, the UK is also singled out as a purveyor of cultural imperialism because it distributes media content across the world through a network of countries that formerly were its colonies. In addition to both countries' role in exporting media content, both countries also play a significant role in training media producers, especially from developing countries. In essence, critics believe the USA and the UK—both English-speaking nations— have too much of a presence in global media operations, and thereby exert too much influence on the cultures of media-importing nations. Some critics argue that the USA and the UK have leveraged this heightened international media presence unfairly through reduced economy-of-scale costs that less developed countries and non-English-speaking countries cannot match. Other critics, as represented in *War, Media, and Propaganda* (2004), edited by Yahya R. Kamalipour and Nancy Snow, argue that "information dominance" of global information flow is part of a comprehensive political, economic, and military strategy by the USA and UK.

One countercriticism to cultural imperialism's focus on the USA and the UK is that the market acceptance of media content and models of media operation from the USA and the UK is merely the result of these countries winning a global business competition. In other words, media companies based in the USA and the UK are offering products and services that people in other countries prefer rather than the options available in their own countries or from other countries in the world.

Another countercriticism argues that countries importing media from the USA and the UK have the ability to absorb pieces of external culture without losing their own cultural foundations. As long as domestic cultures are robust and well established, any traditions adopted by society alongside the importation of media content are said to attain only secondary status in relation to native traditions.

On the larger scale, those who counter negative appraisals of the overall process of globalization argue that what is happening around the world is merely a natural evolution of cultures meshing together as the planet continues to accommodate population growth. These critics argue that in such an evolutionary context, old ways of doing things will naturally be replaced by new ways of doing things. According to this viewpoint, therefore, countries that import foreign media content are merely witnessing changes on the part of people who are open to change and who want to be more integrated with a world culture rather than to remain part of a parochial culture derived from a local country or region.

SUMMARY

Globalization is a process proliferating out of a worldwide business environment that is effectively blurring national boundaries and shrinking the world. The central force that is propelling globalization is corporate commercialism, which generates varying degrees of criticism and countercriticism from a variety of affected groups. The previous discussion of globalization points the way to issues that should be incorporated into comparisons of media systems between two or more countries, because the issues that have been identified are critical to obtaining expansive and meaningful interpretations from the comparisons. The issues identified in this chapter therefore are to be used to derive meanings in subsequent chapters providing comparisons among the media systems of France, Sweden, the UK, the USA, México, China, Ghana, and Lebanon. In the next chapter, Elements of a Media System, the concept of a media system and the elements that make up a media system are introduced. Then, in Chapters 4 through 12, these elements are elaborated on one by one and compared across the media systems of the eight countries.

CHAPTER 3

ELEMENTS OF A MEDIA SYSTEM

PRIMER QUESTIONS

1. What does the term *system* mean to you?
2. What qualifies something as a system?
3. What is a particular system that affects your life? What are the basic elements of that system?
4. How do the elements of the system relate to each other? How do the elements help the system to function?
5. What do you think are some basic elements that make up a media system?

When you set out to explore a new town or city that you are visiting for the first time and that you want to explore, you probably come up with an approach that will help guide where you go. For example, maybe you decide to take a drive around and through the city first to get an idea of how it is laid out. Then maybe you go to a famous historical or cultural site, then to the district where there are a lot of restaurants for lunch, followed by a visit to a good shopping district. Later, maybe you go to the part of the city where the movie theaters or nightclubs are. Having an approach to exploring somewhere new that is based on visiting categories of sites according to your interests at different points in the day allows you to explore the city with a plan—rather than exploring the city randomly, in which case you might miss something for which the city is famous, or waste time going from one end of the city to the other and then all the way back again.

Similarly, before the media systems of the eight countries can be explored, it is important to develop the methodological approach that will guide the comparisons. A **methodological approach** is a way of studying a phenomenon systematically and is composed of a conceptual framework breaking down into the variables that make up this framework. A **conceptual framework** is a set of connecting assumptions that guide the approach and the variables that are used to generate information. **Variables** are categories of information that vary according to different conditions and circumstances. The methodological approach that is used in this book is designed to ensure that the four media are being studied fairly and accurately; that the findings and interpretations are interesting, reasonable, and meaningful; and that the study does not render a snap analysis by examining just one variable related to a phenomenon of media. Particularly in a study comparing media from around the world, the observations will be somewhat sterile unless they go beyond just what is seen, heard, or read in the media—otherwise known as content. In other words, the methodological approach that is designed to compare media from around the world in this book attempts to describe not only the high-profile variable of content but also the less obvious variables that lie underneath the content.

THE METHODOLOGICAL APPROACH OF A SYSTEM

This book uses the methodological approach of "a system" to guide how we explore media from different countries. Though an explanation of what a system is can come across as somewhat abstract and vague, it is necessary to provide one here in order to gain a theoretical understanding of what is discussed in this book and why. This knowledge will in turn enhance the interpretations of the findings. While it is being presented, keep in mind that the theory of a system will be fleshed out with details in the subsequent chapters.

A **system** is a collection of interrelated parts in motion that make up a whole. These parts interact with each other to produce a whole system. There is an organic quality to a system, in that the whole is constantly growing or maturing. At various periods in the evolution of a system's efficiency some parts will flourish, whereas others will flounder or even expire.

Several characteristics help describe how the parts and the whole relate to each other. First, a system is an entity that consists of multiple parts that are mutually influenced by each other. Second, a system draws on a wide range of resources to exist and to function properly. Third, a system is always undergoing change because of external forces but retains a basic stability because of an established internal structure. These resources can include institutions, people, technology, and raw materials. Together, these three characteristics depict a media system as essentially a dynamic, self-perpetuating entity made up of multiple interrelated parts.

Media exhibit characteristics of a system. First, media consist of multiple variables that are mutually influenced by external forces such as technological innovation, intercountry relations, and globalization. Second, media make use of a wide range of resources to produce and deliver content. These resources include equipment, people, and information. Third, media undergo constant change in a variety of areas including content development, industry restructuring, regulatory activity, and market exploration, while retaining a fundamental internal structure. Because media exhibit these characteristics, the concept of a system can be used to describe media.

The conceptual framework that is used in this book to compare media from around the world is that of a media system, the variables of which are called elements. At the end of this chapter, the conceptual framework of a media system and its variables are depicted using a tree as a visual metaphor to make it easier to understand. Before we get to the media system as a tree, however, it is important to identify the connecting assumptions that comprise the conceptual framework of a media system and the variables that make up this framework, as described here:

1. Elements are the fundamental components of a media system. Without the elements, the media system does not function.

2. Each element is directly related to each of the other elements. In addition, a change in one element may lead to changes in some or all of the other elements.
3. Some elements will have a greater influence on the media system in different conditions than other elements. Each element impacts the media system in different ways, under different conditions, and with different effects. Sometimes, one element may have a greater impact on the media system than another element, due to a set of circumstances that exist during a particular time period.
4. One or more elements may illuminate some or all of the other elements. In other words, focusing on one or more element may make it possible to see other elements more clearly than if the focus was initially on the other elements.
5. Sometimes there is a special relationship between a subset of two or three elements that drives changes in all the other elements. By studying this subset, it may be possible to more clearly understand how two or three elements interacting with each other can exert a greater force on other variables than if they were interacting individually with other variables.
6. All of the elements taken together make up a whole media system. Thus, all of the elements must be studied to provide a full understanding of a whole media system.
7. The whole of a media system is greater than the sum of its parts. Viewed individually, each element of a media system has a limited impact on the whole system. But viewed collectively, elements combined into a system comprise a force that has greater power and influence than can be assessed by simply adding up effects of individual elements.

The assumptions listed above provide a plan that will guide the comparison of media presented in this book. It is imperative to keep these qualities in mind when the media systems of the eight countries are being compared, because it will lead to a greater understanding of how the interplay between the selected elements actually results in the manifestation of a particular kind of media system in a given country—that is, a media system with a unique look, sound, and feel. This understanding will in turn lead to a fuller interpretation of the comparisons among media from around the world.

CENTRALITY OF MEDIA CONTENT

Earlier it was stated that **media content** is the most noticeable element that comes into play in a media system. This assertion is based on the reasoning that content is the main point at which audiences mentally come into contact with the media. Though content is a tangible entity, other more obscure but influential elements effectively lie beneath a study of content. Therefore, a study of content alone misses the opportunity to examine more hidden and derivative processes at work in a media system—processes that are revealed by uncovering fundamental elements fronted by content.

Think of a television newscast. It is easy to forget that when you watch and listen to a news story in a television newscast, the story is the product of activities taking place behind the scenes that ultimately give the newscast a particular look, sound, and feel. When you look past the content, however, you can find many factors that lead to the content—such as the people who watch the content; the way the content is regulated, financed, and accessed; the way the society perceives of the role of television in providing content; and the way the culture of the country affects the values expressed in the content.

Therefore, a book that compares media from around the world must study structural elements that facilitate the production of content, as well as the content itself. Still, content should remain a focal point in the comparisons of media systems because it is central to a tangible understanding of media. In essence, to study content in relation to all the other elements of a media system is to illuminate the media system as a whole.

USING A RHETORICAL PERSPECTIVE TO GENERATE ELEMENTS OF A MEDIA SYSTEM

This now brings us to the question of what elements will be used to study media from around the world. This is one place where a rhetorical perspective comes into play. Again, as Sonja Foss, Karen Foss, and Robert Trapp discuss in *Contemporary Perspectives of Rhetoric* (1991), a rhetorical perspective attempts to provide reasonable interpretations of meaning for how the world is seen from a particular vantage point. Accordingly, a rhetorical perspective on the vantage point of a media system attempts to tie potential meanings to knowledge available through a media system. As the discussion of globalization in Chapter 2 suggested, the flow of information around the world is a major influence on what people who access media and people who make media content know. Therefore, a rhetorical perspective provides a way to analyze potential meanings about the look, sound, and feel of media systems in light of circumstances related to globalization.

The following criteria describe a rhetorical perspective for selecting elements that will elicit fair and meaningful comparisons of media systems from around the world:

1. The elements must exist in the media systems of all countries.
2. The elements must be flexible enough and diversified enough to yield interpretations that take context into account.
3. The elements must be basic enough that conclusions are not obscured by a focus on overly specific details.
4. There must be enough parity in the elements across the media systems of all countries.

ELEMENTS OF A MEDIA SYSTEM

In response to the criteria laid out in the previous section, nine elements have been selected to compare the media systems of eight countries in this book:

1. Cultural Characteristics of the Eight Countries
2. Philosophies for Media Systems
3. Regulation of Media
4. Financing of Media
5. Accessibility of Media

6. Media Content
7. News Reporting
8. Media Imports and Exports
9. Media Audiences

These elements were carefully selected according to the criteria promoted by a rhetorical perspective. In essence, the elements are designed to elicit a fair and objective comparison of media across all countries. But above and beyond that goal, the elements are designed to reveal a broad and deep picture of the media systems across the eight countries studied in this book. However, it is important that each element not be seen as a kind of cookie cutter placed on each country's media system to neatly catalogue its elements. Rather, the elements in this text should be seen as commonsense categories of information that generate discussions not only about the media systems of the countries in this book, but also about a media system in any given country.

ELEMENTS OF A MEDIA SYSTEM AS A TREE

To discuss a media system in a form we can easily visualize, it will be helpful from now on to use the metaphor of a tree. There are several reasons for using the image of a tree to depict a media system metaphorically: A tree is an organic system that is constantly changing its shape as new parts grow and older parts die off. A tree is surrounded by a local environment that presents unique conditions—such as air quality, wind speed, soil nutrients, and so on—all of which significantly affect its growth and overall shape. Finally, trees interact with other trees through root systems and pollination, just as media systems from some countries interact with media systems from other countries.

Like a tree, not all elements that comprise a media system are visible at first glance. Underground, there are two inconspicuous but important elements that impact the functioning of a media system as a tree. First, there are local soil conditions containing nutrients that significantly affect the growth and health of the tree. Drawing on this imagery, we can think of the element of **cultural characteristics** as representing local or domestic conditions that influence more subtle attributes of the tree. Similar to how the nutrients in soil affect the texture of a tree, certain cultural characteristics affect the texture of a media system. Also underground is the root network of a tree, which can be half the size of the entire tree. The root network absorbs nutrients from the soil. Drawing on this imagery, we can think of the element of **philosophies for media systems** as being analogous to the root network of a country's media system. Sometimes, the root system of a tree can comingle with the root system of another tree nearby. Similarly, the media system of one country can comingle with the media system of another country.

Above the ground, one portion of the tree that is easily visible is the trunk, which serves as the tree's base, and which supports and gives direction to the other parts of the tree above the ground. We can think of the element of **regulation** as being analogous to the trunk of a media system. Another portion of a tree above the ground is the main branches, which provide the basic parameters and the support for the smaller feeder branches of the tree. Continuing this analogy, we can think of the main tree branches as the element of

FIGURE **3.1** *Elements of a Media System Depicted As a Tree*
Source: Miharu Lane.

financing in a media system, and the feeder branches as the **accessibility** of a media system. The secondary branches exhibit leaves and seeds on a seasonal basis to passersby. Because leaves are the most observable and changeable part of a tree, we can think of leaves as analogous to **content** in a media system. Moreover, some leaves are more sensational than others and thereby stand out among all the leaves of the tree. Continuing this imagery, we can think of the standout leaves in a media system as being analogous to the element of **news reporting**. Just as standout leaves provide commentary on the general welfare of the tree, news reporting provides commentary on the general welfare of a media system and indeed a society. To continue with this imagery, the seeds of a tree are scattered by wind, rainfall, and living creatures to locations near and far away from the tree. Some seeds take root and sprout up as new trees, but others do not, or the seeds make it for a little while and then die off. Therefore, we can think of seeds as being analogous to the element of **imports/exports** in a media system. This brings us also to the final element of a media system. We can think of living creatures that observe a tree as being analogous to an **audience** for a media system. Drawing on this imagery, audiences interact with media content through the accessibility of the content. In other words, the feeder branches of a tree ultimately determine which leaves and seeds are reachable by passersby on the ground.

Figure 3.1 depicts a media system as a tree. This metaphor certainly has shortcomings, but it helps to visually describe and clarify the basic properties of a media system. Thus, when conceptualizing a media system as a tree, it becomes clear that a media system has visible parts as well as some parts that cannot be seen unless you look below the surface. It also becomes clear that audiences are initially drawn to media systems by seasonally produced content which, depending on accessibility, may be reachable by different audiences. Furthermore, it is clear that content is shaped by a host of other elements in the media system including financing, regulation, philosophies, and cultural characteristics, as well as the overall global climate that encloses a media system.

SUMMARY

This chapter laid out an approach for comparing media across different countries by focusing on the media system in each country. A media system consists of nine elements: cultural characteristics, philosophies for media systems, regulation of media, financing of media, accessibility of media, media content, news reporting, media imports/exports, and media audiences. These elements interact with and influence each other—some more than others. Thinking about a media system and its elements as a tree helps to clarity how a media system functions.

It is important to reinforce that the elements compared in this book are applicable not just to media systems in the specific countries discussed but also to media systems in all countries across the world. Therefore, as you read Chapters 4 through 12, you can replicate the kind of analysis in your own studies of other countries and regions representing your own particular interests.

CHAPTER 4

CULTURAL CHARACTERISTICS OF THE EIGHT COUNTRIES

PRIMER QUESTIONS

1. What does the word *culture* mean to you? In general, how does the culture of a country relate to its media system?

2. How has the geography of the country in which you are living influenced the development of media in that country?

3. How has the language of the country in which you are living influenced the development of media in that country?

4. How has the society of the country in which you are living influenced the development of media in that country?

5. How has the government of the country in which you are living influenced the development of media in that country?

Culture is a densely packed and far-reaching term with multiple levels of meanings. To some people, it stands for high culture, and has to do with an appreciation for fine arts such as opera or ballet. To others, *culture* means popular culture, and has to do with hit music or movie stars. To others, *culture* is a specific population of people who live in a particular geographic area, or is a clique of people who share a similar lifestyle or outlook. To still others, *culture* defines ordinary routines that people follow—what they eat and drink, what they wear, what kinds of jobs they have, how they spend their leisure time, and so on. From these thumbnail descriptions, culture is obviously a kaleidoscopic concept that covers a nearly infinite number of dimensions.

This chapter follows a definition of culture articulated chiefly in two books: *Culture's Consequences* by Geert Hofstede (2001) and *Exploring Culture* by Gert Hofstede, Paul Pedersen, and Geert Hofstede (2001). In these works, *culture* is defined as that which distinguishes one group of people from another group of people. This broad definition focuses on how the values of a group of people are manifested essentially in that group's rituals and symbols. At the center of culture is a set of societal norms based on values shared by a population that has experienced a common history. These norms in turn foster the development of social institutions including family, education, government, and media.

When unique cultural characteristics of a country are studied, it leads to a more nuanced understanding of how a media system develops within a particular population of people. The term *characteristics* is used in this chapter's title to indicate that the observations are but tiny snapshots only of the enormously intricate concept of culture. Discussing cultural characteristics will provide readers of this book with some similar background knowledge about the countries and peoples hosting the media systems being compared.

In Chapter 3, the cultural characteristics of a country's media system were likened to the soil surrounding the roots of a tree, because the soil provides the unique combinations of nutrients and minerals that affect the fundamental texture, shape, and overall health of the tree. Accordingly, our purpose here is to profile relevant cultural characteristics that cultivate unique media systems in each of the eight countries.

CULTURAL CHARACTERISTICS OF FRANCE

Geography of France

France covers some 547,030 square kilometers/211,210 square miles. France is the second-largest country in Europe after Russia. France is located in the lower western portion of Europe, and borders several other European countries including: Andorra, Belgium, Italy, Germany, Luxembourg, Monaco, Spain, and Switzerland. (See Map 4.1.) France was one of the original members of the European Union (EU), and the French consider themselves to be

MAP 4.1   *Map of France*

fundamentally European. Because of France's close proximity to many countries in Europe, plus France's early entry into the EU, there is a general disposition on the part of the French that France should be a central player in the affairs of Europe and the EU.

France retains close ties with an extensive network of overseas territories and former colonies, a result of French imperialism mainly during 1870 to 1914. The overseas territories are referred to as DOM-TOMs ("Departments Ouvre Mer" or Overseas Departments, and "Territores Ouvre Mer" or Overseas Territories). Citizens in DOM-TOMs have all the rights of French citizens. The relationship between France, the DOM-TOMs, and the former colonies is manifested in military coordination and relaxed immigration and trade restrictions. Examples of French DOM-TOMs include Guadalupe and Martinique in the Caribbean, French Guiana in South America, and New Caledonia in the South Pacific. Examples of former French colonies include the Middle Eastern countries of Lebanon and Syria and the African countries of Morocco, Tunisia, Senegal, and the Ivory Coast.

Language in France

In general, the French are very proud of their language. At one time, French was the most widely used language around the world but was eclipsed by English in the late twentieth century. Though the French language still has prominence in international diplomacy—for example, it is one of the official working languages of the United Nations—French has significantly less worldwide reach than before. To guard against the erosion of the French language in France, an institution called the Academié was established in 1634. Also, in contemporary times the General Commission on Terminology and Neology publishes Gallic versions of modern words and phrases—for example, instead of using the English-based *le email*, the word *courriel* (a combining of the words *courier* and *electronique*) is preferred (see Henley, 2004). In general, the French regret that the French language no longer has the prominence that it once had. One outcome of this feeling is that visitors to France often receive a cold reception if they try to communicate with French people without trying to speak any French. On the other hand, usually a basic attempt by a visitor to speak a few French words (for example, *bonjour, merci, oui*) elicits an approving attitude from French people.

France also has several secondary languages. Gaelic is spoken in the region of Brittany on the west coast. The importance of preserving Gaelic languages has led local authorities in Brittany to institutionalize its teaching in public schools and to fund the production of Gaelic radio and television programs. German is spoken on the eastern border alongside Germany. And Arabic is spoken in the south of France, where immigrants from Algeria, Tunisia, and Morocco have settled.

The French language was spread through its colonial network. Places where French is spoken as a first language include the African countries of Algeria, Morocco, and Senegal; the Caribbean islands of Haiti, St. Martin, and Martinique; the province of Québec in Canada; and the state of Louisiana in the USA.

Society in France

The population of France is approximately 59 million people. About 20 percent of the French population lives in Paris. France has a 99 percent literacy rate—those aged 15 and up who can read and write. In France, 6.4 percent of the people live in poverty. According to the CIA's *World Factbook* (2002), the largest ethnic group in France by far is White (92 percent), followed by Arab/North African (4 percent), then German (2 percent), Breton (1 percent), and Catalan (1 percent).

In France, people are known for being artistic and for valuing beauty in their surroundings. For example, wine and food are served up with as much attention paid to the presentation as the taste. Similarly, the facades of buildings—both old and new—are often trimmed out with ornamentation. In France, even mundane sights comprising roadside infrastructure— such as light posts, signs, and bridges—are decorated. Figure 4.1 shows the standard ornate newspaper kiosk that can be seen throughout Paris. Street intersections in towns are often embellished with colorful flower displays arranged in intricate patterns. Almost everywhere you look in France, there seems to be some kind of artistic expression. Probably the omnipresence of beauty is a major reason why so many people visit France each year. According to the World Tourism Organization's *Tourism Highlights*, France consistently receives more tourists each year than any other country, and Paris is the most-visited city in the world.

The French are also known for being political. It is said that French people like to talk about politics before talking about the weather. French people normally do not shy away from presenting their political opinions, and when doing so, they have a demonstrative demeanor in their tone and pitch of voice and especially their body movements.

FIGURE 4.1   *Ornate Newspaper Kiosk in Paris, France*
Source: Robert McKenzie.

French people are also known to apply somewhat rigid conventions for how people should greet and depart from each other. On greeting another person in France, there is the expectation that both sides must say "bonjour" before conversation can begin. If a customer does not say "bonjour" to a shopkeeper before asking where a product is, the shopkeeper is likely to take offense. Similarly, French people are often particular about saying "merci" (thank you), "au revoir" (good-bye), or "bon journée" (have a good day) when parting ways. To French people, a conversation is not complete unless it follows certain congenial conventions.

Government in France

Government in France is structured according to a parliamentary democracy with a strong national government, commonly referred to as "the state." The state is a central player in education, culture, the economy, public services, and many other facets of French life. France is also known as a socialist country because of the degree to which state activities are funded by taxation. Underlying the state's role in these and other areas is the objective of promoting French high culture—primarily music, painting, drawing, and literature. In France, the state often works with private commercial interests to achieve this objective. The symbiotic relationship between the government sector and the commercial sector can be traced to President Charles de Gaulle's government from 1958 to 1969. As a result, the term *Gaullism* is used to frame the paradigm for the relationship between government and French media.

French national government has three branches: an executive branch (the president and the prime minister), a legislative branch (Parliament), and a judicial branch (the courts). The head of government is the president, who is elected by the general population. Generally, the president is responsible for France's foreign affairs, whereas the prime minister is responsible for the day-to-day operations of government. Parliament is made up of the Senate and the National Assembly, which is the more powerful of the two institutions. The National Assembly consists of 577 deputies elected by the general public. The Senate is made up of 319 members elected by city and regional electoral colleges.

There are many political parties in France with seats in the National Assembly. The party that gains the most seats in the general election holds a majority in the French Assembly. French political parties cover a broad spectrum of ideologies. The parties on the left of the political spectrum include the ultraleft-wing French Communist Party and the left-of-center Socialist Party. The parties on the right of the political spectrum include the ultra-right-wing National Front party and the right-of-center UDM. The Green Party cuts across the political spectrum.

CULTURAL CHARACTERISTICS
OF SWEDEN (SVERIGE)

Geography of Sweden

Sweden covers some 449,964 square kilometers/173,732 square miles. Sweden is one of five Scandinavian countries. (The others are Norway, Denmark, Iceland, and Finland.) Sweden borders Norway and, in the remote north region of the country, Finland. Sweden is approximately sixteen kilometers or ten miles across the Baltic Sea from Denmark. Also across the Baltic Sea, at longer distances, are Germany, Poland, and the Baltic states of Lithuania, Estonia, and Latvia. The geographical position of Sweden essentially in the middle of these countries makes it a center of trade and commerce in that region (see Map 4.2).

Unlike the UK, France, and the USA, Sweden does not hold a network of overseas territories. However, Sweden retains close ties with the aforementioned countries because of an expansionist period in the seventeenth century that gave it control over Denmark, Finland, Norway, Poland, and the Baltic States. According to Lonely Planet's *Scandinavian Europe* (2003), about 20 percent of the population in Sweden is either foreign-born or has a parent who is not from Sweden.

Language in Sweden

The Swedish language is part of the family of Scandinavian languages, which also includes Norwegian and Danish. However, there are enough differences between the three languages that someone who speaks one Scandinavian language sometimes has difficulty understanding one or both of the other Scandinavian languages.

Two secondary languages are also spoken in Sweden. Finnish is spoken in the far north of Sweden and on some islands off the Swedish coast. Sami is spoken by Laplanders who live in the far north of Sweden. Sami is also spoken in the north of Norway and Finland. Some programs aired on both Swedish television and radio channels are produced in Finnish and Sami.

MAP 4.2   *Map of Sweden*

Most Scandinavians, including Swedes, speak English very well. Because Swedish is rarely studied as a second language in other countries, Swedes have become adept at speaking other languages in order to interact with other countries. Because of English's status as the world's dominant language, Swedes are required to take English-language classes in primary school. Television also plays a large role in teaching English to Swedes in that Swedish television regularly includes American and British programs. Such programs are aired in English, but Swedish translation are provided at the bottom of the screen within a horizontal black bar. The black bar makes it easier to read the Swedish words than if the words were placed just against the camera shot. Figure 4.2 shows what the black bar with a Swedish translation looks like.

Society in Sweden

The population of Sweden is approximately nine million people. Sweden has the largest population in Scandinavia. Approximately 20 percent of the population lives in the capital of Stockholm, at 1.8 million. Sweden has a 99 percent literacy rate—those aged fifteen and up who can read and write. Official record keeping does not show any percentages of people in Sweden who live in poverty. The government provides assistance (e.g., housing

FIGURE 4.2   *English-Language Television Program with Swedish Translation Placed within a Black Bar* ("A risk I won't take.")

Source: SVT Sveriges Television, BBC Worldwide Americas Inc., Hamilton Hodell Ltd., ICM.

and food allowances) to people who qualify so that everyone has a certain basic standard of living. Sweden is very monolithic in terms of ethnicity. According to *Lonely Planet* (2003), Swedes make up 90 percent of the population in Sweden, followed by Finns (3 percent), then Sami (0.15 percent).

Swedish people are known for valuing nature and for taking "natural" approaches to daily living. Martin Gannon in *Understanding Global Cultures* points out that the Swedes' love of and respect for nature permeates the national laws that protect the environment. For example, it is forbidden to commercially develop the Swedish coastline with companies and shops. Figure 4.3 shows a typical view of a Swedish coastline that remains in its natural state. Another example of the Swedes' attitude toward Swedish territory is the centuries-old custom called *Allemansrätten* (right of public access), which allows people to stay on some-one else's property for no more than twenty-four hours, provided that the owners' privacy and immediate surroundings are not violated. Another example of the value Swedes place on nature is the lack of litter in the countryside or even the cities. Swedes extend their concept of nature to the human body, treating it as something natural that does not need to be covered up. In other words, Swedes have little hesitation going naked in certain situations, such as changing clothes at a beach or sitting in a sauna with family and friends.

Swedes are also known for having an open society. The quality of openness has a historical precedent established by the Swedish constitution in 1766 under two acts having to do with freedom of the press and the freedom to express opinion. These acts make it difficult

FIGURE 4.3 *Coastline in Sweden*
Source: Robert McKenzie.

for government to keep information related to the activities of government officials secret. These acts also underline a cultural proclivity wherein Swedish people generally feel that most subjects are appropriate for direct honest discussion in everyday conversation.

Swedes are also known for valuing an egalitarian society in which the needs of society supersede the needs of individuals. This value adheres to the principle that large inequities in the distribution of wealth should not be present in Swedish society because inequality promotes social disharmony. This value in turn promotes the principle that individuals are entitled to high-quality social services (e.g., public transportation, medical care, access to nature) provided by the government. This has led to the common saying that the Swedish government takes care of Swedish citizens from "cradle to grave."

Government in Sweden

Government in Sweden is structured according to parliamentary democracy with a weak monarch as head of state. There are 349 members of the Swedish Parliament. Ministries have limited power in the Swedish political system and are seen more as extensions of the government. Sweden is referred to as a socialist country because of the degree to which the government provides public services. According to Lonely Planet's *Scandinavian Europe* (2003), 74 percent of Sweden's domestic economy is made up of the service sector.

The head of Swedish government is the prime minister, who is elected by the party membership. There are many political parties in Sweden with seats in Parliament. Occupying the left end of the spectrum are the Left Party (formerly the Communists), the Social Democratic Party, and the Greens Party. Occupying the center of the spectrum are the Center Party and the Folk Party (also called the Liberal Party). Occupying the right of the spectrum are the Christian Democrats Party and the Conservatives Party. Swedish politics are known for favoring the left of the political spectrum.

CULTURAL CHARACTERISTICS OF THE UNITED KINGDOM (UK)

Geography of the United Kingdom (UK)

The UK covers some 244,820 square kilometers/94,526 square miles. The UK is made up of England, Scotland, Wales, and parts of Northern Ireland (see Map 4.3). Alternatively, Great Britain refers just to England, Scotland, and Wales. People who reside in the UK are referred to as British. Between the UK and the rest of Europe is a body of water that the British call the English Channel, but which the French call the Sleeve. England and France are separated by about thirty-three kilometers/twenty-one miles at the narrowest crossing of this body of water. This body of water symbolizes a mind-set wherein British people view their country to be fundamentally different from other European countries. Many British, in fact, would say that they are not strictly European. This viewpoint fits into a larger "island mentality" that depicts the UK as on its own, separated from Europe and the rest of the world in a way that is beyond geography.

The UK has special relations with an extensive overseas network of current territories and former colonies. At the peak of the British Empire, about 25 percent of the world's

MAP 4.3   *Map of the UK*

countries were governed by the UK. Many of these countries have since gained independence and are self-governing. The territories that have not sought or gained independence are governed by the UK. These territories include the Falklands off South America, Gibraltar in the Mediterranean, and Trinidad in the Caribbean. Many former British colonies have joined the Commonwealth, a voluntary association founded by the UK in 1971. The Commonwealth facilitates cooperation between the UK and fifty-three sovereign states (former UK territories) in such areas as human rights, economic development, and disease prevention. Examples of member countries in the Commonwealth include Australia, Canada, Ghana, Singapore, and South Africa.

Language in the UK

The dominant language in the UK is English. English is also the language most widely used around the world in terms of political, financial, and media communications. The English language has been propagated across the world mainly through two circumstances. One was Britain's colonization of conquered territories and the establishment of the British Empire: The subsequent emigration of British people to colonial territories spread the English language. This has led to English being spoken as the official language or as a predominant language in such former territories as Kenya, South Africa, and Ghana (Africa); Canada and the USA (North America); Guyana (South America); India, Pakistan, and Singapore (Asia);

and the islands of Barbados, Saint Lucia, and Jamaica in the Caribbean Sea. The second means by which English has been (and continues to be) propagated across the world is through media exports from the USA and the UK. One particular export that has played a large role in the spread of the English language is the BBC World Service, an international radio network established by the UK government to disseminate information, entertainment, and culture from the homeland to British expatriates. Media imports and exports are discussed in more detail in Chapter 11 as an element of a media system.

The UK also has a secondary (and ancient) language that is generally referred to as Gaelic. There are several derivations of Gaelic used in Wales, Ireland, and Scotland. The importance of preserving Gaelic languages has led local authorities in Scotland, Ireland, and especially Wales to institutionalize the teaching of Gaelic in public schools and to fund the production of Gaelic radio and television programs.

Society in the UK

The population of the UK is approximately 59 million people. Most of the population (about 49 million, or 85 percent) resides in England. Approximately 12 percent of the population (about 7 million) resides in London, the capital of England. The UK has a 99 percent literacy rate—those aged fifteen and up who can read and write. In the UK, 17 percent of the people live in poverty. According to the CIA's *World Factbook* (2003), English make up 81.5 percent of the population in the UK, followed by Scottish (9.6 percent), Irish (2.4 percent), Welsh (1.9 percent), Ulster (1.8 percent), then West Indian, Pakistani, and Other (2.8 percent).

In the UK there is a class system that continues to strongly influence social interaction. As Associated Press writer Thomas Wagner puts it, the UK "remains a country ruled by an aristocracy-based social pecking order" (2003, p. A8). Though the class system is in the process of slowly breaking down, clear distinctions between the classes to which people allegedly belong can be observed in terms of dialects, professions, education, politics, and leisure tastes. The class system includes a nobility class, a professional class, a working class, and a farming class—but within these groups further stratifications are visible. Media programs and publications in the UK are often targeted at audiences according to class.

The UK has one of the highest literacy rates in the world. Venturing into almost any aspect of British life reveals a penchant for reading, as people can frequently be seen enjoying books, newspapers, and magazines in public places. Figure 4.4 shows a train car full of people, most of them reading newspapers. Authors and playwrights are featured prominently in talk shows and interview programs on radio and television. Consequently, conversations among British people are often about what they have read. One apparent outcome of this national pastime is a depth of vocabulary that leads British people of all ages and classes to express themselves verbally with a wide range of words at their disposal.

British people are also known for taking a keen interest in studying what they observe—not necessarily in the sense of making an academic study, but rather seeking to understand a subject and talking about it in detail. Martin Gannon in *Understanding Global Cultures* (2001) indicates that historically, people in the UK have striven to be educated about a wide range of subjects. Extended conversations can often be heard in pubs, on trains, and around street corners about wide-ranging domestic and foreign subjects. It is not unusual for a British taxi driver to know details about the American Civil War

FIGURE 4.4   *Travelers Reading Newspapers on a Train in the UK*
Source: Robert McKenzie.

(1861–1865), for instance. British people generally take pride in being able to discuss and debate a subject intelligently and with passion but reason.

Government in the UK

The national government in the UK is structured according to a parliamentary monarchy. The UK is referred to as a socialist country primarily because of the degree to which taxation is used to fund public services such as pensions and medical care. In the UK, the three institutions of national government include the House of Commons, the House of Lords, and the Sovereign. Most power resides with the House of Commons, made up of 659 Members of Parliament (MPs), who represent an equal number of geographic constituencies. MPs are elected by the voting public. The House of Lords is made up of members who inherit their positions because of a family history in government and members who are appointed by the monarchy to their positions. The sovereign is the reigning queen or king.

The head of British government is the prime minister, who is elected by the party membership, not by the voting public. Traditionally, there have been two major political parties in the UK: the Conservative Party and the Labour Party. There are other, much smaller parties that hold seats in the British Parliament including the Liberal Democrats Party and others.

CULTURAL CHARACTERISTICS OF THE UNITED STATES OF AMERICA (USA)

Geography of the USA

The USA covers some 9,631,418 square kilometers/3,718,711 square miles. The USA is the third-largest country in the world, after Russia and Canada. People who live in the USA are known as Americans. Despite its large size, the USA borders just two nations: México to the south and Canada to the north. (See Map 4.4.) The USA is separated from most countries by two vast bodies of water—the Pacific and the Atlantic oceans. These geographical characteristics contribute to what is known as an isolationist orientation in the USA, wherein American people generally feel detached from events in other parts of the world that are not perceived to directly affect the USA.

Like the UK and France, the USA retains an extensive network of overseas territories; these territories are protectorates or outright possessions of the USA. The network has evolved in the context of two activities coinciding with the development of the USA as a world superpower. The first activity has been to provide protectorate or possessive status to islands that have been purchased by the USA or have linked themselves to USA governance. These islands include Puerto Rico, Guam, and the US Virgin Islands. The relationship between the USA and its protectorates and territories is manifested in tariff reductions, voting rights, relaxed immigration policies, and military protection.

The second activity has been the establishment of USA military bases in overseas locations that provide military security in exchange for a USA presence in the territory and the region. The presence of these military bases provides money to local economies. Countries

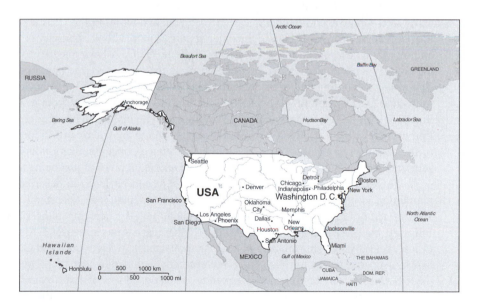

MAP 4.4   *Map of the USA*

where USA military bases are located include Cuba, Israel, Saudi Arabia, Germany, and the Philippines. One way in which the military personnel and the citizens of the territories are linked with USA culture is through the Armed Forces Radio (AFR) Network. The AFR broadcasts music and information at overseas USA military bases to local audiences.

Language in the USA

The primary language in the USA is English. American English shares most of the vocabulary of British English, but differs strongly in dialect. Spanish is a second language that is growing in the USA because of immigration from México, Central America, South America, and some islands in the Caribbean. Other languages, such as Arabic and Chinese, can be found in pockets of first- or second-generation ethnic communities. There is an ongoing dialogue in some states about whether to designate English as the only official language or to permit English and Spanish bilingualism in schools, government, and other public institutions. Though Spanish is officially a second language in the USA, it is unofficially a first language in many communities, both in some big cities such as New York and Miami, and in southern and western states such as Texas and California. Spanish-language media—newspapers, radio programs, and television channels and shows—are commonly found throughout the USA, even in areas well north of the México–USA border.

Society in the USA

The population of the USA is approximately 296 million people, the third-largest population in the world behind China and India. About 75 percent of the population in the USA lives in urban areas. Approximately 2 percent of the population (about 8 million people) lives in New York City, the most populated city in the USA. The USA has a 97 percent literacy rate—those aged fifteen and up who can read and write. In the USA, 12.7 percent of the people live in poverty. Unlike the other countries in this book, ethnicity is somewhat of an amorphous concept in the USA. Most people in the USA have ancestors who came to the country within just over two hundred years. In that time span, the population growth is staggering. According to census data reported by the University of Virginia Geospatial and Statistical Data Center, the population in the USA expanded rapidly from less than 4 million people in 1790 to approximately 283 million people in 2002. This exponential population growth within a relatively short time span has led to an American-folklore description of the country as a "melting pot" of ethnicities. Such a conceptualization has reduced the importance of ethnicity as central to identity formation, in favor of just being an American.

Therefore, race rather than ethnicity as a core concept used to describe a country's population is not usually used to describe the USA population. According to the CIA's *World Factbook* (2002), the majority of the population (77.1 percent) in the USA is White, followed by Black (12.9 percent), Asian (4.2 percent), Amerindian and Alaskan Native (1.5 percent), Native Hawaiian and Other Pacific Islander (0.3 percent), and Other (0.4 percent). A separate listing for Hispanic is not normally included in such racial figures because the US Census Bureau considers Hispanic to mean a person of Latin American descent (including persons of Cuban, Mexican, or Puerto Rican origin) living in the USA who may be of any race or ethnic group (White, Black, Asian, etc.).

American people are known for believing in "the American dream," which is an allegory that anyone who works hard enough can be successful and rise to the top. Martin Gannon in *Understanding Global Cultures* (2001) argues that the American dream is tied closely to the American value of exalting religion in everyday life. More than half of the population attends one of the 400,000 churches in the USA regularly. The American dream negates class barriers as an impediment to social and economic mobility. Instead, the dream promotes hard work as the means by which the average American can pursue a formal education, get a good job, and earn a high income. A chapter by Anders Hayden, "Europe's Work-Time Alternatives," cited in John de Graaf's book *Take Back Your Time* (2003), reports how hard Americans work in comparison with Europeans. When you add up all the overtime hours, the vacation days (Americans typically receive two weeks of vacation per year whereas Europeans typically receive four to five weeks per year), as well as the time that people actually spend at work (instead of when they are scheduled to work), Americans work an average of nine weeks more per year than European employees.

Americans are also known for being practical people more interested in functionality than aesthetics. In other words, generally it is more important to Americans that objects work than whether they are fancy or costly. This practicality can often be observed in the designs of American products. For example, houses are often constructed in a box-type shape, giving more emphasis to spacious inside living areas than outside aesthetic beauty. A further example is the plastic box that Americans often erect on the front lawn by the street for newspaper delivery. Figure 4.5 depicts the practical American house and the plastic newspaper box. Similarly, household furniture is often designed with more of a functional goal than an ornate or stylish goal.

Americans are also known for stressing the importance of the individual. This value system stems from a perception of society as being fundamentally composed of individuals. Under this value system, several assumptions about the individual are implicitly understood. First, the individual is responsible for his or her own destiny in life. Second, the individual should rely on government as little as possible; this assumption grows out of a basic suspicion of government—which is seen as having the potential to be an intrusive force in the lives of people. Third, the individual should promote his or her self-interests to others—also known in the USA as "you've got to sell yourself"—in order to succeed in life.

Government in the USA

Government in the USA is structured according to representative democracy, with power decentralized between a federal government and fifty state governments. The USA is referred to as a capitalist country because of the degree to which the private sector is relied on to provide public services. In USA national government, there are three main branches, which are designed to provide a check and balance against each other. The presidency comprises the executive branch. The president is elected by an electoral-college system in which a popular vote in each state selects a set number of electoral-vote representatives who then cast their votes for a presidential candidate. The legislative branch is a bicameral unit called Congress, which consists of the House of Representatives and the Senate. There are 435 members of the House of Representatives representing geographic constituencies

FIGURE 4.5   *Practical House with Plastic Newspaper Box in the USA*
Source: Robert McKenzie.

across the USA. There are one hundred members of the Senate—two members from each state. The third branch is the judiciary.

There are two major political parties in the USA. The Republican Party is more conservative, whereas the Democratic Party is more liberal. There are other, much smaller parties in USA government—Independent, Reform, Libertarian—but these parties do not have many representatives in government compared to the Democrats and Republicans. American political parties are known for favoring the center of the political spectrum. American parties try to avoid being portrayed as too far to the right or too far to the left.

CULTURAL CHARACTERISTICS OF MÉXICO (ESTADOS UNIDOS MÉXICO, OR MEXICAN UNITED STATES)

Geography of México

The Mexican United States—more commonly known as México—covers some 1,972,550 square kilometers/761,606 square miles. México is the eighth-largest country in the world and the third largest in Latin America, after Brazil and Argentina. México City is one of the three most populous cities in the world (the other two are São Paulo, Brazil, and Tokyo,

Japan). México is flanked by the Gulf of México on one side and the Pacific Ocean on the other side (see Map 4.5). Mexicans generally see themselves as having a dual allegiance to both the USA and to Latin America. México's relations with the USA are strengthened by their membership along with Canada in the North American Free Trade Agreement (NAFTA). México has close relations with most Latin America countries in part because of a shared language (Spanish is the primary language spoken in all Latin American countries except Brazil, Belize, and Guyana), and because México and Brazil are the two largest economies in Latin America.

México has a low-key relationship with the mother country, Spain, in terms of media exchanges. There is some presence of Spanish media content in México, such as *El Pais* (*The Country*) newspaper, and Spanish songs scattered on Mexican radio. But the distribution of Spanish media content to México designed to continue relations between mother country and a former colony is not as prolific compared to France and the UK and their respective former colonies.

Language in México

The dominant language in México is Spanish. Visitors to México will often find that if they do not try to speak any Spanish, they will not be understood very well. As in France, attempts by a visitor in México to speak even a few Spanish words generally will elicit a friendly disposition from Mexican people.

MAP 4.5 *Map of México*

México also has approximately twenty secondary indigenous languages, including two major ones—Mayan and Náhuatl (the predominant language in ancient Aztec civilization)—as well as minor ones such as Zapoteca, Mixe, and Tarasco. Indigenous languages are spoken all over México, but mainly in the southern states. The importance of preserving indigenous languages has led some states such as Oaxaca and Chiapas to institutionalize the teaching of one or more of these languages in public schools and to fund the production of indigenous programs for local radio and television stations.

The Spanish language was spread worldwide through Spain's colonial network. Aside from Spain, places where Spanish is spoken as a first language include the Latin American countries of México, Guatemala, Honduras, El Salvador, Nicaragua, Costa Rica, Venezuela, Colombia, Ecuador, Peru, Bolivia, Paraguay, Uruguay, Argentina, and Chile; most of the Caribbean islands plus the countries of Cuba, the Dominican Republic, and Puerto Rico; and the Canary Islands in Europe.

Society in México

In 2003, the population of México was approximately 105 million people. About 22 percent of the population (approximately 24 million people) in México lives in México City, México has a 92.2 percent literacy rate—those aged fifteen and up who can read and write. In México, 40 percent of the people live in poverty. The majority of the population in México (60 percent) is Mestizo (Indigenous and European), followed by Amerindian (30 percent), White (9 percent), and Other (1 percent).

Like other predominantly warm-climate countries, México is known for having outdoor street vendors just about everywhere you travel. Street vendors are not just in big-city and medium-town marketplaces, but also in rural areas. Some street vendors set up in town squares or on street sidewalks; others walk through car traffic. Street-vendor goods range from crafts such as jewelry and pottery, to food such as roasted corn on a stick, to clothes, to modern-day gadgets such as mobile phones. Street vendors display their goods on blankets, portable racks, tables, the sidewalks, roads, and on their bodies. Figure 4.6 depicts a typical scene of a city square full of street vendors.

Mexican people are also known for finding the subtle humor in almost all situations—simple ones such as people not being on time (a common occurrence), as well as more serious ones such as poverty or government corruption. As Jorge Portilla discusses in *Fenomenologia del Relajo* (1984), Mexicans call this humorous approach to life *relajo*. *Relajo* is a form of social commentary that no matter how bad things seem, humor can preserve a person's dignity. One example of *relajo* that was observed during research for this book is as follows: A tour guide, when talking about the history of Mexican politics, commented in a gentle tone of voice and with a smile that the "The President has been in office for five years and Mexican people are still waiting for the government to do something. . . . Anything."

Mexican people are also known for being very festive. Holidays, birthdays, weddings, and funerals are all celebrated with much zest and fanfare. Regardless of the occasion, usually colorful clothes are worn, loud music is played and sung, and elaborate food layouts are arranged. Mexican festivity is rarely brief and usually lasts many hours.

Mexican people are also known for being strongly influenced by Catholicism. The CIA's *World Factbook* (2003) on México lists Roman Catholicism as being practiced by almost 90 percent of Mexicans. Mexican people often comment that México is more

FIGURE 4.6   *Mexican Street Vendors*
Source: Robert McKenzie.

Catholic than Rome. Examples of the pervasiveness of Catholicism in Mexican life include cathedrals and churches with people worshiping at most hours of the day; an abundance of shops, even in small towns, selling Catholic artifacts; Catholic festivities—the most important of which is Our Lady of Guadalupe—being celebrated with great fanfare; and Catholic clothing, jewelry, and artifacts on people and in their houses and cars. In essence, Catholicism is an integral part of the lives of most Mexicans.

Government in México

Government in México is structured according to a quasi-representative democracy with power decentralized between the federal government and thirty-one state governments. Most (but not all) representatives are elected directly by the people. Mexican democracy is in a transitional stage of development as attempts are made to move away from a long history of government corruption and social poverty, toward political pluralism, economic growth, and the establishment of a body of law that is administered by an independent court system and government bureaucracies. The Mexican Constitution was adopted in 1917 after many years of conflict with other countries (Spain, the USA, and France) and between internal factions. México follows a capitalist orientation by default because of the degree to which the private sector is left to provide most public services, while the government concerns itself with attempting to eradicate poverty, crime, illiteracy, and undeveloped infrastructure.

In Mexican national government, there are three main branches designed to provide a check and balance against each other. The presidency comprises the executive branch. The president is elected directly by the voting public. The Congress is a bicameral unit that consists of the Chamber of Deputies and the Senate. There are five hundred members of the Chamber of Deputies representing geographic constituencies across México. There are 128 members of the Senate; four members represent each of the thirty-one states plus the federal district (*Distrito Federal*). The third branch is the judiciary.

There are three major political parties in México. The Institutional Revolutionary Party (PRI), which has been a center–left party, held the presidency from 1917 until 2000. The National Action Party (PAN), which broke the PRI's seventy-one-year tenure, has been a right-of-center party. The Revolutionary Democratic Party (PRD) has been a left-of-center party. In addition to these three major parties, there are two other minor parties that hold seats in Congress, including the Ecological Green National Party and the Convergence Party, both of which cut across traditional left–right party lines.

CULTURAL CHARACTERISTICS OF CHINA (PEOPLE'S REPUBLIC OF CHINA, OR 中国)

Geography of China

The People's Republic of China (PRC), or China as it is known internationally, covers some 9,596,960 square kilometers/3,705,407 square miles. China is the world's fourth-largest country (after Russia, Canada, and the USA). China is located in Eastern Asia, and borders the East China Sea, Korean Bay, Yellow Sea, and South China Sea. China borders many countries: Afghanistan, Bhutan, Burma, India, Kazakhstan, North Korea, Kyrgyzstan, Laos, Mongolia, Nepal, Pakistan, Russia (northeast and northwest), Tajikistan, and Vietnam (see Map 4.6). China's long history of 5,000 years shows it to be one of the world's earliest civilizations, and reinforces to Chinese people a uniqueness compared to much of the rest of the world. It is only recently that China's rise as an economic power has translated into international recognition of the country as a key player in world affairs.

China has twenty-three provinces (*sheng*), five autonomous zones (*zizhiqu*), and four municipalities (*shi*). Within these administrative divisions, China lays claim to a number of territories and disputed islands. In 1951, China annexed Tibet (*Xizang*) and designated it as one of its autonomous regions. China assumed control of Hong Kong (previously a British colony) in 1997 and the island of Macao (previously a Portuguese colony) in 1999. Designated as Special Administrative Zones, both Hong Kong and Macao function under a "one country, two systems" policy, in which socialist and capitalist ideologies coexist. Taiwan (previously known as Republic of China), and considered by China as the twenty-third province, is labeled by the Chinese government as a "renegade" state. The relationship between China and Taiwan remains tenuous, with both sides fiercely protecting their individual rights of possession and independence, respectively. China is also involved in a number of territorial disputes including the following: the Spratly Islands in the South China Sea (disputed by Malaysia, Philippines, Taiwan, Vietnam, and Brunei); Japanese-administered Senkaku-shoto (disputed by Diaoyu Tai); certain islands in the Yalu and Tumen rivers (disputed by North Korea); China-occupied Paracel Islands (disputed by Vietnam and Taiwan); and Kashmir (China controls a northeastern portion, Pakistan controls a northwest portion, and India controls a central and southern portion).

Language in China

The dominant language in China is Mandarin (or standard Chinese). Mandarin is based on the Beijing dialect and employs a simplified form of written script, as opposed to the complex form of written script used in Taiwan. There are some 6,500 characters in simplified

MAP 4.6   *Map of China*

written Chinese and 13,500 characters in complex Chinese. Following the 1949 revolution, Mao Zedong's Communist government stipulated that Mandarin be used as the standard spoken language in China, and efforts were made to simplify its written script to improve literacy rates among Chinese people. However, other dialects continue to be used in China. Cantonese is used in the southern province of Guangdong and Hong Kong, Shanghainese is used in Shanghai, and Hokkien as well as Hakka and other minority languages are used within pockets of ethnic groups. More recently, there has been a push for Chinese to become bilingual with an emphasis on English as the language of business communication. Accordingly, many national media outlets in China provide an online version of news in English to promote China to the rest of the world as an English-competent country. However, the Chinese continue to protect and promote the use of Mandarin within China.

Society in China

The population in China is the largest in the world, at 1.286 billion people. The majority of the population resides in rural areas (69.6 percent). Approximately 1 percent of the population lives in Beijing, the capital of China. China has an 86 percent literacy rate—those aged fifteen and up who can read and write. In China, 20 percent of the people live in poverty. The largest of the fifty-six ethnic groups living in China fall within the Han nationality

(92 percent), with the other groups constituting approximately 96.5 million people. Those groups with more than one million people include: Zhang, Hui, Uyghur, Yi, Miao, Manchu, Tibetan, Mongolian, Tujia, Bouyei, Korean, Dong, Yao, Bai, and Hani. The majority of the population in China is Han Chinese (91.9 percent). Approximately 8.1 percent of the population is made up of Zhuang, Uygur, Hui, Yi, Tibetan, Miao, Manchu, Mongol, Buyi, and Korean.

The Chinese government used a common language to unite the diverse ethnic groups and to promote Communist thinking—namely, a classless society in which all people have equal social and economic status, creating a community that acts as a whole. In recent years, this system has been replaced by a socialist market economy, in which some divisions between poorer rural and more affluent urban populations, as well as between generations, is tolerated. Chinese youth today are more focused on making money and enjoying life than previous generations.

Chinese people are known for continuing the practice of networking (or *guanxi*) in business dealings by prioritizing the building of relationships through respect and obligation rather than "doing business" in a traditional Western sense. This practice can be traced to Confucianism, one of two philosophies or religious teachings (the other being Taoisim) openly practiced before the Communist Revolution in 1949.

Chinese people are also known for practicing holistic (also known as traditional) medicine in which man is viewed as inseperable from the universe. Martin Gannon in *Understanding Global Cultures* (2001) describes this union as seeking simplicity in life rather than materialistic possessions. Holistic medicine involves a cosmic energy that maintains the sun, moon, and stars as existing within the human body as well. Various subpractices of holistic medicine include the *Yin* and the *Yang* (together as a single energetic force), which represent the balance and the polarity of masculinity and femininity; *Qi*, a life force that circulates energy throughout the body; *Five Elements*, which address the evolution of all materials in the physical world (wood, fire, earth, metal, and water); *acupuncture*, which involves the use of needles on designated energetic points; and *Chinese herbology*, the use and combination of various remedies (tea, pills, tablets, pads, ointments, powder, and lotions) to heal diseases.

Chinese people are also known for valuing artistic performance. One of the most well-known artistic endeavors is that of written Chinese script using sable brushes, ink, and rice paper to create pictographs (for example, 汉, which means "expressiveness") as well as calligraphy. Figure 4.7 shows an artist using these tools to create calligraphy.

Chinese artists also use their tools to create Chinese fables and Chinese opera, which continue to be widely performed in society to create distinct and vivid images that embody the philosophy of life in interesting short stories. Traditional Chinese opera integrates singing, music, dialogue, acting, and acrobatics.

Government in China

Government in China is structured according to a one-party political system representing a central state. The Communist Party of China, founded in 1921, is the ruling party and fought against the Kuomintang during the Chinese Civil War. Following the war, Mao Zedong assumed the role of paramount leader in 1949. Under Mao's leadership, Communist Party

FIGURE 4.7 *Calligraphy Artist in China*
Source: Ian Weber.

ideology was influenced heavily by Leninist Communism, which sought to overthrow capitalism through a workers' revolution and to redistribute the wealth via the working class. During his term, Mao closed off China to the outside world and eventually led the country into its controversial and chaotic Cultural Revolution (1966–1977), which pitted Chinese people against each other as the government attempted to purge nonsupporters of the Communist Party by sending them to "re-education camps" in rural China.

Following Mao's death in 1976, Deng Xiaoping assumed control in 1978 and attempted to rebuild the Communist Party structure. Deng introduced a period of radical change that set the scene for China's gradual move away from a totalitarian structure and toward policies that opened up China to Western investment and influences. The model for achieving these aims of becoming a modern, industrial nation was a "socialist market economy," which as defined under Chinese policy is state control combined with free markets and free trade. This definition reflects the pragmatic nature of Chinese culture.

All government institutions and political committees in China work to see that the Communist Party and state policy is followed and that nonparty members do not create autonomous organizations that could challenge the legitimacy of the government. The Party's highest body is the National Congress of the Communist Party of China. The primary organs of power within the Party are: the Politburo Standing Committee, which consists of nine members; the Politburo, which consists of twenty-two full members (including the Standing Committee); the Secretariat, which is the principal administrative mechanism of the Communist Party; the Central Military Commission; and the Discipline Inspection Commission, which is charged with rooting out corruption and malfeasance among party members.

The Chinese Communist Party holds a National Congress every five years to set national policy. At the National Congress, the Communist Party approves changes to the Party constitution and elects a Central Committee of approximately three hundred people. The Central Committee in turn elects the Politburo. The Party's central locus of power is the Politburo Standing Committee. In practice, positions within the Central Committee and Politburo are determined before the National Congress, so the main purpose of the Congress is to officially announce the Party policies and vision for the direction of China in the next five years.

CULTURAL CHARACTERISTICS OF GHANA (REPUBLIC OF GHANA)

Geography of Ghana

Ghana—formerly called the Gold Coast—covers some 239,460 square kilometers/92,456 square miles. Ghana is located in West Africa just north of the equator. Ghana borders three countries: the Ivory Coast, Burkina Faso, and Togo. To the south, Ghana borders the Gulf of Guinea, which leads to the Atlantic Ocean (see Map 4.7). Contemporary Ghana has strong trade relations with regional West African countries through the Economic Community of

MAP 4.7   *Map of Ghana*

West African States (ECOWAS), the Netherlands, Germany, China, and the UK. As a former colony and current member of the Commonwealth, Ghana's connection with the UK is particularly strong.

Ghana was one of the first countries in the world to become part of a network of global trading. In the 1400s, Portuguese sailors plundered the country's gold and transported it back to Europe. Then, from the 1400s through the early 1800s—in one of the most dehumanizing forms of early globalization—Portuguese, British, Dutch, and Danish traders purchased slaves from local Ghanaian kings, then transported and sold the slaves to owners in the Caribbean islands and the USA. After the slave trade was outlawed by Britain in 1807, Britain purchased land and forts from local Ghanaian kings and eventually declared Ghana a crown colony in 1873. Ghana gained independence from the UK in 1957.

Language in Ghana

All the countries that border Ghana are French-speaking countries. But in Ghana, English is the official language and is compulsory in the public school system. However, English is not universally spoken across the country because of the prevalence of indigenous Ghanaian languages. In Ghana, there are dozens of local languages (across the African continent there are approximately one thousand local languages). Some Ghanaian local languages are strictly oral (there is no written component), and many belong to families of languages. For example, in south-central Ghana, the languages of Ashanti, Fanti, Twi, and Akwapim belong to the larger family of the Akan language. However, if two people speak languages from different families of languages, they probably will not be able to understand each other very well. Both public and private broadcasters in Ghana cater to indigenous language speakers by airing some programs in the major indigenous languages.

Society in Ghana

In 2004, the population of Ghana was approximately 20.75 million people. Approximately 12 percent of the population lives in Kumasi. Ghana has a 74.8 percent literacy rate—those aged fifteen and up who can read and write. In Ghana, 31.4 percent of the people live in poverty. The vast majority of the population (98.5 percent) in Ghana is Black African, which breaks down further into Akan, 44 percent; Moshi-Dagomba, 16 percent; Ewe, 13 percent; Ga, 8 percent; Gurma, 3 percent; Yoruba, 1 percent. European and Other make up approximately 1.5 percent of the population.

Ghana is a developing country. Outside of the major cities, many areas of the country do not yet have basic infrastructure such as paved and curbed roads, electricity, running water, and waste disposal.

Ghana has a societal structure outside of the cities in which villages are organized according to kings, chiefs, and tribal members. The largest village is the Ashanti kingdom. Kings and chiefs are highly respected figures of nobility who wield strong authority over affairs of the kingdom or village. If the national government does not coordinate policies with local kings and chiefs, it is likely that such policies will not be successful. For example, in May 2003 the government had a difficult time getting people living in Afiadenyigba to use public toilets that the government had provided, because the program was not coordinated with or endorsed by the local chief (*Evening News*, 2004).

In Ghana, religion plays a big part in the lives of most people. In *Africa Through Ghanaian Lenses* (2004), edited by Samuel E. Quainoo, author Elom Doulo indicates that religion pervades social, economic, political, and really all cultural settings in Ghana. For example, religious symbols and practices are evident on billboard messages, in the common use of "God" in regular conversation, and in houses of worship consistently full of people. Roughly 63 percent of Ghanaians are Christian (mostly in the south), 16 percent are Muslim (mostly in the north), and 21 percent have traditional (indigenous) beliefs.

Ghanaian people are also known for exhibiting collectivist behaviors, wherein people willingly enter into relationships based on automatic trust because of familial or friendship ties. A common saying in Ghana is that two people who marry each other are also marrying each other's families. Acceptance into a Ghanaian family or friendship brings with it immediate privileges not afforded to strangers. For example, when a Ghanaian meets someone new, he or she will generally present a pleasant but somewhat reserved demeanor. However, if the new person is introduced as a friend or a colleague of someone who is also a friend of the Ghanaian person, typically the Ghanaian person will immediately show great openness and warmth in handshake, tone, and facial expressions. Thus, Ghanaians often try to mention a name of a mutual friend when introducing themselves or exchanging words, to establish a friendly tone to the conversation. Collectivism can also be seen when Ghanaians band together into small groups to spend time together and talk. Ghanaians involved in such group conversations will often be making jokes and laughing out loud. Often, when Ghanaians discuss a subject that turns toward analyzing why a situation is the way it is, someone will introduce an old African proverb to provide insight. For example, a journalist interviewed for this book cited an African proverb to explain why the first civilian government in Ghana had trouble governing and was eventually overthrown by a coup. The journalist stated that there is an old saying, "the first one to go down a road does not see the curves." Such proverbs usually draw on a primal experience of a human being venturing into nature. E. H. Mends explains in *Africa through Ghanaian Lenses* (2004) that the use of proverbs in Ghana reflects "group consciousness" associated with collectivism.

Ghana is also known for having outdoor vendors who casually roam through and beside vehicles on highways brought to a standstill because of traffic or traffic lights. The vendors bring a wide variety of products to the windows of each passenger in the vehicle. It is almost as though if you travel for an hour, you will have been cumulatively approached by a small store's worth of merchandise. Some edible products on offer include water packets, papaya, plantains, and nuts; other products include windshield wipers, newspapers, file folders, sunglasses, and fabrics. Many of these outdoor vendors—both female and male—carry their goods on trays balanced on the tops of their heads, as in Figure 4.8.

Government in Ghana

Government in Ghana is structured according to a parliamentary democracy that is in an infant stage. Kwame Nkrumah led the country to independence from Britain in 1957, became the country's first president, and then changed the name of the country from Gold Coast to Ghana. But subsequent to Ghana's independence, there were several years of coups that eventually resulted in the suspension of a constitution in 1982, the establishment

FIGURE 4.8   *Street Vendors Selling Fruit in Traffic in Ghana*
Source: Robert McKenzie.

of a military dictatorship, and the banning of political parties. Over the next ten years, there was a gradual decline in military rule until 1992, when a new constitution permitting multiple political parties was adopted. Since the establishment of the 1992 constitution, civilian governments have been democratically elected every four years. The year 2000 was particularly important because, for the first time, an opposition civilian government succeeded an incumbent civilian government through a democratic election.

Ghanaian democracy is in a very early stage as efforts are made to build a long-term track record of free and open elections, while developing economic stability for the private sector, the general population, and the government itself. Part of these efforts involve the Ghanaian government divesting itself of public-sector businesses (e.g., energy companies) to get the private sector more involved in the economy. The main intention is to enable the government to reduce expenses, so that it can better focus on uniting regional and tribal localism into a national culture and on improving the quality of life for Ghanaian citizens.

In Ghana's national government, there are three main branches, designed to provide a check and balance against each other. The president and vice president comprise the executive branch, and are elected directly by the voting public. The Parliament is a unicameral chamber that seats 230 elected members representing 230 geographic constituencies from ten regions. The third branch is the judiciary made up of the Supreme Court.

There are many major political parties in Ghana, some of which predate Ghanaian independence. However, it is difficult to characterize Ghanaian political parties according to traditional left–right or liberal–conservative dimensions because the current period of democratic government is so recent. The central focus of all of the political parties tends to be with developing basic services for Ghanaian people (disease immunizations), so the divisions between parties in terms of orientations tend to be more about which services are supported by which political parties. Nevertheless, the following tentative generalizations can be made about the political parties: The two main political parties in Ghana are the New Patriotic Party (NPP), which is known for advocating center-right positions, and the National Democratic Congress (NDC), which is known for advocating left and right positions. Smaller but still significant political parties include the National Independence Party (NIP), which is an offshoot of the NDC, and the People's National Congress (PNC), both of which are known for advocating positions to the center-left, as well as the Convention People's Party (CPP) and the Great Consolidated People's Party (GCPP), both of which are known for advocating positions mainly to the left.

CULTURAL CHARACTERISTICS OF LEBANON (THE REPUBLIC OF LEBANON, OR الجمهورية اللبنانية)

Geography of Lebanon

Lebanon covers some 10,400 square kilometers/4,015.5 square miles and is one of the smallest countries in the Middle East. Lebanon is part of a larger eastern Mediterranean region known as Bilad ash-Sham, sometimes referred to as the Fertile Crescent or Greater Syria. This region includes Lebanon, Jordan, Syria, and Palestinian territories. Lebanon is located in the eastern portion of the Arab world, and borders two countries (Israel to the south and Syria to the east and the north), as well as the Mediterranean Sea (see Map 4.8).

Lebanon has served as an important link between Europe, Asia, and Africa because of its geographic position on the Mediterranean Sea, and because of its multilingual populations that historically have been known for being entrepreneurial. Lebanon's mountainous

MAP 4.8   *Map of Lebanon*

areas are difficult to access and have made the country a refuge for ethnic and religious minorities. Today, Lebanon has eighteen officially recognized religious groups commonly referred to as sects (in Lebanon, the term *sect* does not have the negative connotations it has in some Western countries). Muslim sects form an estimated 60 to 70 percent of the population and the Christian sects form an estimated 30 to 40 percent of the population.

Lebanon was part of the Ottoman Empire for four centuries (from 1516 to 1918). UK and French forces, with the support of the Arab forces, defeated the Ottomans in World War I and subsequently occupied the whole area of Bilad ash-Sham. Arab forces led by Emir Faysal governed a large part of present-day Syria and Lebanon for a short period (between October 1918 and June 1920). The French army forced Arab fighters in 1920 to surrender to its control, and the League of Nations voted to place the Bilad ash-Sham region under the mandate of both England and France.

The terms of the mandate stipulated that England and France encourage local autonomy and facilitate the progressive development of the region toward independence. Accordingly, an agreement (called Sykes Picot) between these two powers divided the area into several new political entities. England managed the affairs of what became known as Iraq, Palestine, and Transjordan (later to become Jordan). France governed the areas of Syria and present-day Lebanon. The French created the State of Greater Lebanon in 1920 and declared this state a republic in 1926. Lebanon and Syria secured their independence from France in 1943.

Language in Lebanon

Arabic is the official language in Lebanon, with French as a second language. Although written Arabic is the same all over the Arab world, each Arab region has a distinct spoken dialect. The spoken Arabic in Lebanon is easily understood by Arabs in all countries of the Arab East (also known as al-Mashrek al-Arabi), which is composed of Bilad ash-Sham, the Arab Nile Valley region (Egypt and Sudan), and the Arab Gulf region (Bahrain, Kuwait, Oman, Qatar, Saudi Arabia, and the United Arab Emirates). Lebanese Arabic is understood with difficulty in Algeria, Morocco, and Tunisia, countries that together form what is known as the Arab West (also known as al-Maghrib al-Arabi). The official Lebanese school curriculum requires students to master two languages. In the past, French was the most common second language taught in Lebanese schools, but with the growing influence of the USA in the region, English is also widely taught in schools. As a result of the history of language use in Lebanon, most Lebanese people use Arabic, French, and English interchangeably in their daily conversations. The use of a foreign language represents a status symbol in Lebanon. For example, Lebanese families often speak English or French on a daily basis in their homes. Street and shop signs are usually in two languages. Restaurant menus are mainly in French, and sometimes have English translations, but rarely are in Arabic. Shop attendants usually respond to questions from customers in French or English, even if the questions are in Arabic.

Other languages are also common in Lebanon. One language is Syriac, an ancient language of the region. This language is often used in the services of some of the old Christian churches such as the Maronite Church, which represents the largest Lebanese Christian sect. A second language is Armenian, used mostly by Armenians who settled in

Lebanon in the second quarter of the past century. Armenians often live in exclusively Armenian neighborhoods and attend Armenian schools. A third language is Kurdish, spoken mainly by Kurds who have migrated from Turkey.

Society in Lebanon

The population of Lebanon is approximately four million people. Approximately 37.5 percent (1.5 million) of the population lives in Beirut (the capital) and its suburbs. Lebanon has a 87.4 percent literacy rate—those aged fifteen and up who can read and write. In Lebanon, 28 percent of the people live in poverty. The largest population in Lebanon by far is Arab (95 percent), followed by Armenian (4 percent), then Other (1 percent).

Lebanese people are known for embracing related values of politeness and saving face. These values dictate that it is improper to make another person look bad in conversation by pointing out faults in the other person. As part of these values, a Lebanese person is expected to show interest in the personal affairs of the people with whom he or she is conversing. This includes entering the personal space of the person with whom a Lebanese person is conversing and showing concern for that person. This cultural value of politeness and saving face sometimes creates communication problems between an Arab (and Lebanese) person and someone from the USA—not because of language disparity but because of cultural differences. For example, it is considered rude for an Arab businessperson to engage in conversation about a business transaction directly on visiting a firm. Instead, the Arab businessperson is expected to start a conversation with personal exchanges. Only after the coffee has been served can business discussions begin.

Lebanese people are also known for having a fluid perception of time. In essence, Lebanese perceive of time as something to be enjoyed rather than something to which people should be enslaved. For example, although Lebanese businesspeople bind themselves to the basic terms of verbal agreements, they do not bind themselves specifically to a fixed deadline. Often, work is submitted when it is finished to the satisfaction of the person doing it rather than according to a prearranged date. It is common for a vendor to tell a customer that the job will be finished "tomorrow," but the word *tomorrow* (*bukra* in Arabic) elusively means "sometime in the future."

Lebanese people are also known for striving to be first in almost every course of action. This desire to be first permeates Lebanese culture in many areas. For example, if a Lebanese customer goes to shop, that person normally will not wait for the shopkeeper to finish with the customer on hand. Instead, the customer entering the shop usually competes for the shopkeeper's attention with a request right away—usually leading the shopkeeper to handle both customers at the same time. As another example, Lebanese vehicle drivers constantly compete to get ahead, disobeying driving rules and causing chaotic traffic jams at almost every opportunity, as depicted in Figure 4.9. A common saying about traffic lights in Lebanon is that green means go, yellow is for decoration, and red is only a suggestion.

Government in Lebanon

Lebanon experienced a devastating civil war from 1975 to 1989. The result is a government in Lebanon that is structured according to a parliamentary republic with a weak national government having fragmented power. The 1990 constitution, which is one of several

FIGURE 4.9   *Competing Drivers in Chaotic Traffic in Lebanon*
Source: Nabil Dajani.

revisions to the original 1926 constitution that was modeled after the French Third Republic, states: "The decisions of the President must be countersigned by the Prime Minister and the Minister or Ministers concerned except the Decree designating a new Prime Minister and the Decree accepting the resignation of the Cabinet or considering it resigned. Decrees issuing laws must be countersigned by the Prime Minister." The 1989 Taif Agreement, which marked the end of the civil war, stipulated that Lebanese government (including the president, prime minister, Parliament, and all senior public officials) represent all the major religious sects in the country, half of which are to be Christian sects, and half of which are to be Muslim sects. Thus, political parties with power tend to represent religious sects and not ideologies. The major political power in Lebanon rests with the notables (*zu'ma*)—or people who represent influential families with a long history of public service—and religious leaders (who are usually in alliance with different *zu'ma*). In contrast, political parties in Lebanon play only a minor role in the political organization of the country. Accordingly, political divisions between the "right" and the "left" are largely a reflection of "confessional" attachments, that is, allegiances based on the belief that each religious community is a separate entity with interests that are distinct from those of other sects. In practice, Lebanese government is more of a tribal coalition of sectarian chieftains than a unified political body.

The National Pact of 1943, and later the Taif Agreement of 1989, distributed all major government positions according to the religious composition of the population as recorded in the 1932 census. Under this system, the presidency is reserved for a Maronite Christian, the position of prime minister is reserved for a Sunni Muslim, and the role of Speaker of the House is reserved for a Shi'ite Muslim. The Lebanese political system puts most of the power in the hands of the Maronite Christian president, who is elected by the Parliament for a nonrenewable term of six years. The Maronites are a local Catholic sect. A prime minister participates with the president in the selection of a cabinet, which has traditionally been a coalition of local sectarian and even tribal interests. Parliament is made up of 128 members elected to four-year terms by popular vote on the basis of sectarian proportional representation.

COMPARATIVE SUMMARY

It is clear that each of the eight countries has a unique and complex set of cultural characteristics that present a particular milieu in which a media system is cultivated. The geography of a country has an influence on the media content that crosses the country's borders. The languages in a country influence the languages in which media content is delivered, as well as the kinds of audiences that can be reached. As we will find out shortly, the cultural characteristics of a country predispose the population toward communicating in person and in media content according to particular conventions and with particular expectations. Moreover, the cultural characteristics of a country give rise to an overarching philosophy that permeates how media might operate within the given country.

CHAPTER 5

PHILOSOPHIES FOR MEDIA SYSTEMS

PRIMER QUESTIONS

1. What are some purposes that media serve for the government of the country in which you are living?
2. What are some purposes that media serve for the general population of the country in which you are living?
3. What are some purposes that media serve for the owners of media as well as media professionals in the country in which you are living?
4. How do purposes of media differ between poorer, smaller, or less stable countries versus richer, bigger, or more stable countries?
5. In what situations are freedoms for the media appropriate, and in what situations are freedoms of the media inappropriate?

Think about what kind of person you usually are when it comes to playing a game. Is it important to you to try to win at all costs, or are you happy just playing the game? Is it important to you that all the players follow the rules exactly as they are specified, or is it okay with you if some rules are modified? Is it important to you that you finish the game, or do you mind if the game gets called off because other things come up? How do your answers to these questions affect the effort you put into the game and the strategies you use? Though you may not think of your game-playing style as being guided by a particular philosophy, it probably is. For instance, perhaps you follow a philosophy that game playing is mainly for fun, which leads you not to have a "killer" instinct when you play a game. Perhaps you have a philosophy that most rules in life are bendable, which leads you to modify rules in a game depending on the situation. Perhaps you believe that just getting the chance to play a game is a nice treat, which leads you not to push to finish the entire game. The main point of laying out these simple scenarios of playing a game is to introduce the idea that your actions are often guided by a philosophy you hold, regardless of whether you are fully conscious of the philosophy while you are pursuing your actions.

Similarly, **philosophies for media systems** lie underneath the decisions that structure the operations of media systems. To refer back to the tree metaphor described in Chapter 3, the element of philosophies for media systems was likened to a root network that feeds the tree with nutrients from the soil but remains hidden from the naked eye. Similarly, a philosophy for a media system is perceived as a root network that feeds the media system with characteristics from the surrounding culture.

There is a large body of research in international media studies on philosophies for media systems. The research was largely initiated in 1956 by a seminal book, *Four Theories of the Press* (1963) by Frederick Siebert, Theodore Pederson, and Wilbur Schramm. That book has spawned decades of research into the provocative question: What is the overall purpose of media? As this area of research has evolved, so has the terminology. In the beginning stages, the research was called **normative theories of the press.** Then, as electronic media became more widespread, the word *press* was dropped in favor of *normative theories of media.*

But normative-theories research became problematic because of a growing recognition that such research was conceptually biased in ways that affected the usefulness of the findings. One bias from the outset was the use of the term *normative* to indicate that an evaluative standard could be developed to assess the relative worth of all of the theories. As Nerone et al. point out in *Last Rights: Revisiting Four Theories of the Press* (1995), the premise lurking in the background of normative-theories research was that certain theories (libertarian, social responsibility) of the media had ethical superiority over other theories (authoritarian, communist). This premise led to skewed evaluations of media systems, such as: government control of the media is never desirable whereas freedom from government control of media is always desirable. Adding to the bias in early normative theories was an assumed meaning of freedom of the media, defined exclusively as freedom from interference by government or the military. Left out of this definition, however, was the acknowledgment that defining freedom of media should also cover independence from corporations and peer pressure. For example, according to the April 2, 2003, *Guardian,* a reporter (Peter Arnett) was fired from NBC News in the USA for saying on Iraqi television during the 2003 Iraq War that the USA-led coalition's initial war plan had failed. Arnett's firing is an example of how media systems operating within a market-based system are also subject to restrictions on communicating values that are perceived to contradict values (patriotic values, in this case) of a media corporation, a government, or a society as a whole. Because of the tacit biases of early normative-theories research, conclusions of the research tended to focus on the dangers of government or military influences on the media, while ignoring dangers of corporate or populist influences on the media.

As a result, normative-theory research increasingly has been conceptualized into **philosophy** research, to better describe a more even line of inquiry into the purpose of media. As Edmund Lambeth explains in John Merrill's *Global Journalism* (1995), a philosophical inquiry helps to identify the values that cultivate the development of a media system. Moreover, by articulating philosophies for media systems instead of normative theories a shift is facilitated from analyzing standard (or normal) procedures for how media systems "should" operate, to analyzing values that guide assumptions about how a media system "might" operate. This transformed analysis of philosophies takes into account significant cultural characteristics that affect the development of a country's media system and presupposes that there are many valid options for setting up a media system given with an overall purpose in mind.

Below, six philosophies for media systems are listed. The first four are legacy philosophies that have histories extending back over decades or centuries. The other two are contemporary philosophies that are more recent. Each philosophy envisions a different overarching purpose for a media system.

Legacy Philosophies (Formerly Normative Theories)

1. Authoritarian
2. Libertarian
3. Communist
4. Social Responsibility

Contemporary Philosophies

5. Developmental
6. Democratic-Participant

Researching the purpose of a media system is only a starting point for discussing how media might serve a particular population. Philosophies for a media system are simply diagnostic, imperfect tools that nevertheless help us to understand how and why media systems appear to have different purposes across various countries.

AUTHORITARIAN PHILOSOPHY

Authoritarian philosophy holds that the head of the country is an all-knowing ruler who deserves obedience and acquiescence. The ordained right of this ruler is to protect the country and to provide discipline and order to its way of life. To this end, authoritarian philosophy often holds that traditional culture should be aggressively maintained against encroaching external or contemporary culture, both of which are seen as eroding sacrosanct traditional values. Examples of encroaching culture that have been considered to be undesirable include revealing clothing, lackadaisical religious practices, and popular arts.

Sometimes the head of state asserts a claim as ruler by virtue of reality royalty, such as a king or queen. Sometimes the head of state asserts a claim to the position through hereditary peerage—that is, by virtue of family lineage, there are inherent rights to the position. Sometimes the head of state asserts a claim to the position as a direct liaison to a supreme being. Often the head of state is a former or current military officer. All of these lineages emphasize the head of state as being someone who has an intrinsic right to the ruler position.

The historical precedents for authoritarian philosophy can be found in ancient Greece and in sixteenth-century Europe. The core writings interpreted to advocate authoritarian philosophy include three works by Plato—*The Republic, Statesman*, and *The Laws*—and *The Prince* (1992) by Niccolo Machiavelli. Authoritarian philosophy views the head of a nation-state as exemplifying Plato's concept of a philosopher-king, and uses Plato's argument that it is a necessity for a nation-state to have a superior philosopher-king. Authoritarian philosophy draws on Machiavelli's justifications and strategies for heads of state to consolidate and exercise power in the name of bringing societal order where there might otherwise be chaos. Some of the ideals that guide authoritarian philosophy have been embraced by proponents of fascism.

Authoritarian philosophy tends to be adopted in countries where elite segments of society—such as those who are formally educated or those who come from wealthy backgrounds—perceive that society is vulnerable to severe internal or external threats. Perceived internal threats include factional conflicts, food supply shortages, disease outbreaks, and natural disasters. Perceived external threats include terrorism, conflicts with other countries, contaminated food imports, and culturally imperial media imports.

Authoritarian philosophy is commonly represented in the governance of society in three main areas. First is the **decree.** A decree is issued by a ruler, and then adhered to by government agencies and citizens without much formal debate or acclamation by vote. Second is the **legislative process.** The process commonly involves the ruler submitting a policy to a deliberative body that debates the policy—perhaps only as a formality—and then enacts it into law. Third is interpretation of **religious doctrine.** Religious doctrines are interpreted from sacred texts by religious leaders and then formulated into policy or law by the government.

When a media system draws on the roots of authoritarian philosophy, at least three principles are commonly followed. First is the principle of **serving the state.** Under this principle, media exist to disseminate information that only the state deems to be appropriate. All information—news, public-service information, entertainment, sports, culture, and so on—must serve the goals of the state. Therefore, any information that has the potential to deviate from state initiatives must be approved by state officials before it can be disseminated by the media.

Second is the principle of **immunity of the state.** Under this principle, media are not permitted to criticize the state. One reason given is that the state is morally superior; therefore, criticism from a morally inferior media organization would be inappropriate. In addition, any criticism of the state by the media may be detrimental to the fragile stability of a country if it causes internal divisions, leaving the country susceptible to anarchy or an invading country. Consequently, authoritarian philosophy holds that there should be no commentary, news reporting, political satire, comedy spoofing, or other kinds of media content that call into question the activities, policies, and laws of the state.

Third is the principle of **state control over the media.** Here, media are either privately or publicly owned, but in either case are controlled by the state. The control is deemed necessary because of a perception that media have too much potential power that could be used to unseat the state or destabilize the country. Therefore, media cannot operate independently of state control. In essence, media organizations function as extensions of the state bureaucracy.

Authoritarian media philosophy is commonly implemented through two procedures. First is the control of content, which can take the form of state censorship or self-censorship. **State censorship** is when a government agency reviews content prior to its dissemination in the media. If the content is judged by the agency to be contrary to state objectives, then the content is not approved for dissemination. **Self-censorship,** within this context, is when the media organization prevents content from being disseminated because it is perceived to be contrary to state objectives; though the media professionals involved may disagree with that categorization, they may also still choose not to disseminate the content because they are wary of retribution from the state.

The concern about retribution introduces a second procedure commonly undertaken to implement authoritarian media philosophy: **punishment.** Under authoritarian philosophy, the state has the right to penalize individuals and media organizations for **seditious libel** (criticism of the state). Such penalties vary according to the perceived seriousness of the crime. At the more lenient end of the scale, punishments can include reprimands, dismissals, and fines. At the harsher end of the scale, punishments can include the closing of a facility, the incarceration of media professionals, and even torture or death. Such punishments may not even be legal, but are carried out nevertheless.

LIBERTARIAN PHILOSOPHY

Libertarian philosophy holds that the individual is responsible for civic participation and the discovery of truth. Central to this proposition is the belief that individuals take responsibility for their own actions. Libertarian philosophy argues that to provide the proper social structure for individuals to pursue their own self-determined destinies, the law must protect individuals from undue interference and retribution from the government. Libertarian philosophy argues that the proper role of government is to concern itself with defending the state against hostile countries or assisting the state during national disasters, rather than intervening in individuals' personal lives by attempting to regulate their morals and interests.

The historical precedent for libertarian philosophy can be found in seventeenth-century England. The core writings that spurred libertarian philosophy include *Two Treatises of Government* (1993) and *An Essay Concerning Human Understanding* (1894) by John Locke, *The Wealth of Nations* (1991) by Adam Smith, and *On Liberty* (1982) by John Stuart Mill. Libertarian philosophy arose out of a concern for the right of an individual to exist without intrusion from the state. As a response to monarchical oppression, libertarian philosophy sought to empower citizens to take control over their own lives. Some ideals that guide libertarian philosophy have been embraced by proponents of capitalism.

Libertarian philosophy tends to take root in societies in which there is heightened suspicion about the power of government. One area in particular in which libertarian philosophy has asserted a minimalist role for government is commerce—the buying and selling of goods and services. Libertarian philosophy holds that if government is too involved in regulating the commerce of the state, then the true needs of the people will be obviated in favor of what the government perceives to be the needs of the people. This assumption implies that there is too much temptation for a government involved in state commerce to pick and choose which makers and sellers of products and services are successful, and ultimately how people are served. Therefore, libertarian philosophy holds that commerce should be subjected not to government objectives but rather to a free marketplace of people—otherwise known as consumers.

Libertarian media philosophy is commonly represented in the governance of society through two main avenues. First is **constitutional law** that provides for the private ownership of property. The thinking is that if citizens can own their own property—which refers to land and housing—then citizens will use that property to chart their own destiny in a way that helps them satisfy a search for truth. In other words, if government owns the property that individuals use, there is little incentive for the individual to explore his or her true potential. The second is **legislative** and **judicial law** that stimulates a free market in which ideas and products can compete against each other. The assumption behind law of this kind is that in a free marketplace, the better ideas and better products will win out over those that are inferior. These two areas of law are seen as central to the ideal of curtailing the role of government so that it is engaged primarily in fostering the growth of individual liberty.

When a media system draws on the roots of libertarian philosophy, at least two principles are commonly followed. First, most media are **privately owned and operated.** This principle establishes the right of media to operate as a commercial activity and to make a profit. The assumption is that profitable media are evidence of an approving marketplace of public opinion. In other words, if the public thinks highly enough of media content, they will vote for it through their habits of television viewing, radio listening, or newspaper reading. In so doing, the public is exercising individual liberty from government mandates or intentions.

Second, government can enter the marketplace only to maintain **fair competition.** Thus, it is appropriate for government to develop laws and policies ensuring that bigger players do not have unfair advantages over smaller players. Fairness extends to enforcing rules so that no media organizations are breaking the law to gain a competitive advantage. For example, **predatory pricing** is when a larger company or individual with multiple product lines temporarily offers an artificially low price on selected products until smaller competitors are driven out of business—after which the prices are raised again.

Third, according to libertarian philosophy, the media **regulate themselves** rather than be regulated by government. According to libertarian philosophy, when marketplace competition drives the development of media products and services, companies will automatically regulate themselves in order to satisfy the needs and interests of the marketplace.

Libertarian media philosophy is implemented through a balance between **rewards** and **punishments** designed to encourage individuals and organizations with media properties to engage in fair competition. As a reward for successful competitive behavior, individuals and companies are permitted to accumulate capital and profit. This financial incentive can extend to property acquisitions, material comfort, and investment. However, if individuals and companies pursue unfair competition, individuals and companies are punished for engaging in illegal activities. The punishment may consist of a government or court-ordered fine if the individual or company is successfully prosecuted.

COMMUNIST PHILOSOPHY

Communist philosophy holds that the role of the state is to be the caretaker for the well-being of society. To this end, a centralized government plans the distribution of both the necessities of sustenance and the pleasures of culture. The role of the individual in this process is to respect the state's objectives and methods for bettering society. In other words, the needs and interests of the individual are de-emphasized in favor of the needs and interests of society. Communist philosophy holds that if individuals work together as a collective whole, then it is possible to achieve an egalitarian society in which there are no wealthy classes and no poverty classes. Such a society would exhibit a roughly equal distribution of wealth across all segments of society.

The historical precedent for communist philosophy was established in the late seventeenth and early eighteenth centuries in Germany. Primary writings that influenced communist philosophy include *Philosophy of Right* and *Philosophy of History* (1956) by Georg Wilhelm Friedrich Hegel and *The Communist Manifesto* (1967) by Karl Marx. The contrast between the ideals of communism and the way in which it has been practiced by some governments has at times obscured a tempered study of communist philosophy as it relates to media systems.

Communist philosophy tends to arise out of a concern for the exploitation of laborers by business owners. This concern centers on the acknowledgment that owners of manufacturing facilities and farms are failing to spread the wealth of their industries to the laborers who produced the actual products. From the vantage point of communist philosophy, the wealth that is being accumulated from these industries causes an undesirable schism between wealthy classes of people (bourgeoisie) and poorer classes of people (proletariat).

Communist philosophy has particular appeal to agricultural societies undergoing rapid industrialization. Communist philosophy warns that the radical transformation from agriculture to industry creates challenges of protecting manual laborers from abusive working conditions created by wealthy industry owners. Such conditions involve the low pay of workers in unsafe conditions and the absence of easy access to health care and education. Communist philosophy also attempts to prevent the populace from succumbing to materialistic tastes and values that have been standardized for the masses. Materialism is seen by communist philosophy as an oppressive force driven by exploitative economic motives rather than by more culturally redeeming motives.

Communist philosophy is commonly represented in the governance of society through two main methods. First is the **decree**, which is issued by the communist party. Decrees may be voted on at the party level, but they normally are not subjected to a voting process participated in by the general population. Second is the **planning objective.** The planning objective is developed and administered by a central government committee. Planning objectives allocate resources to achieve economic targets for goods and services to be provided to the population at fair prices and without surplus waste. Planning objectives may be short term (immediate) or longer term (five years and beyond).

When a media system draws on the roots of communist philosophy, at least three principles are commonly followed. First is **state ownership of property.** Under communist philosophy, private property ownership and the profit motive are seen as unwelcome vices that lead to class division, greed, and the popularization of tastes in such a way as to demean culture. The assumption is that if media are privately owned and commercially driven, the result will be competition that produces content designed to pander to popular tastes—content with little educational or cultural value. Such a strategy is thought of as merely producing content that appeals to the lowest common denominator among people to attract the largest audience possible. In contrast, communist philosophy argues that if media are owned and operated by the government, content can be produced without acceding to a profit-making model—rather, content can edify the populace's knowledge of and appreciation for high arts.

A second, related principle of communist philosophy is the use of media to **elevate public tastes.** Communist philosophy holds that when the general population is left to determine the content of media on their own, the result will inevitably be a dumbing down of the content into primal or sensational themes that have limited societal value. Instead, communist philosophy calls for media to promote more tasteful and sophisticated content such as ballet, orchestral music, ice skating, and gymnastics.

Third, media are to be used as a tool for **teaching communist doctrine.** Using the media for this purpose is considered necessary to guard against the temptations of materialism, which is seen to foster self-interests, detachment from other human beings, and ultimately greater fissures between wealthier and poorer classes. Therefore, communist philosophy holds that media should remind people about the importance of communal values that elevate society to more enlightened levels. Moreover, it is important for media to teach younger people about the virtues of communist philosophy.

Communist philosophy is implemented through two general procedures. First is the control of content through **censorship,** which is administered by government agencies that review the content before it is distributed. Censorship agencies may be located within the government or within a media organization. Second is **punishment.** Under communist philosophy, the state has the right to punish individuals and media organizations for criticizing communist doctrine or for demeaning prescribed cultural values. The penalties range from dismissal from a position to detention in prison.

SOCIAL RESPONSIBILITY PHILOSOPHY

Social responsibility philosophy holds that government influence the media to provide fair and balanced information with a goal of effecting change for the better in society. Much of social responsibility philosophy focuses on news media, though the philosophy also applies to other media content and to media operations in general. According to social responsibility philosophy, government is envisioned as an indirect but persuasive influence in getting the media industry to set codes of conduct to which media professionals voluntarily adhere. Specifically, the role of government is to guarantee that society as a whole benefits from a vigorous and reasoned debate in an effort to achieve a greater public civility, but that the names of people, institutions, and ideas are not unnecessarily smeared in the process. Social responsibility philosophy requires media organizations to regulate themselves, and also required government to step in on behalf of the public when media organizations fail to regulate themselves adequately.

Thus, social responsibility philosophy positions media ownership as a public trust wherein media organizations have certain obligations to society and exist primarily to serve the public. Media are allowed to operate with relative freedom from government control, but the government, acting as a surrogate of the people, is allowed to place expectations on the conduct of media organizations. To facilitate this relationship, media are permitted to have access to government activities and records that not have been classified for national security purposes. In return, media are expected to refrain from promoting unnecessary cynicism and pessimism in public debates. This requires media professionals to approach their roles with great diligence and care.

The historical precedent for social responsibility philosophy was established in the 1940s in the USA, which makes this philosophy a relative newcomer to the typology of philosophies for media systems. The core writings for social responsibility philosophy include a report by a self-appointed public-interest committee called the Hutchins Commission; a book, *Freedom of the Press: A Framework of Principle*, by William Ernest Hocking; and a book some 30 years later, *Responsibility in Mass Communications* (1980), by William Rivers, Wilbur Schramm, and Clifford Christians. The Hutchins Commission was formed during World War II by Robert Maynard Hutchins, then president of the University of Chicago, to study the role of media in modern-day societies. As a result of its work, the commission issued a report, *A Free and Responsible Press* (1947), that incubated social responsibility as a philosophy for a media system. Some ideals of social responsibility philosophy serve as the basis of socialism, whereas others serve as the basis of capitalism.

Social responsibility philosophy arose out of a concern about large newspaper companies during World War II that were publishing increasingly sensationalized stories about domestic corruption and overseas totalitarianism. From the vantage point of social responsibility philosophy, fierce competition among primarily large American newspaper companies had degenerated into a disproportionate amount of seedy journalism that was stirring up public fears about Nazism and Communism. Within this context, social responsibility philosophy questioned the proper role of journalism in disseminating information to society.

Social responsibility philosophy has particular appeal to societies that desire a proactive but nonintrusive role of government in the affairs of the people. In such societies, it is considered appropriate for government to intercede with coercive dialogue or laws in media operations gone awry. Although it is preferable that media professionals correct tonal problems on their own, government leaders retain the option of regulatory or legislative actions to rein in media organizations that exhibit egregiously irresponsible conduct.

Social responsibility philosophy is represented in the governance of society in two areas. First is the **bully pulpit,** wherein government leaders threaten government action, which puts pressure on media professionals to establish their own codes of conduct through professional associations. Second is **regulation,** wherein government enacts legally binding regulations that are designed to preserve a standard of quality to media content. Such regulations may be passed through legislation voted on by elected representatives or issued by government-related agencies.

When a media system draws on the roots of social responsibility philosophy, at least three principles are followed. First, news media routinely provide **factual coverage tempered** with **contextual information.** In news coverage, journalism is expected to provide an appropriate historical context that helps to put the information into perspective. By discussing related events from the past, news media help to guard against cynicism and sensationalism.

Second, media content contains **balanced opinion** and **commentary.** One level of balanced opinion has to do with maintaining equilibrium between the opinions that are presented. For instance, opinions on the political right should be balanced by political opinions on the left; negative news should be balanced by positive news; commentary in favor of a position should be balanced by commentary against a position; and so on. Another level of balanced opinion has to do with sampling a variety of backgrounds of people to voice opinions. Opinions should be solicited from media professionals, government officials, industry leaders, experts from education, common citizens, and other categories of people.

Third, editors and directors should **clarify societal goals and desires.** According to social responsibility philosophy, in addition to just reporting news events, news media are to provide analysis about whether the covered events indicate an adherence to socially redeeming values that are commonly exalted by society. The analysis of societal values can include on-air editorials on radio and television and letters to the editor in newspapers. Such guidelines, which normally are formally published or aired by media organizations, are ultimately meant to elevate the overall quality of media content.

Social responsibility philosophy is commonly implemented through two procedures. The first is **public accountability** through laws and regulations. Such laws stipulate that if there is enough of a public outcry over the activities of a media organization, the government has a right to launch an investigation. If the investigation proves negligent on the part of the media organization, the government can levy a fine against the media organization or take away its right to operate. Second is the use of **public admonishment.** If a media organization engages in activities that the public determines to be at odds with widely held societal values, then the government can engage in a dialogue with the public through the media that effectively embarrasses the media organization and thereby causes it to modify the questionable content or activities.

DEVELOPMENTAL PHILOSOPHY

Developmental philosophy holds that media are to improve the social conditions of developing nations. Such plans have sometimes been interpreted differently through differing ideological orientations. Non-Western thinking generally has envisioned the developmental role for media to be that of strengthening the capabilities of poorer countries to foster stability and autonomy. In contrast, Western thinking generally has envisioned the developmental role for media more specifically to be that of advancing democracy and free-market economics. This basic difference in interpretation has often led to conflicts in situations in which more affluent, Western countries are supplying financial and resource support for development efforts in poorer, non-Western countries.

Divisions in interpretations aside, developmental philosophy requires government to support the role of media as a stimulant for social change. In developing countries there is often little potential advertising revenue or private capital to build media infrastructure. To that end, government is expected to acquire media technology and to deploy it with the purpose of fixing situations that contribute to social hardships. Particular situations that proponents of developmental philosophy have in mind include financial corruption, public health crises, illiteracy, and factional conflict. Developmental philosophy envisions a relationship in which government provides funding for media to actively engage in eradicating such social problems through education. Such a relationship requires government and media to work together in the interests of strengthening each other and in ultimately improving the quality of life in a country.

Developmental philosophy was formulated out of a concern for why developing countries were not making more progress in achieving financial solvency for their governments and a better quality of life for their inhabitants. Previously, it was thought that once developing countries had invested in modern media systems that imported content from the outside world, profound and positive social changes would occur. However, this scenario had not played out as expected in many impoverished countries located mainly in Africa, Asia, and South America.

The historical precedent for developmental philosophy—also sometimes referred to as advancement philosophy—is difficult to pinpoint. Developmental philosophy culminated during the UNESCO debates (see Chapter 2) in a report by Sean MacBride called *Many Voices, One World* (1980). Though developmental philosophy was crystallized by the UNESCO debates, the primary writings for developmental philosophy actually precede the dialogue at the United Nations by about twenty-five years. These writings include

The Passing of Traditional Society (1958) by Daniel Lerner, *The Stages of Economic Growth* (1971) by Walt W. Rostow, *Mass Media and National Development* by Wilbur Schramm, and *Agents of Power* (1984) by J. H. Altschull. Developmental philosophy remains in its nascent stages.

Developmental philosophy is represented in the governance of society in two main areas. First is the **legal establishment of media freedom**—that is, independence from government control. Because governments in developing countries often resist granting media freedom because of government officials wishing to avoid having their activities closely scrutinized, proponents of developmental philosophy call for international pressure to exert what is seen as the necessary leverage to establish freedom for the media to operate autonomously. Specifically, developmental philosophy calls for the legal establishment of media freedom to criticize the government so that governments will be less likely to engage in corruption that effectively stalls the easing of fundamental social problems. Second is the **government mandate,** which requires media to perform certain tasks in exchange for funding. Funding from government is seen as necessary because of a lack of available private investment capital. The government mandate also can be exercised as part of a trade with media, wherein media deploy resources and distribute content to address societal problems and in exchange are provided with access to government operations.

When a media system draws on the roots of developmental philosophy, three principles typically are followed. First, media serve as a **watchdog** on the activities of government, especially efforts to improve physical infrastructure (roads, bridges, water supply, food distribution, and health care). The chief means by which the watchdog function is fulfilled include the news report, the news article, and the documentary. It is argued that such content will lead to more accountability for government activities, as well as increasing aspirations of a country's residents.

Second, media pursue **cultural autonomy.** This principle assumes that for a developing country to remain or become established as an independent and viable nation, the country's media system promotes the country's distinctive culture. Cultural autonomy is seen as particularly important for developing countries that may be subject to overwhelming foreign cultural influences accompanying imported media content. Thus, it is important for media organizations to provide a means of access for indigenous peoples to produce media content for the purpose of passing on authentic cultural traditions such as specialized languages.

Third, media **export domestic media content** to other countries. This serves not only to make the rest of the world more aware of the developing country, but also reinforces the developing country as a sovereign and stable entity in the eyes of the international community. Governments of developing countries may need to fund the production of programs or the marketing of these programs to compete with wealthier countries that have advantages of economies of scale and prior name recognition. Also, developing countries may need to band together into regional alliances to share resources and to put together enough content with enough variety so that the offerings are lucrative to foreign markets.

Developmental philosophy generally is implemented in two main areas. The first is **international assistance.** Such assistance may take the form of World Bank loans, country-to-country loans, debt forgiveness, and equipment and software donations. Furthermore, the threat of withdrawing such assistance should serve as an incentive for developing nations not to shirk from stimulating media development. Second is **public expectation.** Here the thinking is that if residents of a country are led to expect improvements in social conditions by being exposed through media content to a better quality of life in foreign countries, they will be more likely to rise up against their government or exercise what voting options they have to speed up the desired changes if improvement is proceeding too slowly.

DEMOCRATIC-PARTICIPANT PHILOSOPHY

Democratic-participant philosophy holds that citizen-created content is essential to all forms of government. Without the participation of citizens, democratic-participant philosophy sees social policy as unduly influenced by wealthy corporate executives or elitist government officials. Democratic-participant philosophy acknowledges that the role of the citizen in the formation of social policy is meant to vary according to the structure of a country's government. But democratic-participant philosophy argues that the citizen's voice is central to any government that seeks to successfully manage the affairs of its people. Consequently, democratic-participant philosophy proposes formulating media operations in such a way as to involve citizens in all phases of producing media content.

The historical precedent for democratic-participant philosophy—also sometimes known as public-advocacy philosophy—was established in the 1970s through the 1990s in the USA. Seminal writings on democratic-participant philosophy include "Constituents of a Theory of the Media" (1970) by H. M. Enzensberger in the *New Left Review; The New News v. The Old News* (1992) by Jay Rosen and Paul Taylor; *Getting the Connections Right: Public Journalism and the Troubles in the Press* (1996) by Jay Rosen; and *Public Journalism: Theory and Practice* (1994) by Jay Rosen and Davis Merritt. Democratic-participant philosophy is still emerging as a cohesive set of values.

The impetus for democratic-participant philosophy is the perception that disenfranchised groups have been excluded from media production processes otherwise dominated by corporations and governments. The disenfranchised groups include ethnic, religious, political, age, and gender minorities. Together these minorities are seen as common citizens lacking general access to media production, which instead is provided almost exclusively to media professionals.

Democratic-participant philosophy argues that two situations most often create disenfranchisement. One involves countries with media systems operated largely by transnational media conglomerates, which are seen as stultifying the involvement of common citizens in the process of creating content. In such an environment, decisions about media content are made according to highly regimented institutional formulas revolving around audience ratings, advertising pressures, government objectives, and corporate marketing strategies. Consequently, the media content that results from stale corporate formulas is predominantly uniform, commercial, and professional. These qualities of content stand in contrast to that of citizen-created media content, which tends to be heterogeneous, noncommercial, and amateurish. Such nonconformist, creative qualities are seen as desirable because they involve unadulterated creativity and self-expression. Though democratic-participant philosophy concedes that there is a proper place for corporate media content in the universe of social discourse, it insists that there should also be a place for alternative content, including the right of citizens to reply to corporate media content with which they disagree.

A second situation creating disenfranchisement involves countries that have media systems administered largely by government agencies. In such countries, regular citizens typically are prevented from performing an integral role in the creation of media content unless that role supports government objectives. According to democratic-media philosophy, such an exclusionary system is counterproductive even to governments that are not based on democratic participation, because such governments cannot be responsive to their citizens without citizens participating in social discourse through the media.

Democratic-participant philosophy is represented in the governance of society in two main areas. First is **citizen-group pressure.** This entity is a collection of individuals, usually at the local level, that attempts to gain greater access for citizens in both the use of media production equipment and in the creation of institutional media content. Citizen pressure groups operate through letter- and email-writing campaigns as well as phone calls. Often, their successes at opening up media content to citizen input are achieved with media organizations that target local audiences. These media may be owned by larger parent companies, but the companies allow the local community to have a say in the determination of media content.

The second area in which democratic-participant philosophy is represented is through **alternative media start-ups**—that is, organizations formed with the express purpose of providing alternative voices and conventions for producing media content. The people who start up these organizations typically view themselves as outside the political or professional mainstream of content represented in the majority of media choices. Such people are producers, videographers, writers, editors, journalists, and others. Though adequate financing is often a problem, the people involved in alternative media start-ups find a way—usually through volunteer efforts—to produce alternative media based on their professional experience and their resourcefulness.

When a media system draws on the roots of democratic-participant philosophy, two principles are commonly followed. First, media organizations take exception to government-driven objectives and corporate profit motives to make room for **citizen-initiated media content.** This requires a modification in the usual model for creating media content, in that media must allow citizens to have a say in the content that is created by professionals of media organizations. Examples of putting this principle into practice include placing citizens on advisory boards and allowing citizens to write their own newspaper columns and to host radio and television shows. Second, **citizen groups are guaranteed the freedom to express opinions** without fear of retribution from the government or from corporate media. In essence, this boils down to allowing citizen groups to voice criticism without being harassed or imprisoned by government, without having the content censored or modified unnecessarily by the media organization, and without being denied access to the organization's media facilities in the future.

Democratic-participant philosophy is implemented in many ways, but three procedures are most common. First, media content includes **citizen viewpoints** that take on a number of forms depending on the particular medium. Examples include: internet web sites that can provide links for unedited citizen commentary; newspapers that provide space for citizen editorials (appearing as letters to the editor or as expanded articles placed in other sections of the newspaper); radio and television stations providing time for citizen editorials; radio and television stations incorporating citizen voices into talk-oriented programming; and radio and television stations casting citizens alongside stars in selected programs. Proponents of democratic-participant philosophy argue that citizen viewpoints are essential to media content that covers politics—especially campaign coverage. Media are expected to survey citizen opinions to help generate the issues that candidates and elected officials are expected to address.

Second, media organizations allow **citizens to participate in the process of producing content.** In one form of participation, citizens hold seats on advisory boards set up by media organizations to solicit ideas for content. Elsewhere, media organizations provide mechanisms for obtaining citizen feedback that can influence the production process. These mechanisms can include email and post-mail addresses and voicemail phone numbers.

Third, **citizens are provided with access to media facilities** to produce and distribute their own content. This means that corporate or government media must provide funding for citizens to purchase equipment and related resources or provide training programs that certify citizens to use existing equipment and related resources. Several media outlets are thought to provide natural venues for such citizen access, including community radio stations, low-power television stations, community cable channels, community newspapers, and community web sites or user groups.

COMPARATIVE SUMMARY

Philosophies provide a root system of assumptions and values for media systems. Just as a tree's roots mingle with the roots of other trees, so do the philosophies of one country's media system mingle with philosophies of other countries' media systems. Philosophies at work in any given country are increasingly being influenced by philosophies at work in other countries' media systems, because the forces of globalization are facilitating greater connectedness between media industries, governments, and citizens. Table 5.1 presents a summary grid that helps to highlight the main features of the six philosophies for media systems that have been presented in this chapter.

Though no country fits exclusively into one particular philosophy for media operations, every country exhibits attributes that suggest an adherence to one or more philosophy. Think about the country you are living in right now. What laws, rules, procedures, and practices can you identify that illustrate one or more philosophies at work in the country's media system? What does the prevailing philosophy appear to be? What is a secondary philosophy? What is a trace philosophy? Answering these questions can help you draw conclusions about some of the purposes and values of the media system of the country in which you are living.

In France, Sweden, and the UK, the prevailing philosophy influencing media policy has been social responsibility. The main focus of the governments in these countries is to use the power of the state to stimulate cultural content, even if the media content is not commercially profitable. Under this directive, the government provides the financing for electronic and print media content specifically to promote culture and/or education. Libertarianism is present in these three European countries as a secondary philosophy, insofar as

TABLE 5.1   Summary of Philosophies for Media Systems

	AUTHORITARIAN	LIBERTARIAN	COMMUNIST	SOCIAL RESPONSIBILITY	DEVELOPMENT	DEMOCRATIC-PARTICIPANT
Authors	Plato Machiavelli	Locke Mill Smith	Hegel Marx	Hutchins Commission Hocking, Rivers, Schramm, Christians	Lerner Rostow Schramm	Rosen, Taylor, Merrit, Enzensberger
Precedents Leading to Philosophy	Perceived Vulnerability of the State	Freedom from Government Interference	Agricultural to Industrial Society	Sensational Journalism	Stalled Development	Corporate and Government Dominance
Codification of Philosophy	Decree Legislation Religious Doctrine	Constitutional Law Legislative Law Judicial Law	Decree Party Planning Objective	Bully Pulpit Regulation	Government Mandate Legal Right of Media Freedom	Citizen Pressure Groups Alternative Media Start-ups
Principles In Media Operations	Serve the State Immunity of State State Control of Media	Private Ownership of Media Fair Competition Self-Regulation	State Ownership of Property Elevate Cultural Tastes Teach Communist Doctrine	Factual and Contextual Information Balanced Opinion and Commentary Clarified Editorial Goals	Government Watchdog Cultural Autonomy Exported Media Content	Citizen Media Content Freedom of Criticism
Implements of Philosophy	Censorship Prior Restraint Physical or Professional Punishment	Financial Reward Financial Punishment	Censorship Physical or Professional Punishment	Accountability to Public Admonishment in Front of Public	International Assistance Public Expectation	Citizen Viewpoints Citizen Production Citizen Access

Source: Robert McKenzie.

news media have freedoms in a number of content areas, including news reporting and nudity/profanity. Authoritarianism is present in these three countries as a trace philosophy, particularly in regulations stipulating that certain kinds of television content must be delivered (e.g., in France, French-language programming) or regulations that alternatively prohibit certain kinds of television content from being delivered (e.g., in Sweden, advertisements aimed at children).

In the USA, the prevailing philosophy influencing media policy has been libertarianism. The main approach of the USA government toward media policies is to avoid excessive government oversight. This means that the USA government generally is predisposed to allowing the marketplace to determine media policies, preferring to ensure only fair play between media organizations and consumers. Social responsibility is present in the USA as a secondary philosophy, particularly through the licensing process for radio and television stations, which requires broadcasters to serve the interest, convenience, and necessity of the public. Authoritarianism is present in the USA as a trace philosophy, particularly in regulations prohibiting obscenity.

In México, traditionally the prevailing philosophy influencing media policy has been authoritarianism. In the past, the Mexican government has monitored criticism of the government and sought retribution for violations in this area. Increasingly, however, media policy is influenced by libertarianism as a prevailing philosophy, insofar as the Mexican government is allowing the marketplace to play a larger role in the development of media policy and legislation. In addition, developmentalism is present in México as a trace philosophy, insofar as the federal government and state governments pay newspapers, radio stations, and television stations to deliver content that publicizes government efforts to develop the infrastructure of the country.

In China, the prevailing philosophy influencing media policy has been communism, particularly in the state ownership of media. The largest and most prominent media organizations—Central China Television (CCTV), the *People's Daily* newspaper, and the Xinhua News Agency—all are agencies of the government. Authoritarianism is present in China as a secondary philosophy, manifested by heavy government involvement in prohibiting media content that is critical of the government or of the Communist Party. However, a kind of contained libertarianism is increasingly present in China as a trace philosophy because the government now encourages discussion on social and economic issues, as long as it occurs within the parameters set by authorities—which includes no criticism of the government or discussion of state secrets. Accordingly, although the government continues to issue directives to the media and thus maintain some semblance of its previously strong propaganda and control modalities, increasingly the main focus has been to encourage media outlets to compete for viewers and commercial advertising.

In Ghana, the prevailing philosophy influencing media policy since 2000 has been libertarianism. Prior to 1992, all media were state owned. Subsequent to 1992, private print and electronic media began to develop and were instrumental in advocating in favor of democratic rule and against the authoritarian rule that existed until the 2000 elections. Since 2000, the main focus of the government's media policies has been to foster an independent media industry that delivers content that stimulates the democratic discussion of ideas. Developmentalism is present in Ghana as a secondary philosophy, insofar as the government encourages media to contribute to stabilizing democracy and the economy by delivering tolerance and diversity of political opinions. Social responsibility is present in Ghana as a trace philosophy to the extent that regulatory bodies have limited powers of enforcement and instead rely on the goodwill of media organizations to adhere to professional standards of serving the public.

In Lebanon, the philosophies influencing media policy are difficult to identify because of fallout from the civil war and the subsequent political situation in which the central government is weaker than sectarian and ethnic bosses. Authoritarianism is a prevailing philosophy in the government's ownership of an official radio station and the government's restrictions on media ownership and some media content (in particular, potentially inflammatory religious content). Developmentalism is present in Lebanon as a secondary philosophy insofar as the government looks the other way when media violate certain regulations, partly because the government does not have the power to enforce regulations, partly because some media are owned by members of the government, and partly because the government wants media industries to contribute to the country's developing infrastructure and economy. Libertarianism is present in Lebanon as a trace philosophy insofar as newspapers and some radio and television stations are privately owned and are permitted to develop their own standards for producing media content.

CHAPTER 6

REGULATION OF MEDIA

PRIMER QUESTIONS

1. What is regulation?

2. What agencies, organizations, and groups regulate media, and why?

3. How do you think print media are regulated differently from electronic media?

4. How do you think broadcast media are regulated differently from satellite and cable media?

5. What do you think are the main areas of media content that are regulated, and why?

Across the world, media organizations are regulated because of nearly universal perceptions that media content and media operations can significantly impact economies, social policies, political debate, and above all else, the lives of people. People who travel to different countries often notice how different the media content can be from one country to the next. For example, in some countries there seems to be a fair share of violent content in television programs, whereas in other countries there seems to be almost no violent content. The same contrasting statements can be made about political content, advertising content, educational content, and sexual content. Often, such differences in media content are the result of legally binding regulations applied by governments or government agencies in an attempt to achieve societal goals that are consistent with the prevailing philosophies for the given domestic media system.

Regulation is defined as influences on media operations and media content. This broad definition conceptualizes regulation as coming not only from government-related regulatory bodies that have a legal basis for their authority over media operations, but also from nongovernment bodies such as citizen groups, advertisers, audiences, and media organizations themselves. However, because national governments tend to play the most forceful role in regulating media, this chapter focuses on regulation by government-related agencies and branches of government.

Traditionally, broadcast media have been regulated more strictly than print media because of some version of the "scarcity of spectrum space" argument. This argument holds that the broadcasting band can only accommodate a limited number of frequencies for use by broadcasters, but at the same time reaches more people than print because of its pervasiveness in people's lives. In effect, broadcast content is perceived as having a more far-reaching and inescapable impact on audiences than print content and therefore should be controlled. However, two technological developments are causing a reexamination of the scarcity-of-space argument that has guided regulation in the past. One is the growth of cable, satellite, and web technologies, which diminish the importance of radio or television frequencies in distributing content. The second is the use of the internet to distribute broadcast content, as well as its own content. Though most governments have refrained from directly regulating internet content, it has been regulated early on in a somewhat piecemeal fashion through legislation or court cases. For example, the French courts ruled in 2003 that Nazi memorabilia cannot be auctioned on French web sites.

In Chapter 3, regulation was likened to the trunk of a tree. Just as the trunk is the base that holds up the rest of the tree, regulation is the base that holds up a media system. Just as the trunk largely determines the parameters for all the parts of the tree above the ground, regulations set the parameters for the visible elements of a media system, including financing of media, accessibility of media, media content, and media audiences. In other words, regulation influences the basic direction and shape of the outer elements of a media system.

CATEGORIES OF REGULATORY BODIES

There are five basic categories of bodies that regulate media in each country:

Government-Related Agencies

Government-related agencies are bureaucracies that have government oversight of media operations. In some cases, government-related agencies exert direct control over all facets of media operations; in other cases, government-related agencies are only able to exert suggested guidelines over media operations. Usually, government-related agencies report directly to a department or branch of government. But occasionally they operate as independent agencies that interpret and administer regulatory functions required by law. A government-related regulatory agency often is formed to ensure that media organizations serve the public according to country-specific interpretations of what that service should be. Such interpretations of "public service" can differ widely across cultures and countries.

There are three industry-related concepts that governments and media organizations use to describe common categories of content that are consistently regulated. The first term is **watershed** (called *safe harbor* in the USA), which means a specific time period late at night in which certain restrictions on content are relaxed because of the assumption that minors are not watching television or listening to radio. The second term is **minutage,** or the total number of advertising minutes allowed during a prescribed segment of time (usually an hour). The third term is **bumper,** which is a momentary graphic that appears on the television screen between regular programming and advertising to create clear separation between the two types of content.

Media Organizations/Professional Organizations

Media organizations are the television stations, radio stations, production houses, newspapers, internet providers, and so on that produce and deliver media content. Media organizations engage in self-regulation—that is, they enact their own policies about what content is either acceptable or unacceptable. Self-regulation is individualized when a single organization regulates itself—for example, when a company owning many radio stations follows a policy against reporting suicides in news stories to avoid promoting copycat suicides. Self-regulation is collective when an association of media organizations regulates the member organizations—for example, guidelines outlined by a professional organization to which a television station belongs lead that station to rate its own programs according to levels of violent and/or sexual content. Both individual and collective regulation often is implemented by media organizations in accordance with ethical codes of conduct established by industry trade associations.

Media organizations regulate themselves in order to respond to a range of conditions that include competitor strategies, government mandates, citizen pressure groups, interpretation of legislation, and audience media use. Often media organizations negotiate with government to engage in a kind of coregulation in which there is dialogue between the two entities to achieve mutually expected results through mutually agreed-on regulation. Because this process can be laborious, media organizations often attempt to regulate themselves first to avoid government involvement in their operations.

Citizen Groups

Citizen groups typically are nonprofit organizations assembled by activists because of a concern about various aspects of media operations. Citizen groups such as the Parents Television Council (PTC) in the USA can be sophisticated and powerful organizations consisting of advisory boards, officers, and millions of members. Often, citizen groups are motivated by moral concerns about thwarting media content that is perceived to cause great harm to society. Two common areas of concern are the violation by a news program of an individual's right to privacy and the potential of minors to be morally corrupted by viewing debased media content such as unnecessary cosmetic surgery. Citizen groups rarely have authority that makes their recommendations legally binding. As a result, citizen groups often attempt to convince a media organization to comply with requested changes by organizing grassroots pressure on government-related regulators or by seeking to publicly embarrass a media organization into compliance with the desired changes. For example, the PTC continuously reviews prime-time television shows and posts material it considers to be offensive on its web site (www.parentstv.org), which encourages visitors to fill out a complaint form online that the PTC can send to the FCC.

Advertisers and Sponsors

In most private commercial media industries and in some state-owned noncommercial media industries, media organizations rely on advertisers and sponsors for significant revenue streams. When advertising or sponsorship is a major funding source for media operations, a more covert form of regulation can occur. Advertisers (or sponsors) can make requests that media organizations with which they do business refrain from delivering a certain kind of content, with the threat of withdrawing the advertising (or sponsorship) monies, or media organizations may choose on their own to refrain from producing content that might offend advertising or sponsorship clients. For example, it is almost unheard of for a television drama to include dialogue focusing on unhealthy ingredients that are commonly used to make sodas, because soda manufacturers regularly purchase advertising time on television dramas.

Audiences

Audiences regulate media content because the size of an audience often defines the success of media content. If the primary method of financing a media organization is advertising, then the size of the audience plays a paramount role in the regulation of media content. If methods other than advertising are used to finance a media organization, then regulation of media content is determined more by whether there is simply an audience, or a loyal audience, with size being less of a factor.

REGULATION OF MEDIA IN THE EU (EUROPEAN UNION)

France, Sweden, and the UK belong to the European Union (EU), a federation of twenty-five member countries that has regulatory authority over some areas of media operations in the individual countries. Within this context, the EU has approached media regulation as an area over which it should exert influence in member countries. One of the main regulatory provisions is referred to as the Television without Frontiers Directive, described below:

> The directive aims to ensure the free movement of broadcasting services within the internal market and at the same time to preserve certain public interest objectives, such as cultural diversity, the right of reply, consumer protection and the protection of minors. It is also intended to promote the distribution and production of European audiovisual programs, for example by ensuring that they are given a majority position in television channels' program schedules.

Specific regulations addressing these areas stipulate that (1) 50 percent of each member country's television and radio programming must originate within the EU; (2) advertising content must have limited advertising minutage; (3) certain genres of programs (e.g., news and films) must not be interrupted by advertising content; and (4) there must be clear separation between advertising content and regular content. Most EU countries use a bumper to achieve this separation. For example, Figure 6.1 shows a bumper that is aired on television in France both before and after a segment of advertisements. This particular bumper displays the word *publicité* (advertisement) against the background of a countryside view. In keeping with the French propensity to include an artistic touch, abstract graphics of birds have been added.

In the material that follows, regulation of media is discussed across the eight countries. The bulk of the information discussed in this chapter was gathered during on-site interviews with senior officials (acknowledged in the preface) at the regulatory agencies.

REGULATION OF MEDIA IN FRANCE

Following the Gaullist model described briefly in Chapter 4, most of the media law and policy in France is developed by national government assuming a central role in the marketplace of media activity. At the heart of central government is the concept of a state,

FIGURE 6.1   *Publicité Bumper Graphic on* FRANCE *3 Television in France*
Source: FRANCE 3.

which, as Raymond Kuhn explains in *The Media in France* (1995), is used to justify the central involvement of national government in French media activities. Accordingly, the national government is not just an adjudicator of media policy but is also a competitor in the marketplace of media consumption. The government does this by mandating that public broadcasters provide content that meets cultural objectives. This situation, in which the government regulates cultural content on both public and private television and radio broadcasters, is a defining feature of the media system in France.

In France, a press statute enacted in 1881 granted print media freedom from government regulation by guaranteeing freedom of opinion and the right to publish. Similarly, the internet is not regulated by a central, government-related agency in France. However, broadcast media are actively regulated in France by the national government, though the nature of this regulation has changed. For decades, all broadcast media were exclusively owned, operated, and regulated by the national government. After 1982, the National Assembly enacted a law based on the principle that "freedom of communication is free." This law opened up the possibility for private companies to own and operate broadcast media, and it established—as the name implies—that broadcast companies need not pay a license fee for the right to use radio and television frequencies.

The main government-related agency for broadcast regulation in France is the CSA, or Conseil Supérieur de L'Audiovisuel (roughly translated as Higher Council of the

Audiovisual), which was formed in 1989 out of France's first independent regulatory agency established in 1986. The primary oversight body for the CSA is the Ministry of Culture. The governing board of the CSA consists of nine councilors: three of the councilors are nominated for the governing board by the French president; three are nominated by the president of the Senate; and three are nominated by the president of the National Assembly. Councilors come primarily from media industries or academia.

All television and radio operations—terrestrial, cable, and satellite—fall under the regulatory jurisdiction of the CSA. The main authority of the CSA is to apply laws and decrees that are developed by the national government and to issue opinions to the national government about media law and policy. The CSA has the authority to interpret and apply existing regulations, but not to develop new regulations, which is the prerogative only of the national government. CSA regulation covers three central arenas: renewing broadcast licenses for television and radio stations, issuing new licenses for television and radio stations, and disciplining radio and television stations for violating regulations.

The licensing process is as follows. Private broadcast media are licensed by the CSA. Radio stations are licensed for five years, whereas television stations are licensed for ten years. The licensing process is used to ensure that private broadcasters comply with public-service obligations interpreted by the CSA. Public radio and television stations are not licensed; the government's position is that broadcast frequencies are owned by the state, which means that it is not possible to license them or sell them. In exchange for using the frequencies, however, both public and private radio and television stations have obligations to the state in terms of the content that is broadcast. The Ministry of Culture regulates these obligations by issuing decrees. Many of the regulations have to do with promoting culture. The government's Ministry of Culture defines the specific public-service obligations that public radio and television stations are expected to meet.

In France, four areas of content regulation overseen by the CSA are particularly distinctive. The first general area of regulation is **political pluralism on radio.** A precondition for granting a license, commercial French media are obligated to ensure that a wide variety of political voices are represented on television and radio. Owing to this mission, the CSA awards licenses to radio stations with specific plans for program formats that add to a broad spectrum of political opinion. Consequently, in France there is anarchist radio, socialist radio, extreme-right radio, and many other political orientations on radio.

The second general area of government-related regulation in France is the **protection of minors.** In this area, there are two types of content that are prohibited before the watershed, which is defined in France as before 2000 (8:00 PM). One area is erotic programming showing sexual penetration or sexual acts at close range. However, content depicting male and female nudity both before and after 2000 (8:00 PM) is allowed, as long as the programming is not of the erotic kind described above. Profanity in broadcasting content is not regulated by the CSA, but in general profanity is frowned on by French people because it is considered ugly. The second area of content is violent programming, which is not allowed before the watershed if it is deemed to be gratuitous or overly graphic—for example, sounds of human bones being crushed.

A third general area of regulation is **protection of the French language** through domestic content quotas. Adding to the EU policy wherein 50 percent of all television programming must be of European origin, the French government requires that 40 percent of the 50 percent has to be French programming during two time periods: the "peak time" viewing hours of 1800 (6:00 PM) to 2300 (11:00 PM) when most people are watching television and on Wednesdays, or "Children's Day," when children are not in school (instead, children attend school on Saturdays). Additionally, 35 percent of songs on radio stations targeting teenagers must be of Francophone origin (which includes French as well as African-French or Arab-French); 60 percent of songs on stations targeting seniors (age forty-five and over) must be of Francophone origin.

A fourth general area of regulation is **advertising minutage.** A regulation stipulates that public television channels can air no more than eight minutes of advertising per hour, while private television channels can air no more than twelve minutes of advertising per hour. There are no limits on advertising minutage for radio.

The CSA uses two main powers of enforcement to elicit compliance with regulations. The primary power of enforcement is the fine, which the CSA can levy on broadcasters that violate regulations or statutory law. For example, the CSA routinely has fined radio and television stations for noncompliance with minimum quotas for French or Francophone programming. The CSA's second power of enforcement is a mandatory admission of noncompliance, wherein the CSA can force a broadcaster to air a finding resulting from a CSA investigation that concluded the broadcaster was in violation of a regulation.

REGULATION OF MEDIA IN SWEDEN

In Sweden, the national government authorizes newspapers to publish and plays a direct role in regulating broadcast media. The national government itself licenses all national terrestrial television stations and public-service radio stations, while the government-related agency, the Radio and Television Authority, licenses local and community radio stations. The internet is not licensed or regulated by a centralized government-related agency. The Swedish government mandates categories of content on the public-service radio and broadcasters and limits commercial competition against the public-service broadcasters. This situation, in which government broadcasters are positioned more strongly in the marketplace than commercial broadcasters (and more so for television than for radio), is a defining feature of the media system in Sweden.

Though newspapers in Sweden must be authorized by the national government, this process is not used to control or influence content. Rather, authorization is used as a mechanism to register a chain of responsibility for newspaper stories. Specifically, the authorization is administered to hold someone accountable for potential inaccuracies in a newspaper story, by establishing a chain of responsibility for decisions about journalistic content that follows a hierarchy from reporter to editor to publisher.

In Sweden, newspapers were guaranteed freedom from government regulation by two parliamentary acts in 1766: Freedom of the Press and Freedom to Express an Opinion. These acts not only guarantee the freedom of expression, but they also guarantee that the press has access to government information. In addition, the two acts have guided other freedoms afforded to broadcast media. For example, if the government wants to classify public records as secret, it has to petition the Supreme Administrative Court for the right to do so. However, it is quite difficult to succeed in classifying information as secret, and even if such a request is granted, the court may rule that only a small part of the information may be sealed. This provision stimulates investigative research by media journalists.

These two legislative acts have established a strong tradition of self-regulation of print media in Sweden. The centerpiece of the self-regulation approach is an independent Office of the Press Ombudsman, which is financed by various press associations in Sweden. This office consists of an official called an ombudsman, as well as an ombudsman committee. The main purpose of the Office of the Press Ombudsman is to deal with complaints from readers. If the complaint is borne out by the office's research, the ombudsman has the power to sanction a newspaper by requiring it to print a correction or admit that it made a mistake or publish that the committee found a newspaper to be in error. For example, in the spring of 2003, the former leader of the Communist Party won a judgment by the Office of the Ombudsman to levy heavy fines against the national newspaper *Expressen* (*The Express*). This newspaper had printed an article implying that a former political-party leader had participated in a pornographic film, when in fact it was her former husband who was involved with a company that produced pornographic films.

In contrast to the self-regulation concept applied to print media, broadcast media in Sweden are strongly regulated by the government, primarily through the Radio and Television Act of 1996. In Sweden, all broadcasters have to be licensed to deliver content. Prior to 1992, all broadcast media in Sweden except community radio and local nonprofit radio were exclusively owned, operated, and regulated by the national government. But in 1992, law enacted by the Swedish Parliament allowed for the establishment of private commercial broadcasting. The result of this law was to license one television station (*TV 4*) as a commercial broadcaster and to open up the radio band to several commercial broadcasters. Licensing in Sweden is used to ensure that all broadcasters are socially responsible and that commercial television in particular is beholden to public-service requirements similar to those for the public broadcasters (e.g., impartiality).

In Sweden, there are two main government-related agencies that regulate broadcasters. These agencies were formed in 1994 out of existing government agencies. They are kept separate to preserve a balance of power in regulation. The first government-related regulatory agency in Sweden is the Radio and Television Authority. This agency licenses local and community radio transmissions, designates local cable broadcasting companies, and submits proposals to the government as to how licenses for digital terrestrial television should be distributed. The Radio and Television Authority also follows a research directive to provide the government with statistics and other information on the development of ownership, structure, technology, and economics of the radio and television industries. In addition, the Radio and Television Authority collects the fees that broadcasters must pay to renew or to obtain a license to broadcast. The license period for commercial broadcasters is ten years, while the license period is variable for public broadcasters. Because licensing is used as a means of stipulating the inclusion of some kinds of content while precluding or discouraging other kinds of content, the government sets the length of the license period for public broadcasters according to the content goals it wants to achieve. For example, the license period for one Swedish public radio broadcaster was based on quantifying a goal of broadcasting more Finnish-language programming. The one area in which the Radio and Television Authority has the power to issue licenses is for local commercial radio stations.

The second agency is the Broadcast Commission (or, as it is named in Swedish, *Granskningsnämnden för Radio och Television*). The main authority of the Broadcasting

Commission is to apply law that is developed by the national government. This body reports to the national government through the Ministry of Culture, though in practice the Broadcast Commission is largely an independent regulatory agency with the chief responsibility of regulating of content across all broadcast, cable, and satellite technologies. Much of the Broadcast Commission's work is in the area of fielding and investigating consumer complaints. In 2004, the agency received about 1,300 complaints regarding broadcasting content. Most complaints are about journalistic bias, violence, and surreptitious advertising.

In Sweden, two areas of content regulation overseen by the Swedish Broadcasting Commission are particularly distinctive. One area is **advertising**, which was not allowed in Swedish broadcasting prior to 1990. Public broadcasters are prohibited from airing any advertising. Advertising on *TV 4*, the only analog commercial terrestrial television broadcaster, is restricted to ten minutes per hour in prime time—1900 (7:00 PM) to 0000 (midnight)—and eight minutes during non-prime-time hours. Plus, advertising time must not exceed 10 percent of the total television broadcasting time per twenty-four hours. For commercial radio, the maximum advertising minutage is eight minutes. For both radio and television, advertising cannot be placed adjacent to children's programming, and advertising cannot be targeted to children twelve and under; this latter regulation is one that Sweden has tried to introduce to other countries, particularly those in the EU.

A second area of regulation falls under the rubric of **responsibility,** which requires broadcasters to take into consideration the impact of media content in three particular content areas: drug and alcohol use, excessive violence, and sexual content. The Broadcasting Commission has the authority to review whether programming has violated responsibility in these areas. In the area of **drug and alcohol use,** parliamentary regulation specifically prohibits any advertising of alcoholic beverages (including wine and beer) in radio and television broadcasts; the same regulation prohibits the advertising of wine and beer with an alcohol content of more than 15 percent in printed media. In the area of **sexual content,** regulation prohibits erotic programming showing penetration or other graphic sex acts. However, certain sexual activities (including intercourse that is not too graphic) involving both male and female nudity can be shown on television during the watershed time period (after 2100 or 9:00 PM) if those activities are presented in a natural way. In Sweden, profane language is not regulated, so television and radio broadcasters are allowed to air any words at any hour of the day. Finally, in the area of **violence,** television broadcasters are not permitted to air fictional programming outside of watershed hours that contains gratuitous violence. The standards applied in Sweden in the area of violence are typically more restrictive than in other countries, and may, for example, include an actor purposely hitting another actor.

The Broadcasting Commission uses two main powers of enforcement to elicit compliance with regulations. First, fines are levied for violations only of rules pertaining to advertising and sponsorship. The process requires the Broadcasting Commission to go to court to have the fines applied. Though cases can be pending for years, the court normally upholds a fine levied by the Broadcasting Commission. However, for the other areas of content regulation there are no fiscal penalties, a policy that is designed to preserve broadcasters' rights to freedom of opinion. Rather, the Broadcasting Commission can use a second power of enforcement to gain compliance in other content areas: the mandatory admission of noncompliance. Under this power, the Broadcasting Commission can stipulate that a radio or television organization in violation of regulations must broadcast the findings of the Commission.

REGULATION OF MEDIA IN THE UK

Most media law and policy in the UK is developed by national government in concert with the government-related agency OfCom (Office of Communications). At the heart of media law and policy is the position that media have freedom in political and social expression, but have restrictions in advertising and in other content that might be harmful to children. Primarily through the Ministry of Culture, Media and Sport, the government develops policy objectives for broadcast media that are then interpreted by OfCom, which develops the regulations.

To maintain a strong presence of high-quality educational and cultural media content in the overall mix of media content, the government charters the British Broadcasting Corporation (BBC), an independent public-sector broadcaster that distributes content through a variety of mainly noncommercial outlets. Domestically, the BBC is expected to set standards and establish high production values to which the commercial television channels are expected to aspire.

In addition, the BBC is required to adhere to the following code of standards in the production and delivery of content: Impartiality, Accuracy, Fairness, Giving a Full and Fair View of Peoples and Cultures, Respect for Privacy, Respect for Standards of Taste and Decency, Avoiding the Imitation of Anti Social and Criminal Behaviour, Safeguarding the Welfare of Children, Fairness to Interviewees, Respect for Diverse Audiences in the UK, and Independence from Commercial Interests. This situation of a broadcast marketplace in which a strongly positioned public-sector broadcaster backed by the government competes with commercial broadcasters is a defining feature of the media system in the UK.

In the UK, press freedom emerged not by a constitutional statute (there is no constitution in the UK) nor by a pivotal parliamentary act. Rather, press freedom became an acquired right, through persistently aggressive reporting left unchecked by the courts. As long as the content of news reporting is judged by a jury to be in the "public interest," the courts tend to deny libelous actions against the content, thus allowing the press to have wide-ranging freedoms in the UK. Newspapers in the UK are largely self-regulated by the Press Complaints Commission, an independent body that administers a Code of Practice, which contains guidelines developed by the newspaper and periodicals industries. The guidelines include: distinguishing clearly between comment, conjecture, and fact; identifying parents or relatives of someone convicted of, or accused of, a crime; and not interviewing children under sixteen without the presence of an adult. Most newspapers voluntarily adhere to the guidelines of the Press Complaints Commission. Complaints are adjudicated by the Commission, which, if it finds that the code has been violated, will issue findings that suggest a newspaper publish a factual correction, an apology, or a response from the complainant. The commission does not have the power to levy financial penalties.

In the UK, broadcast media are actively regulated by a government-related agency OfCom. OfCom was created by the 2003 Communications Act passed by Parliament. The act stipulated that OfCom has two general duties: to "further the interests of citizens in relation to communications matters" and to "further the interests of consumers in relevant markets, where appropriate by promoting competition." The act further defined these duties as falling into six areas:

1. Ensuring the optimal use of the electromagnetic spectrum.
2. Ensuring that a wide range of electronic communications services, including high-speed data services, is available throughout the UK.
3. Ensuring a wide range of TV and radio services of high quality and wide appeal.
4. Maintaining plurality in the provision of broadcasting.
5. Applying adequate protection for audiences against offensive or harmful material.
6. Applying adequate protection for audiences against unfairness or the infringement of privacy.

OfCom regulates all television and radio operations (terrestrial, cable, and satellite) as well as telecommunications (telephone and computer communication) and wireless communications. Regulation includes licensing, adjudicating complaints, and setting detailed standards for public service. Because of this wide range of areas, and the specificity with which OfCom issues regulations to broadcasters and wireless operators, it is known as a *super regulator.* OfCom has some limited regulatory authority over the BBC, including content standards and complaint handling. But the BBC is mainly regulated by a Board of Governors consisting of twelve members appointed by the Queen. The Board of Governors appoints nine members to an executive board that runs the day-to-day operations of the BBC. The mandate of the Board of Governors is to represent the public interest. Two primary areas of regulation of the BBC by the Board of Governors include impartiality and accuracy.

The governing board of OfCom consists of nine members appointed by the Ministry of Culture, Media and Sport. The members come from media industries and academia. Three of the members must come from OfCom's executive board, which runs the day-to-day operations of OfCom.

In the UK, all broadcasters—even commercial broadcasters—are considered to be public-service broadcasters that have regulatory obligations in terms of both the quality and quantity of certain content types. The BBC receives a charter to operate from the Ministry of Culture, Media and Sport, acting on behalf of the monarch. The time period for each charter theoretically is variable, but traditionally has been set at ten years. The chartering process is used to ensure that the BBC complies with public-service obligations that are different from those of the commercial broadcasters. The public-service obligations for the BBC are framed by the following purpose statement:

> The mission statement of the BBC is to enrich people's lives with great programs and services that inform, educate and entertain. Its vision is to be the most creative, trusted organization in the world. It provides a wide range of distinctive programs and services for everyone, free of commercial interests and political bias. They include television, radio, national, local, children's, educational, language and other services for key interest groups.

OfCom licenses commercial radio stations for a period of eight years, and television stations for a period of ten years. The licensing process is used to ensure that commercial broadcasters also comply with very specific public-service obligations stipulated by OfCom through a "PSB Remit" that contains "terms of the license agreement" in effect for the duration of the license period.

In the UK, four areas of content regulation are particularly distinctive. One area is **television advertising**. There are no advertising minutage requirements for radio in the UK. However, television broadcasters are required to meet the following advertising minutage rules: They cannot air more than twelve minutes of advertising per hour, and cannot average more than seven minutes of advertising per hour over the course of a twenty-four-hour period. Television advertisements are not allowed to be inserted into certain genres of content that run less than thirty minutes, including documentaries, royal ceremonies, religious services, and children's programming. Television advertising breaks must be spaced twenty minutes apart.

Numerous and very specific regulations for both radio and television advertising also cover: use of the word *free,* environmental claims, guarantees, accurate pricing, delivery charges, visual techniques and special effects, testimonials, violence and cruelty, use of animals, stereotypes, pressure to purchase, bullying, vulnerability, sexuality, prescription-only medicines, hypnosis, hypnotherapy, psychiatry, psychology, psychoanalysis and psychotherapy, appeals to fear and exploitation of credulity, smoking deterrents, low-calorie foods, obesity, superstition, religious charities, instructional courses, lotteries, pools and bingo, and alcoholic drinks.

To avoid violations, 90 percent of broadcasters in the UK submit advertisements to a "pre-vetting" organization overseen by the Broadcast Committee of Advertising Practice (BCAP), a government-related body that receives input from OfCom. The pre-vetting organizations (there is one for television advertisements and another one for radio advertisements) screen advertisements to offer advice on whether there are potential breaches of regulations.

A second area of content regulation is **protection of children.** There are many regulations that prohibit certain kinds of content from being aired either during or adjacent to programming targeted at children. Some regulations differ for programs geared to children under the age of eighteen, versus programs geared to children under the age of sixteen, versus programs geared to children under ten. In the UK, the watershed runs from 2100 (9:00 PM) to 0530 (5:30 AM), and is used to protect children from potentially harmful programs. Regulations designed to protect children both during and outside of watershed hours prohibit:

1. Advertisements with personalities or other characters (including puppets, etc.) who appear regularly in any children's television program and who in the advertisements are positively endorsing products or services of special interest to children from airing before 2100 (9:00 PM).
2. Advertisements for merchandise based on children's programs (e.g., toys, puppets, costumes) from being broadcast in either of the two hours preceeding or succeeding episodes or editions of the relevant program.
3. Advertisements from being placed in or adjacent to children's programming that feature: drinks containing less than 1.2 percent alcohol by volume when presented as

low- or no-alcohol versions of an alcoholic drink; liqueur chocolates; matches; medicines, vitamins, and other dietary supplements; trailers for films or videos carrying an eighteen- or fifteen-certificate.

A third area of content regulation is **taste and decency.** This broad area of regulation generally refers to the potential for programming to encourage crime or social disorder or to be "offensive to public feeling." Taste and decency regulations primarily address obscenity and profanity, violence, and stereotyping. However, in the area of obscenity and profanity, regulations recognize the depiction of sexual activity and the naked human body as justifiable programming. Accordingly, nudity on television is justifiable in a nonsexual context before 2100 (9:00 PM). Similarly, representations of sexual intercourse without camera close-ups are permitted with justifiable educational purpose before 2100 (9:00 PM). However, graphic sexual intercourse between 2200 (10:00 PM) and 0530 (5:30 AM) can be shown on subscription-based channels only. Regarding profanity, there is no absolute ban on "bad language," which is allowed before the watershed only if occurrences are in context and are not frequent. The regulations are particularly cautionary against expletives with religious association. Regarding violence, gratuitous violence is not allowed, and all violence has to be justifiable by the context. The regulations are particularly cautionary against imitative violence—violence that children or young people may copy—such as suicide. Sexual violence is rarely justifiable. With regard to stereotyping, programs that stir up racial hatred and, in particular, use racist terms should be avoided. Similarly, programs including people with disabilities must avoid using patronizing terms or humor based on a disability.

A fourth area of regulation involves television **production quotas** for original, regional, and independent production, and for news and public affairs programming. The reasoning behind this area of regulation is that the public is best served when television content that is broadcast has not been produced exclusively by London-based production houses or by global media conglomerates that are distributing the same programming across the world. The public is defined not only as the viewing audience but also the professionals who work in the broadcast industry, particularly those who work in production. The production-quota regulations are outlined in each broadcaster's Public Service Broadcast (PSB) Remit. The regulations stipulate very specific numerical percentages of original, regional, and independent programming for television broadcasters. For example, all terrestrial broadcast programming must include 25 percent of its content that is produced by independent production houses. Another example is that the commercial broadcasters have specific production quotas in several genres: children's drama, children's information, preschools, documentaries, education, arts, schools, and multicultural.

OfCom uses three main powers of enforcement to elicit compliance with regulations. Historically, OfCom and its predecessors have been active in using all three powers of enforcement. First, OfCom has the authority to direct a broadcaster to air a correction or an apology or to cease from repeating a program. Second, OfCom can shorten a license period or revoke a license. Third, OfCom has the power to levy a fine. For example, in March 2003, OfCom levied a fine of 20,000.00 GBP (about 39,000.00 USD at the exchange rate in effect at the time of this writing) on a USA-based home-shopping channel (*YouTV*) for selling dubious products.

REGULATION OF MEDIA IN THE USA

In the USA, media regulation is developed mainly by the FCC, but also by the legislative branch (the Senate and the House of Representatives) and, to some extent, the Supreme Court. Behind the design of this fragmented approach to media regulation is the principle that there should be a check-and-balance system between the branches of government. Media regulation in the USA follows a libertarian outlook in that there is minimal central government control involved in the day-to-day operations of media organizations; instead, the commercial marketplace is the primary influence on media operations and content. This situation of a primarily commercial marketplace of broadcasters in which there is minimal government is a distinctive feature of the media system in the USA.

In the USA, newspapers and the internet are not licensed or regulated by a central government-related agency. Both newspaper and internet content have been protected from regulation by the First Amendment, one of several amendments to the Constitution created by a 1788 congressional act. The First Amendment also serves as a central guiding principle for the legal approach toward broadcast media, though broadcast media have not been afforded the same level of freedom as print media. The rationale for this distinction has been the scarcity-of-space paradigm discussed earlier. However, the proliferation of cable and satellite radio and television channels has diminished the scarcity-of-space argument to the extent that some regulations covering media ownership were relaxed by the Telecommunications Act of 1996.

In the USA, the main government-related agency for broadcast regulation is the FCC, which was formed by the Communications Act of 1934. The impetus for establishing the FCC was to create an expert agency that would implement the policies and statutes of Congress, rather than have Congress engage in a tedious process of crafting legislation for every piece of media policy. Though the FCC to some degree implements court decisions, the primary oversight body for the FCC is Congress, through the Senate Committee on Commerce, Science and Transportation and the House Committee on Energy and Commerce. Both of these committee designations make clear a conceptualization of media primarily as an activity of commerce. The governing board of the FCC consists of five commissioners, each serving a five-year term staggered with the others. The commissioners are appointed by the president and the USA and approved by the Senate. No more than three commissioners may be members of the same political party. The FCC as an independent, government-related regulatory agency for broadcast media has served as a model for other countries that have sought to disassociate media regulation from direct control by central government.

All television and radio operations (terrestrial, cable, and satellite) and all telecommunication operations (telephone and computer) fall under the regulatory jurisdiction of the FCC. The FCC has the authority to both develop regulations grounded in existing legislation and to enforce such regulations. The FCC has the responsibility to consult with Congress by issuing opinions about potential media legislation. Owing to a pervasive libertarian philosophy, the approach of the FCC in terms of regulatory activity is to let effective competition within the commercial marketplace have the first chance to regulate the operations of media, especially in providing content. In other words, the FCC expects self-regulation by media organizations. Usually, the FCC develops new regulations or enforces existing regulations more strongly only when there is a widespread perception by the public, the government, or the media that the marketplace is inadequately regulating the activities of broadcast media. Often, any new regulations will be designed specifically to stimulate effective competition as a corrective means of regulating activities of broadcast media.

In the USA, all broadcasters—both public and private—have to be licensed by the FCC. Radio and television stations both are licensed for a period of eight years. License renewals are staggered across the country so that they do not all come up for renewal at once. Licensing is used to ensure that both public and private broadcasters meet the public's "interest, convenience and necessity," a standard that was stipulated by the Communications Act of 1934, and which covers both media content and media accessibility. However, in practice the FCC does not regulate much media content. The primary mechanism used for determining whether broadcasters are meeting this standard is the commercial marketplace.

In the USA, three areas of content regulation overseen by the FCC are particularly distinctive. One area, as indicated above, is **indecency,** which in the USA has a different legal definition than obscenity (the more punishable of the two activities). In the USA, the Communications Act of 1934 prohibits the broadcasting of obscenity at any time. Obscenity is defined mainly by a three-pronged test arising out of the Supreme Court case *Miller v. California*, 413 U.S. 15, 24 (1973). Essentially, obscenity is defined as whether an average person, applying contemporary community standards, finds that a broadcast appeals to a prurient (appealing to unusual desire) interest. On the other hand, some indecent programming is allowed between the watershed hours (in the USA called the "safe harbor" hours) from 2200 (10:00 PM) to 0600 (6:00 AM). Essentially, indecency is defined by the FCC as "language that, in context, depicts or describes, in terms patently offensive as measured by contemporary community standards for the broadcast medium, sexual or excretory activities or organs" (*Infinity Broadcasting Corporation of Pennsylvania*, 2 FCC Rcd 2705, 1987; see also *FCC Policy Statement*, 2001). Again, the barometer of what is considered to be indecent is the marketplace of consumers, which historically has reacted unfavorably toward broadcast media content containing nudity and profanity.

A second area of regulation is **advertising by noncommercial broadcasters.** In the USA, noncommercial broadcasters—public broadcasters, college and university broadcasters, and community broadcasters—are strictly prohibited from airing advertisements. Under strict guidelines, however, noncommercial broadcasters are allowed to air sponsorships, which are defined by clear boundaries. The main boundaries include the prohibition of programming that urges the audience to buy anything, gives a price for a product or service, or favorably describes a product or service.

A third area of content regulation emphasized by the FCC is **children's programming**. Through a combination of a 1996 FCC Report and Order, along with the 1990 Congressional Children's Television Act, a set of regulations was developed that require all television stations to provide children's programming according to certain guidelines. One requirement is that all stations must provide at least three hours per week of educational/information programming for children, though it is left to broadcasters to define what educational and informational programming is. A second requirement is that bumpers must be aired between children's programming and advertising. And a third requirement is that advertising minutage is limited to ten and a half minutes per hour on weekdays and twelve minutes per hour on weekends (the only restriction on advertising minutage that broadcasters in the USA are required to follow) during children's programs.

The FCC uses two main powers of enforcement to elicit compliance with regulations. The FCC's first power of enforcement involves revoking a license or failing to renew a license, a rarely used power reserved normally for cases in which a broadcaster demonstrates willful and repeated disregard for the law. The second and main power of enforcement is the fine, which the Enforcement Bureau of the FCC can levy against broadcasters that violate regulations or statutory law. For example, in 2001 the FCC fined *KKMG* for airing unmistakable offensive sexual references from an Eminem song called "The Real Slim Shady." For violations of content-oriented regulations, the FCC relies on receiving citizen complaints (as a function of the commercial marketplace).

REGULATION OF MEDIA IN MÉXICO

In México, the national government is directly involved in the regulation of broadcast media, though this involvement has diminished somewhat through México's transition to an open democracy. The national government licenses all television stations and radio stations. Newspapers and the internet are not licensed or regulated by a centralized, government-related agency in México. The Mexican national government does not fund national television. State governments fund regional public television networks. The Mexican national government partially funds a national, twenty-six-station commercial radio network called IMER (Mexican Institute of Radio), that carries many different genres of programming (e.g., rap to classical). The Mexican government owns the country's main news agency, Notimex, which distributes news information primarily to Mexican media. For one hour on Sundays, all radio broadcasters during the *National Hour* must offer their frequencies to transmit government information. This situation of a primarily commercial marketplace with strong government regulation is a defining feature of the media system in México.

In México, newspapers were granted freedom from government regulation by the 1917 Mexican Constitution under Articles 6 and 7, which guarantee freedom of the press and freedom of expression. However, a long-standing tradition of surreptitious intimidation from the government has curtailed freedoms both of newspaper and broadcast media, though the practice has fallen off significantly, but not completely, since 2000. Prior to 2000, during the PRI's seventy-one-year rule, reporters working on sensitive stories about activities of government officials were subjected to such actions as prosecution by the government, threatening phone calls from anonymous people, personal mail being stolen, men in cars following them, and other forms of intimidation ostensibly designed to persuade them into backing away from certain news stories perceived to be unfairly critical. It remains to be determined whether 1998 marks the year in which surreptitious intimidation as a form of regulation is permanently on the wane.

In México there is no national association that promotes voluntary codes of journalism conduct widely subscribed to by newspapers. Thus, most Mexican newspapers and reporters determine their own journalistic codes of ethics and professional conduct.

Broadcast media in México are strictly regulated by the government, primarily through provisions of the 1940 General Law of the Ways of Communication, which was updated by the Television and Radio Federal Law of 1960. In México, all broadcasters have to be licensed to deliver content. The larger climate of Mexican law governing broadcasting can be described as permitting Mexican broadcast media to have general freedom in producing content, but requiring respect for government institutions as a matter of national security. In México, the greatest freedoms from regulation of media are found in entertainment content, whereas lesser freedoms exist for investigative journalism, and even less for depictions of symbols of the state (e.g., the Mexican flag).

In México, there are two main government ministries that regulate terrestrial broadcasters, though various powers of media regulation are scattered across several agencies of government. The formation of these two ministries dates back to the 1940 General Law of the Ways of Communication. Both agencies have department heads who report directly to the president of México. Neither agency has much jurisdiction over multichannel broadcasters.

One agency is the Ministry of Transportation and Communication, which is staffed by officials appointed by the president of México. This agency authorizes the technical licenses needed by broadcasters to operate. Licenses in México take two forms: *Concessions* are licenses granted to commercial broadcasters, who have the right to air advertising. *Permissions* are granted to public broadcasters, who are prohibited from airing advertisements. In México, the license period for all broadcasters is discretionary, with a maximum of thirty years per license period. Typically, however, broadcasters are licensed for fifteen years.

Licensing is used to ensure that broadcasters follow government regulations and to guarantee that transmission time will be provided free of charge for government publicity. There are three obligations required of broadcasters as a condition for being granted a concession, which result in free transmission time for government publicity. One obligation, which has been in place since 1936, is *National Hour* every Sunday morning from 1000 (10:00 AM) to 1100 (11:00 AM). During this time, radio stations must air a government-produced program, which is essentially a series of progress reports on the activities of government ministries and agencies. The second obligation is *state time,* during which radio and television stations must provide thirty minutes in total per day to air short (usually thirty-second) publicity announcements provided by the federal government. The third obligation is a tax known as *fiscal time*. The tax is not paid in money, but in free transmission time for the government in addition to the previous obligation of thirty minutes. Fiscal time is used to air short publicity announcements provided by the federal government. The fiscal time for television is eighteen minutes and for radio is thirty-five minutes. Fiscal time must air between 0600 (6:00 AM) and 1200 (noon).

The second government regulatory agency is the Ministry of Interior, which handles internal affairs, and is also staffed by appointees of the president. The main division that regulates media within the ministry is the Subsecretary of Media of the Secretary of the Government. Within this division, the Department of Radio, Television and Cinematography oversees most of the regulations. This division has the power to implement existing regulations emanating from Congress, but does not have the power to develop its own regulations. This agency monitors radio and television broadcasts to determine whether regulations are being followed.

In México, three main areas of content regulation are particularly distinctive. One area is **advertising.** In México, public television stations are prohibited from airing any advertising. But private television stations, as well as public radio broadcasting on the government's IMER radio network, are allowed to carry advertising. In México, advertising minutage allowances are six minutes per hour on restricted (cable and satellite) television, 18 percent of total transmission time per day on terrestrial television, and 40 percent of total transmission time per day on radio. The advertising minutage allowances for terrestrial radio and television are defined as overall percentages rather than per-hour minutes to allow for advertising to be increased significantly during time periods of peak listening and viewing. When radio programming includes soap operas, sports events, commentaries, dramas, or narratives, there can be no more than twelve advertising breaks per hour; if the radio programming does not include one of these categories, there can be no more than fifteen advertising breaks, and each break can be no longer than two minutes. Similarly, when television programming includes movies, telenovelas, theater, narrative, or drama, advertising breaks cannot exceed six per hour, and each break can be no longer than two minutes; if the television programming does not include one of these categories, there can be no more than ten advertising breaks per hour, and each break can be no longer than one and a half minutes.

A second area of regulation is **questionable programming on television,** or programming that may communicate inappropriate values to certain audiences. The Radio, Television and Cinematography Department of the Subsecretary of Media for the Secretary of the Government uses a classification system to evaluate programming in accordance with ages of audiences that are assumed to be watching television at certain hours. All programs are submitted to the Radio, Television and Cinematography Department to be classified, prior to being aired. The major areas of potentially inappropriate programming that are assessed under this classification system are sex, violence, addictions, and language. The classification system is as follows:

Classification A: programming for all audiences; allowed at any time of the day.
Classification B: programming for teenagers fifteen years old and younger; allowed only after 2000 (8:00 PM)
Classification C: programming for adults; allowed only after 2200 (10:00 PM)
Classification D: "Adult" (sexual) programming for adults; allowed only after 2400 (midnight).

The following two examples illustrate how the classification process is applied. One example is that tobacco can be advertised on television, but not until 2000 (8:00 PM) when a Classification B audience is assumed to be watching. A second example is that hard alcohol and prescription drugs can be advertised on television, but not until 2200 (10:00 PM) when a Classification C audience is assumed to be watching. Before alcohol and prescription advertisements can be aired on television, such advertisements must be submitted to and approved of by the Ministry of Health.

In regard to obscenity, terrestrial broadcasters are not permitted to broadcast nudity or profanity except in the context of a news program. In contrast, cable and television broadcasters are allowed to broadcast some nudity and profanity; if they do so, they are expected to broadcast such programming after 2200 (10:00 PM). There are no regulations regarding profanity on radio, but most broadcasters have responded to informal government requests to refrain from playing songs with profanity or, alternatively, to bleep profanities out when songs are aired.

A third area of distinctive regulation in México is **criticism of government.** In the past, sharp criticism of government was not tolerated. But since 2000, the accelerated transition to an open democracy has paved the way for Mexican media to be more openly critical of government actions. However, Mexican media—including print media—are still expected not to insult government officials and institutions in such a way as to encourage anarchy. Such actions may trigger government prosecution under criminal law.

The Subsecretary of Media uses two main powers of enforcement to elicit compliance with regulations. First, fines can be levied for violations of any regulations. For instance, in 2003, terrestrial broadcaster *Channel 40* was fined for airing corrupting language. (There was also some discussion that year that relatively small financial penalties no longer served as an adequate incentive to comply with regulations, because the amounts had been the same for some forty years.) Second, the Subsecretary of Media for the Secretary of the Government, which tapes all television broadcasters in México City, and all national television broadcasters, can request that the Ministry of Communications and Transportation revoke a broadcast license. In addition to the role of the Subsecretary of Media in enforcing compliance with content, the government-related agency Profeco, which protects the rights of consumers, can censor commercials if enough citizen complaints are received.

REGULATION OF MEDIA IN CHINA

Media law and policy in China is developed by the central government in collective discussions with the Chinese Communist Party (CCP). As such, the government is directly involved in regulating all media. However, the gradual modernization, commercialization, and diversification of the media since 1992 together have resulted in somewhat less direct control by the government as China moves toward a socialist market economy with Chinese characteristics.

Within this changing context, media in China are expected to maintain dual responsibilities of both contributing to the national economy as well as communicating ideology of the CCP. Underpinning this dual responsibility is a government imperative to cease serving as the main funding agency for media development. But even though the media in China are being commercialized, they are not being liberalized. On the one hand, the government is more lenient and tolerant toward entertainment, allowing the media to engage in self-regulation in these areas. On the other hand, the government exercises strict ideological control over information flow in the media; this is achieved through formal measures such as laws, regulations, directives, and guidelines, and through informal measures such as editorial appointments and intimidation.

The primary means of government control over information management in China is through issuing operating licenses to media organizations. In China, private ownership of traditional media (newspapers, radio, television) is not permitted. Also, direct foreign ownership of the media is forbidden. Newspapers must be registered and attached to a government ministry, institute, research facility, labor group, or other state-sanctioned organization. In a departure from this model, however, the government does permit private ownership of internet service providers to allow for investment and growth—but at the same time applies more stringent control mechanisms on internet content providers than on television. This situation, in which there is strong government control concurrent with an expanding commercial marketplace, is a defining feature of China's media system.

In China, regulation of all media content falls under the direct control of the State Council, and the Propaganda Department. In 1987, the government formed the State Press and Publications Administration (SPPA) to draft and enforce press regulations (implemented in 1990 and 1994), and to shift regulatory mechanisms from a political-relationship-based framework to a law-based framework. Reporting directly to the State Council, the SPPA oversees the drafting of laws, regulations, policies, and management development plans and is one of several CCP and government organs responsible for censoring all publications, including newspapers.

In China, freedom of the press is theoretically guaranteed under the 1982 Constitution, which provides rights of freedom of speech, assembly, association, and procession and demonstration. However, these rights are restricted by other clauses relating to social stability and national security, interests of the state, and the primacy of the CCP. In practice, formal regulations, particular informal guidelines direct journalists toward self-censorship of sensitive issues, particularly negative news about the government or about China. Journalists working for CCTV must attend weekly meetings to update their knowledge of the latest government requirements set by the Propaganda Department. An example of a consequence of such practices is that in 2003 the Chinese news media grossly underreported the Severe Acute Respiratory Syndrome (SARS) in early stages of the epidemic.

In China, broadcast media are regulated primarily by the State Administration of Radio, Film and Television (SARFT). Also reporting directly to the State Council, SARFT approves the content of radio, television, and film (domestic and foreign) in accordance with the requirements of the CCP and the Propaganda Department. SARFT supervises the operation of one thousand radio stations, the national television network (CCTV), as well as cable, satellite, and internet services.

In China, the infrastructure of the internet was developed by the government through the China Internet Network Information Center (CNNIC). This body's authority was supplemented by the government's 1997 "Computer Information Network and Internet Security, Protection and Management Regulations," which outlined the duties and responsibilities of service providers and associated punishments for leaking state secrets, damaging state interests, threatening state security, or distributing harmful information. Since 1998, CNNIC has operated under the direction of the Ministry of Information Industry (MII) to oversee the policy development of internet services and content. MII is a superregulator, with authority extending over the internet, telecommunications, multimedia, terrestrial broadcasting, and multichannel broadcasting.

Despite these controls, the internet continues to challenge government regulatory thinking because of a division of responsibilities between the CCP and the central government. For example, the central government is responsible for infrastructure development such as the national broadband network and the internet service providers plus web site registration, whereas the Propaganda Department of the CCP is responsible for internet content providers (ICPs). Similar to the guidelines for print and broadcast media, internet content is not permitted to threaten national security, leak state secrets, attempt to overthrow the government, harm national unity, fan ethnic hatred, undermine the state's religious policy, and spread pornography, superstition, gambling, violence, murder, false rumors, or intimidation.

In addition to the formal regulations outlined above, the government engages in many other strategies to restrict internet content. Routinely, the government conducts surveillance of virtually all the country's email traffic and chat rooms using 30,000 security agents and computer software, initiating periodic arrests and incarceration of individual users posting inappropriate content. In 2002, the government initiated a "Public Pledge on Self-Discipline for China's Internet Industry," which was then signed by over three hundred internet news information service companies. The pledge simultaneously promoted commercial use of the internet while restricting the "posting or dissemination of pernicious information that may jeopardize state security and disrupt social stability."

In China, three main areas of content regulation are common to all media. One area is **criticism of the government.** Media are not allowed to criticize the CCP or specific government policies. The government has allowed the public to engage in some criticisms relating to social or economic justice issues; however, such criticisms still run the risk of transgressing the country's subversion laws. These laws have sometimes been applied to postings on the internet, resulting in "netizens" being jailed for expressing opinions deemed to be politically insensitive.

A second area of regulation is **advertising** in the context of the government mandate that media become more self-funded. According to the "Advertising Law," advertising content is to be censored prior to dissemination to the media by relevant administrative authorities. These bodies consist primarily of the State Administration for Industry and the Commerce and Advertising Censorship Bureau, both of which are administered at the state, provincial, and district levels. Advertising auditors are employed to help businesses enhance their understanding of the specific requirements and interpretations of the law. In 2004, SARFT promulgated regulations relating to "unappetizing advertising," which prohibit advertisements for products such as sanitary napkins, hemorrhoid treatments, and medication for athlete's foot (though advertisements on breast enlargements are permitted). In addition, SARFT sets advertising minutage for television and radio. The government stipulates that television and radio broadcasts can air no more than twelve minutes of advertising per hour. However, regulations limit advertising to nine minutes per hour on television between 1900 (7:00 PM) and 2100 (9:00 PM) and on radio between 2300 (11:00 PM) and 1300 (1:00 PM). Advertisements must be broadcast between most programs on television and radio. However, advertisements can be inserted within television programs that exceed forty-five minutes, so long as the advertising segment do not exceed two and a half minutes. Bumpers are not required between advertisements and regular programming.

A third area of regulation is **culturally appropriate foreign content.** In accordance with the requirements set down by the CCP and the Propaganda Department, SARFT attempts to prevent Chinese people from seeing "programs that offend Chinese sensibilities or challenge the CCP's worldview." Accordingly, certain regulations focus on approving "culturally appropriate" television programming as a way of limiting negative Western influences, particularly on young Chinese people. Generally, authorities define inappropriate programming as content containing sex, violence, or news reflecting negatively on the government or on China. To this end, SARFT applies quotas limiting foreign content to 20 percent of total airtime allocated to television dramas on all channels. Additionally, the government excludes imported television dramas from prime-time viewing (1900 [7:00 PM] to 2100 [9:00 PM]) when more than half the county's 1.2 billion population is watching television.

The Chinese government uses four main powers of enforcement to elicit compliance with regulations. First, censorship can be applied to any media content. The SPPA has the power to ban books and suspend periodicals that engage in promoting indecent material such as pornography; or revealing state secrets, defined as any information that criticizes the government unduly; or reporting inaccurate, fabricated, or sensationalist stories; and disseminating information deemed to have an unhealthy impact on readers. Second, fines can be levied. For example, in 2000, the SPPA and the Propaganda Department fined twenty-seven newspapers because they had published supplements under the same periodical registration number. Third, media facilities can have their licenses suspended. Finally, individuals can be incarcerated. Criticisms of government historically have been met with a swift response by government officials, including physical removal of the offending party of a publication or broadcaster, and government prosecution and incarceration of individuals. According to the French media watchdog organization, *Reporters without Borders*, forty-two cyber-dissidents were jailed in China in 2003.

REGULATION OF MEDIA IN GHANA

In Ghana, the national government plays a limited role in regulating media. Regulations are passed by Parliament, but regulations and policies are administered by government-related agencies. The pace of legislating regulation is cautious because Parliament is hesitant about unintentionally creating a stifled media industry that leads the country back to a military dictatorship and to stalled economic development. The Ghanaian government provides some funding for a state-owned production company, which supplies programming to the state television broadcaster and the state radio broadcaster. The Ghanaian government owns the Ghana News Agency (GNA), which distributes news information primarily to Ghanaian print and electronic media. This situation of an emerging marketplace, in which state-owned media are making adjustments to the flourishing of private media and both private and state-owned media are attempting to upgrade professionalism, is a defining feature of the media system in Ghana.

In Ghana, the 1992 Constitution guaranteed freedom and independence of both print and electronic media. However, up until 2000, when an opposition party unseated the party that had formed the government since 1992, journalists were routinely intimidated into refraining from criticism of the government. For example, a common method of intimidation was for a military official to sit in the studio during a radio or television broadcast that involved news reporting or reporting on politics. In addition, prior to 2000 journalists were imprisoned under a Criminal Seditious and Libel law for reporting that was deemed as undermining the authority of the state. Such conditions led many journalists to conduct self-censorship. The government elected in 2000 to repeal the Criminal Seditious and Libel law in 2001.

In Ghana, two government-related bodies are responsible for regulating media. The National Media Commission is responsible for regulating content, and the National Communication Authority (NCA) is responsible for the licensing of all telecommunication industries, including broadcasters. Both bodies were established by the 1992 Constitution.

The NCA regulates the technical operations of all telecommunication organizations including wireless, cable, satellite, terrestrial, telephone, and the internet. The NCA advises the Ministry of Communications on national telecommunications policy. The NCA is staffed as follows: The Director General is appointed by the president or a minister with presidential authority; the directors are appointed by the board of the NCA; and the senior managers are appointed by the directors with final approval from the board.

A major regulatory function of the NCA is licensing. All telecommunications organizations—including internet organizations—have to be licensed by the NCA. In Ghana, the state owns the airwaves, which are leased to broadcasters through licensing agreements. One area in which applicants for licenses are scrutinized is religion. The NCA ensures a strict separation between church and state. This does not mean that radio and television stations cannot provide religious programming. Rather, the intention is to avoid approving an application for a radio or television station that would offer programming that proselytizes for a religion at the expense of another religion.

In Ghana, broadcasters and internet service providers are licensed for one year. License renewals are obtained by paying an annual fixed fee. Normally, the only circumstance in which licenses are revoked is when an organization fails to pay the fee. Licensing is not used to stipulate that broadcasters or internet service providers carry specific content, but to approve the technical specifications at which broadcasters and internet service providers can operate. However, if a radio broadcaster sets up a transmitter or a signal repeater to extend the transmission of content to areas outside of those specified by the license agreement, the NCA will often ignore the infraction. Such a policy supports a developmental philosophy for a media system and help to develop the industry infrastructure so that radio broadcasting is extended to outlying regions that otherwise would have little or no radio service.

The National Media Commission regulates media content, but does not fall directly under any government ministry. Its main functions include:

1. Promoting and ensuring the freedom and independence of the media for mass communication or information.
2. Ensuring the establishment and maintenance of the highest journalistic standards in the mass media, including the investigation, mediation, and settlement of complaints made against or by the press or other mass media.
3. Insulating the state-owned media from governmental control.

The National Media Commission is composed of eighteen members nominated by various interest groups including religious (Muslim and Christian) representatives, associations of private broadcasters, Parliament, the president, the National Association of Teachers, and the National Council on Women and Development. Technically, the National Media Commission has regulatory authority for both state and private media, and for both print media and electronic media (including the internet), but in practice the National Media Commission has limited financial and other resources and therefore has very limited regulatory power.

As a result, instead of focusing on regulations, the National Media Commission relies largely on the goodwill of media organizations to adhere to guidelines set forth by the Commission. These guidelines are meant to establish a code of ethical conduct and professionalism in the media industry to provide a means of arbitrating complaints made by citizens about media content, and ultimately to foster a vibrant media industry that will help Ghana continue down the path of democracy. The National Media Commission promotes the guidelines by publishing them in pamphlets distributed to media organizations and by conducting workshops for media practitioners—particularly journalists who are in the early stages of their careers.

There are at least three areas of content in the guidelines that are distinctive to Ghana. The first distinctive content area of guidelines is **political reporting.** Most guidelines in this area are designed to ensure free and fair campaigns and elections and include: balancing discussions of personalities with analysis of the issues; making party manifestos intelligible to the electorate; remaining impartial; refraining from activities that compromise the integrity of the journalist; and avoiding the promotion of violent or ethnic conflict. This latter guideline fits in with a national movement to encourage citizens to think of themselves as Ghanaian people first, and to think of regional or tribal people second. When NMC officials wrote this guideline, they were particularly mindful of the generally accepted perception that the media had inflamed ethnic divisions in the neighboring African country of Rwanda, which resulted in a bloody civil war and a protracted campaign of ethnic cleansing. In addition to the political reporting guidelines already mentioned, one of the more strongly asserted guidelines is that the state-owned media must not endorse candidates for political office.

A second area of content guidelines is **rejoinders.** This area relates to a constitutional guarantee that if media content contains a statement about or against a person, that person has the right to require the medium to carry a rejoinder—that is, a reply by the person to statements in the media content. The preface of the pamphlet detailing the Guidelines for the Publication of Rejoinders acknowledges the precarious position of the NMC in relying on the goodwill of media organizations to gain compliance in this area:

> It has not been easy enforcing the constitutional demand for mandatory rejoinders. But if the Commission is to succeed in its endeavors to persuade people not to take the media to court, then their right to rejoinders must be protected.

The guidelines specify that the aggrieved person or his or her authorized agent can write the rejoinder; that the same prominence must be given to the rejoinder as the article or news item that made the statement; that the medium carrying the rejoinder should make it clear that it is indeed a rejoinder; that media organizations must carry a rejoinder within a reasonable amount of time; and that all rejoinders must be copied to the National Media Commission.

A third area of content guidelines is **broadcasting standards.** Some of these standards revolve around promoting a national identity for Ghanaians. For example, two guidelines urge broadcasters to promote national development as a major priority and to facilitate the participation of marginalized individuals and communities in national priority setting. However, most guidelines revolve around protecting Ghanaians from harmful media content. Example regulations include: ensuring that documentaries about sexual themes do not make public and explicit what should be private and exclusive; avoiding presenting drunkenness and robbery not as destructive habits to be avoided or denounced; avoiding advertisements for alcohol that claim it has therapeutic qualities; avoiding the presentation of alcoholic drinks being consumed in a working environment unless it is clear that the working day has ended; avoiding language or scenes likely to incite crime or that glorify war; and broadcasting programs of an adult nature only after 2200 (10:00 PM).

The National Media Commission does not have strong enforcement powers for the guidelines it promotes. The commission cannot levy fines or withdraw licenses. The main procedure for gaining compliance with the guidelines is an arbitration process headed by the Settlement Committee. This process involves the hearing of a case between the aggrieved party and representatives of the relevant media organizations. If a judgment is reached in favor of the aggrieved party, the Settlement Committee will request that the media organization publish or broadcast a retraction, an apology, or the findings of the committee. In 2003, forty-seven cases went before the Settlement Committee. For example, one case involved a complaint by the ownership of a hotel against a newspaper headline, "How Top Hotels Duped Ghanaians." This case was resolved when the newspaper published a retraction of the association of the hotel with the allegations in the story. Often, the Settlement Committee sends out a press statement with the preferred wording to be published or broadcast. Though the Committee can only rely on the goodwill of media organizations to accede to the request, media organizations almost always comply—in large part to avoid government becoming more actively involved in media regulation. If the committee does not find in favor of the aggrieved party, then the party can take the case to the Supreme Court—but not until the Settlement Committee has reached a judgment.

MEDIA REGULATION IN LEBANON

In Lebanon, most media regulations are formulated by Parliament. However, as Nabil Dajani explains in "Disparity between Public Interest and Money and Power" (2003), government attempts to regulate private media are often unsuccessful because the ownership groups have financial backing from other influential groups with ties to members of the government's ruling coalition. In Lebanon, there are private radio and television stations, there is a radio station that operates as an organ of the Ministry of Information, and there is a public television station subsidized by the Ministry of Information. This situation of a fragmented marketplace in which the government struggles to provide public media and to regulate private media against a backdrop of conflicts of interest is a defining feature of the media system in Lebanon.

In Lebanon, newspapers are required to obtain a license from the Ministry of Information. Press laws issued after independence recognize two types of print licenses: political and nonpolitical. Though obtaining such licenses is supposed to be a mere formality according to the Press Law, a 1953 legislative decree put a moratorium on licenses for new political publications until the number dropped down from the fifty-six licenses at that time to twenty-five licenses. The moratorium was enacted in response to pressures from publishers who were alarmed by the growing number of unprofessional newspapers, which were accepting money and "equipment gifts" from businesses and foreign embassies in Lebanon, in exchange for editorially supporting policies and positions of the businesses and foreign embassies. But typical of how regulations are violated in Lebanon, the number of political newspapers had reached 110 licenses in 2004 despite the moratorium.

Newspapers in Lebanon operate according to a modified 1962 Publications Law. The law established four bodies to govern journalists: one body governing publishers (the Order of the Press); a second governing practicing journalists (the Reporters' Syndicate); a third governing foreign correspondents (the Syndicate of Foreign Correspondents); and a fourth overseeing the professional conduct of all groups (the Higher Press Council). To limit the possibility of state intervention, the Order of the Press introduced the practice of self-censorship by setting guidelines for professional conduct, particularly during times of crisis that threaten the stability of the state.

The Publications Law imposed some minimal state censorship and set the limits on freedom of the press. In particular, the law declares that news endangering the national security, unity, or borders of the state, or news that degrades any religion or arouses sectarian or racial grudges constitute punishable offenses. The law also declares that the intentional publication of false news and the use of the newspaper profession for direct or indirect blackmail are punishable offenses.

In 1994, Parliament enacted the Broadcast Law regulating radio and television stations within two main bodies. The first is the National Council for the Audiovisual Media, which reports to the Ministry of Information. The second is the Ministry of Telecommunications. The law requires public and private broadcasters to secure a license from the Council of Ministers on the recommendation of the National Council for the Audiovisual Media. The law was based on a French model, which is often how laws in Lebanon are developed.

Broadcasting was a government monopoly until the beginning of the civil war in 1975, which weakened government control in most areas of the country and produced fragmented control by militia groups. During this time, illegal "pirate" media thrived and operated freely. By the end of the civil war, these media received de facto recognition from the government. The 1994 Broadcasting Law formally legalized some of the illegal pirate stations. The law also made a condition for granting a broadcasting license that all broadcast stations must be owned by a group that represents different ethnic and religious backgrounds, with each member owning no more than 10 percent of the shares. However, as is the case for newspapers, the government has applied the law unevenly. For example, in 1995, radio and television licenses were approved for the following applicants: the Sunni Muslim prime minister, the Shiite Muslim Speaker of the House, the Greek Orthodox Christian Minister of Interior, and the Maronite Christian Minister of Health. These licenses violated the law that prohibits an individual from owning more than 10 percent of a broadcast station. At the same time, several applications for radio and television licenses by opposition groups were declined, though at least three of them met the licensing standards. These licenses were later approved in 1999 when a new government came to power. But by then two of the television stations were unable to operate because of a lack of funds.

The governing board of the National Council for the Audiovisual Media consists of ten members: five are appointed by the council of ministers, and five are elected by Parliament from a list of nominees prepared by its steering committee. Members are selected primarily to represent the prominent politicians (known as political bosses), and also to represent the major religious sects.

All television and radio operations (terrestrial, cable, and satellite) fall under the regulatory jurisdiction of the Ministry of Information, as represented by the National Council of the Audiovisual Media, and the Ministry of Telecommunication. Although the Broadcasting Law does not spell out the authority of the National Council of the Audiovisual Media clearly, the law describes its main role as monitoring that laws passed by Parliament as well as decrees passed by the national government are practiced. Another role is to issue opinions to the government about broadcasting law and policy.

Though the Broadcasting Law provides the National Council for the Audiovisual Media with the authority to regulate cable and satellite broadcasters, no guidelines were drawn up to define the operation of these systems. Therefore, they operate without any proper official control. Similarly, the Broadcasting Law provides the Ministry of Telecommunications with the authority to regulate the internet, but the regulations deal only with the technical specifications of the medium.

In Lebanon, both radio stations and television stations are licensed for a renewable period of sixteen years—if the station applies three years prior to the expiry date of the license. Broadcasters are obliged to meet terms of conditions drawn up by the TV and Radio Transmission Organization Committee, which reports to both the Ministry of Telecommunications and the Ministry of Information. The terms of conditions make stipulations about both technical requirements and content.

There are three areas of content regulation in Lebanon that are particularly distinctive. One area is **domestic programs.** Regulations stipulate that programs originating in Lebanon must comprise 16.6 percent of the total programs aired on both radio and television stations. The purpose of this regulation is to avoid programming being dominated by foreign content. Another requirement is that radio and television stations transmit national-orientation, educational, health, intellectual, and tourist programs at the rate of one hour per week. These programs are to be aired free of charge, and the information required for their transmission is to be supplied either by the Ministry of Information or from a station's archives. However, both of these regulations are vaguely defined and are not widely followed by stations.

A second area of content regulation is **political opinion.** In comparison with neighboring Arab countries, a fairly broad range of political opinions can be presented in Lebanese media content. However, as Nabil Dajani notes in *Disoriented Media in a Fragmented Society* (1992), this freedom has led Lebanese media to criticize policies and officials of other governments (such as Saudi Arabia, Jordan, Syria, and Iraq) in the Middle East. In turn, some of these governments have imposed economic "punishments" on Lebanon, such as when tourists from Iraq and Saudi Arabia were not permitted to visit Lebanon. In response to the punishments, the Lebanese government issued a legislative decree forbidding the Lebanese media from criticizing all foreign heads of states. Additional media regulations in the area of political content prohibit content that may endanger national security or arouse sectarian conflicts. For example, Lebanese media are not allowed to promote relations with Israel, with which Lebanon has been in a state of war since 1948.

A third area of content regulation is **advertising.** The regulation stipulates that advertisements should be presented clearly and differently—in both audio and videoform—from the programs during which they are aired. Advertisements typically air between programs but can be aired during a program provided that the unity and the value of the program are intact, and in a manner not harmful to the owners of the program's literary and artistic rights. Additionally, radio and television stations must refrain from airing any advertisement that might misinform the consumer or harm the consumer's health or interests, which includes violating public morals. The law does not set limits for advertising minutage.

A fourth area of regulation involves **religious programming.** One regulation prohibits private broadcasters from airing continuous religious programming, but permits religious programs to be broadcast up to a maximum of one hour per week. Alternatively, the government permits religious groups to air religious programs via a designated channel on the public television broadcaster *Tele Liban.* However, a number of religious broadcasters (e.g., television broadcasters *Tele-Lumiere* and *ad-Da'wa* as well as radio broadcaster *al-Bashayer*) continue to operate without a license, and the government has been unable to stop them.

The Ministry of Information and the Ministry of Telecommunication have two main powers of enforcement to elicit compliance with regulations: the fine and court suspension of broadcasting, which either ministry can request the courts to enforce against a broadcaster for violating regulations or statutory law. For example, the government secured a court decision to revoke the license of *MTV* for violating regulations of political advertising during a parliamentary election. The government presented evidence that the financial backer of MTV in Lebanon, a member of the opposition and running for Parliament, used the news programs to advertise his candidacy and attack his opponents. However, other television stations committed similar violations advertising other political candidates but were not referred to court by the government.

COMPARATIVE SUMMARY

Table 6.1 summarizes the comparisons of regulation in each country. One area of comparison to highlight here is the main government agency with which regulatory agencies are most closely linked, as well as the purview of the agency. Countries with regulatory bodies located mainly within government ministries that oversee both noncommercial and commercial media include México, China, Ghana, and Lebanon. Of these, China has the most centralized regulations, whereas Sweden, México, and Lebanon each split functions of regulations mainly across two governmental bodies. Countries with regulatory bodies located mainly within government-related but independent agencies include the UK, France, Sweden, and the USA—though in France and Sweden the actual development of regulations is handled by government ministries or the legislative process. Countries with government departments or ministries that directly regulate media content in public-service media include France, Sweden, and China. The one country with a quasi-regulatory agency that has mainly a nonbinding advisory role is Ghana.

Countries where broadcast media operations are conceptualized primarily as an extension of culture include France, Sweden, and the UK. In the USA, media operations are conceptualized primarily as an extension of commerce. In México, media operations are conceptualized as an extension of the interior and of transportation and communication. In China, media operations are conceptualized primarily as an extension of propaganda. In Ghana, media operations are conceptualized primarily as an extension of communication. And in Lebanon, media operations are conceptualized primarily as an extension of information.

A second area of comparison to highlight here is the power of regulators across the eight countries. China has the greatest concentration of power in a government regulator, the State Council and Propaganda Department, which actively controls multiple facets of

TABLE 6.1   Summary of Regulation of Media Across Eight Countries

	GOVERNMENT BODIES	MEDIA CONTENT REGULATED	PRIORITY CONTENT AREAS	ENFORCEMENT OPTIONS

France	CSA	Radio
		Television
			Political Pluralism
			Television Advertising
			Protection of Minors
			Protection of French
			   Language
				Fines
				Acknowledgment
				   of Noncompliance

Sweden	Radio and
	   TV Authority
	Media
	   Commission
		Radio
		Television
			Advertising to Children
			Drugs and Alcohol
			Violence
				Forced Broadcast
				   of Findings of
				   Broadcasting
				   Commission
				Fines for
				   Advertising
				   Violations

UK	OfCom	Radio Television	Children Television Advertising Taste and Decency Production Quotas	Fines Forced Broadcast of Apology License Revocation

USA	FCC	Radio
		Television
			Indecency
			Advertising by
			   Noncommercial
			   Broadcasters
			Children
				Fines
				License
				   Revocation

México	Ministry of Interior
	Ministry of
	   Transportation and
	   Communication
		Radio
		
		Television
			Advertising by
			   Questionable Television
			   Programming
			Criticism of Government
			   Institutions
				Fines
				License Revocation

China	State Council and
	   Propaganda
	   Department
		Newspapers
		Radio
		Television
		Internet
			Criticism of Government
			Advertising
			Foreign Content
				Censorship
				Fines
				Closure of Facility
				Incarceration

Ghana	National
	   Communication
	   Authority
	National Media
	   Commission
		*Newspapers
		*Radio
		*Television
			Political Reporting
			Rejoinders
			Broadcast Standards
				Arbitration Process
				License Revocation

Lebanon	National Council for
	   Audiovisual Media
	Ministry of
	   Information
		Radio
		Television
			Domestic Programs
			Political Opinion
			Advertising
			Religious Programming
				Fines
				Court Suspension

* Regulations are guidelines, not legal requirements.
Source: Robert McKenzie.

newspaper, broadcast, and internet media, including developing regulations and enforcing regulations. The next most powerful regulator is the UK's OfCom, which actively develops and enforces regulations to mandate categories of broadcast content. Next comes the USA's FCC, which in theory has the power to develop and enforce regulations, but in practice is reluctant to do so in most areas, except in the area of potentially indecent content. Then, the next most powerful regulators are found in France (the CSA) followed by Sweden (the Broadcasting Commission). Regulators in both France and Sweden actively enforce ministerial and parliamentary regulations, but do not have the authority to develop regulations themselves. Sweden's Broadcasting Commission lacks some enforcement powers that France's CSA has. Next come México's regulators, the Subsecretary of the Government and the Ministry of Transportation and Communication, both of which apply regulations developed by the government, but cannot develop regulations. In addition, the regulations do not cover as wide a range of content areas as the regulations in place in the previously mentioned countries. Next comes Lebanon's two regulators, the National Council for the Audiovisual Media and the Ministry of Telecommunications. Both of these regulators have the authority but lack the resources and political independence to be actively involved in applying regulations evenly. The weakest concentration of power is in Ghana's two regulators, the NCA and the NMC. The NCA sometimes puts aside existing regulation to help encourage the development of a telecommunications infrastructure, and the NCM lacks authority to develop binding regulations and to levy financial penalties.

A third area of comparison to highlight here has to do with which of the four media—newspapers, radio, television, internet—are regulated, and to what extent. France, the UK, the USA, and México concentrate regulations only on radio and television. Sweden, Ghana, and Lebanon regulate radio, television, and to some extent newspapers, though the newspaper licensing process is rather minimal. China is the only country out of the eight that comprehensively regulates newspapers, radio, television, and the internet.

A fourth area of comparison to highlight here involves the content areas that are targeted by regulations. Most content regulations are in some way subjugated to some variation of taste and decency principles. Though all the countries strongly regulate the presentation of sexual intercourse on television, three countries in particular—the USA, China, and Lebanon—have regulations to prevent basic nudity and profanity. France, Sweden, the UK, and the USA have high-profile regulations protecting children, though the regulations are stronger in Sweden than they are in the USA. Many of these regulations are also connected with regulations limiting advertising. The European countries—France, Sweden, and the UK—have strong regulations limiting advertising in broadcast media in an effort to avoid too much commercialization of content, especially news content. France, the UK, and China have regulations to protect national culture and domestic media production. México, China, and Lebanon have regulations restricting criticism of government, though China's regulations are much more wide-ranging. China, Ghana, and Lebanon have regulations limiting religious media content that might promote social instability.

CHAPTER 7

FINANCING OF MEDIA

PRIMER QUESTIONS

1. What do you think are some advantages of using advertising to finance media content? Using a license fee (a fee that a person pays for owning a television set or a radio receiver)? Using government allocation? Using user fees (also known as subscriptions)? Using donations?

2. What do you think are some disadvantages of using advertising to finance media content? Using a license fee? Using government allocation? Using user fees? Using donations?

3. What do you think are some underlying assumptions about why it is appropriate to finance media with advertising? With license fees? With government allocations? With user fees? With donations?

4. How do you think the philosophies for media systems affect the financing of media content? What philosophies for media systems tend to lead to what methods of financing media content?

5. How do you think media content is affected when it is financed by more methods versus fewer methods?

When reading a newspaper, listening to radio, watching television, or surfing the internet, it is easy to overlook how much the content is affected by how it is financed. That is because financing is really in the background of how people experience media content. Put another way, it is more enticing to be drawn to whether a television advertisement is funny, outrageous, or silly than to analyze, for example, how the use of advertising as a revenue source affects the look, sound, and feel of the television programming. Yet advertising, like all methods of financing, has a monumental impact on the design and the delivery of media content.

This chapter discusses the element of **financing,** defined as the provision of money or services to facilitate the production and distribution of media content. The chapter focuses on identifying the primary sources of financing for media systems in the eight countries. Financing is a critical element of a media system, because money shapes the media content that is produced, as well as the audiences that are served by media content, plus the audiences that are underserved by media content. Generally, the broader the mix of financing used by a media organization, the less beholden a media organization is to producing and delivering media content that meets the goals and objectives of a single source of financing.

In Chapter 3, financing was likened to the main branches of a tree that set its basic parameters by providing support and direction for the feeder branches (referred to in this book as representing the element of accessibility). If a main branch on a tree deteriorates or dies off, then the feeder branches (accessibility) and the leaves (content) that connect to it will also wither away or expire. The main branches of a tree do not draw as much attention from passersby as the trunk or the leaves of a tree. Similarly, as the first paragraph pointed out, financing does not draw as much attention from the audience as the regulations (the trunk) or the content (the leaves) of a tree.

As might be expected, there is no standard formula for financing content in newspapers, radio, television, and the internet across a country's media system. Rather, as Robert Hilliard and Michael Keith point out in *Global Broadcasting Systems* (1996), different media content is paid for by different combinations of financing models that have developed within the constraints of prevailing geopolitical and economic forces. For example, in some developing countries, there are not enough people with enough money to purchase advertised products to support a viable advertising industry. However, against this backdrop is the larger climate of globalization in which global media conglomerates are seeking new international audiences for media content via new technological delivery systems, wherein advertising and user fees have become more widespread as methods of financing media content. In contrast, government allocation as a method of financing has generally been on the decline or has held steady, as governments have sought to reduce expenditures on public services, including public-service media. Readings that discuss the financing of media include *Electronic Media and Industrialized Nations* (1999), by Donald R. Browne; *The Economics of Television* (1988) by Richard Collins, Nicholas Garnham, and Gareth Locksley; and *New Media Politics: Comparative Perspectives in Western Europe* (1986), edited by Denis McQuail and Karen Siune.

METHODS OF FINANCING

Advertising

Advertising is a method of financing in which a provider of media content sells space or time to a vendor so that the vendor can promote a product or service to the audience. Advertising is commonly used to finance newspapers and the internet and, to a lesser extent, radio and television. Normally, a vendor pays a media organization to advertise a product or service to the targeted audience. Newspapers sell space, broadcasters sell time, and web sites sell both space and time. Media professionals typically describe this process as selling the ability to access an audience to advertisers. Academics sometimes describe this process more bluntly as media selling audiences to advertisers.

Sponsorship is a variation of advertising in both commercial and noncommercial media content, wherein space and time are underwritten by a vendor. In a typical underwriting agreement, the vendor is mentioned throughout the media content, in exchange for money. Sponsorship agreements with noncommercial broadcasters ordinarily stipulate restrictions on how the vendor's product or the vendor itself can be described during the mentions. Such restrictions can include limitations on the size of the sponsorship and the qualitative claims that can be made to describe the product or service.

Advertising tends to be used in countries influenced by a libertarian philosophy of media operations in which there is a market-based economy. Two main assumptions lie behind the perceived worthiness of advertising as a method of financing. One assumption is that government should not be involved in financing the business of media, and individuals should not be required to pay for media. Rather, the financing of media should be a voluntary outgrowth of a commercial marketplace in which individuals freely select media content from the choices that are available. In this marketplace, a vendor pays for media content that is popular with audiences, by purchasing time or space within that content to advertise products and services. The second assumption is that individuals can indirectly select the choices of media content to be offered when they form audiences large enough to entice vendors to pay for the content through advertising. Alternatively, media content that is not accessed by large-enough audiences might be canceled because of the failure to generate enough advertising revenue.

Advertising as a method of financing media content is criticized for two major reasons. One criticism argues that when media organizations rely exclusively or predominantly on advertising as a source of revenue, misplaced priorities are given to advertising content over the arrangement of other media content. For example, newspapers are usually produced according to a system in which advertising content is laid out before the news content. Similarly, try this test with radio: Turn on the radio and do a "band sweep." That is, listen for a moment to the radio frequency at the far left of the band, and then scan to the right until you reach the last radio frequency, while stopping on each radio frequency in between for a few seconds. When you have reached the last frequency to the right, count up how many times you stopped on regular programming, and how many times you stopped on an advertisement. Critics contend that if advertising occupies a large percentage of the space or the time available in the delivery of media content, there is little room to deliver content that is devoid of profit-making potential, such as public-service announcements, educational messages, artistic expressions, or just silly humor. Similarly, if advertising occupies too large a percentage of space and time, other content gets squeezed into short and fast-paced segments that then become superficial and hurried.

A second criticism is that advertising effectively harms society in a host of areas. In particular, countries with leanings toward a social responsibility philosophy tend to place greater governmental restrictions on advertising in favor of protecting society from the innocence of children being exploited; social and political discussions having less prominence in public discourse than corporate commercialism; consumers being misled by false advertising; artists' creations being altered by advertising; and media content being dumbed down to accommodate the advertiser goal of making content understandable to the largest possible number of people.

Supporters of advertising argue that it provides media producers with a financing model that allows media organizations to be more innovative and responsive to audience tastes. That is, because advertising revenue can be increased depending on the popularity of media content, media organizations theoretically have a strong financial incentive to invest in technology and content that meets audience tastes and continues to grow audience numbers.

License Fee

A **license fee** used to finance broadcast media requires people to pay an annual fee for the privilege of owning and using television sets. Sometimes, license fees are also levied on the ownership and use of radio receivers. But usually, one license fee is required only of people who own television sets, and the revenue that is generated is then used to pay for both radio and television public-service broadcasting. License fees as a method of financing should not be confused with the use of the term *licensing* to describe the procedure in which a government requires that a media organization (usually a broadcast organization) be officially approved and registered before it can operate. Figure 7.1 shows an example of the application and fee for a television license used in the UK in 2003 to fund the BBC.

Usually, a person who owns a television set or a radio receiver pays a license fee to the government for the right to use the television set or the radio receiver to access media programming. The monies collected through license fees are then used to fund the production of government-sanctioned media content. Some governments in countries mandating license fees use vehicles with transmission-detection equipment to drive through neighborhoods to discover—and fine—television viewers or radio listeners who have not paid license fees.

Mandatory license fees tend to be used in European countries with media systems grounded in a social responsibility philosophy, and in some countries that are former

FIGURE 7.1 *Application Form for a Television License in the UK*
Source: Robert McKenzie.

colonies of European countries. Typically, there are three assumptions behind the worthiness of using a license fee to finance media operations: that media use is a luxury that consumers should pay for directly out of their own pockets; that the design of media content should not depend solely on advertising financing, because it caters to mass tastes; and that direct government appropriation (discussed next) is unreliable because it can change with the political orientation of the government. The use of a license fee is designed to generate a stable revenue source that allows media organizations to produce content.

The government usually decides the cost of a license fee and collects, or hires a surrogate to collect, the monies. Typically, license-fee monies are allocated exclusively to public broadcasting services. Commercial broadcasters, newspapers, and internet content providers typically do not receive license fee monies.

License fees are criticized for three main reasons. Media professionals charge that they stifle investment and growth: Because the revenue from license fees is dependent on a fixed segment of the population that owns television sets or radio receivers, the collectable revenue is also fixed. Consequently, broadcasters might have little incentive to improve the quality of content or the delivery of content if improvements will not increase revenue. Media professionals also criticize license fees by arguing that media organizations receiving such monies have unfair advantages (a stable and guaranteed revenue stream) over media organizations that do not receive license-fee monies. Such critics contend that media organizations having to look elsewhere for sources of financing are more dependent on the economic cycle and the popularity of their media products to sustain operations. Some critics argue that some people are forced to pay license fees for media content that they do not access. Other critics argue that some people who should pay license fees refuse to do so without getting caught. In response, supporters of license fees counter that license fees enable media organizations to produce and deliver high-quality media content without the pressure of meeting the expectations of advertisers or achieving sizable audiences.

Government Appropriation

Government appropriation as a method of financing is when the government allocates monies or resources for the production and delivery of media content, usually on an annual cycle as part of the budgeting process for everything the government is going to fund. Government-appropriated monies are usually allocated either as cash or as tax credits to the provider of media content. When government allocation makes up only part of the operating expenses of a media organization, the allocation is known as a **government subsidy.** Government appropriation resources can also include free postal service or utility expenses. Usually, individuals and businesses pay income tax to the government. Drawing on this general revenue, a government agency or legislature approves a portion of the monies to be allocated to the designated media—normally public-service media.

There are two main assumptions behind the worthiness of government appropriation as a source of financing. One assumption is that certain media—usually select broadcast media—should be set aside as public services made available to the general population and produced without profit-making directives. The second assumption is that society in general should share the cost of providing public-service media content.

Government appropriation is commonly used as a financing source in countries following communist, authoritarian, or social responsibility philosophies, which seek to actively control media content, and in developing countries, which lack large enough middle or wealthy classes. As mentioned already under license fees, developing countries often cannot sustain an exclusive advertiser-supported system because of a lack of consumer demand for commercial products and services. By ensuring annual government financing, therefore, both fledgling and established media organizations can plan long-term objectives for the production and delivery of content.

Government appropriation as a method of financing is criticized for three main reasons. One is that the revenue created through general taxation is connected to unpredictable swings. This in turn makes it difficult for media organizations to plan the production and delivery of content. A second criticism is that, like license fees, government appropriation forces some people to pay for media content they do not access. A third criticism is that government appropriation of financing for media permits the government to have too much control over media content; critics warn that if a media organization provides content that is considered to be inappropriate by powerful government officials, financing will be reduced or withheld in order to terminate the content.

User Fees

User fees as a method of financing permit a media organization by law to charge a fee to individual audience members who access that organization's media content. The user fee normally comes in two forms. One is a **subscription,** wherein the user pays a flat and predictable fee for regular access to a newspaper, a selection of television and radio channels, or a web site. Subscriptions are normally paid out on a monthly or yearly basis. The other form of user fee is the **per-use** fee, wherein a user pays for each instance of access to media content.

Both subscriptions and per-use fees are used in various ways to finance newspapers, multichannel broadcasting, and internet web sites. In the newspaper industry, per-use financing is referred to as *sales.* Financing by sales means the reader pays for a newspaper on the spot. In the multichannel broadcasting industry, per-use financing is referred to as *pay-per-view.* Subscription fees and pay-per-view fees are usually used to finance premium channels (particularly movie channels). In the internet industry, subscription financing is commonly referred to as an *access fee.* Almost all private internet users pay an access fee for internet service. In contrast, employees at organizations that connect to the internet, and students attending universities, usually do not have to pay an access fee. Though most web sites are free once access to the internet is gained, for some web sites, internet users have to pay either a subscription fee or an additional access fee to get to certain kinds of content including financial research, music, and sexually explicit photos and videos, to name a few. In addition, internet providers often charge user fees to people and organizations seeking to post information on the web, such as blogs or home pages.

User fees are generally determined in response to a perception of what the marketplace will support. However, user fees required to access content delivered by cable and satellite broadcasters are often regulated by a local or national government if the company has a monopoly in a particular geographic market.

There are two basic assumptions behind the appropriateness of user fees as a source of financing. One assumption is that user fees allow audience members to pay only for the media content they access. This assumption is somewhat blunted in the case of satellite and cable broadcasting because user fees normally cover a package of channels, many of which audience members do not access or want. A second assumption is that user fees provide a more direct relationship between audience needs and resulting media content because the financial path between user fees and media organizations is more direct.

User fees tend to be used as the preferred model for financing in two situations. One situation has to do with whether a libertarian philosophy for a country's media system underlies the prevailing outlook for how a content provider should operate. If a libertarian philosophy predominates, the financing model of user fees is seen as an appropriate mechanism for allowing the marketplace to determine the selection of media content. The second situation is when certain media content is accessed by a niche audience. In that case, user fees are seen as a more appropriate financing method than a license fee or government allocation, which is premised on providing media content benefiting society as a whole.

The user fee as a method of financing is criticized for two main reasons. One is that user fees only lead to the production and distribution of media content that appeals to the largest audience possible, not to a small but loyal audience. A second criticism is that user fees—particularly subscription fees for broadcast content—tend to increase on a regular basis. This criticism holds that providers of media content are in a coercive position to raise user fees for content that is delivered by satellite and cable technologies because audience members are reluctant to discontinue using expensive equipment connected to wiring that has been installed and already runs through the households.

Donation

Donation is a method of financing in which an individual or an institution (a company or a public trust) voluntarily contributes money to a provider of media content. Usually, donations are made to nonprofit radio and television stations. Donations normally go directly from the donor to the media organization.

Generally, money is donated by two sources. One group includes people who perceive their donations to be critical to the survival of media content reaching niche audiences—content that would otherwise be discontinued if the marketplace were left to determine its viability. A second source includes people and institutions seeking tax relief. Donations are rarely the chief method of financing for content dispersed widely by major media organizations because donation monies typically pale in comparison to other methods of financing.

The main assumption behind donation as a method of financing is that it allows individuals and institutions, of their own volition, to contribute to media content that they alone desire to be produced and distributed. A second assumption is that donation engenders a sense of community and civic duty by encouraging citizens to take an active part in determining the media content that is produced and distributed.

Donation as a method of financing is criticized for two main reasons. One criticism is that donations rise with economies in an upturn and fall with economies in a downturn. Once again, such unpredictability makes it difficult for providers of media content to plan for production and distribution on a long-term basis. A second criticism is that large institutional donors sometimes contribute monies for media content that will promote ideological causes. Such institutions, it is argued, are in a better financial position to promote their causes than individuals or smaller institutions. However, proponents of donations regard them as a welcome method for financing specialty media content—often considered to be artistic and cultural— to reach audiences that otherwise would be underserved.

FINANCING OF MEDIA IN FRANCE

Financing of Newspapers in France

In France, advertising and sales are used to finance most newspapers. Figures from 1999 show that sales makes up a larger percentage (just under 56 percent) of total financing than advertising (just over 44 percent).

In addition, the state has provided subsidies to small-circulation newspapers that offer minority political viewpoints in an effort to promote political pluralism. To this end, indirect subsidies in the form of tax relief are provided for the purchases of new equipment, as well as postal, telephone, and train transportation costs associated with distributing the newspaper. To a lesser extent, direct subsidies are provided to a few daily newspapers in Paris with low advertising revenue, again to stimulate political pluralism.

Financing of Radio and Television in France

In France, two private, terrestrial radio and television broadcasters (*TF1* and *M6*) are financed entirely by advertising, whereas *Canal+* is financed by a combination of advertising and subscription fees.

Private multichannel (cable and satellite) broadcasters receive financing from a mix of two sources: advertising and user fees (both subscription and per-use fees).

Public broadcasters are financed by a combination of advertising revenue and a mandatory television license fee. French law requires that financing of public broadcasting be a 50–50 split between revenues raised by license fees and revenues raised by advertising. The monies that are collected through these two methods of financing are used for the production and delivery of content by the French public broadcasters. For the license fee, a person who installs television-receiving equipment must fill out an application and pay a fee for the right to use that equipment. This license fee is the same regardless of how many televisions are in use. The Ministry of Culture sets the amount of the license fee. In 2003, the cost of a French television license fee was 116.50 euros—about 136 United States dollars (USD). (Note: All figures given are calculated according to the exchange rate in effect at the time of this book's writing.)

A television owner receives a bill (*taxe audio-visuelle*) in the mail from the Department of Licensing for Audio-visual Services (Service de La Redevance de l'Audiovisuel), which is a division of the state's general tax collection authority (Le Tresor Public). The television owner is responsible for mailing in payment for the license or having the money debited from the owner's bank account. The monies that are collected are then allocated to France Télévisions and France Radio, two state-owned companies that produce and distribute programs. France Télévisions distributes television programs to the three public television stations, *France 2, France 3,* and *France 5/Arte;* France Radio distributes radio programs to the five public radio stations (*France Musiques*, *France Culture*, *France Info*, *France Inter*, and *France Blue*). *Arte*, which shares a broadcast frequency with *France 5*, is financed by a combination of both French and German license fees. License-fee monies are also allocated to partially subsidize the French film industry.

Financing of the Internet in France

In France, stand-alone internet content providers (those that do not serve as additional outlets for government agencies or broadcasters) do not receive any government financing. Stand-alone providers of internet content draw on a combination of advertising and user-fee financing.

FINANCING OF MEDIA IN SWEDEN

Financing of Newspapers in Sweden

In Sweden, advertising and sales are used to finance most newspapers. Figures from 2000 show that advertising makes up a larger percentage (about 56 percent) of total financing than sales (about 44 percent).

In addition, the state provides subsidies to newspapers that rank second in terms of advertising revenue across geographic markets compared to the leading newspapers, in an effort to promote a plurality of opinion. To this end, the government allocates monies to the number-two newspaper in major cities. An example of such a newspaper that has received government subsidies financing is *Svenska Dagbladet,* published out of Stockholm.

Financing of Radio and Television in Sweden

In Sweden, private terrestrial radio and television broadcasters are financed entirely by advertising. Private multichannel (cable and satellite) broadcasters receive financing from a mix of two sources: advertising and user fees (both subscription and per-use fees). Public broadcasters are financed entirely by revenues from a mandatory television license fee; they are not permitted to carry advertising. License-fee monies are used for the production and delivery of content by the Swedish public broadcasters. For the license fee, a person who installs television-receiving equipment must fill out an application and pay a fee for the right to use that equipment. Regardless of the number of televisions in use in a household, the fee is the same. The cost of the fee is set by a government agency called Radio Service (*Radiotjänst*). In 2003, the cost of a Swedish television license was 1,740 Swedish crowns—about 227 USD. These monies pay for the operations and the programming on the two public television stations (*SVT 1, SVT 2*) as well as the seven public radio stations (*P1*, *P2*, *P3*, *P4*, *P5*, *P6*, *P7*).

A person who owns a television set must report it to Radio Service. This agency then mails out a bill for the license fee to that person. To ensure compliance, the Swedish government dispatches vehicles with transmission detection equipment to neighborhoods to identify radio receivers or television sets that are in use. The government announces beforehand where the vehicles will be dispatched, to encourage voluntary compliance.

Monies collected through license fees are then distributed by the government to one of three **ownership foundations:** Swedish Radio, which manages public radio; Swedish Television, which manages public television; and Swedish Educational Broadcasting, which manages educational content for both public television and radio. The three ownership foundations oversee the production of content provided to the public radio and television stations. Each ownership foundation has a board of directors made up of members who are appointed by the Swedish government.

Financing of the Internet in Sweden

In Sweden, stand-alone providers of internet content (those that do not serve as additional outlets for government agencies or broadcasters) do not receive any government financing; instead, they draw on a combination of advertising and user-fee financing.

FINANCING OF MEDIA IN THE UK

Financing of Newspapers in the UK

In the UK, advertising and sales are used to finance most newspapers. Figures from 2000 show that advertising makes up a larger percentage (about 64.5 percent) of total financing than sales (about 35.5 percent). The government provides no press subsidies to newspapers.

Financing of Radio and Television in the UK

In the UK, private terrestrial radio and television broadcasters are funded entirely by advertising. Private multichannel (cable and satellite) broadcasters receive financing from a mix of two sources: advertising and user fees (both subscription and per-use fees).

Public broadcasters are financed entirely through a mandatory television license fee paid by people who own televisions sets. The Department for Culture, Media and Sport sets the amount of the license fee. In 2003, the cost of a British license fee for color television was 116 Great Britain Pounds (GBP) per year—about 192 USD. The fee differs depending on whether a person owns a color or black-and-white television set, but the fee is the same whether a person owns one or more television sets. These monies pay for the operations and the programming on the BBC's public terrestrial television channels (*BBC 1*, *BBC 2*), multichannel television channels (*BBC 3*, *BBC 4*, *CBeebies*, *CBBC*, *BBC News 24*, and *BBC Parliament*), and five radio services (*Radio 1*, *Radio 2*, *Radio 3*, *Radio 4*, and *Radio 5 Live*). The internationally distributed BBC World Service radio is funded by government appropriation.

A person who installs television-receiving equipment must fill out an application and pay a license fee for the right to use that equipment. The license fee is paid at a local post office or via the internet. License-fee monies are processed by a division of the BBC called TV Licensing. These monies are passed on to the government, and then allocated to the

BBC for the production and delivery of content. TV Licensing uses a number of means to detect people evading the license fee, including a database of television owners, a nation-wide team of enquiry officers checking on unlicensed addresses, television detector vans, and officers on foot with handheld TV detection scanners.

Financing of the Internet in the UK

In the UK, stand-alone providers of internet content (those that do not serve as additional outlets for government agencies or broadcasters) do not receive any government financing. Stand-alone providers of internet content draw on a combination of advertising and user-fee financing.

FINANCING OF MEDIA IN THE USA

Financing of Newspapers in the USA

In the USA, advertising and sales are used to finance most newspapers. Figures from 1997 show that advertising makes up a much larger percentage (about 87 percent) of total financing than sales (about 13 percent). The government provides no subsidies to newspapers, but there are indirect subsidies from municipal governments, which are legally required to publish "public notices" in local newspapers. Some examples of public notices include hearings, bids for government contracts, and available committee memberships.

Financing of Radio and Television in the USA

In the USA, private terrestrial radio and television broadcasters are funded mostly by advertising. Private multichannel (cable and satellite) broadcasters in the USA receive financing from a mix of two sources: advertising and user fees (both subscription and per-use fees).

Public broadcasters in the USA are financed by a broad mix of sources. The two primary sources of financing are donations (membership and business donations) and government appropriation (federal and state). The monies collected through these two methods of financing comprise about two-thirds of the financing of the production and delivery of content on radio stations that are members of National Public Radio (NPR) and television stations that are members of the Public Broadcasting System (PBS). Other sources of financing include sponsorships and foundations. Advertising is not permitted on public broadcasting.

Individuals or institutions (for-profit and nonprofit) that seek to become members of a public broadcast station can pay a monthly or yearly fee. Typically, there are various levels of membership, depending on the dollar amount that is donated. Or, individuals or institutions can donate to public broadcasters during campaigns known as fund-raising drives, which normally occur two to four times a year. During a fund-raising drive, the public broadcaster uses airtime to solicit donations (criticized by some as "begging") from the audience. The monies that are collected from both types of donations go directly to the local public broadcaster to cover the cost of production and distribution of content.

During annual appropriations for all public expenditures, Congress allocates a portion of this fund to the Corporation for Public Broadcasting (CPB), a private, nonprofit, nongovernment corporation. The CPB then provides partial financing for the operations of public broadcasters, as well as full or partial funding for the production of content for NPR and PBS that is then distributed to member stations.

Financing of the Internet in the USA

In the USA, stand-alone providers of internet content (those that do not serve as additional outlets for government agencies or broadcasters) do not receive any government financing and must draw on a combination of advertising and user-fee financing.

FINANCING OF MEDIA IN MÉXICO

Financing of Newspapers in México

In México, newspapers are financed by advertising, sales, and government subsidies. Government subsidies are provided to newspapers through three methods. One method—called "paid insertions"—is where the national government, state governments, and municipal governments pay for advertisements in newspapers. This method of subsidy effectively encourages some favorable coverage of the government by the given newspaper. At the national level, the government purchases paid insertions as needed. At the state level, usually the government enters into annual contracts with regional newspapers to reserve daily or weekly space on a particular page for government publicity. Usually, paid insertions contain publicity about recent accomplishments made by a government department. Figure 7.2 shows an example of a full-page paid insertion, which appeared in a regional newspaper based in the state of Veracruz. This particular insertion is a report by the Veracruz agriculture department concerning growing more crops, increasing exports, opening up more jobs, and establishing new trading partners.

There is no law requiring that newspapers disclose their financing, so percentages of revenue sources often are kept secret. However, it is estimated that many newspapers receive 40 percent to 60 percent of revenue from government-subsidized paid insertions. Some papers receive even more than 60 percent of their revenue from government-subsidized paid insertions, and some newspapers receive as low as 3 percent of revenue from the government.

A second method of government subsidy involves the direct payment from state government to a regional newspaper with statewide circulation. And a third method involves secret payments by government representatives to journalists to elicit coverage of a story in such a way as to present a positive image of government. This method is not condoned publicly, but nonetheless has been somewhat common.

Financing of Radio and Television in México

In México, private terrestrial radio and television broadcasters are financed entirely by advertising. Private multichannel (cable and satellite) broadcasters in México receive

FIGURE 7.2 *Government Advertisement in Regional* Milenio *Newspaper*
Source: Milenio.

financing from two sources: advertising and user fees (both subscription and per-use fees).

State governments—not the national government—fund public television. A combination of federal, state, and, to a lesser extent, private-sector funding is provided for a public radio broadcast network called *IMER* (Mexican National Institute of Radio). IMER comprises twenty-six radio stations, each formatted individually, ranging from rap to classical music. IMER stations carry advertising as well. In addition to the IMER stations, seven public radio networks are funded by state governments. These state public radio networks are allocated funding on a yearly basis, and are not allowed to carry advertising.

The basic path that government appropriation takes is as follows: During annual appropriations, state legislatures in México allocate funding to public broadcasters operating within individual states. The monies are generated at the state level by state income taxes. The monies are generated at the federal level from revenues from the sale of oil and electricity.

Both private and public broadcasters receive additional subsidized financing from state governments and the federal government through agreements to guarantee the dissemination of government publicity, similar to the notion of paid insertions in newspapers. Under these agreements, the government purchases time from broadcasters to disseminate information about government initiatives that are ostensibly in the public interest. Examples include road construction projects, health initiatives, and annual department reports.

There are two main sources of government monies for these methods of government subsidies. At the state level, financing is generated by income or property taxes. At the federal level, financing is generated by oil, gasoline, or electricity revenues.

Financing of the Internet in México

In México, stand-alone providers of internet content (excluding those that serve as additional outlets for government agencies or government broadcasters) do not receive any government financing. Such stand-alone providers of internet content draw on a combination of advertising and user-fee financing.

FINANCING OF MEDIA IN CHINA

Financing of Newspapers in China

In China, newspapers are funded mainly by advertising, sales, and government subsidies. Figures from 2001 show that advertising revenue accounted for 60 percent of total financing compared with sales, which made up almost 40 percent of financing.

In 2004, the government relinquished its monopoly on newspaper distribution under the World Trade Organization (WTO) agreement, which allows foreign companies to enter the market and compete with *China Post* for distribution rights. However, the government continues to allocate subsidies to influential national newspapers, including the *People's Daily, Guangming Daily,* and *Economic Daily.* The subsidies take the same path as for broadcasters, with direct payments made to selected newspapers via government agencies and Party branches. The main purpose of subsidizing preferred newspapers is to allow the government to maintain at least one financially viable Party newspaper within key competitive markets.

However, another method used to finance newspapers is under-the-table payments to journalists or publications by businesses and individuals for positive coverage of the products and services of a company. Though the government has instructed the media to expose such breaches publicly, the practice continues as media organizations pursue profitability, and as journalists feel the pressure to supplement poor salaries. In 2004, the government's Xinhua News Agency released the names of eleven journalists—including four from its own agency—who were paid hush money by a mining company to cover up the extent of a workplace disaster that killed thirty-eight miners in northern China's Shanxi province.

Financing of Radio and Television

In China, public broadcasters (there are no private broadcasters) are financed mainly by a mix of advertising, subscription fees, and government appropriation. About 55 percent of financing comes from advertising, and about 15 percent of financing comes from central and local government (Communist Party branch) subsidies. Other broadcasting revenues are derived from subscriptions, program and video sales, and promotional publications for sale related to television and radio programming.

The annual meeting of the Communist Party and National Congress decides on the monies to be parceled out to Party branches and government agencies such as the State Administration of Radio, Film and Television (SARFT) and the Ministry of Information Industry (MII). The monies are allocated directly by these Party branches and agencies to designated public broadcasters, with priority given to national broadcasters such as China Central Television (CCTV), Central People's Radio, and international broadcaster China Radio International. The monies generated at the level of central government are from the sale of electronics, petroleum, and chemical engineering. The monies generated at the level of local government are from income taxes and business taxes.

Multichannel (cable and satellite) broadcasters receive revenues from a mix of two sources: advertising and user fees (subscription and per-use fees). Users subscribe to the per-use digital services, paying additional fees to digital cable television operators in each city. These digital services include stock reports, movies, and sports scores.

These monies are used by television and radio broadcasters to purchase, produce, and deliver content that is approved by the two main regulatory bodies, SARFT and the MII. The monies are also used by broadcasters to expand the rollout of digital services by the year 2015, as mandated by the central government.

Financing of the Internet in China

In China, internet content and service providers are funded by advertising, user fees (subscription and per-use fees), approved overseas investment, and government appropriation. Funding of the internet is based on three classifications. The first classification is traditional media. In 2000, the government introduced "The Development Outline of Internet Publicity," and selected five traditional media web sites to receive government appropriation: *People's Daily*, Xinhua News Agency, CCTV, China Radio International, and China Central Radio. The second classification is commercial web sites such as Sina.com, Sohu.com, and Netease.com. These web sites mostly include companies listed on the NASDAQ, which receive strong financial support from approved overseas investors. For example, Chinese portals Sohu.com (Disney Corporation), Netease.com (Viacom/*MTV*) and Sina.com (Google) have formed joint-venture partnerships to fund expansion of online services. Commercial web sites also finance operations by developing a range of business services including mailbox services, e-commerce, wireless services, and online games. The third classification is joint-venture web sites, which are provided by traditional media and commercial operations (for example, Qianlong.com and Southcn.com). Joint-venture web sites finance their operations from traditional media and commercial companies, as well as from advertising and user fees (subscription and per-use fees for business services).

FINANCING OF MEDIA IN GHANA

Financing of Newspapers in Ghana

In Ghana, advertising and sales are used to finance both state-owned and private newspapers. Figures from 2000 show that advertising makes up a larger percentage (about 64.5 percent) of total financing than sales (about 35.5 percent). The government provides no press subsidies to newspapers. The state-owned newspapers do not receive any direct government funding, but are eligible for government loans at reduced interest rates.

Financing of Radio and Television in Ghana

In Ghana, private terrestrial radio and television broadcasters are funded entirely by advertising. Private multichannel (cable and satellite) broadcasters receive financing from a mix of two sources: advertising and user fees (both subscription and per-use fees).

Public broadcasters are financed by a mix of financing generated by advertising and by a quasi-mandatory television license fee. The Ghana Broadcasting Corporation sets the cost of the license fee with approval from Parliament. The fee differs depending on whether a dwelling has one television set or more than one television set. In 2004, the cost of a license fee was 3,000 Cedis (about 30 US cents) for one television set, and 20,000 Cedis (about 2 USD) for more than one television set. License-fee monies are used to pay for the operations and the programming on the public television network (GTV, or Ghana Television), and on the public radio channels (*Radio 1*, *Radio 2*, *FM Radio*) run by GBC Radio. However, on a fairly widespread basis, some owners of televisions elect not to pay the license fee because they consider it unfair to pay for content on GTV or on GBC Radio when these organizations also receive advertising monies and because they perceive that they do not watch enough GTV or listen to enough GBC radio to warrant a fee. Though the government does fine television owners who do not pay the license fee, not enough surveillance resources are allocated to ensure universal compliance.

A person who installs television-receiving equipment must go to one of the Ghana Broadcasting outlets (basically small stores or stands located in the cities) to pay for the license. The monies that are collected are then allocated to GBC production expenses. To gain compliance, Ghana Broadcasting infrequently sends employees into the field to knock at random on doors of houses to see if televisions are on the premises, and if so, whether residents have paid a license fee. The fine for an unpaid license fee is 100,000 Cedis (about 11 USD).

Financing of the Internet in Ghana

In Ghana, stand-alone providers of internet content (those that do not serve as additional outlets for government agencies or broadcasters) do not receive any government financing; instead, they draw on a combination of advertising and user-fee financing.

FINANCING OF MEDIA IN LEBANON

Financing of Newspapers in Lebanon

In Lebanon, advertising, sales, and political subsidies finance most newspapers. Figures from 2000 show that sales financing makes up a much larger percentage (just under 72 percent) of total financing than advertising financing (just over 28 percent). But financing figures are regularly questioned by media experts in Lebanon because newspaper publishers are not normally forthcoming with such figures. Rather, it is widely accepted that the bulk of media financing in general—and newspaper financing in particular—comes from secret political or commercial subsidies.

Subsidies to Lebanese newspapers come in a variety of forms. One is when a politician, a political party, or—in the case of Libya—secretly "rents out" the entire publication for a yearly or monthly fee. Accordingly, all costs of production and staffing are paid for during the period of the contract. Subsidies to journalists are also provided by the government or by individual politicians in the form of equipment, paper, long-term low-interest loans, or outright payment. Sometimes, subsidies take the form of salary payments to newspaper employees. Sometimes, payments are made to employees directly and without knowledge of the media institution, particularly when that institution is supposed to be neutral, as in the case of the government-run radio station and the government-supervised television station. Still another form of subsidy is when companies advertise in Lebanese newspapers on the basis of the paper's editorial policy or the political identity of the editor.

In addition, bribes are commonly paid to newspapers and journalists. Bribes have come from companies, local organizations, foreign embassies in Lebanon, and even the Lebanese government. Though bribes are frowned on in some Western countries, in some Middle Eastern countries bribes are considered a normal part of conducting business. The presumption behind a bribe is that the newspaper is expected to propagate the policies of the briber or the institution to which the briber belongs to.

Financing of Radio and Television in Lebanon

Almost all radio stations in Lebanon (the exception being the official *Radio Lebanon*) are financed by advertising and political or business subsidies. As the official radio station, *Radio Lebanon* operates as a department within the Ministry of Information.

Private satellite broadcasters receive financing from a mix of two sources: advertising and subsidies from owners or business/political groups. Multichannel cable broadcasters are financed primarily from user fees, with little or no advertising. Cable broadcasters in Lebanon typically are small operations that cover a number of neighborhoods with some seventy channels that are often illegally pilfered from larger regional cable systems. The government does not pursue the illegal retransmissions because of a perception that such actions would cause a public uproar. The regional systems do not pursue the illegal transmissions because they boost the number of viewers, which increases advertising revenue.

The only public television station, *Tele Liban,* is financed mostly by advertising. However, the government subsidizes *Tele Liban*'s losses. Drawing on general tax revenues, the government allocates money to *Tele Liban* during annual appropriations if the broadcaster is losing money, which is regularly the case.

Financing of the Internet in Lebanon

In Lebanon, stand-alone internet content providers (those that do not serve as additional outlets for government agencies or broadcasters) do not receive any government financing. Stand-alone providers of internet content draw on a combination of advertising and user-fee financing. In Lebanon, internet providers rent out bandwidths from the Ministry of Posts and Telecommunications. Many internet companies are owned by members of the government or their relatives or both.

COMPARATIVE SUMMARY

In summary, five methods of financing are frequently used by media organizations to pay for the production and delivery of media content: advertising, license fees, government allocation, user fees (subscription fees and per-use fees), and donation. Certainly there are other methods of financing the production and distribution of media content that are not described in this chapter—such as investment returns, copyright fees, the sale of goods and services, barter trades, and the rental or leasing of production facilities to outside parties. However, the five methods of financing described in this chapter represent the bulk of financing models for most media organizations across the globe.

Table 7.1 provides a summary comparing financing of media across the eight countries. In each country, the most predominant source of financing is advertising. All eight countries have newspaper content, radio content, television content, and web content

TABLE 7.1   Summary Comparing Financing of Media in Eight Countries

	NEWSPAPERS	*PUBLIC RADIO	*PRIVATE RADIO	*PUBLIC TELEVISION	*PRIVATE TELEVISION	INTERNET
France	Advertising Government Subsidy User Fees	Advertising License Fee	Advertising	Advertising License Fee	Advertising	Advertising User Fees
Sweden	Advertising Government Subsidy User Fees	License Fee	Advertising	License Fee	Advertising	Advertising User Fees
UK	Advertising User Fees	License Fee	Advertising	License Fee	Advertising	Advertising User Fees
USA	Advertising User Fees	Government Allocation Donations	Advertising	Government Allocation Donations	Advertising	Advertising User Fees
México	Advertising User Fees	Government Allocation	Advertising Government Publicity	State Government Allocation	Advertising Government Publicity	Advertising User Fees
China	Advertising Government Allocation User Fees	Advertising Government Allocation		Advertising Government Allocation		Advertising Government Allocation User Fees
Ghana	Advertising Government Loans User Fees	Advertising License Fee	Advertising	Advertising License Fee	Advertising	Advertising User Fees
Lebanon	Advertising Political Subsidies Private Subsidies User Fees	Government Allocation	Advertising Political Subsidies Private Subsidies	Government Allocation	Advertising Political Subsidies Private Subsidies	Advertising User Fees

* Terrestrial broadcast radio and television.

Source: Robert McKenzie.

funded by advertising. In the USA, advertising makes up a much larger percentage of the total financing of media than in the other countries. For example, according to *World Press Trends* (2002), advertising makes up the following percentages of total financing for newspapers in each of the eight countries: USA (87 percent), Sweden (64.5 percent), UK (64 percent), Ghana (64 percent), China (60 percent), France (44 percent), Lebanon (28 percent), and México (unknown).

In terms of broadcasting, the countries where advertising is not permitted to finance public television and radio include Sweden, the UK, the USA, and México. Countries where advertising is permitted to fund public television include France, China, Ghana, and Lebanon. Countries where advertising is permitted to partially finance public radio include France, China, and Ghana.

Government appropriation is used to finance media content in six of the countries. In China, government appropriation is used to fund newspaper, radio, television, and internet content. In France, government appropriation is used to finance small-circulation newspapers offering minority political viewpoints. In Sweden, government appropriation is used to fund second-tier competing newspapers in major cities. In the USA, government appropriation is used to partially fund public radio and public television. In México, government appropriation for advertising government activities is used to fund newspapers. Also in México, government appropriation from the national government is used to fund public radio, whereas government appropriations from state governments are used to fund public television in individual Mexican states. In Ghana, government appropriation is used to make loans to newspapers, and to partially fund public radio and public television. In Lebanon, government appropriation is used to write off losses incurred by the public television station, and to fund the official radio station.

License fees are used to finance public radio and television content in four of the countries. France, Sweden, the UK, and Ghana all require people who own television sets to pay a license fee, which is then used to fund public radio and television. In Sweden and the UK, public radio and public television content are financed almost wholly through license-fee monies, but in France and Ghana, public radio and public television content are financed through a combination of advertising and license-fee monies. However, enforcement of the license fee in Ghana is weak, effectively preventing the license fee from being mandatory.

The pattern of user-fee financing is the same for most of the countries. User fees in the form of subscriptions are used to finance newspapers, along with advertising. User fees in the form of subscriptions and per-use fees are used to finance multichannel television. And user fees in the form of monthly subscriptions are used to finance internet access in the home, whereas per-use fees are used to finance internet access in internet cafés. Both monthly subscription fees and per-use fees are combined also with advertising to finance internet content.

In the USA, donations are substantially used to finance public radio and public television.

In addition to the five methods of financing summarized, under-the-table payments (otherwise known as bribes) commonly have been used to finance newspaper content in México, China, and Lebanon. Because of the clandestine nature of this method of financing, it is difficult to say to what extent it occurs in the other countries as well.

CHAPTER 8

ACCESSIBILITY OF MEDIA

PRIMER QUESTIONS

1. How accessible is television where you are living? How about cable television and satellite television? How about digital television?

2. How accessible is radio where you are living? How about satellite radio? What is the approximate proportion of public television compared to private television? What about the approximate proportion of public radio compared to private radio?

3. How accessible are newspapers where you are living? What shops or vendors normally sell newspapers? Which newspapers can you receive where you are living?

4. How accessible is the internet where you are living? Can you easily access the internet in your home? Can you easily access the internet outside of your home?

Think about the selection of newspapers, radio frequencies, television channels, and internet technologies that you regularly come into contact with during your daily routines. Now think about which of those media are easy to access because they are convenient or inexpensive or readily available. Now think about which newspapers, television channels, radio frequencies, or internet technologies are hard to access because they are inconvenient or expensive or scarcely available. Now think about the television programs, radio programs, newspapers, and the internet web sites that you know exist, but cannot access because they simply are not available where you live. Finally, try to think about unfamiliar types of newspapers, radio programs, television shows, and web sites that may exist out there—somewhere. That last kind of thinking is especially challenging because it requires you to imagine media outlets that possibly exist, but at present are outside of your known media experiences.

Putting all of these lines of thinking together raises some basic questions about the access you have to media in your local environment, namely: What kinds of media surround you? What kinds of media do you come into contact with during your daily routines? What kinds of media are easy to access without going out of your way, or without having to pay a lot of money you really cannot afford? What kinds of media are virtually impossible to access because the economy and/or the infrastructure in the country is too underdeveloped (as discussed in Chapter 5, Philosophies for Media Systems)? These questions will help you assess the accessibility of media at your particular location. When you combine that knowledge with additional, more comprehensive information about the accessibility of media at other locations across the world, you can gain insight into just how varied the media choices really are where you are living.

In other words, studying the accessibility of media initiates an understanding of the range of media content to which people are exposed, by revealing the limitations and the possibilities of the selection of media choices available in a given country. In the course of studying the accessibility of media, it is possible to compile a rough inventory of what kinds of media are available to people in their homes, workplaces, modes of transportation, places of recreation and leisure, and so on. Such an inventory highlights the media choices that are available, and also whether people can access certain media as they go about their normal daily routines, or whether people have to make a specific trip or a concerted effort to access certain media. Therefore, an inventory of accessibility of media also helps put a rhetorical perspective on how the available media choices translate into cognitive and emotive points of reference that invite audiences to adopt certain feelings, beliefs, and behaviors related to the content that is accessed.

In Chapter 3, accessibility of media was compared to the feeder branches of a tree. This imagery symbolizes that just as the branches of a tree present leaves and seeds to passersby, media outlets similarly present content to audiences. Those feeder branches that place leaves and seeds within the reach of passersby are in effect making those leaves and seeds easily accessible, whereas those that are unreachable from the paths of passersby are in effect making certain media content difficult or even impossible to access. Similarly, media outlets that display leaves and seeds that are reachable from the paths of passersby are in effect making certain media content easy to access.

This chapter provides information that compares the accessibility of newspapers, radio, television, and internet. The main objective is to present the big picture of the accessibility of media across the eight countries studied in this book through the available data, rather than a comprehensive and standard numerical inventory of all the newspaper, radio, television and internet outlets that exist in each country. During the discussion, qualitative evaluations such as "low," "moderate," or "high" are used to describe aspects of a medium's accessibility in comparison with the other countries.

NEWSPAPER DISTRIBUTION TERMS

It is helpful here to define terms used in this chapter to describe the distribution of newspaper content:

- A **broadsheet** is a newspaper whose shape is more horizontal than it is vertical before it is opened up. Broadsheets open up vertically, and then horizontally as the pages are turned. Contentwise, broadsheets usually are "serious newspapers" focusing on politics, crime, culture, business, education, and other related subjects.
- A **tabloid** is a newspaper whose shape is more vertical (it looks like a tablet) than it is horizontal before it is opened up. Tabloids are usually smaller than broadsheets, and are easier to page through in smaller spaces (for instance, while sitting on a train seats). Contentwise, tabloid-size newspapers can either be "serious" newspapers focusing mainly on factual news, or they can be "sensational" or "entertainment newspapers," focusing mainly on dramatic news related to crime, celebrities, scandals, outrages, gossip, and so on.
- **Circulation** is the number of copies of a newspaper that are printed and delivered. Circulation figures do not necessarily indicate the number of newspapers that have been purchased or read. For example, *USA Today* is commonly circulated free of charge to hotel guests in the USA. Therefore, circulation refers simply to how many newspapers are distributed.

RADIO AND TELEVISION DISTRIBUTION TERMS

It is also helpful to define several terms used in this chapter to describe the delivery of radio and television content:

1. A **station** is a single facility that delivers a program. The station may broadcast its own programming, or it may broadcast programming obtained from another source.

2. A **network** is a group of *affiliate* stations or *member* stations (radio or television) that receive programming at select times of the day from a program supplier, which is usually a studio or a flagship radio or television station. Affiliate stations are usually commercial stations that forfeit local advertising time to the network in exchange for the right to broadcast network programming during portions of the broadcast day. Member stations are usually noncommercial stations that pay the network to broadcast the network's programming during portions of the broadcast day.

3. An **ownership group** is a collection of stations that belong to the same private corporation. Sometimes the programming is the same across all stations, and sometimes the programming differs between the stations.

4. A **channel** is a numerical brand used to identify a media outlet to allow the audience to easily identify a single source of the programming. Usually a radio or television channel is offered by a single media organization, and can be viewed or listened to in different geographic regions through the use of multiple transmitters, repeaters, or translators. Sometimes, a channel is used to represent the main public identity of the radio or television content; elsewhere, a station's call letters (e.g., WCAU) or a bandwidth frequency (90.3 FM) is used to represent the main public identity of the radio or television content.

5. **AM radio** refers to the distribution of programming on the Amplitude Modulation band (540 KHz to 1.7 MHz) of the frequency spectrum.

6. **FM radio** refers to the distribution of programming on the Frequency Modulation band (88 MHz to 108 MHz) of the frequency spectrum.

7. **Long Wave** refers to the distribution of programming on the Long Wave band (30 to 300 KHz) of the frequency spectrum.

8. **Short Wave** refers to the distribution of programming on the Short Wave band (5.9 MHz to 26.1 MHz) of the frequency spectrum.

9. **Terrestrial broadcasting** refers to content that is delivered through the airways to an antenna connected to a television set or a radio receiver.

10. **Broadcasting** refers to the delivery of content not just through the airwaves, but also through cable and satellite technology. In the past, the term *broadcasting* was used strictly to mean a process by which a transmitter delivers content through the airways to a television set or radio receiver. But television news programs that originate on terrestrial broadcast stations are often picked up and then redistributed by satellite and cable providers, or on the internet. Thus, because of the intertwining of cable, satellite, and terrestrial broadcasting, *broadcasting* and its derivations, *broadcast* and *broadcasters,* are increasingly being used to describe radio or television content received via the airways, satellite, or cable.

11. **Multichannel broadcaster** is a phrase used to categorize satellite and cable broadcasters together as essentially the same kind of entity. The main reason is that both satellite

and cable providers distribute multiple television and radio channels. A second reason is that the proliferation of global media conglomerates has led to similar television channel lineups on a given country's satellite and cable delivery systems.

12. **Penetration** refers to the percentage of households that are reached by a particular medium (newspapers, radio, television, or internet). Penetration does not necessarily indicate the percentage of homes actually using a particular medium, but rather the percentage of potential households that could be accessing the medium. This definition differs somewhat from the cable television industry's definition of penetration as the percentage of homes subscribing to cable out of all the homes passed by a cable system.

SOURCE CITATION FOR STATISTICAL DATA PRESENTED

In an effort to avoid cluttering the flow of this chapter with citations for every sentence or figure presenting statistics, the sources are cited in this paragraph. Statistics on newspaper accessibility were obtained from *World Press Trends* (2003, 2002). Statistics on the internet were obtained from *InternetWorldStats* (2004) at internetworldstats.com. Statistics on broadcast accessibility were obtained from government-related regulatory agencies in the eight countries, either through interviews with agency spokespeople or through official agency documentation. The available statistics varied somewhat across each country.

NEWSPAPER TITLES AS IDIOMS

In this chapter, Chapter 9 (Media Content), as well as Chapter 10 (News Reporting), newspaper titles are presented in their domestic languages, but also with literal English translations. Usually, domestic newspaper titles become idioms when translated into English—that is, a group of words in a newspaper title take on a different meaning than the separate words would have in translation. For example, the French newspaper *Le Monde* translated into English as *The World* loses meanings that can be understood only by communicating in the French language. This makes translating newspaper titles into English titles somewhat of a misleading enterprise. Yet, to leave the titles in their domestic language without attempting to convey their meanings in English would miss an opportunity to help demystify totally foreign words and convey similar as well as different names of newspapers across the eight countries. Therefore, at the first mention of a non-English newspaper title in the next three chapters, an English translation will be provided—however imperfect it may be—but in subsequent mentions the titles will be listed only in the domestic language.

ACCESSIBILITY OF MEDIA IN FRANCE

Newspaper Access in France

In France, the penetration of daily newspapers in 2001 was low, at 33.1 percent of adults. This percentage is affected by the fact that France has a strong magazine industry. Total daily circulation for national newspapers in 1999 was 2,437,000. In France, there are five national daily newspapers: *Le Canard Enchaineé* (*The Enchained Duck*); *Le Figaro;*

L'Humanité (*The Humanity*); *Le Monde* (*The World*); and *Libération* (*Liberation*). All of the national dailies are serious newspapers. Four have a broadsheet shape, whereas one, *Libération,* has a tabloid shape. National daily newspapers in France are published in the morning. All of the national newspapers are published out of Paris, the capital. All national newspapers can be purchased in most towns throughout France.

In 1999, there were sixty-four different regional/local newspapers distributed per day in France, a low number compared to the other countries. Regional/local newspapers tend to be associated with geographic regions of France. For regional/local newspapers, the total daily circulation in 2001 was 6,026,000. In France, the newspaper with the largest circulation is not a national publication but rather the regional *Ouest France* (*West France*). A sample front page of this newspaper is shown in Figure 9.2 in Chapter 9 on Content.

Table 8.1 shows the penetration numbers for the top ten circulating newspapers in France. In France, newspapers are distributed primarily through three methods. In 2000, single-copy sales accounted for 47.1 percent of total newspaper sales, a moderate number compared to the other countries; home deliveries accounted for 38.8 percent, also a moderate number; postal deliveries (deliveries through the mail) accounted for 14.1 percent, a somewhat high number compared to the other countries. Newspapers in France are commonly sold either at a stand-alone kiosk in the big cities, or in a *bureau du tabac* (tobacco shop)—a shop that is usually located on just about every other street block in most cities and towns, large or small. A *bureau du tabac* that sells both domestic and foreign newspapers normally displays a diamond-shaped yellow sign displaying an old-fashioned quill pen. This sign is normally hung on the wall outside the *bureau du tabac,* but perpendicular to the wall so that it can be spotted easily from down the street as well as across the street. Often, a *bureau du tabac* serves as an exclusive distribution agent for a regional newspaper, and displays an ad for that regional newspaper outside the shop. Figure 8.1 shows a *bureau du tabac* that serves as a distribution agent for the regional newspaper *L'Est Republican* (*The East Republican*), and one that sells both foreign and domestic newspapers (as represented by the diamond-shaped yellow sign).

TABLE 8.1   Top 10 Circulating Daily Newspapers in France

DAILY NEWSPAPERS	CIRCULATION	MAIN CONTENT
Ouest France (*West France*)	760,000	Serious
Le Parisien/Aujourd'hui (*The Parisien/Today*)	485,000	Serious
Le Progrès (*The Progress*)	393,000	Serious
L'Equipe (*The Team*)	387,000	Serious
Le Figaro	349,000	Serious
Le Monde (*The World*)	348,000	Serious
Sud Ouest (*South West*)	337,000	Serious
La Voix du Nord (*The Voice of the North*)	320,000	Serious
Le Dauphiné Libéré (*The Free Dolphin*)	256,000	Serious
La Nouvelle Républic (*The New Republic*)	247,000	Serious

Source: World Press Trends (2003).

FIGURE 8.1   Bureau du Tabac *Selling Both Domestic and Foreign Newspapers in France*
Source: Robert MᶜKenzie.

The *bureau du tabac* sells newspapers, magazines, tobacco, and lottery tickets. Sometimes, a *bureau du tabac* sells alcohol and offers a place for people to sit down and read newspapers or magazines. Newspapers at the *bureau du tabac* are usually displayed on racks inside the shop. Figure 8.2 shows a typical wide selection of domestic and foreign newspapers sold at a *bureau du tabac* with a yellow diamond-shaped sign.

Radio Access in France

In France, the average household has between three and four radio receivers. Terrestrial radio in France is delivered on FM, AM (medium wave), and LW (long wave). In France, national radio is delivered mostly by Radio France channels (funded by state-mandated license fees plus advertising), and to a lesser extent by commercial radio networks. Radio France operates five public-service radio channels, four of which carry national programming, and one of which (*France Bleu*) carries local programming on forty-two stations. The Radio France channels are carried on approximately 1,500 radio frequencies across France, and as a result can be heard on more than one radio frequency in some parts of the country where coverage overlaps. The Radio France channels and their general program formats are listed in Table 8.2.

In France, private radio is mostly local. In 2003, there were approximately 1,500 private commercial radio stations, a fairly large number in comparison with the other countries. Like the national government radio services, some regional radio stations can be heard on more than one frequency. Between state broadcasters and private commercial broadcasters, there are 3,000 radio broadcasters in France, also a fairly large number in

FIGURE 8.2   *Selection of Domestic and Foreign Newspapers Sold at a* Bureau du Tabac *in Paris, France*

Source: World Press Trends (2003).

comparison with the other countries. In Paris alone, there are fifty-two different radio broadcasters delivering content on forty frequencies.

In addition to domestic radio, France has the Radio France International (*RFI*) network. This network is delivered internationally in 19 languages on short-wave frequencies and through internet streaming. Much of *RFI*'s programming is targeted at the French DOM-TOMs described in Chapter 4.

In France, radio content is delivered primarily via terrestrial broadcasting, though it can be accessed via satellite and cable broadcasting. National terrestrial broadcast penetration for radio is 100 percent of households in France.

TABLE 8.2   Public-Service Radio Channels in France

RADIO FRANCE CHANNELS	CONTENT
France Bleu (French Blue)	Regional Radio Stations
France Culture (French Culture)	Traditional French Music, Drama, Discussion
France Info (French Information)	News and Information
France Inter (French Inter)	Contemporary Music
France Musiques (French Music)	Classical Music

Source: Robert McKenzie.

Television Access in France

In France, the average household has two television sets. Television content in France is distributed mostly via terrestrial broadcasting. Data from 2003 show terrestrial television penetration at approximately 98 percent of households, which is high, but in keeping with penetration in most of the other countries. Satellite penetration is fairly low at about 10 percent of households, and cable penetration is very low at about 10 percent of households. Satellite accessibility tends to be most common in towns and rural areas. Cable accessibility is most prominent in medium and large cities, to a great extent because laws are designed to protect the beauty of classical buildings from being compromised by modern telecommunications-receiving equipment.

Digital television penetration in France in 2003 was at approximately 10 percent of households, and was delivered by both cable and satellite. The government planned to implement terrestrial digital television in 2005.

In France, there are six terrestrial broadcasting channels that deliver programming to a national audience. Three television channels are public (license-fee funded) channels, and three are private channels. These channels and their general programming formats are listed in Table 8.3.

Some of the channels listed in Table 8.4 do not fit neatly into the public/commercial dichotomy. *TFI* is a former public channel that was privatized. *France 5* and *Arte* actually share a frequency. *France 5* broadcasts in the morning and afternoon, and at 1900 (7:00 PM) switches over to *Arte*, which is a cooperative venture between the French and German governments. *Canal+* is both a terrestrial and a cable/satellite broadcaster, but in both cases is a subscription-based, scrambled television channel.

TABLE 8.3   National Television Channels in France

PUBLIC-SERVICE TERRESTRIAL BROADCAST TELEVISION CHANNELS

CHANNEL	MAIN CONTENT
France 2	General interest with cultural emphasis
France 3	General interest with cultural and regional emphasis
*France 5	Educational and cultural emphasis
*Arte	French/German artistic emphasis

* These two channels share broadcast time on the same frequency.

COMMERCIAL TERRESTRIAL BROADCAST TELEVISION CHANNELS

CHANNEL	MAIN CONTENT
TF1	General interest
Canal+	General interest
M6	General interest

Source: Robert McKenzie.

There are twelve local terrestrial television stations in France, most of which operate in French DOMs (described in Chapter 4, Cultural Characteristics).

In France, there are five main cable providers and two satellite providers. Both satellite and cable channel lineups include the five terrestrial channels already mentioned. A viewer who begins at the first channel that comes up when the television is turned on and then surfs upwards will come across the three public-service television channels within the first five channels surfed.

Internet Access in France

Internet penetration in France in 2004 was at 40.6 percent of the population, which is on the lower side compared to the other countries, especially Western countries. In the household, the internet is normally accessible through either a cable (high-speed access) or telephone (dial-up access) connection, wherein users pay a monthly service fee to an internet service provider to get online. The internet is accessible in cities and in medium-size towns at cyber cafés. Figure 8.3 shows the inside of an internet café in France. Internet cafés are not as common in French cities as in other European cities.

Computer keyboards in French internet cafés are usually configured according to the French alphabet. This results in some letters (e.g., the letter "Y") being assigned to a different key on the French-alphabet computer keyboard than on the English-alphabet computer keyboard. Some internet cafés offer one or two computers with keyboards using an English-alphabet configuration. Likewise, some internet cafés have software installed that allows the user to use the keyboard as a foreign-language keyboard (e.g., English, Chinese). The software makes it possible for the user to type the keys on the computer, but the result that appears on the computer screen is in the translated language.

ACCESSIBILITY OF MEDIA IN SWEDEN

Newspaper Access in Sweden

In Sweden, the penetration of daily newspapers in 2001 was 88 percent of adults, by far the highest percentage among the eight countries. In 2001, the total daily circulation for national

TABLE 8.4   Top 10 Circulating Daily Newspapers in Sweden

NEWSPAPER	CIRCULATION	MAIN CONTENT
Aftonbladet (*The Evening News*)	402,000	Sensational
Dagens Nyheter (*Daily News*)	361,000	Serious
Expressen (*The Express*)	334,000	Sensational
Göteborgs-Posten (*The Gothenburg Post*)	254,000	Serious
Svenska Dagbladet (*The Daily Swedish Sheet*)	175,000	Serious
Sydsvenska Dagbladet (*The Daily South Sweden Sheet*)	138,000	Serious
Dagens Industri (*Daily Industry*)	125,000	Serious
Nerikes Allehanda (*Nerikes Miscellaneous*)	66,000	Serious
Östgöta Correspondenten (*The Östgöta Correspondent*)	66,000	Serious
Upsala Nya Tidning (*Upsala New Times*)	63,000	Serious

Source: Robert McKenzie.

FIGURE 8.3 *Interior of an internet Café in France*
Source: Robert McKenzie.

newspapers was 885,000. In Sweden, there are seven daily newspapers considered to have national or nearly national reach, also a high percentage, especially given Sweden's size. Four are serious newspapers: *Dagens Nyheter* (*Daily News*), *Svenska Dagbladet* (*The Daily Swedish Sheet*), *Dagens Industri* (*Daily Industry*), and *Göteborgs-Posten* (*The Gothenburg Post*). Three are sensationalist-oriented: *Aftonbladet* (*The Evening News*), *Expressen* (*The Express*), and *Kvällposten* (*The Evening Post*). The serious newspapers in Sweden are published in the morning, whereas tabloids are published in the afternoon. Most national newspapers are published out of Stockholm, the capital. All national newspapers can be purchased across the majority of Sweden.

In 2001, there were ninety different regional/local newspapers published per day in Sweden, which is comparatively high, given its size. For regional/local newspapers, the total daily circulation was 2,799,000 in 2001. Regional/local newspapers tend to be associated with geographic regions in Sweden—for example, the *Skånska Dagbladet*. A sample front page of this newspaper is shown in Figure 10.4 in Chapter 10, on News Reporting.

Table 8.4 shows penetration numbers for the top ten circulating newspapers in Sweden. In Sweden, newspapers are distributed primarily through three methods. In 2001, home delivery accounted for 72 percent of total newspaper sales, the highest percentage among the eight countries. Single-copy sales accounted for 23 percent of sales, a moderate to low percentage; and postal deliveries accounted for 5 percent of sales, an average percentage. Most single-copy sales take place at a *pressbyrån* (press bureau). Most small towns have at least one *pressbyrån*; the big cities of Malmö, Stockholm, and Göteborg have several. *Pressbyråns* are normally located within walking distance of train stations. Newspapers at *pressbyråns* are usually displayed on shelves or racks inside the shop. Sometimes domestic newspapers

FIGURE 8.4   *Newspapers Sold outside a* Pressbyrån *in Sweden*
Source: Robert McKenzie.

are displayed outside the *pressbyrån* on the sidewalk, as in Figure 8.4. *Pressbyråns* and other newspaper shops often advertise newspapers by posting cylinder-shaped ads displaying newspaper headlines on the shop-front wall, as in Figure 8.5.

Radio Access in Sweden

In Sweden, the average household had six radio receivers in 2003, a high number. Terrestrial radio in Sweden is delivered primarily on the FM band. Some stations can be heard on more than one radio frequency in some parts of the country where coverage overlaps. In Sweden, there are seven public-service radio channels funded by state-mandated license fees. Four channels broadcast programming to a national audience (one of these, *P4*, splits time broadcasting local programming as well). Three are regional public-service radio channels that are funded by license fees and fed to twenty-six stations that broadcast localized programming. The general program formats of these channels as well as the national channels are listed in Table 8.5. The P before each channel number stands for Program. The SR stations can sometimes be heard on several frequencies on a radio band, depending on the area of the country; some broadcasts may overlap. Programming on *P7* is broadcast only on digital radio (DAB), the internet, and cable.

In Sweden, commercial radio is local and regional. In 2003, there were eighty-nine private commercial radio stations in Sweden, a very low number compared to the other

FIGURE 8.5 *Cylinder Placards for Front Pages of Newspapers Sold inside a Newsagent in Sweden*

Source: Robert McKenzie.

countries. Like the public-service radio channels, some regional commercial radio stations can be heard on more than one frequency in certain parts of Sweden.

In addition to domestic radio, the radio network *Radio Sweden* is distributed internationally in seven languages—including Swedish, English, German, Russian, and Baltic languages—and targeted mainly at Swedes living in other countries. *Radio Sweden* is delivered by short wave, medium wave (AM), and internet streaming.

In Sweden, radio content is delivered primarily via terrestrial broadcasting, though it can be accessed via satellite and cable broadcasting. National terrestrial broadcast penetration for national radio channels is at 100 percent of households in Sweden. In 2003, satellite digital radio penetration was at approximately 30 percent of households.

Television Access in Sweden

In Sweden, there were approximately eight million analog television sets in 2003. The average household in Sweden has two television sets. Approximately 97 percent of the Swedish population aged nine to seventy-nine have access to a television set in the household. In Sweden, television content is distributed via terrestrial, cable, and satellite broadcasting. Data from 2003 show terrestrial television penetration at approximately 97 percent of households,

TABLE 8.5   Public-Service Radio Channels in Sweden

SWEDISH RADIO (SR) NATIONAL RADIO CHANNELS IN SWEDEN

CHANNEL	MAIN CONTENT
P1	The talk channel (news, culture, theater, debates, science, life outlook, international questions)
P2	The music channel (classical, modern art, jazz, folk, symphony, radio choir, Swedish and foreign artists, ethnic languages)
P3	The young channel (pop music, culture, community programming, live concerts, young humor and entertainment, news)
P4	*National* The adult channel (news, pop music, entertainment, sports, and current affairs)
P7	Finnish-language programming (only DAB, cable, and internet)

SWEDISH RADIO (SR) REGIONAL/LOCAL RADIO NETWORKS IN SWEDEN

CHANNEL	MAIN CONTENT
P4	*Local* The local adult channel (26 local channels; local news, activities and culture, local entertainment, music, local and national sports, national government announcements, local Finnish programming (programming varies according to locality)
*P5	Radio Stockholm (modern music, news) (heard in Stockholm)
*P6	The multicultural channel (international affairs broadcast in 17 languages; based in Stockholm)

* Delivered as both analog and digital radio—over the internet and by satellite.

Source: Robert McKenzie.

TABLE 8.6   National Terrestrial Television Channels in Sweden

PUBLIC-SERVICE TERRESTRIAL BROADCAST TELEVISION CHANNELS IN SWEDEN

CHANNEL	MAIN CONTENT
SVT 1	General interest with educational/cultural emphasis
SVT 2	Special interest with factual and experimental emphasis

PRIVATE TERRESTRIAL BROADCAST TELEVISION CHANNEL IN SWEDEN

CHANNEL	MAIN CONTENT
TV 4	General interest with educational/cultural emphasis

FIGURE 8.6   *Exterior of an Internet Café in Malmö, Sweden*
Source: Robert McKenzie.

an average percentage compared to the other countries. Satellite penetration was at approximately 22 percent of households, a slightly better than moderate percentage. Cable penetration was at approximately 37 percent of households, a fairly high percentage. Satellite accessibility tends to be most prominent in towns and rural areas. Cable accessibility tends to be most prominent in cities, towns, and communities.

Digital television penetration in Sweden in 2003 was at approximately 20 percent of the segment of the population aged nine to seventy-nine. Digital television in Sweden is distributed by terrestrial, cable, and satellite broadcasting. The government intends to close down terrestrial analog television in favor of digital broadcasting by the year 2008.

In Sweden, there are three terrestrial broadcasting channels that deliver programming to a national audience. Two television channels are public-service broadcasters, and one is commercial. These channels and their general programming formats are listed in Table 8.6.

In addition to these three channels, there are two other channels—*Channel 3* and *Channel 5*—that deliver Swedish programming to Sweden via cable and satellite. But *Channel 3* and *Channel 5* technically are not national Swedish channels: These two channels are registered in England and thereby governed by regulations in the UK.

There are no local terrestrial broadcasters in Sweden, though both of the public-service broadcasters—*SVT 1* and *SVT 2*—provide regional programming (programming that is of interest mainly to a particular region of the country), in addition to the predominant content of national programming.

In Sweden, there are two national cable providers and satellite providers, offering dozens of channels. Both satellite and cable channel lineups include the five broadcast channels already listed. The public television channels occupy the first and second channel positions in the channel lineup, followed by commercial channels.

Internet Access in Sweden

Internet penetration in Sweden in 2004 was the highest, not just among the eight countries, but also in the world, at 74.6 percent of the population. The internet is typically accessible in the household through a cable or telephone connection, which users pay for through a monthly service fee. The internet is accessible in cities and medium-size towns at cyber cafés, such as the one with a bicycle rack outside, pictured in Figure 8.6. Computer keyboards normally have keys assigned to the Swedish alphabet, which presents a different keyboard configuration than that of an English-alphabet keyboard.

ACCESSIBILITY OF MEDIA IN THE UK

Newspaper Access in the UK

In the UK, the penetration of daily newspapers in 2001 was 50.3 percent of adults, a moderate percentage compared to the other countries. In 2001, the total daily circulation for national newspapers was 12,546,000. In the UK, there are ten national daily newspapers. There is a tradition of Sunday national newspapers that are different from the national dailies. Though most of the Sunday newspapers are owned by the parent companies that own the daily newspapers, the Sunday newspapers usually have their own editorial staffs and financial operations. There is a large number of national newspapers (and especially sensational tabloids), considering the size of the UK. All national newspapers can be purchased in almost every town in the UK. Most national newspapers in the UK are published in the morning. Five are serious broadsheets, listed as follows: *Financial Times* (*The Business*), *The Guardian* (*The Observer*), *The Independent* (*The Independent on Sunday*), *The Telegraph* (*The Telegraph on Sunday*), *The Times* (*The Sunday Times*). Five are tabloids—four of which are sensational and one of which is serious—listed as follows, with the Sunday counterpart in parentheses: *Daily Express* (*Sunday Express*), *Daily Mail* (*Mail on Sunday*), *Daily Mirror* (*Sunday Mirror*), *The Sun* (*News of the World*), *The Star* (*Daily Star Sunday*).

All of the top ten circulating newspapers in the UK are national daily newspapers. Table 8.7 shows the numbers for them in 2002. The most widely circulating newspaper was the *Sun*, a sensationalist tabloid.

In 2001, there were 5,353 titles of regional/local newspapers in the UK, by far the highest percentage among the eight countries. In 2001, total daily circulation for national newspapers was approximately 18 million, and for regional/local newspapers was approximately 12.5 million. Many regional newspapers are associated with Scotland, Wales, or Ireland—for example, the *Scotsman*. Local/regional newspapers tend to be associated with a town, as in the case of the *Seaford Gazette* (pictured in Figure 9.4 in Chapter 9 on media content).

In the UK, newspapers are distributed primarily through two methods. In 1999, single-copy purchases accounted for 87 percent of sales, the highest percentage by far, in

TABLE 8. 7   Top 10 Circulating Newspapers in the UK

NEWSPAPER	CIRCULATION	MAIN CONTENT
The Sun	3,473,000	Entertainment
The Daily Mail	2,477,000	Serious
The Mirror	2,188,000	Entertainment
The Daily Telegraph	1,021,000	Serious
Daily Express	958,000	Sensationalist
The Times	720,000	Serious
Daily Star	620,000	Entertainment
Financial Times	479,000	Serious
The Guardian	408,000	Serious
The Independent	231,000	Serious

Source: World Press Trends (2002).

comparison with the other countries. Home delivery of newspapers accounted for only 13 percent of sales, a very low percentage. Most single-copy sales take place at newsagents, which are plentiful in the UK. Even small towns routinely have several newsagents, sometimes just a few shops away from each other. Newspapers are usually displayed inside the newsagent in a rack or on shelves. Outside on the sidewalk, newsagents sometimes display stand-up placards that advertise headlines of local newspapers sold inside. Figure 8.7 shows sidewalk placards displaying handwritten quotes from local newspaper headlines; Figure 8.8 shows a selection of newspapers sold at a British newsagent.

Radio Access in the UK

In the UK, the average household had six radio receivers in 2003, a high number. In the UK, radio is delivered primarily via terrestrial broadcast and satellite broadcast. Terrestrial broadcast penetration for national radio is 100 percent of households in the UK. Satellite digital radio coverage was at approximately 95 percent of households in 2003. Terrestrial digital radio coverage was approximately 85 percent of households.

Terrestrial broadcast radio in the UK is delivered primarily on the FM and AM (medium wave) bands, though one of the public-service broadcasters (*Radio 4*) is delivered also on the long wave (LW) band. In total, there are eight terrestrial radio channels and networks that broadcast programming to a national audience. Five of the eight are BBC public-service channels funded by state-mandated license fees, and three of the eight are commercial broadcast networks. In many parts of the UK, a national radio channel or network can be heard on more than one radio frequency because of overlapping coverage by two or more stations. These radio channels and networks and their general program formats are listed in Table 8.8.

In 2003 in the UK, there were 269 commercial radio stations, a fairly low number compared to the other countries. There were also forty public-service (BBC) national stations and eight public-service (BBC) regional radio stations. All together, about half of the UK's radio stations are noncommercial.

FIGURE 8.7   *Placards Quoting Newspaper Headlines outside a Newsagent in the UK*
Source: Robert McKenzie.

In addition to domestic radio, the UK has a government-funded international radio network, the *BBC World Service*, which began as a primarily short-wave radio service aimed at British expatriates living in other countries. It has since evolved into a radio service delivering world news and other programming in forty-three different languages to 140 million people in almost all regions of the world. The *BBC World Service* delivers content via short wave, FM broadcasting, and internet streaming.

All of the national public radio services, as well as the national commercial radio stations and the regional BBC stations, are broadcast in digital format either through terrestrial or internet delivery.

Television Access in the UK

In the UK, almost all households (approximately 99 percent) had one television set in 2003. Most households (approximately 81 percent) in the UK have two television sets. In the UK, television content is distributed via terrestrial, cable, and satellite broadcasting. Data from 2002 show terrestrial television penetration to be at approximately 99 percent of households, an average number compared to the other countries. Satellite penetration was very high, at approximately 45 percent of households, and cable penetration was also on the

FIGURE 8.8   *Selection of Newspapers at a Newsagent in the UK*
Source: Robert McKenzie.

high side, at approximately 22 percent of households. Satellite accessibility tends to be most prominent in towns and rural areas. Cable accessibility tends to be most prominent in major cities such as London and Manchester.

In 2002, 37 percent of households had access to digital television. The government is requiring all television distributors to deliver digital content by the year 2010. The government has promoted conversion to digital programming by funding a digital transmission service called Freeview, which distributes a lineup of commercial and BBC channels carrying digital content to users who purchase a set-top box.

In the UK, there are five terrestrial television channels that deliver programming to a national audience. Two television channels (*BBC1* and *BBC2*) are funded by government-mandated license fees, one television channel (*Channel 4*) is a publicly owned commercial broadcaster, and two channels (*ITV* and *Five*) are privately owned commercial broadcasters. *ITV* stands for Independent Television (in Wales, the broadcast frequency used by *Channel 4*

TABLE 8.8   National Radio Channels and Networks in the UK

LICENSE-FEE FUNDED (BBC)

CHANNEL	MAIN CONTENT
Radio 1	Contemporary music
Radio 2	Broad range of music, light entertainment, documentaries, public-service broadcasting and popular culture
Radio 3	Classical and jazz music, drama, documentaries, discussion
Radio 4	News and current affairs, drama, science, arts, religion, natural history, medicine, finance, gardening, Parliament
Radio 5 Live	News, current affairs, sports
*1Extra	Hip hop, garage, R&B, dancehall, drum and bass, documentaries
BBC Asian Network	Music, news, views
*BBC 6 Music	Thrash, funk, rock, reggae, ska, other
*BBC 7	Comedy, kids, drama

COMMERCIALLY FUNDED

CHANNEL	MAIN CONTENT
Classic FM	Classical music, news, information
Virgin 1215	Rock and pop
Talk Sport	Sport

*Digital broadcast audio only.

Source: Robert McKenzie.

in the rest of the UK is allocated to a channel called *S4C*, which delivers Welsh-related programming, much of which is in Gaelic). *ITV* is owned by a handful of regional companies and is the only television channel that delivers local/regional programming. These channels and their general programming formats are listed in Table 8.9.

In the UK, there were two major cable providers and one satellite provider in 2003, offering dozens of channels. The two BBC terrestrial broadcasters (*BBC1*, *BBC2*) occupy the first two positions in the channel lineup, followed by the commercial channels. Multichannel *BBC3* and *BBC4* occupy channels 14 and 15, respectively.

Internet Access in the UK

Internet penetration in the UK in 2004 was at 58.5 percent of the population, a fairly high percentage compared to the other countries. In the household, the internet is normally accessible through a cable or telephone connection, wherein users pay a monthly service fee to an internet service provider to get online. In most towns, large or small, the internet is accessible in two locations: at cyber cafés, where users pay a per-minute fee; and at local libraries, where the user can get online for free. In London, the internet is accessible in some phone booths, such as the one pictured in Figure 8.9.

TABLE 8.9   National Terrestrial Television Channels in the UK

BBC TERRESTRIAL BROADCAST TELEVISION CHANNELS IN THE UK

CHANNEL	MAIN CONTENT
BBC1	General interest with educational emphasis
BBC2	Special-interest with intellectual/cultural emphasis

COMMERCIAL TERRESTRIAL BROADCAST TELEVISION CHANNELS IN THE UK

CHANNEL	MAIN CONTENT
ITV	Regional interest
Channel 4	Innovative, experimental
Five	General interest

FIGURE 8.9 *Internet Phone Booth in London, England*
Source: Robert McKenzie.

ACCESSIBILITY OF MEDIA IN THE USA

Newspaper Access in the USA

In the USA, the daily penetration of newspapers in 2000 was 55 percent of adults, a moderate to high percentage compared to the other countries. In 2001, the total daily circulation for newspapers was 55,578,000. In the USA, there is one purely national daily newspaper with distribution at virtually every newspaper vendor across the country: *USA Today* (published out of Virginia). Two other newspapers—the *Wall Street Journal* and the *New York Times*, both published out of New York City—have extensive but not comprehensive national circulation. In addition, the *Christian Science Monitor* is distributed nationally mainly through the post. These four newspapers are all broadsheets and are all published in the morning. In 2001, the most widely circulating newspaper was *USA Today*, a broadsheet that in some ways resembles the look and feel of a television news program. Table 8.10 lists the top ten circulating newspapers in the USA for 2001.

In the USA, almost all papers are regional or local. Regional newspapers are normally associated with a big city. Examples include the *Philadelphia Inquirer*, the *Chicago Tribune*, and the *Houston Chronicle*. Local newspapers are normally associated with a town or a cluster of counties. In 2001, there were 1,468 titles of newspapers in the USA, the second-highest number next to the UK.

In the USA, newspapers are distributed primarily through three methods. In 2000, single-copy purchases accounted for 76 percent of sales, a high percentage compared to the other countries. Home delivery of newspapers accounted for 19 percent of sales, on the low to middle side. Other sales (postal, street vendor, newspaper dispensers) accounted for only 5 percent of sales. Single-copy sales take place at a variety of places including convenience stores, grocery stores, newsagents, newsstands (in big cities), and freestanding dispensers, which are often located on sidewalks outside restaurants and hotels. Figure 8.10 shows a typical row of newspaper dispensers in the USA. Note how the dispenser for *USA Today* newspaper resembles a television set.

In the USA, convenience stores are more common than newsagents as outlets for selling newspapers. Convenience stores are plentifully located throughout big cities, small towns, and even rural areas. Usually, convenience stores are located where there is frequent vehicle traffic—either along streets or at gas stations. Convenience stores usually sell newspapers, magazines, food products, tobacco, lottery tickets, and gasoline. Newspapers at convenience stores are usually displayed inside on shelves. Figure 8.11 shows an example of the selection of newspapers sold at a convenience store in the state of Pennsylvania.

Normally, newspaper carriers working directly for a newspaper deliver the local newspaper to the home. The carrier usually throws the newspaper on the driveway on the ground outside the front door, or places it in a roadside newspaper box used exclusively for newspapers, such as the one pictured in Figure 4.5 in Chapter 4, Cultural Characteristics. In the USA, a postal mailbox on a homeowner's property cannot be used for newspaper deliveries because of a federal law prohibiting tampering with a person's mail.

Radio Access in the USA

In the USA, the average household had five radio receivers in 2003. In the USA, radio is delivered primarily via terrestrial broadcast. In 2003, terrestrial broadcast penetration for

TABLE 8.10   Top 10 Circulating Newspapers in the USA

NEWSPAPER	CIRCULATION	MAIN CONTENT
USA Today	2,150,000	serious
Wall Street Journal	1,781,000	serious
New York Times	1,109,000	serious
Los Angeles Times	944,000	serious
Washington Post	760,000	serious
New York Daily News	734,000	sensationalist
Chicago Tribune	676,000	serious
Long Island Newsday	577,000	serious
Houston Chronicle	552,000	serious
New York Post	534,000	sensationalist

Source: World Press Trends (2002).

radio was about 98 percent of households in the USA, and satellite digital radio penetration was at approximately 0.8 percent of households.

Terrestrial broadcast radio in the USA is delivered primarily on the FM and AM (also known as medium wave) bands, though there is some short-wave broadcasting. In the USA, terrestrial radio is primarily local. There are no national terrestrial radio channels in the USA. Rather, most radio stations affiliate with national networks or belong to multiple ownership groups. Most of the national networks are commercial. Noncommercial radio networks include Public Radio International (PRI) and National Public Radio (NPR). Though NPR is not routinely considered to be a network in the traditional sense of the word

FIGURE 8.10   *Newspaper Dispensers in the USA*
Source: Robert McKenzie.

FIGURE 8.11   *Selection of Newspapers inside a Convenience Store in the USA*
Source: Robert McKenzie.

(when a network pays an affiliate to carry the network's programming in exchange for advertising time that the network gets), NPR is a network according to the definition outlined at the beginning of this chapter (it supplies programming to member stations). In some parts of the USA, a radio network can be heard on more than one radio frequency because of overlapping coverage by two or more stations. Some major radio networks are listed in Table 8.11. These networks typically own multiple radio stations in multiple geographic markets. Sometimes a network owns more than one station in a market. A network will broadcast any program format on a station that it perceives will serve listeners' needs in a given market. Therefore, networks are not normally tied to exclusive radio formats, content-wise. Multiple ownership groups such as Clear Channel often distribute programming through the technique called **voice tracking,** in which a program that originates in one part of the country is distributed to networked stations across the country, but with local programming (such as news or commercials) at each individual station mixed into the voice-tracked program in such a way that the overall program sounds locally originated.

In the USA, there were more than 13,000 radio stations in 2003. To put this number into some perspective, about one-third of the radio stations in the world are located in the USA. In 2003 there were about 11,500 commercial radio stations in the USA, by far the largest number among the eight countries (France is a distant second with 1,500

TABLE 8.11   National Radio Networks and Ownership Groups in the USA

NETWORKS	OWNERSHIP GROUPS
ABC	*Clear Channel*
CBS	*Infinity*
CNN	*Cox Radio*
ESPN (Sports)	*Entercom*
*NPR	*Citadel*
	Radio One
	Cumulus Media
	Univision
	Emmis

* Partially government-funded.

Source: Robert McKenzie.

commercial stations); and there were about 1,500 noncommercial radio stations (mostly NPR member stations, university/college stations, and community-run stations).

In addition to domestic radio, the USA has a government-funded international radio network called Voice of America (VOA). This service began as a primarily short-wave radio service aimed at promoting democracy and the "American" way of life to nondemo-cratic countries, but evolved into a service delivered by short wave, AM and FM radio, as well as satellite television and the internet. In 2003, the VOA delivered world news and discussion-oriented programming in fifty-five different languages to approximately 94 million people in almost all regions of the world.

In 2003, just under three hundred terrestrial radio stations in the USA were broadcast-ing in digital format. All satellite radio broadcasting is in digital format. In the USA, satellite radio broadcasting began in 2002. In 2003, there were two satellite radio providers.

Television Access in the USA

In the USA, almost all households (approximately 98 percent) in 2003 had at least one television set, with an average of 2.4 television sets per household—a higher figure than the other countries for which these data were available. In addition, television sets are set up for viewing in all kinds of commercial and public establishments, such as bars, restaurants, and car repair businesses, as well as doctors' offices, hospitals, and government social-service facilities. In the USA, television content is distributed via terrestrial, cable, and satellite broadcasting. Data from 2002 show terrestrial television penetration at approxi-mately 98.2 percent of households, an average percentage. Cable penetration was very high, at approximately 67 percent of households. Satellite penetration was on the low side, at approximately 19 percent of households. Cable accessibility tends to be most prominent in rural areas, suburbs, and big cities such as New York City and Chicago. Satellite accessi-bility tends to be most prominent in suburbs and rural areas.

In 2003, approximately 36 percent of households had access to digital television. The government is requiring all television stations to deliver digital content by the year 2007.

In the USA, the large proportion of commercial (advertising-funded) media in comparison to the relatively small proportion of nonprofit and/or government-funded media is a defining feature of the selections of media content that are available. There are eight terrestrial television networks that deliver programming to a national audience via television affiliate stations. Seven of the networks are commercial, and one (*PBS*, or Public Broadcasting System) is noncommercial. The ten networks and their general programming formats are listed in Table 8.12.

Out of the ten commercial networks, four are considered to be in a top tier (NBC, CBS, ABC, Fox) because of the large numbers of television stations they have as affiliates, plus their nationwide audience reach, whereas the others are considered to be in a second tier. The two Spanish-language networks are Telemundo and Univision.

In the USA, there are two satellite television providers and dozens of cable providers, offering dozens of channels. Satellite and cable-channel lineups include the eight networks already listed. But sometimes a network television show appears on more than one cable channel because cable providers broadcast the programming of affiliate stations from different geographic markets (for example, Philadelphia and New York City). Viewers normally do not come across noncommercial PBS channels until they surf upwards through more than ten to twenty channels.

TABLE 8.12   National Terrestrial Broadcast Television Networks in the USA

COMMERCIAL TERRESTRIAL BROADCAST TELEVISION NETWORKS IN THE USA

CHANNEL	MAIN CONTENT
ABC	General-interest programming
CBS	General-interest programming
NBC	General-interest programming
Fox	General-interest programming
UPN	General-interest programming with emphasis on programming for youth and ethnic minorities
PAX	General-interest programming with emphasis on family programming
Telemundo	Spanish-language programming
Univision	Spanish-language programming
WB	General-interest programming with emphasis on pop-culture programming

NONCOMMERCIAL TERRESTRIAL BROADCAST TELEVISION NETWORK IN THE USA

CHANNEL	MAIN CONTENT
PBS	Arts and cultural programming

Source: Robert McKenzie.

Internet Access in the USA

Internet penetration in the USA in 2004 was on the high side, at 68.8 percent of the population. In the household, the internet is accessible through a cable or telephone connection, wherein users pay a monthly service fee to an internet service provider to get online. Most people in the USA have access to the internet in the home. In big cities and some small towns, the internet is accessible at cyber cafés, wherein users pay a per-minute fee. Cyber cafés are not as plentiful in the USA as they are in Europe.

ACCESSIBILITY OF MEDIA IN MÉXICO

Newspaper Access in México

In México, figures on the penetration of daily newspapers are unavailable. However, research indicates that a newspaper is read on average by five people once it is finished circulating among family, friends, and acquaintances.

In México, there are ten newspapers with national circulation, a large number of newspapers, especially considering the relatively high rate of illiteracy in México. These newspapers can be accessed across most of the country, but not in all towns and cities. All the national newspapers are morning dailies. Seven of the ten newspapers have a tabloid shape: *ESTO, La Prensa* (*The Press*), *Diario de Yucatan* (*Diary of Yucatan*), *El Financiero* (*The Financial Report*), *La Jornada* (*The Day*), *El Graphíco* (*The Graphic*), and *Uno Más Uno* (*One on One*). Five of the tabloids are serious, whereas *El Graphíco* is sensationalist, and *ESTO* is a sports newspaper. Three of the ten newspapers have a broadsheet shape: *El Universal* (*The Universe*), *Excelsior,* and *Reforma* (*Reform*). In 2002, the most widely circulating newspaper was the sports-oriented tabloid *ESTO.* Table 8.13 lists the top ten circulating newspapers in México for 2002, all of which are distributed nationally.

In México, national, regional, and local newspapers are also abundant. In 2001, there were 340 daily newspaper titles. National newspapers are normally associated with México City. *Millenio* has both a national edition and individual state editions. Regional newspapers are normally associated with a state or a cluster of towns in a state. *El sol de México* has individual state editions in most of the states. Local newspapers are normally associated with a town. Examples of regional newspapers from the state of Veracruz include *Millenio* and *Punta Yaparte.* In México, newspapers are distributed primarily through three methods: single-copy purchases at newsstands, single-copy purchases from walking streetside vendors, and home delivery of newspapers. Newsstands are plentifully located in town squares and on sidewalks throughout towns and cities. Because most of México has a warm climate year-round, freestanding newsstands are more common than newsagents housed inside stores. Figure 8.12 shows a typical Mexican newsstand. In addition, streetside vendors (men and boys) sell newspapers by walking between vehicles stuck in traffic jams or waiting at red lights.

Radio Access in México

In México, the average household had three radio receivers in 2004. In México, radio is delivered primarily via terrestrial broadcast. In 2000, terrestrial broadcast penetration for radio was about 96 percent of households.

FIGURE 8.12   *Newsstand in México City*

Source: Robert McKenzie.

TABLE 8.13   Top 10 Circulating Newspapers in México

NEWSPAPER	CIRCULATION	MAIN CONTENT
ESTO	385,000	sports
La Prensa (*The Press*)	330,000	sensationalist
El Universal (*The Universe*)	182,000	serious
El Graphíco (*The Graphic*)	150,000	sensationalist
El Financiero (*The Financial Report*)	147,000	serious
Reforma (*Reform*)	126,000	serious
El Norte (*The North*)	119,000	serious
La Jornada (*The Day*)	101,000	serious
Diario de Yucatan (*Diary of Yucatan*)	50,000	serious
El M (*The M*)	50,000	serious

Source: World Press Trends (2002).

In México, there were more than 1,471 radio stations in 2004 (855 AM, 616 FM). Terrestrial broadcast radio in México is delivered primarily on the FM and AM bands. In México, terrestrial radio is primarily local. There are no twenty-four-hour national terrestrial radio channels in México. Rather, most radio stations belong to statewide networks

TABLE 8.14   **Regional Radio Networks in México**

Califormula Radio	*MVS Radio San Luis Potosi*
Corpocation Mexicana de Radiodifusion	*MVS Radio Tampico*
Estereo Sol	*Nucleo Radio Mil*
Grupo Acir	*Nucleo Radio Monterrey*
Grupo Acir Puebla	*Nuestra Cobertura*
Grupo Avanradio	*Promomedios de Occidente*
Grupo Empresarial RCG	*Promomedios Norte de Sinaloa*
Grupo Radio Estereo Mayran	*Radio Centro*
Grupo Radio Miled	*Radio Formula*
Grupo Radio Nucleo	***Radio Nuevo Leon*
Grupo Radio Sonora	*Radio y Television de Aguascalientes*
Grupo Rivas	****Radio y Television Mexiquense*
Grupo Siete	*Radiopolis*
Grupo Uniradio	*Radiopolis Guadalajara*
*IMER - Instituto Mexicano de la Radio	*Radiosistema del Noroeste*
Multimedios Estrellas de Oro	*Rodrigo Lemus*
MVS Radio	*Unidifusion*

* Federal-government funded.
** State-government operated.
*** Public-network.

Source: Robert McKenzie.

and carry the same programming as other stations in the network. Most radio networks are private and commercial. Some of the major radio networks are listed in Table 8.14. These networks typically own multiple radio stations in multiple geographic markets across a particular state. Radio networks typically air shared news and commercial programming as well as selected radio shows, but leave it up to the individual radio stations to determine their own particular radio formats based on perceptions of market needs.

In addition to the federally funded IMER network (discussed in Chapter 6, Regulation of Media), there are seven state-government-funded public radio networks. In 2003, digital radio broadcasting had not yet been developed in México.

Television Access in México

In México, almost all households (approximately 98 percent) in 2003 had at least one television set in 2003, with two television sets in the average household. In México, television content is distributed via terrestrial, cable, and satellite broadcasting. Data from 2002 show terrestrial television penetration at approximately 70.5 percent of households, a very low percentage compared to the other countries. Cable penetration was also low, at approximately 12 percent of households, as well as satellite penetration at approximately 9 percent of households. Cable and satellite accessibility tends to be most prominent in bigger cities such as México City, Guadalajara, and Monterey. In 2003, the government was considering but had not yet set a mandatory date for conversion from analog to digital television.

TABLE 8.15   National Private Terrestrial Television Channels in México

CHANNEL	MAIN CONTENT
Azteca 7	Youth focused
Azteca 13	Family focused
Televisa 2	Telenovelas (soap operas) and entertainment
Televisa 4	Home shopping/USA shows in primetime
Televisa 5	Children's shows/USA films
Televisa 9	Telenovelas and movies

In México, there are two terrestrial television networks—Televisa and Azteca—that deliver programming to a national audience. Both Televisa and Azteca are private commercial networks, distribute programming on national network channels, and own individual stations. Azteca has two national television channels: *Channel 7* and *Channel 13*. Televisa has four national network channels: *Channel 2*, *Channel 4*, *Channel 5*, and *Channel 9*. These channels can be viewed across most of México. The general programming formats for these network channels are listed in Table 8.15.

There is no national public television network or channel. But at the state level, there are seven public television networks and seventeen combined public television and radio networks. Overall, there were 740 television stations in México in 2004.

In México, there are two satellite television providers and several cable television providers, offering dozens of channels. Satellite and cable-channel lineups sometimes include the six networks already listed. Public television channels are not normally in the beginning selection of channels when surfing from the first channel upwards.

Internet Access in México

Internet penetration in México in 2004 was at 11.9 percent of the population, the fourth-lowest percentage out of the eight countries. The internet is not usually accessed in the home. Rather, most people in México have access to the internet in internet shops, as depicted in Figure 8.13. These shops normally do not include a place to eat or have a drink. Keyboards in Mexican internet shops are usually configured according to the Spanish alphabet. This results in some letters (e.g., the letter "ñ") on the Spanish-alphabet keyboard taking the places of different keys than on the English-alphabet keyboard. In México, users often pay for the internet after they have used the service.

ACCESSIBILITY OF MEDIA IN CHINA

Newspaper Access in China

In China, the penetration of daily newspapers in 2001 was 74.3 percent of adults, the second-highest percentage among the eight countries (behind Sweden). There are ten main national daily newspapers. *Cankao Xiaoxi*, which reports mostly government policy, has the largest circulation figures. Beijing's *People's Daily* (*Renmin Ribao*), a China Communist

FIGURE 8.13   *Exterior of an Internet Café in México*
Source: Robert McKenzie.

Party (CCP) organ, is the most popular traditional newspaper. The majority of other popular publications are tabloid newspapers published in the evening. Total circulation for the nationals in 2001 was 25,241,000. The country's newspaper readers are found mainly in urban areas, and in major downtown districts. Table 8.16 depicts the top ten circulating national daily newspapers in China in 2003.

In 1999, there were 734 different regional/local newspapers distributed per day in China, a high number overall, but also somewhat of a low number considering the size of the country. The total daily circulation for regional/local newspapers was 117.8 million copies in 2000. Newspapers are distributed primarily through three methods. In 1999, subscription-based (postal delivery) sales accounted for 61 percent of total sales, the highest percentage by far among the eight countries. Subscription-based sales involve the state agency China Post delivering the newspapers through the mail. Home deliveries accounted for 29 percent of sales, a percentage on the low side. Single purchases, mainly from roadside newspaper

TABLE 8.16   Top 10 Circulating Newspapers in China

NEWSPAPER	CIRCULATION	MAIN CONTENT
Cankao Xiaoxi (*Reference Information*)	2,530,000	serious
Renmin Ribao (*People's Daily*)	1,773,000	serious
Yangcheng Wanbao (*Yangcheng Evening News*)	1,650,000	entertainment
Guangzhou Ribao (*Guangzhou Daily*)	1,600,000	entertainment
Yangcheng Wanbao (*Yancheng Evening News*)	1,500,000	entertainment
Xinmin Wanbao (*Xinmin Evening News*)	1,218,000	entertainment
Chutian Dushi Bao (*Chutian Metro News*)	1,213,000	entertainment
Nanfang Dushi Bao (*Nanfang City News*)	1,030,000	entertainment
Beijing Wanbao (*Beijing Evening News*)	980,000	serious
Qilo Wanbao (*Quilo Evening News*)	850,000	entertainment

Source: Ian Weber.

FIGURE 8.14   *Newspaper Viewing Frames Attached to the outside of a Building in China*
Source: Ian Weber.

stands, accounted for 10 percent of sales, the lowest percentage among the eight countries. One of the most traditional ways to access daily national and prominent local newspapers is to view selected pages of them at streetside frames, as shown in Figure 8.14. Each frame generally displays the front and two inside pages (and sometimes the sports page) of selected newspapers. These frames are erected on the walls of buildings along major roads and thoroughfares where people walk or commute by bicycle.

Another common way to access newspapers is by buying them from streetside vendors. Figure 8.15 depicts a selection of newspapers sold off a tricycle used by a streetside vendor in China.

Radio Access in China

In China, there are 184 radios per 1,000 people. It is estimated that there are 1.3 radio sets in the average household. In 2002, there were 306 radio stations in China, broadcasting 22,838 hours of programming on 1,983 frequencies every day with radio penetration at 93.34 percent of the national population, a low percentage compared to the other countries. Terrestrial radio in China is delivered on AM, FM, and LW bands. In China, national radio is delivered by China National Radio (CNR), a government-operated network broadcasting on seven channels. The CNR channels and their general program formats are listed in Table 8.17.

FIGURE 8.15 *Newspapers Sold off the Tricycle of a Streetside Vendor in China*
Source: Ian Weber.

In China, there are also regional radio networks that are government controlled but commercially funded. Whereas the government once subsidized radio operations, it now requires radio stations to be financially self-sufficient. As a result, almost all radio stations in China carry government propaganda free of charge, as well as commercials paid for by the private sector.

In addition to domestic radio, the Chinese government also operates an international radio network called China International Radio (CRI), which is delivered by satellite. CRI broadcasts to a global audience in thirty-eight foreign languages, Mandarin Chinese, and four Chinese dialects. The government mandate for CRI is to deliver programming that introduces China to people around the world.

Television Access in China

In China, almost all households (approximately 98 percent) had at least one television set in 2004. The average household in 2001 had 1.2 television sets. Television content is distributed via a combination of satellite, terrestrial, and cable broadcasting. Data from 2002 show terrestrial television penetration at approximately 97 percent of households, an average percentage compared to the other countries. Each of the forty-six satellite-delivered channels is available via satellite downlink within designated cities throughout China, which then redistribute programming over terrestrial and cable services to households. In 2001, cable television penetration was at 27.5 percent of households, which is a moderate

TABLE 8.17   National (Government-Operated) Radio Channels in China

CHANNEL	MAIN CONTENT
Channel 1	News, broadcasting throughout China in Mandarin
Channel 2	Business and economy, science and technology, and lifestyle
Channel 3	Music and arts channel on FM stereo
Channel 4 and *Channel 8*	Programming in languages of ethnic minority groups such as Mongolian, Tibetan, Uygur, Kazak, and Korean
Channel 5 and *Channel 6*	Programs for listeners in Taiwan
Channel 7	Programs catering for the region of the Pearl River Delta, including Hong Kong and Macao

Source: Ian Weber.

percentage compared to the other countries. Cable accessibility tends to be most prominent in major eastern seaboard and central provincial cities. The government in China outlawed direct-to-home (DTH) satellite transmission in 1993 to curb the importation of nonapproved foreign programming. Therefore, satellite penetration in China is technically 0.0 percent, though some of CCTV's satellite television programs are picked up by terrestrial and cable television suppliers in China and redistributed to households.

The Chinese government designated 2001 as the "Year of Broadband," launching test trials of digital television in four municipalities (Shanghai, Beijing, Guangzhou, and Tianjin) in 2002, and expanding services to thirty-three cities in 2003. The government has also stipulated that by 2005, 25 percent of television stations must broadcast programming digitally, and by 2010 all television broadcasts must be digitally delivered. Analog transmissions will cease in 2015.

In China, there are fifteen national television channels under the banner of China Central Television (CCTV). All CCTV channels are operated by the Chinese government. CCTV channels distribute more than 270 daily hours of news, economics, arts, opera, music, sport, movies, military affairs, science and technology, agriculture, and children's programs. These channels and their general programming formats are listed in Table 8.18.

In addition, each of the major cities has at least one television station, such as Beijing Television (BTV) and Shanghai Television (STV), which also broadcast to surrounding provinces.

In China, there are 750 city-run cable television networks typically broadcasting up to thirty-five channels of programming. Shanghai has the largest cable television operation with 3.1 million subscribers. Other major cities such as Beijing, Tianjin, Guangzhou, Shenzhen, and Chongqing have well-developed cable television networks offering a range of Chinese and Western programming.

Internet Access in China

In 2003, internet penetration in China was at 6.8 percent of the total population, the third-lowest percentage of the eight countries. Internet service in the household is usually through a dial-up connection, where users pay a monthly fee to an internet service provider.

TABLE 8.18 National (Government-Operated) Television Channels in China

CHANNEL	BASIC CONTENT
CCTV-1	Comprehensive news channel
CCTV-2	Economic news
CCTV-3	Chinese culture
CCTV-4	Foreign politics, economy, society
CCTV-5	Sports, health, education
CCTV-6	Dedicated movie channel
CCTV-7	Children's, military, and agricultural
CCTV-8	Drama: domestic (48.8 percent); foreign (35 percent)
CCTV-9	English language news, documentaries
CCTV-10	Modern science and technology
CCTV-11	Traditional Chinese opera
CCTV-12	Western (China) regional programming
CCTV-13	Children
CCTV-14	Music Channel
CCTV-15	French-Spanish Channel

Source: Ian Weber.

Internet cafés are banned by the government from opening within 200 meters of schools because of a perception that children will have access to "harmful cultural information." In the major cities, high-speed internet access is available at cyber cafés (*wang ba*). Computer keyboards in China typically contain a reduced set of Chinese characters, such as the one depicted in Figure 8.16.

However, many computers in China have English keyboards and software that allow users to type up the Chinese language using English-language keys. The software makes it possible for the user to type "pinyin" letters—a Romanized alphabetic system (like English)—on an English-language computer keyboard, which bring up Chinese characters on the computer screen. For example, typing the pinyin term *ni3 hao3* (which means *hello*) will bring up 你好 (*hello* in Chinese) on the computer screen.

你好

FIGURE 8.16 *Computer Keyboard with Reduced Set of Chinese Characters*
Source: Ian Weber.

ACCESSIBILITY OF MEDIA IN GHANA

Newspaper Access in Ghana

In Ghana, figures on the penetration of newspapers are unavailable. There are three daily newspapers with national news and national circulation: *Daily Graphic*, the *Ghanaian Times* and the *Evening News,* All three are state-owned (public) newspapers based in the capital of Accra, and are serious newspapers. The *Ghanaian Times* has a broadsheet shape, while the *Daily Graphic* and *Evening News* have tabloid shapes. However, these three newspapers cannot be found in all towns and villages because the lack of viable roads does not permit easy transport to all areas of Ghana. In addition to the state-owned newspapers, there are several major private newspapers that have been proliferating since the 1992 constitution guaranteed their right to freedom and independence, including the following: *The Chronicle* (serious), *The Independent* (serious), *The Daily Dispatch* (serious), *The Statesman* (serious), *The Crusading Guide* (serious), *P&P*, or *People and Places* (entertainment-oriented), *Ghana Palaver* (serious), and *The Daily Guide* (serious). These private newspapers carry national news and have wide circulation mostly across the south of Ghana, and are increasing their reach to the north, but lack the circulation and the resources (financial, technological, human) of the state-owned newspapers. Almost all newspapers in Ghana are published in the morning. The exception is the *Evening News*, published by the parent company of the *Ghanaian Times.*

In Ghana, there is also a tradition of Saturday newspapers, because Sunday is a day in which most Ghanaians organize activities around churchgoing. Some of the Saturday newspapers have the same ownership as daily newspapers. For example, the *Mirror* shares the same parent company as the *Daily Graphic*, and the tabloid-shaped *Spectator* (serious) shares the same parent company as the *Ghanaian Times*. Other Saturday newspapers are freestanding.

Some of the top ten circulating newspapers in Ghana are national daily newspapers, and some are national biweekly or weekly newspapers (Table 8.19). The most widely circulating newspaper is the *Daily Graphic.*

TABLE 8.19   Estimated Top 10 Circulating Newspapers in Ghana

NEWSPAPER	MAIN CONTENT
Daily Graphic	Serious
Mirror	Entertainment
Ghanaian Times	Serious
Daily Guide	Serious
Chronicle	Serious
Graphic Sports	Sports
Graphic Showbiz	Entertainment
The Spectator	Serious
People & Places (*P&P*)	Entertainment
Crusading Guide	Serious

Note: Circulation figures unknown.

Source: Robert McKenzie.

In 2004, there were seventy-nine titles of regional/local newspapers registered with the National Media Commission in Ghana, a low number overall, but somewhat of a high number considering the size of the country. Most of the newspapers tend to be associated with one of the two largest cities, Accra or Kumasi. Almost all newspapers are published in English.

In Ghana, newspapers are distributed primarily through single-copy sales at newsstands or from walking streetside vendors. Newsstands are located somewhat sparsely along well-traveled roads and in cities and towns. Usually, newsstands sell newspapers and/or magazines and no other products. The inventory of newspapers offered both by newsstands and by street vendors usually is low; frequently, newspapers have sold out by the afternoon. Typically, newspapers are fastened to the outside of a newsstand with clothespins in such a way that the outside walls of the structure are almost completely covered with newspapers except for a small, chest-high opening to hand money through to the vendor, as depicted in Figure 8.17.

Streetside vendors selling newspapers walk through congested traffic or position themselves on the side of well-traveled roads. Usually they carry a selection of newspapers displayed across their arms or held in their hands, as depicted in Figure 8.18.

FIGURE 8.17   *Newsstand in Accra, Ghana*
Source: Robert MᶜKenzie.

FIGURE 8.18   *Street Vendor Selling Newspapers in Accra, Ghana*

Source: Robert McKenzie.

Radio Access in Ghana

In Ghana, data on the ownership and penetration of radio and television are estimates. Because broadcasting—particularly television broadcasting—is in an early stage of development, neither the government nor private industry has committed resources to collect this information.

In Ghana, most households have at least one radio receiver. In 2004, more than half of homes had three or four radio receivers. In Ghana, radio is delivered primarily via terrestrial broadcast. Terrestrial broadcast penetration for radio in Ghana is about 80 percent of homes, a low figure compared to the other countries. Homes in Ghana include not only houses and apartments, but also huts. In 2004, there was no satellite digital radio coverage and no terrestrial digital radio coverage.

Terrestrial broadcast radio in Ghana is delivered primarily on the FM band, with some state-operated radio being delivered on the short-wave band. There are three national radio networks in Ghana—as listed in Table 8.20—all delivered by the state-owned Ghana Broadcasting Corporation (GBC). Two of the networks are carried on the short-wave radio band: *Radio 1* is mostly a public service with little advertising that is broadcast in multiple African languages; *Radio 2* is mostly a commercial service with abundant advertising that is broadcast in English. The third, *FM Radio*, is a news network only carried on ten regional GBC stations that are programmed locally when they are not networked with news.

In 2004, there were 127 radio stations in Ghana, a low number compared to the other countries. Of this total, ninety-seven were private broadcasters, and thirty were public service or community broadcasters. A few of the stations—both public and private—are licensed to foreign organizations. These stations include Radio France International and the BBC and Sky (both from England). Because both public and private broadcasters in Ghana carry advertising, most radio stations in Ghana are commercial stations.

TABLE 8.20   National State-Funded Radio Networks in Ghana

CHANNEL	MAIN CONTENT
Radio 1	Local talk stations in indigenous languages, and music
Radio 2	All types of music
FM Radio	Music, news, and information

Source: Robert McKenzie.

Television Access in Ghana

Again, data on television access in Ghana are estimates only. In 2004, only 50 to 60 percent of households had at least one television set, a very low number compared to the other countries. In Ghana, television content is distributed via terrestrial, cable, and satellite broadcasting. Data from 2004 show terrestrial television penetration to be at approximately 90 percent of people, a low percentage compared to the other countries. The main reason the percentage is as high as it is, considering how many people have television sets, is because many people watch television communally at the homes of friends and family. Data from 2004 show cable penetration to be 0.06 percent of households, the lowest percentage among the eight countries, and satellite penetration to be at approximately 0.01 percent of households, also the lowest among the eight countries. Both cable and satellite accessibility tend to be most prominent in higher-income homes and in hotels in Accra and Kumasi.

In 2004, digital television was not available. The government was holding discussions on requiring conversion from analog to digital transmission in 2006 or 2007.

In Ghana, television broadcasting is in a rapid stage of development. In 2004, there were twenty television stations licensed for operation, some of which had not yet begun broadcasting. Several television stations already broadcasting to regional audiences had plans to broadcast nationwide, though in 2004 only one television station was delivering programming to a national audience: the state-owned Ghana Television (GTV), a subsidiary of the Ghana Broadcasting Corporation (GBC) funded by license fees and advertising. Stations with plans to broadcast nationwide, plus GTV, along with their general programming formats, are listed in Table 8.21.

In Ghana, there were two major cable providers and one satellite provider in 2004, offering dozens of channels. Satellite and cable-channel lineups normally include the private broadcast channels already mentioned, but not the state-owned GTV, which is normally accessed by antenna. Table 8.22 lists most of the television-program suppliers delivered by satellite and cable providers in Ghana. It shows a significant presence of foreign television programming.

Internet Access in Ghana

Internet penetration in Ghana in 2004 was about .08 percent of homes, by far the lowest percentage among the eight countries. Internet access in the household is not very common,

TABLE 8.21   Terrestrial Television Stations Either Broadcasting Nationally or with Plans to Broadcast Nationally in Ghana

CHANNEL	MAIN CONTENT
*GTV	News, information, education, films, telenovelas
TV3	News, entertainment, political talk, telenovelas, and soaps
Metro TV	News, film, African and Western music, soap operas, sports
TV Africa	African languages and culture, political talk

* State-owned, funded by license fees and advertising.

Source: Robert MᶜKenzie.

TABLE 8.22   Satellite and Cable (Multichannel) Television in Ghana

ActionTV	M-Net Domestic
Activate	Movie Magic
Africa 2 Africa	MTV
Africa Magic	National Geographic
Animal Planet	Parliamentary Service
BBC Food	Reality TV
BBC Prime	Rhema Network
BBC World	RTPi
Bloomberg Information TV	SABC 1
BVN TV	SABC 2
Canal+ Horizons	SABC 3
Cartoon Network	SABC Africa
CCTV4	Sci-Fi Channel
China Central Television 9	SIC
CNN International	SONY Entertainment
Deukom	Summit
E tv	SuperSport
ESPN	TBN
Eurosport	TellyTrack
Fashion TV	The Series Channel
Go	Travel Channel
Hallmark Entertainment Network	Turner Classic Movies
History Channel	TV Globo
Kworld	TV5
K-TV World	VHI
KykNet	ZEE TV

in large part because many homes do not have landline telephones. Most people in Ghana access the internet at internet cafés, which are plentiful in major cities. Users in internet cafés pay a per-minute fee. Internet speed in these cafés is comparatively slow. Internet cafés can also be found in some of the most remote of villages—those with electricity or satellite

FIGURE 8.19   *Internet Café Sign on a Tree in Accra, Ghana*
Source: Robert McKenzie.

access. Signs for internet cafés can often be seen posted outside the cafés, at street corners near the cafés, and even on trees down the road from cafés (Figure 8.19).

ACCESSIBILITY OF MEDIA IN LEBANON

Newspaper Access in Lebanon

In Lebanon, the penetration of daily newspapers in 2000 was 24.9 percent of adults. This low figure is due to several factors. First, Lebanese citizens do not generate a strong demand for newspapers because of the high cost of newspapers compared to their incomes. Second, Lebanese newspapers tend to be unattractive to readers because they focus mostly on political news and give little or no attention to the daily concerns of average citizens. Third, prior to the civil war, the Lebanese press served as a forum for the Arab world to debate ideological and political conflicts between different Arab regimes. However, by the end of the Civil War (1975–1989), the Lebanese press had lost significant readership and advertising.

In Lebanon, there are thirteen main national daily newspapers: *al-Anwar* (*The Lights*), *al-Balad* (*The Country*), *al-Bayrak* (*The Banner*), *ad-Dyar* (*The Homeland*), *al-Kifah al Arabi* (*The Arab Struggle*), *al-Liwa* (*The Flag*), *an-Nahar* (*The Day*), *as-Safir* (*The Ambassador*), *ash-Sharq* (*The Orient*), *Aztak* [Armenian], *L'Orient-Le Jour* [French], *The Daily Star* [British], and *Zartoung* [Armenian].

This is the largest number of national newspapers among the eight countries, though it is easier to create a national newspaper in Lebanon because it is the smallest of the eight countries. All national newspapers in Lebanon are serious in content and are based in the capital city of Beirut, but can be purchased throughout Lebanon. All of these newspapers are morning newspapers, and almost all of the newspapers are broadsheets; the exception is the tabloid-shaped *al-Kifah al Arabi.*

Circulation figures for newspapers in Lebanon are usually unavailable, and when released for purposes of advertisers are highly exaggerated. The May 2004 issue of *ArabAd*, the industry's trade magazine, reported that circulation figures for three Lebanese newspapers—*al-Balad*, *as-Safir*, and *al-Anwar*—exceeded 100,000. However, according to a panel discussion held at the Lebanese American University early in 2004 and including the publisher and editors of three leading newspapers (*an-Nahar*, *as-Safir*, and the *Daily Star*), the average collective distribution of all daily newspapers in Lebanon in 2004 did not exceed 60,000 copies. Thus, Table 8.23 shows two sets of penetration numbers for the top ten circulating newspapers in Lebanon.

In 2004, there were twelve regional/local publications in Lebanon, a very low number compared to the other countries. Only four of the regionals are published daily. The fact that Lebanon is a small country that can be driven through both from north to south and from east to west in less than half a day diminishes a need for local newspapers. Regional/local newspapers are associated mainly with the major towns. For regional/local newspapers, the total daily circulation is not made available by publishers but is estimated to range from one to two thousand copies for each publication.

TABLE 8.23   Top 10 Daily Newspaper Circulation in Lebanon

NEWSPAPER	*CIRCULATION	BASIC CONTENT
an-Nahar (*The Day*)	50,000/10,000	Serious
as-Safir (*The Ambassador*)	45,000/8,000	Serious
ad-Diar (*The Homeland*)	20,000/9,000	Serious
al-Anwar (*The Lights*)	20,000/5,000	Serious
l'Orient le Jour	20,000/4,000	Serious
Daily Star	15,000/3,000	Serious
al-Liwa (*The Flag*)	15,000/1,500	Serious
al-Nayat al-Hayat (*The Life*)	10,000	Serious
(Saudi Arabia–based newspaper published in London but with a Lebanese edition)		
ash-Sharq al Awsat (*The Middle East*)	6,000	Serious
(Saudi Arabia–based newspaper published in London but with a Lebanese edition)		
ash-Sharq (*The Orient*)	6,000/2,000	Serious

* The first figure is circulation estimated by *World Press Trends 2003*. The second figure is circulation estimated by Lebanese professionals in the newspaper industry.

Source: World Press Trends (2003).

In Lebanon, newspapers are distributed primarily through four methods. In 2004, single-copy sales accounted for about 25 percent of total newspaper sales, a moderate percentage compared to the other countries; home deliveries by newspaper peddlers accounted for about 48 percent of sales, a high percentage compared to the other countries; home and institution deliveries by newspaper distributors accounted for about 25 percent of sales; and postal deliveries accounted for less than 3 percent of sales, a roughly average percentage compared to the other countries. Single-copy sales usually take place in bookshops, displays on street pavements, newspaper stands, kiosks, and through newspaper peddlers at street intersections. Kiosks are located in upper-class neighborhoods and are a more upscale version of newspaper stands. Kiosks and newspaper stands sell both domestic and foreign newspapers as well magazines, periodicals, popular books, and lottery tickets. Newspapers are usually displayed on racks standing on the ground in front of a kiosk or a newspaper stand. Figure 8.20 below shows a Lebanese newspaper stand. Figure 8.21 shows a typical selection of newspapers sold at a Lebanese newspaper stand.

Newspaper subscriptions are not as common in Lebanon as in other countries, mainly because newspapers cost more through subscription than through newsstands or peddlers. The primary reason for the inflated subscription prices is that large institutions are willing to pay such prices because they perceive that in return they will receive favorable news coverage. Thus, newspaper publishers in Lebanon are often less interested in individual subscribers than in "bulk" institutional subscribers.

FIGURE 8.20 *Newspaper Stand in Lebanon*
Source: Nabil Dajani.

FIGURE 8.21 *Selection of Newspapers Sold outside a Newsagent in Lebanon*
Source: Nabil Dajani.

Radio Access in Lebanon

In 2003, Lebanon had 678 radio receivers per 1,000 people, the highest ratio of radio receivers among Arab countries. Terrestrial radio in Lebanon is delivered on the FM and AM bands both by the government's *Radio Lebanon* and by the twelve commercially licensed radio stations, a low number compared to other countries. As the area of Lebanon is small, all AM radio stations and most FM stations are national. In addition to the licensed stations, a number of illegal stations that are protected by political bosses broadcast on FM frequencies. Most radio stations can be heard on more than one radio frequency. Table 8.24 lists the licensed radio stations operating in Lebanon.

In Lebanon, radio content is delivered primarily via terrestrial broadcasting. However, a few radio stations also broadcast via satellite and cable. National terrestrial broadcast penetration for national radio is estimated to be 100 percent of households in Lebanon.

Television Access in Lebanon

In Lebanon, it is estimated that the average household has two television sets. Television content in Lebanon is distributed mostly via terrestrial broadcasting. In 2003, terrestrial television penetration was at approximately 98 percent of households, an average number

TABLE 8.24   National Radio Stations in Lebanon

Radio ash-Shark	France FM
NBN Radio	Light FM
Radio Free Lebanon	Radio Strike
Radio ash-Sha'b	Radio One
Voice of Lebanon	Sound of Music
Saut al-Ghad	Pax Network
Radio Delta	Mix FM
Radio Scope	Nostalgie
99FM	Liban Star

Source: Nabil Dajani.

TABLE 8.25   Licensed Television Stations in Lebanon

CHANNEL	MAIN CONTENT
Tele Liban	General programming
LBCI terrestrial	General programming
LBCI satellite	General programming
Future TV	General programming
New TV	General programming
NBN	News
Al-Manar TV	General programming

Source: Nabil Dajani.

compared to the other countries. Cable television penetration in Lebanon is estimated at 78 percent, the highest percentage out of the eight countries, and, according to a March 26, 2004 report by the *Lebanese Daily Star* newspaper, one of the highest percentages in the world. This is mainly because of the low cable subscription fees described in Chapter 7. Satellite penetration in Lebanon is less than 10 percent of television homes, an average to low percentage compared to the other seven countries. Satellite accessibility tends to be mostly in rural areas where cable operators do not operate. Cable accessibility tends to be most prominent in the capital city and towns. Table 8.25 lists the television stations in Lebanon, which are all national.

There are nine national television stations. Eight of these are officially licensed, and one is not. Six of the eight licensed stations were on the air in 2004; two were not. The eight licensed television stations include the only public broadcaster, *Tele Liban*, and the five private commercial broadcasters: the Lebanese Broadcasting Company International (*LBCI*), *Future Television*, the National Broadcasting Network (*NBN*), *al-Manar* (organ of the Islamic Hizbollah Party), and New Television (*NTV*). In addition to these licensed stations on the air, two stations—the Independent Communication Channel International (*ICNI*) and United Television (*UTV*)—were licensed but not on the air in 2004. In addition to the officially licensed stations, the Christian-religious station *Tele Lumiere* broadcasts without a license but with tacit government approval.

Digital television penetration in Lebanon is growing, but in 2004 there were no reliable figures available as to the number of households with digital television. Digital television is available through both multichannels and by terrestrial broadcast.

In Lebanon, there are numerous cable providers, but more than two-thirds of these operators are technically illegal. Cable operators usually limit their operations to city or town neighborhoods. Cable-channel lineups normally include the local broadcast channels in addition to some seventy other channels covering all official and private Arab satellite channels. There are two main satellite television providers in Lebanon.

Internet Access in Lebanon

Internet penetration in Lebanon in 2004 was at 2.3 percent of the population, the second lowest percentage among the eight countries. In the household, the internet is normally accessible through dial-up access, wherein users pay a monthly service fee to an internet service provider to get online, in addition to paying the government-managed telephone company (named OGERO) for the time spent online. The internet is generally accessible in internet cafés in cities and in a number of the villages. In addition, some organizations and universities lease dedicated bandwidth from the Telecommunications Ministry, thus providing users with high-speed access. Keyboards in most Lebanese homes and internet cafés are configured in both English and Arabic alphabets.

COMPARATIVE SUMMARY

In this chapter, patterns in the accessibility of newspapers, radio, television, and the internet were compared across the eight countries. Accessibility of media is a phrase that is meant to portray what it is like for a person who lives in a given country to come into contact with different kinds of newspapers, radio programs, television shows, and web sites. Accessibility of media is analogous to the feeder branches of a tree—or the parts of the tree that deliver the leaves of content to passersby. As people pass by the branches of a media system, what kinds of newspapers, radio programs, television shows, and web sites do those people come into contact with because those media are convenient to reach? For example, are the available newspapers that people come into contact with local newspapers, regional newspapers, or national newspapers? Are the radio programs that people find on the dial distributed by public stations, government stations, or private stations? Are the television shows that people find on the dial distributed by public stations, government stations, or private stations? Are the television channels accessible through terrestrial broadcasting, through cable broadcasting, or through satellite broadcasting? Is the internet commonly available in people's homes, or in internet cafés? In the final analysis, when you look at a media system as a tree, what kinds of media are regularly delivered to people?

Table 8.26 summarizes numbers that quantify the accessibility of media in each of the eight countries.

TABLE 8.26   Summary of Accessibility of Media Across Eight Countries

	FRANCE	SWEDEN	UK	USA	MÉXICO	CHINA	GHANA	LEBANON
Penetration of Newspapers	33.1 percent	88 percent	50.3 percent	55 percent	7.9 percent	74.3 percent	N/A	N/A
Total Circulation	2,437,000	885,000	12,546,000	555,578,000	39,000	25,241,000	N/A	N/A
Number of National Newspapers	5	7	10	4	10	10	2	12
Number of Regional/Local Newspapers	64	90	5,353	1,468		734	79	12
Regional/Local Circulation	6,026,000	2,799,000	18,000,000		117,800,000			
Distribution of Newspapers								
Single Copy	47.1 percent	23 percent	87 percent	76 percent		10 percent		25 percent
Home Delivery	38.1 percent	72 percent	13 percent	19 percent		29 percent		48 percent
Postal Delivery	14.1 percent	5 percent		5 percent		61 percent		3 percent
Average Number of Radio Receivers Per Household	3-4	6	6	5	3	1.3	3.5	?
National Public Radio Networks	5	4	5	2	1	7	3	1
Private Radio Stations	1500	89	269	11,500		0	97	12
Average Number of Television Sets per Household	2	2	2	2.4	2	1.2		2
Penetration of Television								
Terrestrial	98 percent	97 percent	99 percent	98.2 percent	70.5 percent	97 percent	90 percent	98 percent
Satellite	10 percent	22 percent	45 percent	19 percent	9 percent	30 percent	1 percent	10 percent
Cable	10 percent	37 percent	22 percent	67 percent	12 percent	27.5 percent	6 percent	78 percent
National Television Networks								
Government	3	2	2	1	0	13	1	1
Private	3	1	3	7	6	0	1	3
Internet Penetration per Population	40.6 percent	74.6 percent	58.5 percent	68.8 percent	11.9 percent	6.8 percent	0.8 percent	2.3 percent

* Note: The years for these data vary. Please see the text within this chapter to note the year for each statistic.

High penetration of daily newspapers occurs in Sweden and China. Medium penetration of daily newspapers occurs in the USA, the UK, and, to a lesser extent, France. Low penetration of daily newspapers occurs in México, Ghana, and Lebanon. Countries with the largest number of national newspapers are the UK, México, China, and Lebanon. Countries with comparatively moderate numbers of national newspapers are France and Sweden. The remaining two countries—the USA and Ghana—have just one and two purely national newspapers, respectively. It is possible to identify a general relationship between a country's size and the accessibility of national newspapers versus regional/local newspapers: The larger the country, the more likely it will be that regional newspapers are more readily accessible than national newspapers. This, along with its large population, is why China has the greatest sheer volume of daily national newspaper penetration at 25,241,000. Conversely, the smaller the country, the more likely it will be that national newspapers are more readily accessible than regional/local newspapers.

The greatest proportions of single-copy sales occurs in France, the UK, and the USA. These numbers for France and the UK are largely explained by their large populations of commuters. In the USA, this number is partly explained by the density of populations in major cities plus the role of convenience stores and gas stations in selling newspapers. In the other countries, home-delivery sales account for the largest portion of sales. In Sweden, home delivery accounts for almost three-quarters of all newspaper sales, a fact that is largely explained by the sparse distribution of Sweden's population of only 8 million people.

Government-operated or -supervised radio has a strong presence in the radio-channel selections in France, Sweden, the UK, and China. All four countries have multiple channels and frequencies for public-service radio. China and Sweden both operate seven radio networks, though not all of them are national. The high profile of public-service radio in these four countries is partly explained by the central position of the state in promoting culture and education. Commercial radio has the strongest presence in the USA, and a significant presence in México and France. Digital radio has high penetration in the UK and Sweden.

The percentage of terrestrial broadcast penetration is in the high nineties in almost all of the countries. Only México has a much lower terrestrial broadcast penetration at 70.5 percent, a situation that is influenced both by México's relatively large size, and the inability of a large segment of the population living in poverty to purchase or have a need for a television set. Though Lebanon and Ghana both have significant portions of their populations living in poverty, their terrestrial broadcast penetration numbers are not as low as México. For Ghana, the high penetration numbers are mainly explained by communal television viewing. For Lebanon, the penetration numbers are large because the country is so small it can easily be covered by television signals. After terrestrial television distribution, the next most common form of penetration in the other countries (except the UK) is cable broadcasting. Cable television has the highest penetration in Lebanon and the USA. The high proportion of satellite broadcasting penetration in the UK can be explained partly by an aggressive marketing strategy involving free installation and heavily discounted programming offered by the satellite supplier Sky Television, a division of News Corporation.

National television channels or networks funded by government-mandated license fees have a strong presence in the landscape of channel listings in the European countries of France, Sweden, and the UK, as well as China. China has fifteen government-operated channels, by far the most. The pattern of government-funded television in the European countries as well as in China is attributable largely to the central presence of the state in the distribution of cultural, educational, or party-political programming. México has a strong presence of state-government-funded television. The USA has a small presence of government-funded national television in the television channel-selection landscape.

Internet penetration varies widely. Because the internet is a new and rapidly advancing medium, user numbers and penetration will continue to increase dramatically. Sweden and the USA have the highest internet penetration. The UK and France have moderate internet penetration. There is a huge drop-off from those four developed countries to the remaining developing countries. This is illustrated by comparing France, the developed country with the lowest internet penetration at 40 percent of the population, with México, the developing country with the highest internet penetration at 11.9 percent of the population. México, China, Ghana, and Lebanon all have low internet penetration.

CHAPTER 9

MEDIA CONTENT

PRIMER QUESTIONS

1. How would you define *media content*?

2. What newspaper content is typical of where you are living? What newspaper content do you think is unique to where you are living?

3. What radio content is typical of where you are living? What radio content do you think is unique to where you are living?

4. What television content is typical of where you are living? What television content do you think is unique to where you are living?

5. What web site content is typical of where you are living? What web site content do you think is unique to where you are living?

Think about what you notice the most about a tree when you pass it by—probably the leaves. Earlier in this book, media content was likened to the leaves of a tree. Just as leaves serve as a focal point for people who pass by a tree, so too does content serve as a focal point for potential audiences in the vicinity of media outlets. So great is the presence of content during the audience's experience of a media system, that the audience can be largely unaware of the previously discussed elements that are combining to form a media system.

This is the first of three chapters that deal with media content. In this chapter, media content is discussed in a broad sense of the term. In the next two chapters, more specialized areas of media content—news reporting and imports/exports—are discussed as separate elements of a media system in their own right. In previous chapters, content was positioned as the element that would best exhibit the impact of all the elements on each other and on the media system.

DEFINING MEDIA CONTENT

The Traditional Definition

Media content traditionally has been defined as quantifiable data contained within a medium, and identifiable through a research methodology called content analysis. Unfortunately, this definition treats media content versus media form as separate, discrete, and mutually exclusive concepts. Two important books that address the traditional definition of media content are Klaus Krippendorff's *Content Analysis: An Introduction to Its Methodology* (1980) and Roger Wimmer and Joseph Dominick's *Mass Media Research: An Introduction* (2003).

To illustrate how the traditional definition of media content splits content from form in a messy and somewhat artificial way, consider a hypothetical study of the form of a newspaper, wherein the order of the news sections is analyzed. Perhaps such a study would identify the first section as current events, the second section as feature news, the third section as sports, and the fourth section as business-classifieds. Though this is a study of the form of the newspaper, it is also possible to infer that certain content is given greater importance than other content. For example, placing sports third indicates that sports news is perceived to be the third-most-important category of news after current events and features. This simple example shows how form and content are so inextricably linked that conceptualizing them as two mutually exclusive categories of information can be difficult.

Another problem with the traditional approach to defining media content is that it has promoted the idea that content is primarily what drives an audience to access selected media, while treating form merely as a secondary motivator. Yet, as Marshall McLuhan declared long ago in *Understanding Media* (1964), "the medium is the message." This famous statement suggests that audiences sometimes seek out media forms—as in "getting on the internet"—more enthusiastically than the specific information carried by a given medium. Media form is especially relevant to an audience that is being exposed to foreign-language media content because the tone of the conversations between characters can play a more pivotal role in helping the audience to make any sense of the foreign dialogue than the dialogue itself, which may not be understandable. Therefore, in essence, the traditional definition of media content has failed to properly acknowledge the importance of form in certain contexts of media use.

Defining Media Content as Form and Substance

To address the problems with the traditional definition, **media content** is defined here as a combination of **form** (the way in which the substance of a medium is presented) and **substance** (the information contained within a medium), neither of which can be perfectly separated from each other. *Substance* is a better term for our purposes than *data*, which usually is understood to mean just numbers. In essence, defining media content as a combination of substance and form provides for a broader, more descriptive analysis of similarities and differences across the content of media systems in various countries.

DISTINCTIVE THEMES IN MEDIA CONTENT

This chapter focuses on **distinctive themes** in the content of newspapers, radio, television, and the internet in the eight countries. Distinctive themes reveal interesting facets of one particular media system compared to facets of another media system. The following variables will be used to analyze distinctive themes in the form and substance of media content in the eight countries:

Themes of Form in Newspaper Content
- Format (Tabloid versus Broadsheet)
- Proportions of Text, Advertising, Graphics, Photographs, Cartoons

Themes of Substance in Newspaper Content
- Sections/Typical Coverage
- Violence
- Nudity, Profanity, Sexuality

Themes of Form in Radio and Television Content
- Published Radio Program and Television Program Listings
- Private versus Public Broadcasters
- Start and End Times of Programs
- Advertising Minutage
- Actual Time Length of Program Content

Themes of Substance in Radio Formats and Television Genres
- Typical Radio Formats/Television Genres
- Unique Radio Formats/Television Genres
- Violence
- Nudity, Profanity, Sexuality

Themes of Content on the Internet

As discussed previously, the internet follows patterns in the distribution of content that are radically different from the other three media. One pattern that is different is that search engines automatically use **geolocation** technology to bring up content that is local to where the internet is being accessed. For example, geolocation technology is at work when a search engine automatically comes up in the first language of the country in which the computer is being accessed. In other words, if someone accesses the web site google.com in Lebanon, the web pages will automatically come up in Arabic language, as depicted in Figure 9.1.

A second pattern involves localized pop-up ads that automatically appear according to where the computer being used to access the internet is located. Even if a person logs on to a computer in one country, and then accesses an email service based in another country, pop-up ads that come up will often be about local products and services in the country in which the computer is being accessed.

Because internet content is not automatically confined by the country in which it is distributed (as other media are), the analysis of internet content in this book focuses on content that audiences access. Accordingly, the bulk of the analysis of internet content takes place in Chapter 12 on Media Audiences. In the meantime, however, internet content is analyzed briefly in terms of the two variables that, taken together, represent basic themes of form and substance: (1) start-up web page content and (2) restricted web site content.

MEDIA CONTENT IN FRANCE

Newspaper Form in France

In France, the five national newspapers all have a different size. *Libération* and *L'Humanité* (*The Humanity*) both have a tabloid shape but are slightly different sizes. *Le Figaro*, *Le Monde* (*The World*), and *Le Canard Enchaîné* (*The Enchained Duck*) are all broadsheets,

FIGURE 9.1   *Google Web Page in Arabic Language*
Source: Google, Inc.

but *Le Monde* is a much smaller newspaper widthwise and heightwise, compared not only to French newspapers but also to broadsheets in other countries.

The national newspapers are all quite serious and formal. The formality is seen in the dominance of text over photos or graphics, the use of academic language, and the coverage of serious subjects. Even *Le Canard Enchaîné,* which is full of cartoons and text that communicate ironic humor, focuses mainly on serious political subjects. Though the word *canard* in French can be used to mean *duck,* it also is a nickname for a newspaper. Regional newspapers are less formal and tend to be more colorful with more graphics. Figure 9.2 shows the front page of the regional newspaper, *Ouest France,* which also happens to have the largest circulation in France. There are no national sensational tabloids. Sensational journalism in France appears mostly in magazines.

In France, the national newspapers generally have a high proportion of text compared to advertising, photos, and graphics. Again *Le Canard Enchaîné* is an exception, with cartoons accompanying most major stories. A rough estimate would put text at about 80 percent in French newspapers, and photographs, advertising, and graphics at about the remaining 20 percent of newspapers. The tabloid-shaped *Libération* tends to run more photos than the others. Most major stories in *Libération* are accompanied by one photograph covering one-fifth to one-third of the page.

FIGURE 9.2   *Front Page of Regional Newspaper* Ouest-France

Source: Robert McKenzie, permission granted by Journal *Ouest-France.*

Unique to French newspapers, testimony is usually signified with left and right arrowheads around italicized words (as in << *quote* >>). Often quotes are scattered throughout a paragraph, either as phrases or as whole sentences. For example, in the September 2, 2004, *Le Monde*, there was a story about the wording of a document that was drafted as part of the treaty that produced the failed 2004 European Constitution. The story, published on *Le Monde's* web site, contained the following paragraph:

> For several months, Mr. Valls has cultivated his difference and takes the opposite course to the direction on subjects such as the offence of insult to the flag, which it approved, or on the case of the Italian refugee Cesare Battisti, who affirmed it << *is not a good combat for the PS.* >> But, this time, the situation is considered to be more serious and testifies to the climate of tension and of suspicion which reigns with the Socialists.

Advertising occupies a relatively small portion of newspapers—in most, only about 5 to 10 percent of the content. Advertising typically does not appear on the front page of *Libération* and *L'Humanié; Le Monde* and *Le Figaro* usually display one boxed in the lower righthand corner on the front page. It is typical to see several pages of a French national newspaper containing no ads.

In national newspapers, photographs are used sparingly. Usually there are one or two photographs in color on the front page, but many articles inside have none. Of the articles that have photographs, most are in black and white. The quality of photos in terms of clarity (pixel resolution) is generally very good, even in regional and local newspapers. Photographs in French newspapers often are very small and contain headshots of people. The regional newspapers in France tend to be more graphic and colorful in terms of photographs, and use them more frequently.

Graphics and cartoons are somewhat common across all national newspapers. Both hand-drawn and computer graphics are used to illustrate stories, especially in *Le Monde.* Across most newspapers in France one sees fairly detailed, hand-drawn cartoons, especially in *Le Monde* and *Le Figaro.* The cartoons usually function as political commentary and are placed next to stories on which they are commenting. In *Le Canard Enchaîné,* there are usually different cartoons accompanying two or three stories per page. The cartoons almost always point out ironies not only in politics but also in the absurdities of daily life. For example, on page 5 of the April 16, 2003, edition of *Le Canard Enchaîné,* a cartoon accompanies a story about efforts by the French government to eliminate red tape—created by the multiple documents that French citizens often have to produce when they use government services. The caption reads, "Trying to Start a Simplified Bureaucracy." In the cartoon box, a woman is seen placing several documents on the counter in front of a government bureaucrat. In response, the bureaucrat replies: "We are not going to! Because you have *too many* documents."

Newspaper Substance in France

In France, sections in national newspapers vary, but typically include: International, European Union, Societé (general-interest news around France), Politics, Culture, and Sports. Sports news usually includes Football (soccer), the Tour de France (in the summer), tennis, rugby, and horse racing. *Le Monde* and *Le Figaro* also have insert sections. *Le Monde* has a well-known insert on Books, and *Le Figaro* has an insert on Financial News.

The formality of most French national newspapers leads them to read somewhat like literary magazines. Particularly in *Le Monde* and *Le Figaro,* sentences are long, vocabulary is elevated, and newsworthy subjects are often esoteric. For example, a front-page story in the August 2, 2004, *Le Monde* ran the headline "Questions around Some *Alicaments.* *Alicaments* is a newly coined term describing an esoteric category of foods that have medicinal value. Most coverage in French national newspapers is about politics, and often about French politics that interface with European Union politics.

Stories about violent crimes are somewhat common in newspapers in France. Often when violent crimes are covered, stories focus on a romantic or passionate relationship between two or more people connected in some way to the crime.

Stories with photos of nudity are not very common, though they can be found. Usually, if nudity is found in a French newspaper, it is a topless woman in a work of art that appears in an exhibition discussed in a newspaper story; or a topless female in an ad for a body product such as perfume. Profanity is rare but not unheard of in French newspapers. If profanity is printed, it is likely to be in the context of a quote from a newsmaker.

Radio Form in France

In France, radio listings generally are not normally published by newspapers. Partial radio listings are published in the weekly magazine *Telérama* for three of the Radio France networks (*France Musiques, France Culture, France Inter*), and for a few of the major private radio stations including *BFM, Europe 1, Le Mouv, RCF, RTL, Sud Radio, Campus, RFI* (the state-funded Radio France International), and *TSF*. Radio programs on commercial stations usually begin at exactly the top of or the bottom of the hour. On state-owned radio networks, programs can begin and end at any minute on the half hour. For example, on *France Musiques* a daily music program begins at 7:07, and on *France Culture,* a daily discussion program on anthropology begins at 13:38. These start times are usually consistent from one day to the next.

On both state-owned and private radio, ads can be heard frequently. Typically, actual programming varies from twenty to twenty-four minutes per half hour because of advertising.

The Radio France networks are usually pervasive in the selection of accessible radio frequencies in a given area. When scanning through radio frequencies on the FM band, as the radio receiver locks onto the next available frequency, it is about as likely to be a Radio France service (either on a local station or a national network station) as it is to be a private radio station.

A lot of talk can be heard across the spectrum of radio programming. On talk and discussion programs—and particularly political programs—conversations with callers are emphatic and can often last five to fifteen minutes.

Radio Formats in France

Radio France networks are programmed according to the following niche formats: *France Bleu* broadcasts music, news, and discussion programs that differ by region. For example, a *France Bleu* station on the eastern coast of France may broadcast a gardening program focusing on flowers that can grow in sandy soil. *France Culture* broadcasts traditional French music, drama, and discussion. *France Info* broadcasts news and information. *France Inter* broadcasts contemporary music including pop, rock, and jazz. *France Musiques* broadcasts traditional classical music and contemporary classical music, interspersed with discussions about the music.

Commercial radio is programmed according to moderately narrow niche formats. Many formats revolve around ethnic or political content. For example, there is anarchist radio, Jewish radio, and Muslim radio. Pop stations tend to broadcast contemporary music from across several decades.

French radio represents some of the most diversified radio there is. Moving across the radio band, the listener will hear many samples of discussion programs, news programs, sports programs, contemporary music, classical music, traditional French music, ethnic music, and music that does not fit neatly into a particular category. Within this diversified radio universe, there are three themes that are distinctive to French radio. First is classical music, defined in its broad sense as symphony, operatic, sonata, baroque, renaissance, contemporary classical, and the like. A second theme in French radio is intellectual radio. Symbolized by the *France Culture* radio network, intellectual radio includes lectures, documentaries, and discussions on biology, astronomy, history, archaeology, literature, the fine arts, and other academic subjects. For example, on August 16, 2004, *France Culture* broadcast a discussion and interview program with François Jacob, described as "one of the great names of biology of the twentieth century, and one of the pioneers on the research of AIDS." A third theme in French radio is opinionated discussion programs. These programs usually involve passionate but polite debates between participants with strong opinions about current events.

On French radio, profanity is somewhat of a regular feature in imported rap and other pop-music songs, though lower-scale profanity such as *merd* (shit) can also be heard in French pop music. But normally, even though regulations do not prohibit profanity, guests and hosts do not regularly utter profane words on French radio.

Television Form in France

Television listings are published in the national weekly magazines, *Télérama* and *Télé7Jours,* as well as in magazine inserts in regional newspapers, and by most daily newspapers. Listings of channels in the national magazines contain detailed information in color, such as channels, program titles, start and end times, short descriptions of what each program is about, and some screen grabs (a photo of a scene) to promote certain evening programs. The listings also include a number code that users can program into a videotape machine or DVD recorder to record a television program.

Television programs on both public and private channels usually start and end at the :5s around the clock. It is not very common for programs to begin at :00 or :30 on the hour. Television program segments vary according to multiples of five-minute increments (i.e., programs can run for 5, 15, 30, 40, 55 minutes, etc.). Usually, when a program finishes, there is a still graphic accompanied by a voiceover that first promotes a program coming up later in the day or the week, and then promotes the show that immediately follows.

In France, one advertising break each is permitted during and outside of a thirty-minute program (after a program ends and before another program begins). Some programs—news, documentaries, films—are not permitted to have advertising breaks within the programming. Allowing for promos, which are not included in the advertising minutage limits, the actual program length on the public stations is approximately forty-seven minutes per hour, and for private stations is about forty-one minutes per hour.

As Table 9.1 shows, television program listings in France are split equally between the state-owned public channels and the privately owned channels, both of which carry advertising.

TABLE 9.1 Sample Television Program Listings from France, April 24, 2003

TIME	TF1	TIME	FRANCE 2	TIME	FRANCE 3	TIME	CANAL 1	TIME	M6	TIME	FRANCE 5 ARTE
6:05pm	Red Zone	6:05	Urgencies	6:15	It Is Not a Wizard	6:15	Results and Sports	6:50	The Chameleon	6:00	In the Air
6:55	The Bigdil	6:55	There Is All Tests	6:20	Questions for a Champion	6:25	The Simpsons	7:50	Camera Cafés	7:00	Steps in Italy
8:00	News: The Journal	7:50	Johnny	6:55	News: The Journal	6:50	Spin City	7:55	Six	7:45	Arte Information
8:40	The Result of the Races	8:00	News: The Journal	8:15	All the Sport	7:15	The Zapping	8:05	Our Beautiful Family	8:15	Reports: Child Soldiers of Poutine
8:55	Julie Lescaut	8:55	100 Minutes to Convince	8:25	The Fabulous Destiny of . . .	7:20	Against Journal	8:40	Camera Cafés	8:45	An Angel Has My Table
10:40	The Derniere Tracking	10:45	Double I	8:55	Empire of the Sun	7:55	The Guignols of Information	8:50	Research of the New Star	11:15	India between Tradition and Modernity
12:20am	Slides of the Economy	12:20	Newspaper of the Night	12:00	In Search of Asylum	8:05	Joke Has Share	11:10	Freaky Links	12:00am	Aphrodite of Amristar
						8:35	Sports News	12:05	Normal, Paranormal?		
						8:45	Cinema News				
						8:55	The Zapping				
						9:00	Feroce				
						10:35	Mensomadaire				
						11:40	Requiem for a Dream				

Source: Robert McKenzie.

Television Genres in France

In France, much of the terrestrial television programming—especially on the public channels—is oriented toward promoting French culture, though both the public and private channels carry a good portion of entertainment-oriented programming. Cultural programming often includes film, documentaries, and magazine programs (programs containing two to four minifeature stories). One way in which the importance of French culture can be observed has to do with the way that imported television programs containing foreign languages are handled. When an imported program is broadcast, the voices of French actors are dubbed over the original foreign-language dialogue, which promotes French culture by protecting the French language.

All terrestrial broadcasters air programming twenty-four hours a day, except *France 5/Arte.* Some television channels on satellite or cable discontinue programming from 0200 (2:00 AM) until 0600 (6:00 AM). The following general statements can be made about programming across the day on the terrestrial broadcasters: In the early morning, there are news programs and children's cartoons. In the late mornings, there are game shows and cuisine shows. In the afternoon, there are dramas, films, and documentaries. In the evenings, there are documentaries, dramatic series, magazines, and films. *Canal+* is well-known for broadcasting films and soccer.

One distinctive television genre is the "magazine," scheduled across most time slots of the broadcast day, and often as a series. These programs can run up to two hours, during which reporters cover two to four feature stories. A common theme among magazine feature stories is to examine how people lived in another part of the world during a particular period of time. The program *Thalassa* on *France 3* exemplifies this genre. For example, on May 10, 2004, *Thalassa* focused on the Sahara Desert. *France 3's* description of this episode was: "In May, a long narrow wrinkle will be explored—the Sahara, of Mauritania and Niger—while passing by Mali, borrowing the caravan tracks which connect Maghreb to black Africa and the Atlantic with the Red Sea." This particular edition contained seven different reports by reporters focusing on different regions of the Sahara Desert.

A second distinctive genre on television in French is the "parody comedy," which involves characters—real people or puppets—acting out caricatures of politicians and other famous people. One program that is typical of this genre is *Les Guilgenols (The Puppets)*, on *Canal+*. This ten-minute program involves skits between puppets with exaggerated facial features and mannerisms. The puppets are designed to capture the likeness of well-known politicians, in terms of facial features, body movements, and vocal quality, in order to accurately impersonate the politicians. The dialogue of the puppets often makes them and the real people they represent look hapless. Frequently, the president of France and other government officials are parodied by the puppets, but famous people from other countries are parodied as well. Often, Americans are portrayed on this program as muscle-bound and brutish.

A third distinctive television genre is the *téléfilm,* which usually lasts one and a half hours and is broadcast by both the public and the private broadcasters at 9:00 PM. Usually, the basic plot of the *téléfilm* revolves around a mysterious murder that the characters in the *téléfilm* as well as the television audience try to solve. Sometimes, the plot involves sexual indiscretions that cause problems in intimate relationships. Sometimes the basic plot of a *téléfilm* involves a detective who solves a mysterious murder. Such *téléfilms* often take place in contemporary times, but draw on historically accurate facts from a past time period. For example, the *téléfilm* "Navarro," aired by the private broadcaster *TF1* as a series during the summer of 2004, regularly featured characters with connections to the Algerian War (which lasted from 1954 to 1962 and resulted in Algeria securing independence from France). *Téléfilms* can be French productions, or joint French–German or French––Canadian productions.

In general, violence on television in France is somewhat common. Some violence can be seen in the evening hours on dramas, movies, and news programs. The violence on news programs can be graphic, but usually the camerawork will not focus on a close-up shot of the people who have been hurt. Nudity can be seen on French television (terrestrial and multichannel) almost every night, in regular programs involving sexual activity including lovemaking, in promotions for upcoming programs, and in ads for body care products such as like shower gel and perfume. Female nudity is much more common than male nudity on television in France, though both can be seen. It is not common to hear profanity on television in France.

Internet Content in France

Aside from the court-ordered prohibition of selling Nazi memorabilia discussed in Chapter 6, web sites in France normally do not restrict content, regardless of how they are accessed. Chain internet cafés typically provide a start-up page on their computers designed especially for the café. The start-up web pages typically include paid advertising.

MEDIA CONTENT IN SWEDEN

Newspaper Form in Sweden

In Sweden, four national newspapers—*Dagens Nyheter* (*Daily News*), *Svenska Dagbladet* (*Daily Swedish Sheet*), *Göteborgs-Posten* (*Gothenburg Post*), and *Dagens Industri* (*Daily Industry*)—are serious newspapers. Only one of them—*Göteborgs-Posten*—is a broadsheet. The other national newspapers, as well as the sensationalist newspapers *Aftonbladet* (*Evening Sheet*), *Expressen* (*The Express*), and *Kvällposten* (*The Evening Post*), have a tabloid shape.

Swedes often refer to their national newspapers either as the "morning papers" (the serious newspapers) or as the "afternoon newspapers" (the sensationalist tabloids) because of when they are printed. In Sweden, the national newspapers are all serious to a large degree. The two main national newspapers, *Dagens Nyheter* and *Svenska Dagbladet*, are strictly serious newspapers. But even the sensationalist-oriented tabloids published in the afternoon focus much more on crime and politics than they do on popular-culture-type news such as the activities of celebrities.

Swedish newspapers have a clean look. They generally have clear print and sharp photos, without a lot of clutter. In Sweden, the tabloid-shaped newspapers and the version of *International Herald-Tribune* newspaper that is printed in Sweden have either a stapled or glued binding, preventing pages or sections from slipping out.

The proportion of text compared to advertising, photos, and graphics does not vary tremendously. Most newspapers have plenty of photos and graphics in addition to text.

FIGURE 9.3   *Front Page of the Sensationalist Tabloid* Expressen *from Sweden*

Source: Robert McKenzie, reprinted with permission by *Expressen*, June 2, 2003.

A rough estimate would put text at about 60 percent in Swedish newspapers and put photographs, advertising, and graphics at about the remaining 40 percent of newspapers.

In the sensational tabloids, headlines are often bolded to such an extent that the letters in the words look very black and very thick. A lot of color—especially blue, yellow, and red—is used to border words, to provide a background to words, or to point out something in a photograph. Figure 9.3 shows the front page of the June 2, 2003, *Expressen*, which provides a good representation of how Swedish sensational tabloids look.

Advertising occupies a relatively small portion of newspapers—in most newspapers, only about 10 percent of the content. In national newspapers, there is a strip at the bottom of the front page used for advertising, and frequently the second page is a full-page ad. However, it is typical for several pages in a row in the national newspapers to contain no advertising.

In Swedish national newspapers, photographs are very popular. Usually there are three or four in color on the front page. Inside the newspapers, most pages have one or two photographs. In all the national newspapers, most photographs are in color and can take up one-fourth to one-third of a page. The quality of photographs is generally very good in both national and local newspapers. Graphics commonly appear in Swedish newspapers, usually to show maps of areas where a newsworthy event is described, or in the business section to illustrate a financial trend. Political cartoons are not very common in Swedish newspapers.

Newspaper Substance in Sweden

In Sweden, sections in national newspapers vary, but typically include: Current World Events, Swedish News, Debates, Culture, Consumer, and Sports. The debate pages in the serious newspapers play a large role in political discussions in Sweden. The culture section in Swedish newspapers—even the sensational tabloids—is usually substantial and is located toward the front of the newspaper. *Dagens Nyheter* is particularly well-known for its culture section. Sports news usually includes football (soccer), hockey, and track and field. *Aftonbladet* is known for its sports section printed on pink newspaper pages.

Stories about violent crimes sometimes appear in newspapers in Sweden, especially in the afternoon newspapers. When violent crimes are covered, stories often focus on the plight of victims and the failed role of the state in fostering social and economic conditions that might have prevented the crime.

If nudity appears in a Swedish newspaper, as it does occasionally, it is likely to be a naked man or woman in a work of art that appears in an exhibition covered by a newspaper story, or sometimes a topless woman in the news—for example, in a beach setting during the summer. Nudity is somewhat commonly portrayed in newspaper graphics accompanying stories about the human body. For example, in the Culture section of the June 2, 2003, *Dagens Nyheter*, an article discussed how a USA television talk show (*Dr. Phil*) discusses private problems in public, and how the host tries to discuss subjects from the perspectives of both men and women. The article was accompanied by a graphic that included: a photograph of Dr. Phil's head superimposed on a drawing of a man crouched in a sports jacket holding a beer and a remote control; a graphic of a woman standing up in a shirt, skirt, and boots; and a graphic of a naked woman thrusting out her chest and holding on to her bottom. This graphic depicted the female's breasts (including nipples) but not her genitals. Usually, if profanity is printed in Swedish newspapers, it is likely to be lower-impact words such as *fan* (the devil) or *jävla* (damn), as they are quoted from a statement by a newsmaker. However, stronger words can also be found in Swedish newspapers, particularly in educational reports attempting to describe how young people talk about sex.

Radio Form in Sweden

Program listings for the public-service radio networks (*P1, P2, P3, P4*) are regularly published in national morning and afternoon newspapers. Radio listings for the Swedish Radio networks are also published in the national magazine *SE TV,* and in weekly magazine inserts (such as *Aftonbladet TV*), which come with the national newspapers. In Sweden, radio programs on the Swedish Radio networks begin and end at almost any minute on the hour. For example, on May 29, 2003, on *P1* a discussion program called "People and Beliefs" ran from 0703 (7:03 AM) to 0755 (7:55 AM). Many programs run at the same time every day, but others are unique to a particular time slot on a particular day—such as a radio play that ran from 1903 (7:03 PM) to 1913 (7:13 PM) on June 2, 2003 on *P1*; the following night, this time slot was filled with a consumer discussion program, "Money and Your Rights." Programs on commercial radio stations usually begin at exactly the top of or the bottom of the hour. There are no ads on the Swedish Radio networks, but they can be heard somewhat frequently on commercial radio stations; actual programming is typically twenty-six minutes per half hour (minus promotions) because of advertising minutage regulations.

The Swedish Radio networks generally are more pervasive than commercial networks in the selection of accessible radio frequencies in a given area. When scanning through radio frequencies on the FM band, as the radio receiver locks onto the next available frequency, it is about twice as likely to be a Swedish Radio network than a commercial station.

Talk can be widely heard across most radio programming. Much of the talk on Swedish radio is rather slow-paced compared to other countries—even by pop radio hosts and political discussion hosts. On talk and discussion programs—and particularly political programs—conversations with callers are often slow-paced and sometimes include several pauses of silence.

Radio Formats in Sweden

Swedish Radio networks are programmed according to the following niche formats: *P1* broadcasts a lot of discussion programs, including in-depth news analysis, current affairs, and debate. *P1* also airs drama, documentaries, and talk shows about the arts, science, and social and philosophical issues. *P2* broadcasts classical music (traditional, contemporary, jazz, folk) and ethnic-language programming. *P3* is geared to a younger audience and broadcasts pop music, news, cultural, and social programs. *P4* broadcasts regional programs focusing on local culture, music, and news. *P5,* accessible only in the Stockholm area, broadcasts modern music aimed at a younger audience. *P6,* available in the Stockholm area as well as internationally via shortwave radio and the internet, broadcast news, and discussion programs. And *P7* broadcasts Finnish music, culture, news, and discussion programs. Commercial radio is programmed according to moderately narrow niche formats, many of which revolve around pop-music content—such as hip-hop, rave, reggae, house, and rock.

There are at least three distinct themes on Swedish radio. First is Swedish culture. Particularly on *P1*, but also on the other Swedish Radio networks as well as some commercial stations, programs are aired that have a cultural focus to them. These programs discuss subjects specific to Sweden such as the welfare state, music, poetry, literature, and nature and the environment. The subject of taking care of nature is particularly pervasive across Swedish radio, whereas the welfare state is pervasive on *P1* and *P3*. Often there are debates about whether the welfare state is working or whether it is too expensive (that is, whether taxes are too high). A second theme of Swedish radio is the discussion program, which airs on all the *P* channels. Often, discussion programs center on themes that have to do with nature. For example, on August 9, 2004, *P4* aired a program about a "sea tower" root that grows naturally in the south of Sweden. During the program, the host discussed with several callers how this root has a lot of vitamins and nutrients, how it makes a nice marmalade, and how a shampoo can be made out of it. Discussion programs on *P3* and on some commercial stations are geared to youth audiences, and often feature young people who come in to or call the station to talk with a host about such subjects as youth culture, romantic relationships, and friendships. A third theme of Swedish radio is traditional Swedish folk music—characterized by singing accompanied by a violin, guitar, and accordion. Folk music is commonly played on *P1*.

Profanity is somewhat of a regular feature on Swedish radio. Higher-impact words such as *fuck* can sometimes be heard in imported English-language rock or rap music. And both higher-impact and lower-impact profane words can be heard during discussion programs—particularly on educational youth discussion programs focusing on sexual relations.

Television Form in Sweden

Television listings are published widely in the national weekly magazine *SE TV*, as well as in magazine inserts in national newspapers, and by most daily newspapers. Listings include essentially the same information as French television listings.

   Television programs on both public and private channels usually start and end at any of the :5s around the clock, and can run for five, fifteen, thirty, forty, or fifty-five minutes, and so on. On terrestrial television, when a program finishes, usually a host comes on the screen for about sixty seconds to tell viewers about the programs that are coming up later, and the program that immediately follows.

   In Sweden, advertising is not allowed on the two state-operated Swedish Television channels (*SVT 1* and *SVT 2*). On *TV4*, there is usually just one advertising break per thirty minutes of programming. Some programs (news, documentaries, films) are not permitted to have advertising breaks within the programming. Allowing for promos, which are not included in the advertising minutage limits, the actual program length on the SVT channels is about fifty-six minutes per hour, and for private stations is about forty-eight minutes per hour during prime-time evening hours and fifty minutes per hour during other hours.

   As Table 9.2 shows, the SVT channels dominate television listings in Sweden, at a two to one ratio with the one commercial terrestrial channel.

Television Genres in Sweden

In Sweden, most terrestrial television programming on the public channels is oriented toward educational programming, though these channels also carry some entertainment-oriented programming. Educational programming is often in the form of discussion programs and documentaries. For example, on May 29, 2003, a discussion program on *SVT 2* called "The New Sweden: Two Languages Are More Than One Elephant," addressed problems with racism in Sweden. Educational programs air at all hours of the day on *SVT 1* and *SVT 2*. On the commercial broadcaster *TV 4*, most of the programs are entertainment oriented, and many are from the USA.

   In Sweden, the terrestrial television broadcasters do not broadcast twenty-four hours a day. *SVT 1* usually broadcasts from 0600 (6:00 AM) to just after midnight, *SVT 2* sometimes signs on as late as 1725 (5:25 PM) and signs off just after midnight, and *TV 4* usually signs off at 0200 (2:00 AM) in the early morning for a couple hours. There are also some television channels on satellite or cable that sign off the air, usually from 0200 (2:00 AM) until 0600 (6:00 AM). In Sweden, the following general statements can be made about programming across the day on the terrestrial broadcasters: On *SVT 1* and *SVT 2*, there are news programs, children's programs, educational programs (book talks, history discussions, learning about nature, sex education), and documentaries across the early morning and through the afternoon. In the early evenings, there typically are cartoons and game shows. In the evening and late evening, there are dramas and documentaries. On *TV 4*, in the early morning there are children's programs and game shows. In the afternoons there are USA comedies, dramas, and talk shows. In the evenings there are USA dramas, comedies, documentaries, films, and British drama.

   In Sweden, there are at least three distinctive themes of television genres. One distinctive television genre is the "enjoying nature documentary" scheduled across most time slots

TABLE 9.2   Sample Television Program Listings from Sweden, September 29, 2004

SVT 1		SVT 2		TV 4	
TIME		**TIME**		**TIME**	
6:30pm	Richard Scarry's World of Adventure	6:00pm	Current Events	6:25pm	Keno
		6:15	Star Trek Enterprise	6:30	News
6:55	Around the Globe			6:54	Weather
		7:00	Short Film: Lovesick and Tarzan Type	7:05	Dr. Phil
7:00	A Square Meal			8:00	The Dream Pad
7:15	How Lucky Leif Discovered America	7:30	Sex, Room and Kitchen	10:00	News
				10:26	Weather
		7:55	Leunig	11:25	Will and Grace
7:30	News Reporting	8:00	Book Review	11:50	A Publisher's Nightmare
7:50	Radio Aid: The Victoria Fund	8:30	The New Sweden		
8:00	Dirty Dancing	9:00	Current Events		
9:00	American Feature Film	9:15	Sports News		
		9:30	Festival Heroes		
9:40	Trust Daddy	10:30	Special: Film Festival in Cannes		
10:00	He Led Our Politics				
11:00	News Commentary	11:00	Play Room		
		11:30	K Special: Japanese Shapes		
11:05	With Joy of Your Life				

of the broadcast day. This programming can run anywhere from thirty minutes to just under two hours, and sometimes is run as a series. What makes this genre unique is not that the documentary is about nature per se, but about Swedes having fun in and coexisting with the environment. For example, a fishing documentary that aired on *SVT 1* on June 6, 2003, included scenes of about twenty Swedes participating in the following activities: driving their caravans to a lake in Finland; swimming naked in the lake; sitting naked in a sauna floating on the lake; eating a large meal together as a group; partying at night with beer and wine and toasts of schnapps; singing songs inside and outside of their caravans; and fishing.

A second distinctive genre on television in Sweden is the talk/variety/sing-along program. This program often is aired as a one-time program during a holiday season. Usually the program revolves around a host who brings on famous Swedes to chat about what they are doing for the holiday, and what the holiday means to them. The guests typically are politicians, journalists, and artists. Usually the artist performs his or her art. For example, a poet may deliver a poem, or a singer may sing a song. There is a cozy atmosphere created on these programs through the diffused lighting, the familiarity with which people talk to each other, and the lack of a produced feel to the segments. This type of program often ends with all of the participants getting up, dancing, and sometimes singing national songs that are known by almost all Swedes.

A third distinctive television genre is the investigative documentary. These programs usually investigate a perceived failure on the part of the state—Swedish or foreign—to provide a basic living standard for certain human beings in particular circumstances. In the investigative documentary, it is typical for reporters to interview people who have fallen on hard times, and to provide background information on what may have led to a problematic situation. Sample subject areas include: refugees living in Sweden who are not integrated into Swedish society; people with mental problems living in society without proper assistance; Swedish farmers trying to compete with other farmers from EU countries.

In general, violence on television in Sweden is not common. Some violence can be seen in the evening hours on news programs, but usually the camerawork will not focus on a close-up shot of the people who have been hurt. However, one exception is news coverage of war, which often features close-up camera shots of violence. Male and female nudity is fairly common on terrestrial and multichannel television. Typical genres that show nudity include documentaries, movies in which there is a sexual relationship between the characters, and sexual education programs geared toward young adults. Such educational programs typically involve segments on practicing safe sex in which, for example, it is demonstrated how to put a condom on an erect penis. Nudity in this kind of circumstance is quite graphic, though penetration is not shown. Profanity is not common on Swedish television, but can be heard on Swedish television in discussion programs, news programs, and documentaries.

Internet Content in Sweden

In Sweden, web sites do not normally restrict content, regardless of how they are accessed. internet cafés typically provide a start-up page on their computers designed especially for the café. The start-up web pages typically include paid advertising.

MEDIA CONTENT IN THE UK

Newspaper Form in the UK

National newspapers with mostly serious content usually have a broadsheet shape; however, the *Times* and the *Independent* are published in both a broadsheet and a tabloid version. National newspapers with mostly sensational content have a tabloid shape, as do many local newspapers with mostly serious content, such as the *Seaford Gazette*, shown in Figure 9.4. Physically, UK newspaper pages have high quality. They feel thick compared to newspaper pages in other countries, and have very sharp photographs and text.

The proportion of text, advertising, photos, and graphics in newspapers varies according to whether the newspaper is a serious or a sensational newspaper. The serious newspapers—most notably the national broadsheets—are made up mostly of text, but also have significant portions of photographs, advertising, and graphics. A rough estimate would put text at about 60 percent of the newspaper, and put photographs, advertising, and graphics at about the remaining 40 percent of the newspaper. The sensational newspapers—most

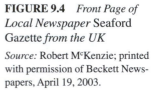

FIGURE 9.4   *Front Page of Local Newspaper* Seaford Gazette *from the UK*

Source: Robert McKenzie; printed with permission of Beckett Newspapers, April 19, 2003.

notably the national tabloids—have more photos, ads, and graphics than text. Advertising occupies a substantial portion of newspapers. In most newspapers, advertising occupies from 20 to 30 percent of the content. Advertising typically does not appear on the front page of tabloids, with the exception of promotions by the newspaper for information and contests inside the newspaper. But the broadsheets often have one advertisement in a strip along the bottom of the front page.

Photographs are omnipresent in UK newspapers. Most photographs in the sensational tabloids are in color, while most photographs in the serious broadsheets are in black and white (except for the front pages of individual sections). Usually, most pages of newspapers in the UK have at least one photograph—frequently headshots of people. Often in the sensational tabloids, photographs are laid over and blended with background graphics. The quality of photos in terms of clarity (pixel resolution) is generally very high—even in local newspapers.

In the UK, graphics and cartoons are not very common across newspapers. Some broadsheets (e.g., the *Guardian*, the *Times*, and the *Daily Telegraph*) print a small box cartoon that offers social commentary on a subject that has contemporary and national relevance. Another distinctive use of a cartoonlike approach is featured in a series in the *Sun* called "Deidre's Photo Casebook," which presents photographs of real people in a cartoon-strip, soap-opera format discussing relationship issues usually involving infidelity.

Newspaper Substance in the UK

In the UK, most broadsheet newspapers—national and regional/local—have three common sections in the following order: current events, sports, and business. The most popular sports coverage includes football (soccer), rugby, cricket, and horse racing—which often has several pages dedicated to it. Other sports that are routinely covered include snooker (a game like billiards), track and field, and tennis. Many broadsheets also have special insert sections (such as the *Guardian*'s "G2," which specializes in public sector job advertisements).

Much of the coverage in the UK broadsheets is about politics. Articles on domestic politics tend to focus on new government policies and government reports. In addition, much of the political coverage is about the UK's political posturing within EU politics, and within world politics in the context of a close political relationship with the USA.

Other sections are common to the broadsheets, but not on a daily basis. These sections include: Culture, Home, Travel, and Special Inserts (mentioned earlier). The Culture section focuses not only on high culture but also on popular culture. The Travel sections are somewhat distinct in that multiple destinations are listed from all over the world, along with a variety of package deals covering various forms of transport and accommodations. Elaborate photos of two or three locations often accompany listings in a Travel section.

The sensational national tabloids in the UK (known also as the London Tabloids, and the "red tops" because of the red banners across the top of them) are some of the most notorious newspapers across the world. The tabloids cover both gossip-type news and serious news, and are known for being extremely sensational in terms of exaggeration, scathing criticism, and sordid details. Articles in tabloids often engender outrage over the conduct of government officials, criminals, and celebrities (especially pop stars and movie stars). Usually the conduct has to do with sex, drinking, or drugs. Frequently, tabloids serialize aspects of a person's life by covering a story for several days in a row on the front pages, and then perhaps revisiting the issue throughout the year and maybe even across several years. Often, articles in tabloids are accompanied by paparazzi photos of famous people seemingly cavorting together in foreign countries.

Stories about violent crimes are somewhat common in newspapers in the UK. Often when violent crimes are covered, stories focus more on the suffering of the victims and families rather than on the alleged crime itself. Stories with nudity and profanity are occasionally published, though not among all newspapers. The *Sun* and the *Daily Star* popularly publish a lot of photos of topless women, including photos of topless celebrities sunbathing on holiday. Both publish a topless "Page 3 Girl" almost every day. Figure 9.5 shows a Page 3 from the March 7, 2003, edition of the *Sun*. In addition to the topless photo, stories on the same page claim that celebrities Gwyneth Paltrow and Sharon Stone are bargain shoppers. In the broadsheets, nudity typically is seen in the context of a nude painting or sculpture on exhibit. Nudity can also be seen in broadsheets in photographs accompanying stories with a medical focus, such as breast cancer.

Both low-impact and high-impact profanity appears with some regularity in the broadsheets—especially the *Guardian*—often in two kinds of circumstances: (1) when a newsworthy figure provides a quote that includes profanity, and (2) when profanity is used in a writer's editorial, such as the following commentary by Rod Liddle in the *Guardian* (May 7, 2003):

FIGURE 9.5 Page 3 of the *Sun* Newspaper from the UK

Source: Robert McKenzie; *Sun* (London), March 7, 2003; www.thesun.co.uk; reprinted by permission, ©NISyndication Limited, London.

I once read a four-word album review of some hopeless band in the NME. It said simply: "You're shit, fuck off." It was, I suppose, a childish and intemperate review. But it had a certain ring to it. (Sect. G2, p. 5)

Profanity does not normally appear in the sensational tabloids. If a quote is printed in the sensational tabloids that contains a profanity, the profane word is replaced with a string of symbols such as &*!* %.

Radio Form in the UK

In the UK, listings for public-service (BBC) radio and for some commercial radio stations are published in most newspapers and in the weekly magazine *Radio Times.* In the UK, radio programs on both commercial and public stations typically begin at exactly the top of the hour or the bottom of the hour. Some programs on the publicly funded BBC radio services begin at :5s on the hour. On BBC radio channels, the start times and end times of program slots can be different from one day to the next. For example, on a Monday a discussion show might begin at 2000 (8:00 PM), but on Tuesday a music show might begin at 2000 (8:00 PM),

FIGURE 9.6   *Sample Radio Program Listings for* Radio1, Radio2, *and* Radio 3 *from* Radio Times *Magazine in the UK*

Source: Radio Times, *March 29–April 4, 2003.*

with a discussion show beginning at 2100 (9:00 PM). Figure 9.6 reproduces a page from the *Radio Times* magazine listing radio programs aired on April 3, 2003, by three of the BBC radio services. Note how detailed the listings are, and how many different start and end times there are for the programs. These radio program listings are very similar to those for public-service radio programs in France, Sweden, and other European countries.

On commercial stations, advertising breaks are frequent. Typically, actual programming varies from eighteen to twenty-two minutes per half hour because of inserted advertising. On big-city commercial stations such as London's *Heart 106.2*, two minutes of ads typically are aired after two songs in a row. There are no ads on BBC channels. BBC radio frequencies are usually pervasive in the selection of accessible radio frequencies in a given area. When scanning through radio frequencies on the FM band, as the radio receiver locks onto the next available frequency, it is about as likely to be a BBC network (either on a local station or a national network station) as it is to be a commercial station.

Pop radio hosts normally keep a brisk pace and witty style to their talk. Often, hosts read listener emails—usually song requests—on the air. On most stations, there are often live conversations with callers lasting two to three minutes per segment. On talk stations, conversations with callers are somewhat slow-paced and can last five to ten minutes.

Radio Formats in the UK

BBC channels are programmed according to the following niche formats: *Radio 1* broadcasts contemporary music, which essentially is pop music but also includes pop songs from the past. *Radio 2* broadcasts a range of music (just about anything other than classical music), as well as light entertainment, documentaries, public-service announcements, and popular culture. For example, on March 31, 2003, there was a documentary called "Live from the Stables," a series on British swing greats from jazz and contemporary pop. *Radio 3* broadcasts classical and jazz music, drama, documentaries, and discussion. Typically, music from composers is featured along with a panel discussion about the music. *Radio 4* essentially broadcasts news and talk; programming includes news and current affairs, contemporary drama, science, arts, religion, natural history, medicine, finance, gardening, and Parliament. *Radio 5 Live* broadcasts news, current affairs, and sports.

Commercial radio is programmed according to moderately narrow niche formats. *Virgin Radio*, one of three national commercial stations, plays pop-rock hits not just from today but also from past eras (e.g., a Britney Spears song is followed by an Elvis Presley song). This is true also for the BBC's *Radio 1* and for regional radio stations that broadcast pop-rock music *Classic FM*, a second national commercial radio station, broadcasts classical music. *talkSPORT* broadcasts sporting events and talk shows focusing on sports.

In the UK, there are at least three distinctive themes in the radio formats. First, most radio—even commercial radio—includes a lot of discussion and analysis. Whether the radio program is about political issues, sports, or a book, a sizable portion of the broadcast involves segments in which the host and panelists discuss and analyze the content. A second distinctive theme is that a music bed often plays underneath news and sometimes underneath discussion. And a third theme is the "overseas documentary"—which is to say that UK radio documentaries often take place on location in foreign countries. For example, on March 31, 2003, a program on *Radio 4*, "The State of Africa," examined wildlife in Africa in a discussion format between the radio host and discussants in Africa.

Profanity is a somewhat regular feature of two areas of programming on radio in the UK. Profane lyrics can be heard in music—particularly contemporary music such as hip-hop (rap)—and profane words are sometimes uttered by talk-show participants. But profanities are not regularly spoken by on-air personalities or hosts.

Television Form in the UK

In the UK, detailed television listings are published by the national magazine *Radio Times*, as well as by most newspapers (see Figure 9.7).

Television programs on both commercial and BBC channels usually start and end at the :15s around the clock—:15, :30, :45 or :00—but can begin at the :05s on the hour, such as :50 or :25. Television program segments vary according to multiples of five-minute increments. Usually when a program finishes, there is a still graphic accompanied by a voiceover that first promotes a program coming up later in the day or the week, and then promotes the show that immediately follows.

There are no ads on BBC channels. On commercial channels, one advertising break is permitted during, and one outside of a thirty-minute program (after a program ends and before another program begins). Some programs—news, documentaries, and children's shows—are not permitted to have advertising breaks within programs. Allowing for promos, which are not included in the advertising minutage limits, the actual program length on the BBC channels is about forty-seven minutes per hour, and for private channels is about forty-one minutes per hour.

Figure 9.7 reproduces a page from the BBC's *Radio Times* magazine listing television programs aired on April 3, 2003 by the three terrestrial noncommercial television channels (*ITV*, *Channel 4*, *Five*). Note how detailed the listings are, how many different start and end times there are for the programs, and how a coded number is provided to allow the audience member to tape a program without having to program the specific day and hours into the recorder. France, Sweden, and other European countries have magazines with very similar formats to list television programs.

Television Genres in the UK

In the UK, much of the television programming, and especially on the BBC channels, is oriented toward teaching the audience something. On commercial channels, programming is mostly entertainment oriented, but programming over the course of several hours often has an educational emphasis. For example, during a three-hour time block on April 1, 2003, *Channel 4* ran three such programs, which were described in *Radio Times* (March 29–April 4, 2003) as follows:

> 1955–2000; a 5-minute program called "Ramallah Daily": "Continuing the daily films about pressures faced by Israelis and Palestinians in the West Bank and Gaza."
>
> 2000–2030; a half-hour program called "The City Gardener": "The cluttered Sheffield home of Darren and Maxine Stansall presents a big challenge to property expert Andrew Winter in the second of a new 11-part makeover series in which he transforms homes that refuse to sell into highly desirable residences. Drastic measures are required to achieve a sale, including the whole family and their dog moving out."
>
> 2000–2100; a half-hour program called "The City Gardener": "In the first of a new ten-part gardening series, horticultural expert Matt James reveals how even the most neglected city

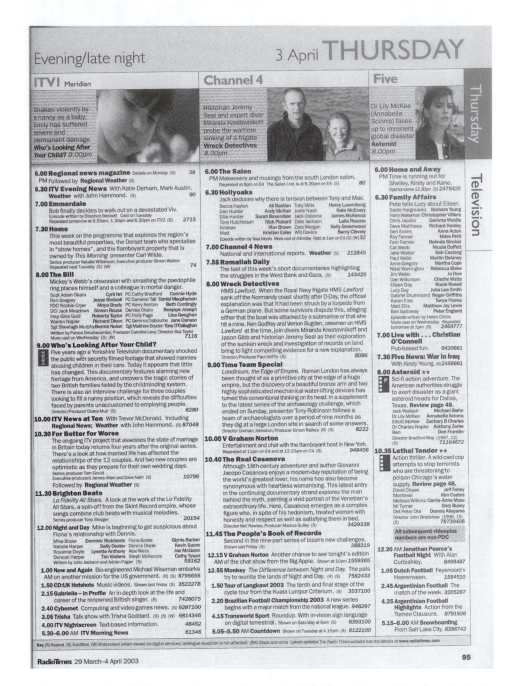

FIGURE 9.7   *Sample Television Program Listings for ITV, Channel 4, and Five from* Radio Times *Magazine in the UK.*

Source: Robert McKenzie; printed with permission by *Radio Times,* March 29–April 4, 2003.

garden can be turned into a lush paradise, beginning with a desolate wasteland in Southampton that careful cultivation soon transforms into a stunning outdoor room."

Terrestrial television channels broadcast programming twenty-four hours a day. Some satellite and cable channels discontinue programming from 0200 (2:00 AM) until 0600 (6:00 AM). In the UK, it is difficult to characterize television genres across channels and time periods of the day because there is a lot of diversity. However, two regular genres in the morning are news programs for adults and various programs for children (such as quiz shows, variety shows, cartoons, and make-believe shows with characters made out of clay, wood, and other materials). In the afternoon, typical genres include children's programs and game shows. In the evening, typical genres include dramas, documentaries, gardening shows, home improvement shows, comedies, and movies (often from the USA).

In the UK, one distinctive television genre is the "detailed documentary," scheduled across most time slots of the broadcast day. The documentary's subject matter on UK television ranges from traditional nature to historical documentary, from travel to ordinary life. Often the documentary chronicles how a person handles a challenge. For example, *Channel 5*'s program, "The Child Who's Older Than Her Mother," was described in *Radio Times* (April 2, 2003) as "A moving documentary about five-year-old Hayley Okines, who was born with progeria—a rare aging disease. By secondary school age her body will be like that of a 90-year-old woman." The detailed documentary usually includes a lot of research and unscripted reality-video clips to tell a story.

A second distinctive television genre is the "intellectual quiz show" exemplified by two shows: "University Challenge" and "Countdown." The intellectual quiz show challenges contestants on detailed knowledge of history, the arts, culture, science, and mathematics, rather than on more trivial subjects such as entertainers. On "Countdown" there is a segment in which the contestants are given a sequence of different numbers as well as a total number. The object is to figure out how the set of numbers can be added, subtracted, divided, or multiplied in any order in 30 seconds to arrive at the total number.

A third distinctive television genre in the UK is "interactive teletext." This genre is a kind of television service in which the viewer can use the television remote control to scroll through hundreds of pages of information containing different categories such as current events (headlines), sports (scores, player trades), financial news (currency rates, stock values), music news (hit records), travel news (airplane arrivals, holiday packages), and weather forecasts. Teletext programming is provided in both digital and analog form by the BBC, *Channel 4*, Sky Television, and *CNN*. The information available on teletext is continuously updated throughout the day. Figures 9.8 and 9.9 show two pages of Ceefax, the BBC's teletext information service. The numbers on the right-hand side of the page indicate additional page numbers that viewers can bring up with the television remote to see each story.

In general, violence on television in the UK is somewhat common. Some violence can be seen in the evening hours on dramas and movies, though it usually is not very graphic. The violence on news programs can be particularly graphic. For example, a violent clash between two groups of people on a news program might include close-up shots that vividly show people being hit with weapons. The close-ups might also show injured or dead people with clearly visible blood stains.

Nudity is commonly broadcast on terrestrial television channels in the context of dramas, movies, and sometimes news programs. Usually, there is some form of nudity every

BBC HEADLINES
SADDAM LOSING GRIP ON IRAQ, PM SAYS 116
People of Iraq "turning towards us"

First US tanks "move across Tigris" 104
Media's hotel "hit in shell attack" 107
US troops will burn in tanks – Iraq 111

Saddam targeted in US bombing raids 106
UK soldiers focus on Basra supplies 112
US pilot safe after plane goes down 114

SMOKING Light-up ban at work sought 119

JOBS Tesco expansion creates 11,000 121

HEDGEHOGS First night of cull fails 124

CATCH UP WITH THE NEWS FOR LONDON 160
News Index 102 Flash 150 Weather 400

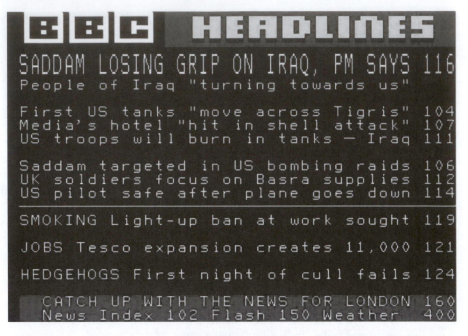

FIGURE 9.8 *Index of Pages on the BBC's Teletext Service,* Ceefax, *from the UK*
Source: Ceefax.

BBC SPORT
SIR ALEX FACES UEFA RAP OVER CLAIMS 304
FOOTBALL Draw remarks lead to probe
Vialli linked to position at Fulham 303
Souness wants to keep striker Sukur 303

CRICKET King turns down Windies job 342
Paceman McGrath confirms tour plans 342

GOLF Monty eyes top 10 Masters spot 487

TENNIS Ivanisevic set for operation 337

BOXING Johnson makes pay cut pledge 381

US MASTERS – CEEFAX SPECIAL SECTION 480
Football 302 Cricket 340 M/Sport 360
Rugby 370 General 380 Racing 660
Golf 330 BBC Sport 358 Tennis 330
MORE NEWS IN REGIONAL SPORT PAGE 390

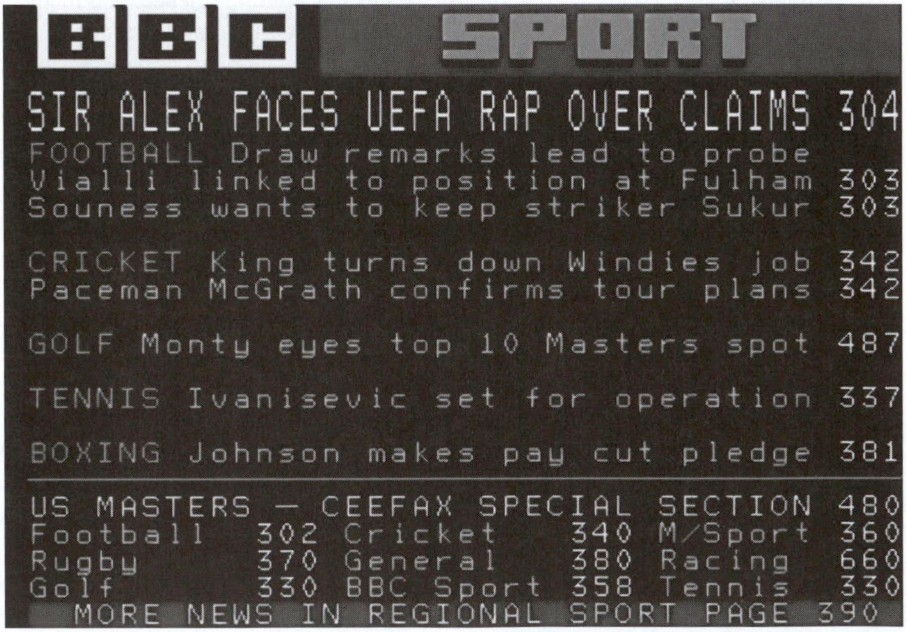

FIGURE 9.9 *Sports Stories on the BBC's Teletext Service,* Ceefax, *from the UK*
Source: Ceefax, BBC.

night. Typically, scenes with nudity are brief, and naked body parts are sometimes partially obscured by other objects within the scene. Female nudity is much more prevalent than male nudity on television in the UK. It is fairly common to hear profanity on television in the UK in the evening. Almost all words—including *fuck*—can be heard on broadcast television in the UK, on both live and taped comedy shows, talk shows, dramas, films, and on certain newscasts reporting on events at which profanity is used. Though profanity is not routine, it generally is not edited out if it is considered to be relevant to the program.

Internet Content in the UK

Start-up web pages are designed especially for internet cafés. These pages usually contain preferred browsers and search engines, as well as advertisements for products and services sold both inside and outside the café. In chain internet cafés, access to adult web sites is often blocked by a filter installed by the café. British Telecomm also blocks access for its dial-up and broadband users to web sites containing pornographic images with potential minors.

MEDIA CONTENT IN THE USA

Newspaper Form in the USA

Most USA newspapers are broadsheets in both form and substance, though some big cities have daily tabloids. *USA Today* is narrower than the *Wall Street Journal* and the *New York Times*, as well as most big-city broadsheets. Ink often rubs off USA newspapers onto the reader's hands. There is great variation in the proportion of text, advertising, photos, and graphics. Generally speaking, the largest proportion of a newspaper is text. Typically, most newspaper text will be in a single font, with emphasis provided by bolding the font or by increasing its pitch in a story headline.

In the USA, the national *USA Today* is considered to be a highly visual newspaper that mimics the form of television in two main respects. One is through the television-like design of the street dispenser used to sell *USA Today* (as depicted in Figure 8.10 in Chapter 8 on Accessibility of Media). The other is through a layout design that presents a lot of color photos and graphics, while keeping text to a minimum in terms of length and level of vocabulary compared to other newspapers. The success of *USA Today* has led other newspapers to become somewhat more visually appealing through greater use of color and graphics.

In the USA, advertising occupies a substantial portion of most newspapers. In the *New York Times,* for example, the proportion of advertising—including classifieds—is about 45 percent of the total space. Advertising typically appears on all pages of newspapers in the USA except the front page; an exception to this convention is *USA Today*, which typically runs one or two smaller ads on the front page. On Sundays, most newspapers become thick and weighty because of extra sections and multiple advertising inserts for retail stores, which fall out from the newspaper as it is handled.

In the USA, photographs and graphics are somewhat common in newspaper stories. In general, photographs accompanying news stories on the front page are in color, and on succeeding pages are in black and white. Photographs in newspapers in the USA—particularly local newspapers—often have a grainy quality, or show double images.

Computer-generated graphics are often used to illustrate stories containing information about finances and technology.

The local newspaper pictured in Figure 9.10 shows a typical broadsheet, as well as the proportions of photographs, graphics, and a common font that is used in the USA.

Cartoon strips are a regular feature in newspapers, especially in big-city and small-town newspapers. Cartoon strips are typically found in sections toward the back of the newspaper. In addition to cartoons, newspapers in the USA typically print one or two political cartoons, usually on an editorial page.

Newspaper Substance in the USA

Most broadsheet newspapers—national and regional/local newspapers—typically feature sections in the following order: Current Events, Feature, Sports, Business, and Classified. The Classified sections of newspapers in the USA usually occupy a substantial portion of the newspaper. Big-city newspapers often have a Metro section, and a special-insert section that runs one day a week—for example, the *New York Times*'s "House&Home" section. In addition, big-city and regional newspapers often contain local sections that typically vary according to the county in which the newspaper is distributed.

In the USA, there is a group of three newspapers known as the "prestige press" because of their impact on stories that are run in smaller newspapers and their impact on the subjects discussed on television talk shows. The *New York Times* is known for publishing editorials that are quoted in local newspapers and discussed on radio and television on

FIGURE 9.10 *Front Page of Local Newspaper* Pocono Record *from the USA*

Source: Robert McKenzie; reprinted with permission by *Pocono Record*, February 3, 2004.

politically oriented talk shows. The *Wall Street Journal* is known for extensively covering business news, including economic policy, investments, money management, and banking. The *Washington Post* is known for investigative stories related to government.

Much of the content in the prestige press involves coverage of (1) events related to national politics based in Washington, DC (wherein the content often breaks down issues into strategies employed by Republicans and Democrats to gain competitive advantages against each other); (2) violent crime that is relevant to the city in which the newspaper is based, but has wider national interest because of circumstances surrounding the crime; and (3) investigations that uncover potential corruption or wrongdoing by public officials or companies.

Big-city tabloids in the USA tend to focus on news stories exhibiting high drama. For example, a New York City tabloid's two main front-page stories were: A fire "hero" who was "hurt" by falling debris; and "outrage" over Janet Jackson's breast being exposed during the Super Bowl (*Daily News*, February 2, 2004).

Regional/local newspapers in the USA typically cover local crime stories and upcoming events. For example, front-page stories for a local Pennsylvania newspaper (*Pocono Record*, February 7, 2004) included: a state teacher's union and the state government reaching agreement on a contract; the updated expense of a highway welcome center; houses being added onto by building a lower level; and a local musical group that is gaining attention.

There are three newspaper sections that are commonly found in most broadsheets in the USA: Current Events; Business, which covers news ranging from stock-market reports to consumer spending data to corporate activity; and Sports. Sports sections tend to focus on the four major seasonal sports in the USA: baseball, "American" football, basketball, and hockey. College and high-school sports also are covered in big-city and regional/local newspapers.

Newspapers routinely include stories about violent crimes. Such crimes are described with detail in regard to whether the violence resulted in injury or death. The sentence here, taken from a story in the *Washington Times*, typifies how violent crimes are described in terms of the end results: "A police standoff ended after nine hours yesterday with a gunman and two other persons dead and four officers wounded" (November 13, 2003, p. A9). However, photos in newspapers in the USA generally do not show close-ups of victims, or vivid bodily harm such as bruising and blood; nor are graphic details about the specifics of the injuries to human body parts described.

The approach to nudity and profanity in newspapers in the USA follows a similar pattern to broadcasting content, which is to say that it is rare to see a photograph of a nude person. However, if a nude person does appear in a photograph in a newspaper, the genitals usually are blurred or blackened. Very rarely, a newspaper story covering an art exhibition might show a woman's breasts. Similarly, profane words typically will be presented by blocking parts of the words using symbols like _ _ _ _ or *%$*#.

Radio Form in the USA

In the USA, radio program listings are not normally published in newspapers. Sometimes newspapers publish the radio station call letters and frequencies that are available in the immediate area. In the USA, radio segments on both commercial and public stations almost always begin and end exactly at either the top of the hour or the bottom of the hour. Except for news, program segments usually last three to four hours. Per half hour, regular programming varies from eighteen to twenty-two minutes because of advertising.

Radio listings are normally printed only in local newspapers. The typical newspaper listing includes radio stations, radio frequencies, and formats, but not radio programs or shows. On radio in the USA, there is a predominance of commercial programming over noncommercial programming, and privately funded programming over government-funded programming. Public broadcasting channels are available in a channel selection but ordinarily are outnumbered by commercial channels by a ratio of around ten to one.

Radio programming in the USA normally includes multiple breaks for advertising—usually prior to the start of, several times during, and again after the program concludes. Advertising breaks typically run for three to four minutes but can run much longer. Prior to the start of a radio program, advertising typically runs five to seven minutes. Advertising minutage usually ranges from eight minutes per half hour to twelve minutes per half hour.

Almost all radio hosts in the USA keep a very brisk pace to their talk. Interchanges on the air with callers are often hurried, with the on-air personality guiding the caller to "get to the point." However, as Kate Bachman points out in an article in *Mediaweek*, the "live deejay" on many music stations is no longer a mainstay because of "voice tracking," a practice in which the on-air host prerecords talk segments on computer that are then inserted between songs during "real-time" programming at one or more radio stations.

Radio Formats in the USA

Radio content in the USA is mostly determined by a radio station's niche format. Typical formats include Contemporary Hit Radio, Hot Country, and News/Talk. Radio formats tend to be narrowly defined. For example, a station with a Hot Country format will normally broadcast songs from contemporary artists such as Faith Hill or Alan Jackson, but not usually songs of artists from twenty or thirty years ago such as Johnny Cash or Conway Twitty. In most regions of the USA, the selection of radio formats available will include "top 40," adult contemporary, classic rock, country, talk, and classical or jazz (usually aired by a public broadcasting station).

Much of the programming on radio is locally originated, but some programming originates from networks, syndicates, and from other radio stations that are part of the same ownership group. Usually, the only programming that originates from a network and is aired on a local station is national news. The programming that originates from a sister station or a syndicate is typically a music show or a talk show with a well-known and popular on-air personality. However, when local stations broadcast syndicated or sister-station radio programs, there is usually an attempt to mix that content with some local content (for example, weather, commercials, and news) to give the impression that the programming is coming from the local station.

There are at least three distinctive themes in USA radio formats: (1) the "Contemporary Hit Radio" (CHR) formula, which is structured according to what music is selling the best ("hit" songs are played multiple times at set intervals throughout the day); (2) Country, which ranges from older, "twangy" country music to newer country music with somewhat of a rock-and-roll sound; and (3) Talk, which is accessible mostly on the AM band, and is typified by a right-wing political orientation. On talk radio programs, the host and callers typically advocate policies and positions using a bombastic delivery style. Callers are often told before they speak that they have "30 seconds" to respond, or that they must be brief in their response. Often, the host interrupts a caller's sentences.

Profanity is generally not spoken on broadcast radio. Some words that are considered to be less profane—for example, *ass* and *shit*—can be heard in music played on radio in the USA, but usually only if the words are buried by music. Otherwise, one of three methods is employed to prevent profanities from being aired. One method involves airing songs that have alternate "clean" lyrics designed just for radio play. Another method is when, if a conversation takes place live on the air, the radio station runs a "delay," which gives the host or another staff member a few seconds to press a button that can delete profane words uttered by guests before the words are broadcast. Another method is when both songs and on-air conversations with potential profanities are muted or replaced with a bleep or another sound effect. For example, on December 21, 2004, radio station KKLZ in Las Vegas, Nevada, ran a contest in which listeners were asked to call in and identify the year of a song that was played. One caller correctly guessed that the year for the song was 1976. The conversation between the host and the caller was recorded off the air while the song was being aired, and then played back on the air, after the song had ended. The conversation consisted of the host telling the caller that he was correct, and that he had therefore won free tickets to a concert. The caller then exclaimed "holy sh . . . (bleep) . . . t." Thus, the beginning of the word, "sh," could clearly be heard, as well as the ending of the word, "t." But the middle of the word, "i," was only partially muted by the bleep. Immediately afterwards, the caller remarked, "I mean, holy cow"—while the on-air host laughed. On-air hosts at stations—particularly those with edgier formats—often/avoid directly saying a profanity by using code word or words that sound similar to a specific profane word. An example is using the word *friggin* instead of *fucking*. This technique is a way for the on-air personality to follow the letter of the law, but at the same time to violate the spirit of the law. As I (2002) argue in "Contradictions in U.S. Law on Obscenity and Indecency in Broadcasting: A Bleeping Critique," such methods of partially disguising profanity only serve to invite radio listeners to solve a puzzle presented by a code word or a piece of a missing word or phrase. In such a rhetorical exercise, listeners ironically become more mentally involved in the programming—and therefore are more vividly exposed to meanings of the pseudo-masked profanities.

Television Form in the USA

Television program listings are published in most newspapers and in the weekly magazine *TV Guide*. Television programs on both commercial and public stations almost always begin and end exactly at either the top of the hour or the bottom of the hour. Programs segments usually last half an hour or one hour. However, in 2004, networks were experimenting with running some prime-time shows one minute past the hour to keep the audience from changing channels to another television show. Normally, the actual time length of a television program varies from eighteen to twenty-two minutes per half hour because of inserted advertising. As Table 9.3 shows, the typical listing of television channels and programs available shows a predominance of commercial programming over noncommercial programming, and privately funded programming over government-funded programming. Public broadcasting channels are available in the average channel selection but ordinarily are outnumbered by commercial channels by a ratio of around ten to one.

TABLE 9.3 Sample Television Program Listings from the USA, October 28, 2004

TIME	ABC	TIME	NBC	TIME	CBS	TIME	FOX	TIME	PAX	TIME	PBS
6:00pm	Action News	6:00pm	News at Six	6:00pm	News 22 at Six	6:00pm	King of Queens	6:00pm	Pyramid	6:00pm	News Hour with Jim Lehrer
6:30	ABC World News	6:30	NBC Nightly News	6:30	CBS Evening News	6:30	Everybody Loves Raymond	6:30	Shop 'til You Drop		
7:00	Jeopardy	7:00	Wheel of Fortune	7:00	Seinfeld	7:00	King of Queens	7:00	Newswatch	7:00	Nightly Business Tempo
7:30	Wheel of Fortune	7:30	Jeopardy	7:30	Entertainment Tonight	7:30	Everybody Loves Raymond	7:30	Family Feud	7:30	The New This
8:00	Extreme Makeover	8:00	Joey	8:00	Survivor: Vanuatu	8:00	King of Queens	8:00	On the Cover	8:00	Old House
		8:30	Will & Grace			8:30	Everybody Loves Raymond	8:30	Balderdash		
9:00	Life As We Know It	9:00	Apprentice: Part 2	9:00	CSI: Crime Scene Investigation	9:00	Tru Calling	9:00	Cold Turkey	9:00	Pennsylvania's Historic Firehouses
10:00	Prime-Time Live	10:00	ER	10:00	Without a Trace	10:00	Special: TV's Funniest Game-Show Moments	10:00	Diagnosis Murder	10:00	Shroud for a Night Tingle
11:05	Jimmy Kimmel Live!	11:35	The Tonight Show with Jay Leno								
		12:35	Late Night with Conan O'Brien								

Source: Robert McKenzie.

Television programming normally includes multiple breaks for advertising. Usually there is an advertising break prior to the start of a program, then about ten minutes and again about twenty minutes into the program, and again after the program concludes. Advertising breaks are typically three to four minutes per break. Advertising minutage per half hour usually ranges from eight to twelve minutes per half hour, though infomercials consist entirely of advertising. The multiple advertising breaks as well as the length of the breaks on both television and radio put a squeeze on the regular programming. In other words, regular programming often sounds and looks shortened and rushed because it must make way for advertising. Similarly, during the advertising segments, typically there are quick cuts from one sound to another and/or from one camera shot to another, while viewers are urged to hurry "before it's too late" or "while the offer is still valid," in regard to making a purchase.

Television Genres in the USA

The vast majority of television programming is commercial and entertainment oriented, starting with lower-number cable and satellite channels that tend to be accessed first as viewers begin to surf through programs. Cultural-oriented and information-oriented programs tend to be found on one channel between ten and twenty carrying a PBS-member station, and then not again until upper channels in the thirties and higher. Almost all television channels broadcast programming twenty-four hours a day. Certain genres typically are scheduled during portions of the broadcast day. From 1900 (7:00 PM) to 2100 (9:00 AM), network affiliates usually carry network programming, which typically involves a two-hour news program presented by multiple anchors. These news programs are presented in a less formal manner than more serious news programs in the evening. Hosts typically converse with each other and make light jokes in between presentation of the news. From late morning up until noon and again in the afternoon, typical television genres include soap operas, game shows, and talk shows. Local and network news typically air in the early evening. During the mid- to late evening, typical program genres include comedies, dramas, reality programs, and news magazines. Standard late-night programs are comedy-based talk/variety shows. During overnight hours, typical program genres include infomercials and reruns of sitcoms and dramas.

One distinctive television genre in the USA commonly broadcast in the evenings is the formulaic sitcom. Usually taking place in an upper-middle-class household, the set is designed in such a way as to represent a spotless household with nothing out of place. Often the plot involves a central problem presented at the beginning of the show, which leads the cast to having humorous moments up to the end of the show when the problem is solved in a tidy way.

A second distinctive television genre is the televangelist sermon, broadcast mostly in the evenings and on Sundays. Programs usually involve a male or female preacher reading scripture and telling stories with a moral ending to an auditorium packed with worshipers. Often the studio and television audience is asked to pray during the program and to donate money to the religious organization.

A third distinctive genre is the infomercial, usually seen from 0200 (2:00 AM) to 1200 (noon) any day. Infomercials are especially common on weekend mornings. An infomercial is usually a half-hour program during which a product or service is sold by one or two hosts demonstrating the product in front of a studio audience. Various types of products are sold during infomercials, including household cleaners, food-related appliances and gadgets, exercise equipment, weight-loss treatments, and get-rich-quick schemes. Infomercials typically incorporate multiple opportunities during the program for the product or service to be purchased outright, or in installments, or with financing.

Violence on television in the USA is a common theme. Violent programming can be seen at most hours of the day. Dramas, cartoons, and movies often have various levels of violence ranging from gun shoot-outs to fistfights. News programs also regularly cover violence. Promotional trailers for prime-time dramas regularly show someone pointing a gun in a moment of suspense. However, across all genres in which violence is part of the content, rarely does the program show blood or injured body parts in graphic, close-up camera shots.

In the USA, nudity is a regular theme usually on premium cable and satellite television channels only. On terrestrial broadcast channels, nudity is rarely seen. Occasionally, a medical or scientific documentary will provide a quick glimpse of a woman's breast or buttocks, or a man's buttocks. More typically, when a program's plot involves a scene with nudity, camera angles show the character in such a way that foreground objects in the scene (for example, a chair) obscure the character's genitals from being fully seen by the viewer.

Nudity on a television program outside of a medical or scientific context generally causes widespread uproar in the USA. Such was the case when Justin Timberlake pulled down part of Janet Jackson's top, exposing one of her breasts during a half-time show of the national football championship game (the Super Bowl) broadcast by the CBS network, a division of the Viacom global media conglomerate. The next day, the chairman of the FCC announced that he was ordering an immediate investigation into the incident. A few days later, the FCC reported that it had received over 200,000 complaints about the incident from television viewers (AP story, *Pocono Record*, February 7, 2004). About six months later, CBS affiliate stations that broadcast the segment were fined $27,500 each (totaling $550,000) by the FCC. Similarly, profanity is not regularly seen or heard on terrestrial television in the USA. If a character utters a profanity during the taping of a show, usually the sound of the profanity gets muted or bleeped out in the postproduction process before the show is broadcast.

Internet Content in the USA

Internet content in the USA is rarely restricted because most people access the internet where they reside. If internet content is restricted in the USA, it is mainly that of adult web sites. Parents, businesses, and some internet cafés employ filters to restrict access to such sites. Because the internet is frequently accessed in the home, most start-up web pages are selected by the main person using the computer, and typically consist of portal home pages, email sites, or personal home pages.

MEDIA CONTENT IN MÉXICO

Newspaper Form in México

In México, newspapers are a fairly even mix of broadsheets and tabloids in terms of size. Though there are some sensational national newspapers, most newspapers are serious in substance. A distinctive feature of newspapers in México is that there are so many of them—nationals, regionals, and locals—most of which have been founded or reconstituted since the 1990s. Several newspapers in México have a national brand but publish different regional news depending on the state where the newspaper is distributed. Examples include *Diario* (newspaper), *Milenio*, and *El Sol* (the *Sun*).

There is great variation in the proportion of text, advertising, photos, and graphics in newspapers. Generally speaking, the largest proportion is text, though more so for the broadsheets than the tabloids. Sometimes, headlines or words in headlines are emphasized with an upside-down exclamation point before the words and a right-side-up exclamation point after the words, just as in the Spanish language. The proportion of advertising varies tremendously, both in terms of private-sector versus government (paid insertion) and advertising. In top-circulating newspapers such as *El Universal* (*The Universal*) and *La Prensa* (*The Press*), advertising is mostly from the private sector, and typically occupies from 35 to 40 percent of the space. In lesser-circulating national newspapers and most regional (state) newspapers, government advertising versus private-sector advertising is roughly equal, and typically occupies from 10 to 20 percent of the newspaper. Advertising can appear on any newspaper pages.

Photographs are fairly common in newspaper stories. In general, photographs accompanying news stories on the front page are in color, whereas about half of the photographs on succeeding pages are in black and white. Graphics are not very common to most newspapers, but political cartoons are a regular feature in many newspapers. Political cartoons can be found not only on editorial pages but also on other pages. One particular regional newspaper, *La Política* (see Figure 9.11), fills its pages with satirical cartoons to report information. The cartoon in the upper-left corner, showing a woman on crutches who is missing her legs, depicts a Housing minister who was fired but vows to return to government.

Newspaper Substance in México

In México, many broadsheet newspapers feature five sections in the following order: Current Events, Culture and/or Society, Finance, Sports, and Classifieds. The nationals usually have a Metro section, and a special-insert section that runs one day a week—for example, *El Universal's* Destinations (Travel) section. State newspapers often contain local sections that vary according to the region in which the newspaper is distributed. The four big sports that are covered are football (soccer), bullfighting, baseball, and—increasingly—American football.

Most newspapers in México provide heavy coverage of politics, current events, the economy (often related to economic relationships with the USA), religion, and sports. The political coverage focuses not only on legislation and policy announcements—considered to be standard news events in most countries—but also on speeches by political officials as news events in and of themselves. Both the national tabloids and broadsheets focus on allegations of corruption, government policies, political-party activities, crimes, and sports. The two main differences are that broadsheets offer more factual reporting, whereas the tabloids often sensationalize their reporting; also, the tabloids focus more on crime or alleged criminal activity than the broadsheets. State newspapers focus on politics, crimes, and developments in México's infrastructure.

Newspaper content in México routinely includes stories about crimes, most of which involve allegations of government corruption, or robberies related to illegal drug trafficking. Such crime stories are often described in graphic detail. For example, in *El Universal*, a

FIGURE 9.11   *Regional Newspaper* La Politica *from México*

Source: Robert McKenzie; printed with permission from Consejera Editorial Ivonne Gutiérrez Carlin, *La Politica,* December 4, 2003.

front-page story about two police agents who were "executed" contained the following sentence: "Inhabitants of the community of San Juan Ixtayopan lynched and burned two intelligence agents of the Preventive Federal Police (PFP) and brutally struck another, which placed her in the hospital" (December 2, 2004). In addition, photos in Mexican newspapers—usually the tabloids—are known to show graphic details of victims of violence. Such photos often include a clear view of a victim who has been severely injured or killed, with disfigurement and blood clearly visible. For example, on the back page of the November 16, 2004, *La Prensa*, five photos in color accompanied a story on the robbery of a restaurant allegedly committed by three men, one of whom was shot and killed by the police during the robbery (see Figure 9.12). The photos show guns used in the heist, the car windshield that was shot out, and one of the robbers lying on the ground in a clearly visible pool of bright red blood.

In México, newspaper content does not normally include nudity or profanity. One exception is in news coverage of art, which will regularly include photographs of male and female genitals. If a profane word is covered in a newspaper story, almost always portions of the word are blocked out using symbols such as **** or something like *%$#.

Radio Form in México

Radio listings are normally printed in local newspapers, but not in many other publications, including national newspapers. The typical newspaper listing includes radio stations, radio

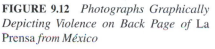

FIGURE 9.12   *Photographs Graphically Depicting Violence on Back Page of* La Prensa *from México*

Source: Robert McKenzie; printed with permission by *La Prensa,* November 16, 2004.

frequencies, and formats, but not radio programs or shows. Radio segments on both commercial and public stations almost always begin and end exactly at either the top of or the bottom of the hour. Except for news, program segments usually last three to four hours. Per half hour, regular programming varies from eighteen to twenty-two minutes because of advertising. There is a predominance of commercial programming over noncommercial programming, and privately funded programming over government-funded programming in México. Public broadcasting channels are available in a channel selection but ordinarily are outnumbered by commercial channels by a ratio of about ten to one.

Radio programming in México normally includes multiple breaks for advertising. Usually there is an advertising break prior to the start of a program, again anywhere from five to ten minutes and then eighteen to twenty-two minutes into the program, and again after the program concludes. Within programming, advertising breaks typically run one and a half minutes because of minutage regulations. Prior to the start of a radio program, advertising typically runs five to seven minutes. Advertising minutage per half hour usually ranges from eight to ten minutes.

On pop-music stations, hosts often act out comedy skits involving outrageous pranks. For example, a skit might involve an on-air host calling a mother and telling her that her daughter was seen drunk at a party. While the host is describing the incident, loud laughter from the studio typically is heard by listeners. The mother might respond by being upset or embarrassed, after which the host will eventually reveal that the information is false. On talk stations, interchanges with callers are somewhat extended.

Radio Formats in México

Radio content in México is mostly determined by a radio station's niche format. The two most common formats are Contemporary Music and Regional; others include Pop Music, Rock en Espanól, News and Sports, Tropical (salsa, merengue, cumbias), Cultural (dance, art, painting, politics), University Radio (diversified programming), Religion, and Discussion. In most regions of México, the selection of radio formats available will include a few ranchero stations, a rock station, and a discussion station.

In México, there are at least two distinctive radio formats. One is the popular regional format, which includes mariachi, ranchera, banda, and norteña music. Mariachi music typically consists of four or five men singing and playing acoustic guitars, violins, and trumpets. Ranchera music—also called cowboy music—originates in country towns and usually consists of guitars, horns, and vocals. Norteña music has elements of waltz, polka, and country music. Two defining features of norteña music are the accordion and the lyrics that often tell stories about the "underworld"—for example, stories involving drug traffickers, famous criminals, or undocumented immigrants crossing the border. Banda music is characterized by percussion instruments and large brass ensembles—mainly trumpets, trombones, and tubas. A second distinctive format is community radio, found mainly in the south of México among economically poorer, mainly indigenous populations. Community radio typically consists of local music and discussion programs in indigenous languages. Often, community radio is politically oriented and agitates for greater political freedoms or even secession from the Mexican government. Community radio operates using low-power transmitters or even just a pair of loudspeakers placed outdoors in a public area where people congregate. Though most community radio broadcasts technically are illegal, the government tends to overlook their operations.

The IMER radio stations in México—those funded by the federal government (discussed in Chapter 7)—have individual formats that collectively present tremendous variety. Though the stations are government funded, some IMER stations are primarily public-service oriented whereas others are geared to popular tastes. Below, consider the web site descriptions for two IMER radio stations, which demonstrate just how different one IMER station can be from another.

XEQK 1350 AM "Radio of the Citizens"

To promote democratic culture through citizen participation exerting freedom of expression and the right to information. The station proposes and makes program contents innovating formats of communication that stimulate knowledge, analysis and solutions of the subjects of public interest, as well as reflects the diversity of sectors of Mexican society, allowing informative plurality.

XHOF 105.7 FM "Reactor 105"

Reactor 105 programming is essentially musical and is the only station of México City that programs exclusively rock and alternative rock in English and Spanish. The rock is the musical expression of the youth culture of the great cities, and the alternative rock proposes structures and sounds different from the commercial tendencies and limited promotion campaigns. Reactor 105 is the new option for the young public of México City who always looks for the newest and provocative alternative rock in Spanish and English.

Profanity is generally not spoken on broadcast radio. Normally, profanities in songs played on Mexican radio are muted or replaced with a bleep, a sound effect, or different lyrics designed just for radio play. The lack of profanity is mainly the result of programmers deciding not to air it, since profanity on radio is not specifically prohibited by regulation in México.

Television Form in México

Television program listings are published in some newspapers and in the weekly magazines *Tele Guia* (*TV Guide*) and *Mi Guia* (*My Guide*). Most television programs on both commercial and public stations begin and end exactly at either the top of the hour or the bottom of the hour, but there are also many programs that begin at :15 and :45 on the hour. Program segments that begin at the top of the hour or the bottom of the hour usually last thirty minutes or one hour. Program segments that begin at :15 or :45 on the hour usually last fifteen minutes. As Table 9.4 shows, the typical listing of television channels and programs available shows a predominance of commercial programming over noncommercial programming, privately funded programming over government-funded programming, and a lot of programming from the USA. Public broadcasting channels are usually available in the average channel selection but ordinarily are outnumbered by commercial channels by a ratio of around ten to one.

Television programming in México normally includes multiple breaks for advertising, usually before, during, and after the program. Advertising breaks are typically three to four minutes long. Advertising minutage per half hour varies, depending on the category of programming. Those specialty programs such as news or telenovelas (soap operas) have advertising minutage that ranges from one and a half to three minutes per half hour, while other programming—particularly during evening hours—can range from nine to ten minutes per half hour (see Chapter 6 on Regulation). Television programming in México during evening hours is condensed to accommodate advertising, which results in a fast-paced feel to the programming.

Television Genres in México

The majority of television programming is commercial and entertainment oriented, and is found on the lower-number cable and satellite channels that tend to be accessed first as viewers begin to surf through programs. Cultural and information-oriented programs tend to be found on the upper channels reached secondarily as viewers surf through programs. However, cultural and educational documentaries and discussion programs can be seen with some frequency on entertainment-oriented channels as well. Most terrestrial television channels sign off some time after midnight and resume programming at 0500 (5:00 AM). Certain genres of television programs are typically scheduled during portions of the broadcast day. In the mornings, programming is typified by news/talk programs similar to the morning news/talk programs in the USA, as well as documentaries, and lots of cartoons (mainly from the USA). From late morning up until noon and again in the afternoon, typical television genres include cartoons, talk shows, entertainment news, and lots of telenovelas. In the evenings, films, dramatic series, comedies, music videos, network news, and lots of telenovelas dominate the programming.

One distinctive television genre is the Mexican version of the soap opera, known as the *telenovela*. Telenovelas are on several channels every day, at almost all times of the day; as

TABLE 9.4   Sample Television Listings from México, December 16, 2003

TIME	CANAL 2	CANAL 4	CANAL 5	CANAL 7	CANAL 9	CANAL 13
6:00pm	Life TV	Paradise	The Wild Thorn-Berries Cartoon		The Ear	Opening the Window
6:30			Jimmy Neutron-Boy Genius Cartoon			
7:00	Clap! The Place of Your Dreams	Dr. Quinn	Malcolm in the Middle			Watch Out for the 2 Boys in the City
7:30			Dragon Ball Z Cartoon	Oh Boy!		
8:00	The Wedding Veil of the Girlfriend	Law And Order	El Chavo Cartoon	The Simpsons	First Impact	The Daughter of the Gardener
8:30						
9:00	Mariana of the Night	New Vision	Shock Cinema Presents: Robin Hood Prince of Thieves	Made at 7	ER: Emergency Room	Look of a Woman
10:00	Top of the Hour	The Bathroom		Seventh Rhyme	Spectacular	Nightly News
11:00	Singing to the Virgin of Guadalupe	Golf	Taken Freedom			Commentary: The Protagonist
12:00am	Mass in Honor of the Virgin of Guadalupe and San Diego		Jackass	Opening of Mexican Golf	Special of R. T. C.	Singing to the Virgin of Guadalupe

Source: Heather Metz.

already discussed, the programming on two of the national channels is oriented around telenovelas (see Figure 9.4). A telenovela usually runs for about six months and then it is finished. Actors from one telenovela then often move on to play different roles on other telenovelas. A telenovela's plot often centers on a love story between two people who face conflicts because the lovers come from different social classes. Usually, the telenovela has a happy resolution in which the two lovers get together, presumably for life. Often, religious images and practices permeate telenovela scenes in the form of priests, praying, churches, crucifix jewelry, and household decorations. And the "bad guy" is often a ranch owner who wears black.

A second distinctive television genre in México is the "parody comedy," seen mostly in the evenings. This is a style of humor that cuts across a lot of television comedies, in which all aspects of acting are exaggerated to achieve laughter from the audience. In a Mexican parody, comedy, clothes, hair, and faces can be outrageous in color and presentation, voices can be unnaturally high, and reactions can be overly emotional. Actors in parody comedies can have purple hair, oversized ears, large painted freckles, big glasses, painfully squeaky voices, honking laughter, and so on. Examples of parody comedies include *El Chavo Del 8* (*The Boy in Apartment Number 8*), *La Parodia* (*Parody*), and *Borzo*. Often, but not always, parody comedies poke fun at politicians and celebrities. A plausible scene in a parody comedy involves a politician who sits at a bar and is portrayed as a big alcohol drinker, then goes home to sleep, and then dreams of his or her political opponent in a terrifying way.

A third distinctive television genre in México is the political speech. Politicians from all levels of government—national, state, local—frequently deliver political speeches. Typically, a politician organizes a press conference and stands in front of a microphone with colleagues at his or her side. Television stations often preempt regularly scheduled programming to carry the politician's whole speech, or at least a major portion.

Violence on television in México is a fairly common theme at most hours of the day, mostly because of imported USA programs that contain violence. Dramas, cartoons, and movies on television often have varying levels of violence ranging from gun shoot-outs to fistfights. News programs also regularly cover violence, and sometimes show blood, injured body parts, or a deceased person in fairly close-up camera shots.

In México, nudity is not normally seen on terrestrial broadcast channels. Occasionally, a medical or scientific documentary will show a woman's breasts and buttocks, or a man's buttocks. When the plot of a program involves a scene with nudity—for example, a situation in which two people make love—camera angles do not show the character's genitals. However, topless females can be seen occasionally on basic cable and satellite channels. Profanity is not regularly seen or heard on television. Some profanity can be seen on regular cable channels or on premium cable and satellite channels, but on terrestrial television profanity is generally bleeped out or muted during the postproduction process.

Internet Content in México

Internet content in México is not normally restricted. Internet cafés will sometimes restrict the content of adult web sites. In México, start-up web pages are typically in Spanish and consist of portal home pages, email sites, or personal home pages.

MEDIA CONTENT IN CHINA

Newspaper Form in China

In China, almost all national newspapers are broadsheets, such as *Renmin Ribao* (*People's Daily*), *Zhongguo Qingnian Bao* (*China Youth Daily*), and *Guangming Ribao* (*Guangming Daily*). However, the most distributed national newspaper, *Cankao Xiaoxi* (*Reference Information*), is a tabloid. A distinctive feature of newspapers in China is that they all must run front-page lead stories on Communist Party or government-related information and officials.

There is tremendous variation in the proportion of text, advertising, photographs, and graphics in newspapers. Generally, the largest proportion is text. Headings are typically larger and are emphasized using bold text to attract the reader to key stories. Generally, headings follow the Western style with Chinese characters (*han zi*) arranged from left to right across the page, but the pictograph format of Chinese writing allows headings to follow the more traditional style of top to bottom.

The use of color in newspapers differs across newspapers. For example, the national broadsheet *Beijing Qingnian Bao (Beijing Youth Daily)* is highly visual and uses bright colors (lots of red and blue) throughout the body of the publications. Often, a token color photograph of a key government official is placed on the front page of a newspaper to comply with rules stipulating that lead stories focus on government information. As an opposite example, *Cankao Xiaoxi* uses no color, instead publishing small black-and-white photographs throughout the publication.

Advertising occupies an increasing portion—usually from 30 to 40 percent—in Chinese newspapers because of reductions in government funding as well as increased production costs. Typically, advertising appears on the majority of newspaper pages in China, but varies considerably across the vast number of publications. Some newspapers have large color advertisements on the front page, with the majority having at least one smaller front-page advertisement. A distinctive feature of advertisements in *Cankao Xiaoxi* is a strip of small, single-column advertisements running from top to bottom along the middle fold of each of the internal pages of the newspaper, which has the effect of hiding half of the advertisements, unless the pages are pulled apart.

Photographs generally dominate the front, and the majority of subsequent, pages of both broadsheet and tabloid newspapers. Photographs accompanying news stories on the front page are generally in color, but do vary with a mix of color and black and white in tabloid newspapers. Photographs generally are small and of relatively poor quality. Graphics are less common in mainstream national and city newspapers; the exceptions are economic newspapers, which use computer-generated graphics to illustrate financial trends.

The newspaper pictured in Figure 9.13 shows a typical broadsheet in China, as well as portions of photographs, graphics, and the style of font and headings already described.

In China, comic strips are rarely seen in newspapers. However, political cartoons are sometimes used to comment on current international events. For example, *Cankao Xiaoxi* printed a cartoon of USA President George W. Bush as a commentary on the USA's military action in Iraq in 2003 (December 18, 2003, p. 3). In the cartoon, Bush is pictured as a chef preparing food, but refusing orders from those countries that opposed the USA's military action.

Newspaper Substance in China

In China, most broadsheet newspapers—both national and local—are organized into two sections. One section features daily news relating to Chinese politics, economics and finance, culture and society, and international issues. The other section features health advice, book excerpts, television programming, movie times and venues, personality profiles, lifestyle and historical/tradition features, weather, and the popular sport section—which tends to focus on soccer (football), tennis, table tennis, Formula 1 racing, and NBA

FIGURE 9.13 *Front Page of* Shanghai Evening Post *January 7, 2004 from China.*

Source: Ian Weber.

basketball (in the USA). Tabloid newspapers typically have four sections: daily news (violent crimes, urban life, and international news), sports, and editorial; economic news, food, and health; entertainment news, cultural issues, and sports and historical places, individual personalities, housing, and consumer information.

The commercialization of the media has resulted in a number of categories of newspapers that determine the stories. Chinese define one main category as "Party newspapers" (*Dang Bao*). For example, *Renmin Ribao, Beijing Ribao (Beijing Daily)*, and *Jingji Ribao (Economic Daily)* are broadsheets that focus specifically on government policies, leaders, and political issues. A second category is mainstream broadsheets such as *Beijing Qingnian Bao* and Shanghai's *Xinmin Wanbao (Xinmin Evening News)*, which have a more commercial orientation focusing on urban lifestyle and social and cultural issues, rather than having an exclusively political focus. A third category is city-based tabloid newspapers such as *Xin Jing Bao (New Beijing Paper), Huaxia Shibao (China Times)*, and *Jinghua*

Shibao (Beijing Times). These newspapers usually report on gritty aspects of urban lifestyle in China such as violent crimes and celebrity scandals. For example, *Xin Jing Bao* featured the heading "Feng Kuang Nan Zi Hui Dao Kan Si San Nu Zi" (Crazy man kills three women with knife). The story reported:

> "Help, help, my sister was killed!" a woman shouted for help in the Gong Ti Bei Li residency block in Dong Cheng District on 03:30/3:30am yesterday. A man cruelly killed his girlfriend and the other two women. He was caught by policemen and guards when escaping. (December 18, 2003, p. A11)

However, the government has attempted to control the content of such racy publications because they have become more popular than Party newspapers. The State Press and Public Administration (SPPA) advises offending newspapers of possible suspension of publishing licenses for printing sensationalist stories and for disseminating information deemed to have an unhealthy impact on readers.

Most city tabloid newspapers feature fairly comprehensive coverage of international news issues. Newspapers generally focus on issues in countries that relate to China geographically (e.g., Japan), economically, politically (e.g., the USA), and globally in terms of national security.

Newspapers in China do not publish nudity or profanity of any kind. These subjects are considered taboo by the government because it believes such influences corrupt people, especially youth, and undermine the march toward a socialist spiritual civilization.

Radio Form in China

In China, radio programs usually begin at the top or the bottom of the hour. A number of programs start at five minutes or quarter after the hour. National radio program schedules are strictly controlled with little flexibility for change. For example, China Central Radio posts its programming schedule at the start of each year on its web site. Programming is delivered in two formats: weekday and weekend. However, on major holidays such as National Day, radio stations replace regular programming with patriotic programs that promote nationalistic spirit among the population.

Radio programming in China typically includes advertising at the start and end of programs, with some short ad breaks in between programs. Advertising breaks run from four to five minutes in length. However, advertising minutage restricts the combined length of these breaks to nine to twelve minutes per hour, depending on the time of broadcast. Advertising has become a common feature in radio programming. However, there are no purely commercial stations.

Radio listings are also published in national daily newspapers and in specific weekly broadcast publications. For example, the *Shanghai Guangbo Dianshi Zhoukan (Shanghai Radio and TV Weekly)* publishes programming schedules, listing the radio channel, its frequency, and program times. These publications also profile programs and celebrity events. *Shanghai Guangbo Dianshi Zhoukan* published a two-page color center spread on a famous Shanghai on-air host's marriage. The story featured photographs of the couple at various stages of their lives (January 12–18, 2004, pp. A1, 8–9).

Radio Formats in China

Radio content in China is mostly a mix of moderatly defined niche formats. Those radio stations in larger city markets such as Beijing, Shanghai, and Guangzhou have niche formats including Top 40, Pop, or Classical. Most radio programming in China falls under entertainment (music and sports), education (children and English language), and information (news, traffic reports, and talk shows).

Almost all the programming on radio originates locally. More recently, programming is distributed to radio stations from the network of Chinese radio, television, and film companies that produces government-approved programming for syndication throughout China's radio stations. This content supplements radio station's localized talk shows, weather, commercials, Chinese music, and national news drawn from the government flagship information source, Xinhua News Agency.

In China, there are at least three distinct radio formats. One distinctive format is Asian pop music, which is defined by the popularity of Canto-pop (Hong Kong), Mando-pop (Chinese), and J-pop (Japan). Audience interactivity is an important part of this format as younger listeners commonly use mobile telephones to send SMS (Short Message Service) messages to request favorite songs. A second distinctive format on radio (and television) is foreign-language education programs. Local radio stations such as Beijing People's Radio broadcast programs that teach English, Japanese, German, and Spanish. A third distinctive format is talk radio, which offers a much freer exchange of views than other media content in China. The emergence of talk radio has shifted the emphasis from authorities addressing people, to people addressing authorities, resulting in radio becoming a crucial avenue for the government to gauge the mood of the nation. Sometimes listeners discuss social, economic, and even taboo political subjects such as human rights. A fourth distinctive format is "professional advice," particularly on health-related issues. Such health programs are classified as profit or nonprofit. An example of a nonprofit program is when psychological assistance is provided to help people with family or work-related crises. An example of a profit-oriented program is when doctors from hospitals diagnose call-in patients, and encourage them to come to their hospitals for traditional Chinese or Western treatment.

Profanity and sexual references are not spoken on broadcast radio in China. If callers begin to approach these taboo subjects, broadcast directors monitoring the programs cut the caller off.

Television Form in China

In China, television programs begin and end at varying times. Programs can start and end at the top or bottom of the hour, at the quarter hours, at five-minute intervals throughout the hour, or simply at the end of the advertisements. Many of the popular programs broadcast during the "golden period," 1900 (7:00 PM) to 2100 (9:00 PM), start on the hour. For example, CCTV's *Xinwen Lianbo* (*News Broadcasting*) starts at 1900 (7:00 PM) and ends at 1930 (7:30 PM). However, there is no standard length for such programs, with some running five or fifteen minutes long, and others running for forty-five or fifty-five minutes.

After one program ends, a still graphic usually accompanies a voiceover that introduces the next program; the exception is important political programs or cultural events such as the Spring Festival celebrations. In China, advertising regulations contribute to the irregularity of start and end times over a day's viewing. Because advertising is generally not allowed during the majority of programming, all advertisements are shown in blocks of nine to twelve minutes at the end of programs, creating a situation whereby programs start and end at odd times. The exception to this convention is in the broadcasting of television episodes of melody drama, within which regulations allow a two and a half-minute advertising break. A melody drama is a kind of soap opera that blends communist ideology with cultural entertainment (described in more detail in the next section). Table 9.5 shows sample television program listings in China.

Television Genres in China

Television programs can be generally classified into entertainment and education orientations. Entertainment programming includes sports, melody dramas, movie, music, and game shows. Education programming includes news, talk shows, and documentaries. The national broadcaster CCTV has fifteen channels, eight of which are dedicated entertainment-oriented, broadcasting music, movies, Beijing opera, sport, children's programs, and melody dramas. CCTV's other channels broadcast a comprehensive mix of education and entertainment content, covering news and game shows. Comparatively, local city and provincial television stations are more entertainment oriented than the national broadcaster CCTV, with fewer obligations to serve as a government propaganda tool. Television stations broadcast up to twenty hours a day, usually ceasing transmission between 2300 (11:00 PM) and 0100 (1:00 AM).

In general, television broadcasts typically begin with a morning fitness program at 0600 (6:00 AM), and then national (CCTV) and local news (city or provincial stations) from 0700 (7:00 PM) to 0830 (8:30 AM). These news programs are presented in a formal manner by one anchor. From 0900 (9:00 AM) to 1100 (11:00 AM), typical television genres include education programs for younger children, health and retirement programs for elderly viewers, and melody dramas. Newscasts generally follow the morning programming schedule at 1100 (11:00 AM). Afternoon programming typically includes talk shows whereby experts are invited to discuss business, legal, social, and cultural topics and issues. For example, a typical afternoon program is *Daode Guancha* (*Observing Morals*), which focuses on moral issues such as abortion that traditionally have not been talked about publicly. Late afternoon programming includes cartoons and quiz shows for younger children and teenagers. The "golden period" includes a national news broadcast, an investigative reporting program such as *Jiaodian Fangtan* (*The Focus*), and a popular melody drama.

One distinctive television genre in China is the investigative news report. In general, this kind of program is thirty or forty-five minutes in length, and focuses on a particular news event, providing audiences with in-depth background information and analysis on the topic. Programs such as *The Focus* and *Xinwen Diaocha* (*News Probe*) aim to uncover corruption in society such as official abuse of power, copyright piracy, or counterfeit products.

A second distinctive television genre in China is the education-oriented talk show. The host typically invites several experts to discuss political, economic, technology, or cultural topics. For example, the talk show *Duihua* (*Dialogue*) usually focuses on successful entrepreneurs. Talk shows usually invite either a local or foreign entrepreneur who has a successful business operation in China.

TABLE 9.5 Sample Television Program Listing from China, September 23, 2004

TIME	CCTV 1	TIME	CCTV 2	TIME	CCTV NEWS	TIME	CCTV 4	TIME	CHANNEL 9 ENGLISH
6:14pm	Oriental Time	6:00pm	Artwork Investment	6:00pm	News International Information	6:00pm	Global Information	6:00pm	Financial and Economic Report
7:00	Xinwen Lianbo	6:20	Serve You	6:10	Information	6:30	Exploration and Findings	6:30	Across China
7:38	The Focus	7:10	Golden Earth	6:30	Wonderful China	7:00	News Briefing	7:00	Global Outlook
7:55	TV Series: Hongqipu (24)	7:35	The Frontier	7:00	Xinwen Lianbo	7:10	TV Series: Stick to Innovation (11)	7:28	Screen Guide
8:49	TV Series: Hongqipu (25)	8:00	Life	7:35	The Focus	8:00	News Briefing	7:30	Today's Topic
9:45	The Probe	8:30	Law and Economy	7:55	Weather	8:10	All across China	8:00	Today's Asia
10:35	Night News	9:00	Economic Information	8:00	News	8:40	Two Sides of Taiwan Strait	8:30	Cultural Report
11:07	TV Series: Red Rose (39)	9:30	Half Hour for Economy	8:30	News Saloon	9:00	China News	9:00	Comprehensive News
12:02am	TV Series: Red Rose (40)	10:05	China Economy Report	9:00	Today	9:30	Today's Focus	9:30	China in Foreigner's Eyes
12:56	TV Series: Red Roses (41)	10:25	China Security	9:30	Global Observation	10:00	China Literature and Art	10:00	Financial and Economic Report
		11:00	Earth Story	9:55	Weather	10:20	China Theatre	10:30	Documentary
		11:30	Absolute Challenge	10:00	Xinwen Lianbo (Rebroadcast)	10:50	Language Anecdotes	11:00	Comprehensive News
				10:30	CCTV Forum	10:55	China Civilization	11:15	Sports Report
				11:00	News	11:00	Financial and Economic Report	11:30	Nature and Science
				11:30	Social Record	1:30	Today's Topic	11:55	China Culture
				12:00	Midnight News	11:30	Updates across the Strait	12:00am	Comprehensive News
				12:30	Sports Report	11:45	Taiwan Encyclopedia	12:30	Across China
						11:50	Science and Technology Expo	1:00	Financial and Economic Report
						12:00am	News Briefing		

Source: Lu Jia.

231

A third distinctive television genre in China is the modern melody drama, already mentioned. The term *melody* is used because the drama attempts to bring together (harmonize in the musical sense) political ideology with entertainment values, to produce programming that is both popular and thought-provoking. This genre draws from the Western concept of melodrama, which depicts exaggerated emotions, stereotypical characters, and interpersonal conflicts. However, though melodramas are certainly designed to entertain, they are also used to educate Chinese citizens. Melody dramas generally focus on government officials fighting corruption to help remold a new ethical and moral spirit that is conducive to promoting the government's vision of a socialist market economy.

Violence, nudity, and sex on radio and television are officially prohibited in China under the government's mandate to build a morally strong society. However, regulations do not prohibit Chinese *gongfu* (kungfu) programming from being aired, because fight scenes are heavily choreographed. Children's cartoons, most of which are imported from Japan or the USA, are strictly regulated to avoid programming containing excessive violence.

Internet Content in China

As discussed in Chapter 6, internet content in China is restricted in various ways by service and content providers, as well as government regulatory bodies. Most home pages are in Chinese (*putonghua*) and consist of official Chinese news, entertainment, or information portals, or email, chat, and personal web sites. Many younger users go online using internet cafés (*wangba*) to play online games or chat with friends, but the government applies time restrictions on users or requires identification cards because of concerns about teenagers ignoring schooling. In addition, security agents or email-scanning software are employed to monitor emails and chat rooms to prevent criticism of the government.

MEDIA CONTENT IN GHANA

Newspaper Form in Ghana

Almost all newspapers are serious newspapers having a tabloid shape. The two newspapers that are published in broadsheet form (the *Ghanaian Times* and its sister newspaper the *Evening News*) are smaller in size than broadsheets in other countries. A distinctive feature of newspapers in Ghana is that politics and implications for democracy are the predominant focus of the coverage. The *Daily Graphic* is considered to be the most prestigious newspaper, followed closely by the *Ghanaian Times*. But since the establishment of democratic civilian government in 1992, the papers are making transitions from serving as official outlets of government news to outlets for independent journalism. The two state-owned newspapers have established readerships and resources (unlike the private newspapers), to get the newspapers to outlying regions of the country.

Most newspapers in Ghana have poor print quality. The two state newspapers—the *Daily Graphic* and the *Ghanaian Times*—tend to have the best quality. But for the private newspapers, pages are thin, ink is often faded or smeared, letters and words are sometimes not horizontally aligned, and photos often have poor resolution.

There is a good deal of parity among the newspapers in the proportion of text, advertising, and photos. In general, about 80 percent of a newspaper is text, and advertising occupies a small portion of most newspapers. One reason is that there is relatively soft consumer demand for advertised products. Another is a holdover perception from previous times that causes advertisers to be reluctant about placing advertisements in newspapers that criticize the government, in case there are retributions. Thus, it is common for only one or two ads to appear in an entire issue of a newspaper. Most newspapers do not have a Classifieds section. If a newspaper carries advertising, typically it will be a boxed advertisement that can appear on just about any page except the front page. More often than not, advertisements appear toward the back of the newspaper.

Photographs are very common in newspapers. Most newspaper stories are accompanied by at least one photograph. In general, photographs accompanying news stories on the front pages of the *Daily Graphic* and the *Ghanaian Times* are in color, with photos on subsequent pages in black and white. For the other newspapers, photos are usually in black and white on all pages. Photographs are often grainy and somewhat blurry. Graphics, cartoon boxes, and cartoon strips are not very common in Ghanaian newspapers.

Newspaper Substance in Ghana

The vast majority of newspaper coverage in Ghana focuses on political news. In some private newspapers, all or almost all of the coverage is political news. In the state-owned newspapers, additional sections include Sports, Business, and Features—a section that sometimes includes editorials, though they are not identified as such. In the private newspapers, a Commentary section labeled as such is a common feature. In both the private and the state newspapers, significant page space is devoted to notices of deaths. Often a full page is devoted to a photo of a citizen who has passed away, and a list of family members who are survivors of the deceased person. The friends and family members usually pay for these full-page notices, because it is a tradition in Ghana to inform as many people as possible about a person's death, so they can come to the funeral to acknowledge the passing of a member of the community. Much of the content of the state-owned newspapers leans toward supporting the government simply because in the past the government funded the newspapers and provided most of the information that was compiled into news stories. Ironically, most content in the private newspapers also leans toward supporting the government because it is not the government that was in power from 1992 to 2000, and it is not like the previous governments. An exception is the *Ghana Palaver*, which often criticizes the post-2000 government and looks back favorably on the 1992–2000 government.

Since 1992, the state newspapers have had the freedom to criticize government, but are in the process of testing how far the criticism can go. More frequently, the state newspapers tend to endorse government activities and officials—often with words not considered appropriate for journalism in other countries. For example, in the *Ghanaian Times* Features section, an article with the headline "Defending the Republic," led with this paragraph:

> Two Sundays ago on *Metro TV,* the Defence Minister, Dr. Kwame Addo-Kufor, put in a masterly performance which by any yardstick was most commendable. He was not only answering tough questions about his work as Minister, but also explaining off some misconceptions about the Ministry and its work. This polished, highly educated man showed that he is fit not only to occupy a cabinet seat in Ghana, but indeed in any part of the world. (May 11, 2004, p. 6)

Often, state-owned newspapers tend to focus on government initiatives by highlighting the activities of a particular ministry.

The private newspapers tend to be more outspoken than the state-owned newspapers. Much of the coverage focuses on activities that took place during the first civilian government that ruled with an authoritarian style, and was voted out of office in 2000. For example, on the front page of the *Statesman*, a paragraph with a story headlined with "NDC Gives Up" stated:

> Humiliated by six successive by-election defeats since losing power in the general election of 2000, information reaching *The Statesman* is that the NDC is frantically looking for face-saving routes to escape fielding a candidate for the forthcoming by-election. (May 20, 2004, p. 1)

A common type of content in Ghanaian newspapers is reactions of Ghanaian chiefs to government policy. For example, Figure 9.14 shows the lead story in the *Evening News*, in which a local chief refuses to apologize to the president of Ghana for the villagers' reluctance to use government-supplied public toilets. problems with a local village accepting and using public toilets from the government. This photo conveys the look and feel of many Ghanaian newspapers.

Newspapers in Ghana also tend to regularly cover social-welfare and health-related issues. Often the coverage seeks to provide basic information to educate the reader about procedures related to sexuality and the human body. Examples of such topics include HIV, safe sex, vasectomy, and menstruation. Such information normally is less about new research in these fields and more about teaching the reader what the terms mean or what the procedures are, and how they affect the human body.

The subject of democracy is also routinely covered in Ghanaian newspapers. Such coverage analyzes what democracy means, and what is involved in promoting it. For example, a page 2 article of the May 20, 2004, *Chronicle* with the headline "The Old African Democracy, is the Way Forward" promoted a kind of pluralism found in traditional village life. Post-2000, it is typical for Ghanaian newspaper stories to promote democratic ideals such as pluralism, tolerance, and fair elections.

Violent crime is not very prominent in Ghanaian newspaper coverage. Nudity and profanity are not printed inn Ghanaian newspapers. These subject matters are considered to be immoral and not appropriate media content.

Radio Form in Ghana

In Ghana, radio segments on both commercial and public stations almost always begin and end exactly at either the top or the bottom of the hour. Except for news, program segments often last two to four hours. Per half hour, regular programming typically varies from twenty to thirty minutes because of inserted advertising. Radio hosts in Ghana normally have a slow to moderate pace to their speech. On talk-oriented stations, interchanges with callers often run up to fifteen minutes or more.

Radio frequencies and programs are printed only in the *Ghanaian Times*. Radio listings are not printed in other newspapers or in other publications. Many of the stations have

FIGURE 9.14 Front Page of *The Evening News* newspaper in Ghana

Source: Robert McKenzie; printed with permission by *The Evening News*, May 13, 2004.

emotive titles—for example: *Joy FM, Peach FM, Radio Uniiq* (a GBC station), *Choice FM,* and *Vibe*. On radio in Ghana, there is a predominance of commercial programming over non-commercial programming, and privately funded programming over publicly funded programming. Public broadcasting channels are usually available in the average channel listings but are typically outnumbered by commercial channels by a ratio of around ten to one.

Radio programming in Ghana normally includes a few breaks for advertising. There is no typical pattern to set advertising breaks on Ghanaian radio, but usually there are two or three breaks per half hour. Advertising breaks typically run for one to two minutes. Advertising minutage can range from four to twelve minutes per half hour.

Radio Formats in Ghana

Radio content in Ghana is highly diversified and loosely formatted. Most radio stations offer a lot of talk/discussion/information/news programs. Local languages are often spoken. Of the music stations, most play many different types of music within radio programs, rather than a specific format. It is common, for example, to hear a sequence of songs that includes reggae, gospel, jazz, and pop. There are at least three distinctive kinds of programming that can be heard on Ghanaian radio. One is the "magazine" program, which typically features a five to ten-minute news report on a health-related issue that is then followed by phone calls from listeners about the report. Next is the "breakfast show," where the radio host typically chooses an issue written about in the newspapers, then discusses the issue with studio guests in between songs. A third kind of distinctive programming is a review of the English-language newspapers but given in local Ghanaian languages, during which the hosts discuss newspaper headlines and main stories. A fourth kind of distinctive programming that is heard more in the outlying areas is the "folklore advice" program, which for some listeners is perceived more as fun entertainment than as factual information. Hosts with alleged knowledge of herbal medications and other naturally occurring phenomena discuss concoctions that may cure ailments or fix personal problems, such as how to capture a man.

Profanity is considered to be at odds with traditional (mainly religious) Ghanaian values, and is not spoken on broadcast radio in Ghana.

Television Form in Ghana

Television program listings are printed only in the *Ghanaian Times*. Television programs on both public and private television almost always begin and end exactly at either the top or the bottom of the hour. Programs segments usually last thirty minutes or one hour. The actual time length of a typical program varies from twenty to twenty-five minutes per half hour because of inserted advertising. Typical broadcast and multichannel television listings available contain only commercial programming, and a predominance of privately funded programming over license-fee funded programming. *GTV* is available in an average channel selection but is typically outnumbered by commercial channels at a ratio of around four to one.

Television programming in Ghana normally includes three breaks for advertising. Usually there is an advertising break prior to the start of a program, then again about fifteen minutes into the program, then again after the program concludes. Advertising breaks typically are two minutes long. On the evening programs, paid-for sponsorships—also called "rolling announcements"—often precede a regular program and run for ten minutes. Examples of rolling announcements from May 19, 2004, on *GTV* include: a Tennis Open, the Recall of Parliament from Recess, and a Holy Child PTA Meeting. When rolling announcements are not part of the programming, regular advertisement segments add up to anywhere from of five to ten minutes per half hour. In addition, advertising sometimes takes the form of a business logo appearing on the screen for the entirety of a regular program being aired.

Advertising on television in Ghana sometimes has an uneven and amateurish production quality. For example, the sound level of one ad can be followed by another ad with markedly louder or quieter sound, which might also be distorted or muffled. Similarly, the visuals in advertising on television in Ghana can have problems with lighting, making the faces of actors somewhat difficult to see. Some advertisements appear to be loosely scripted.

Television in Ghana sometimes includes text information between regular programming. This information can consist of announcements about community events, health advice, or African proverbs, such as this one from "Yoruba—Nigeria," which appeared on *TV Africa* throughout May, 2004: "Trust not to an inheritance; The product of one's hands is sufficient for one." As Table 9.6 shows, the commercial private broadcasters outnumber the commercial public broadcaster *GTV* by a 3 to 1 ratio.

Television Genres in Ghana

There is a fairly even balance between political and entertainment-oriented programming on private television channels. The public television broadcaster (*GTV*) leans more toward

TABLE 9.6   **Sample Television Program Listings from Ghana, May 20, 2004**

TIME	GTV	TV3	TV AFRICA	METRO NEWS
6:00pm	Initiative Africa	Treasures of Wisdom	DW-TV	Boston Public
6:20		In Loving Memory		
6:30	Adult Education	Evening News	Local Language News	African Movie
7:00	Major News	Children's Hospital	DW-TV	
7:30		Small World	News	
8:00	Press Briefing	Auto-Wheels	Media Today	
8:30	Documentary	Efie Wura	Your Health	
9:00	Tentacles		Documentary	Metro News
9:30	Dada Boat	Charmed		Good Evening Ghana
10:00	ABN Sunset Beach	Esmeralda	Turning Point	
10:30	Late News	Late News	Late News	Metro Telejournal
11:00	LRC		DW-TV	Newsline
11:30		Late Night Movie	Close Down	Advertising Circle
12:00am	DW-TV	BBC		Close Down

Source: Robert McKenzie.

cultural and information-oriented programming, but still offers entertainment-oriented programming. Ghanaian terrestrial television stations do not broadcast twenty-four hours a day. Most sign off around midnight and begin programming at 0500 (5:00 AM). It is difficult to identify portions of the day that are characterized by certain genres of programming, because many program offerings are influenced by what is available that is low cost. Often, this results in airing foreign-produced television programs. However, in terms of domestically produced programs, two generalizations can be made: First, throughout the broadcast day, but particularly in the morning and early evening, television channels typically carry low-budget magazine and news programs such as *GTV*'s *Breakfast Show* and *Metro TV*'s *Market Watch.* Second, during the afternoon, early evening, and late evening, typical genres of programs include music videos, imported films, both imported and domestic soap operas, dramas, and to a lesser extent, comedies.

One particularly distinctive television genre in Ghana is the discussion program. This genre covers magazine, talk, and interview programs. Examples include *TV Africa*'s *Media Today, TV3*'s *Insight,* and *GTV*'s *Straight Talk Africa.* These kinds of programs often have a host who leads a discussion among a panel of experts debating an activity or policy of the government. The sets of these programs are often rather basic, consisting mainly of a countertop behind which participants sit, and a basic prop on the wall behind the participants, often showing the name of the program. Sometimes, these programs are in local languages. Participants often converse in an energetic and emphatic manner in both tone and body language (waving arms and hands), and sometimes wear traditional African dress.

A second distinctive television genre in Ghana is "television church." This program usually involves a minister preaching to a crowd of worshipers, who are infrequently shown on camera. The minister usually cites scripture and speaks about what he considers to be exemplary moral behavior that the audience should follow. Donations are not typically asked for during television church.

A third distinctive television genre in Ghana is the "indigenous culture" program. The main purpose of these programs is to promote and preserve native African culture, which is perceived by some to be in danger of extinction because of the prevalence of imported foreign (mainly Western) programs. Often this genre promotes African culture by communicating what Africa has contributed to the world—for example, medicinal herbs such as aloe, and minerals such as iron. Many of these programs also feature traditional dress, dance, and music—especially drums and other percussion instruments. *TV Africa* in particular is focused on promoting African culture as a counterbalance to Western culture, brought in by imported media, as is indicated in the following two promotional messages that aired throughout May, 2003, on *TV Africa*: "Promoting African Values" and "For Africans, By Africans, To Africans." Similarly, figure 9.15 shows two anchors from a *TV Africa* newscast wearing traditional African dress instead of the Western-style dress of jackets, ties, and blouses.

Violence on television in Ghana is a somewhat common theme, mainly because of imported films from the USA and Nigeria. News programs do not regularly contain violence. However, across all genres in which violence does appear, rarely does the program show blood or injured body parts in close-up camera shots. Nudity is not seen on terrestrial television programming. Topless women can occasionally be seen on premium cable and satellite television channels only. Similarly, profanity is not seen or heard on terrestrial television in Ghana. Some profanity can be heard on basic and premium cable channels and satellite channels, but much less so than in other countries.

Internet Content in Ghana

Internet content in Ghana is not generally restricted at the level of distribution. But some internet cafés—which is where most people access the internet in Ghana—employ filters to restrict access to adult web sites.

MEDIA CONTENT IN LEBANON

Newspaper Form in Lebanon

In Lebanon, almost all newspapers have a similar broadsheet size. The exception is *Al-Kifah al-Arabi*, which has a tabloid size. Newspapers are for the most part serious. All newspapers in Lebanon use classical Arabic and employ academic language that focuses

FIGURE 9.15   *News Anchors in Traditional African Dress on* TV Africa *in Ghana*
Source: TV Africa.

on serious political subjects, rather than the daily concerns of the average Lebanese person (this theme is further discussed in the next chapter on news reporting).

Lebanese newspapers generally have a high proportion of text compared to advertising, photos, and graphics. A rough estimate would put text at about 60 percent, photographs at about 25 to 30 percent, advertising at about 7 to 12 percent, and graphics at about 1 to 2 percent. *Al-Balad* is an exception, with many more photos and graphics.

Most newspapers are printed in cursive style because Arabic letters are not printed in block style as in English, where every letter has a small version and a capital version. Instead, Arabic letters typically have six or seven cursive forms, depending on several factors. For example, the letter "t" has one shape in the beginning of a word, another in the middle, and several shapes at the end of a word, depending on the meaning and/or gender of the word. To facilitate the mass printing of Arabic, a special standardized format was designed, which is practical for newspapers but diminishes the beauty and nuances of true Arabic.

Advertising does not occupy much space in Lebanese newspapers. Usually, several ads are boxed next to one another on the front page. It is also common for newspapers to run a full-page ad on the last page or to place ads in the top left and right corners of the front page, near the newspaper logo. Ads in Arab-language newspapers in Lebanon frequently are printed in English or French.

FIGURE 9.16   Front Page of National Newspaper *as-Safir* from Lebanon

Source: Nabil Dajani; printed with permission by *as-Safir*.

In Lebanon, photographs are somewhat popular. Usually, photographs are few and small on the front page. Often, larger photographs of important news events are run on the inside pages and are keyed to smaller ones on the front page. Graphics and comedic cartoons are not common, but political cartoons are found in leading newspapers such as *an-Nahar, as-Safir, ad-Diyar,* and *al-Balad.* Usually, these cartoons deal with local politics and are placed on the last page.

Figure 9.16 shows the national *as-Safir*, which has a typical look of newspapers in Lebanon. Note the advertisement in the bottom right-hand corner, which is presented in cartoon form.

Newspaper Substance in Lebanon

In Lebanon, most newspapers have common sections. Front-page articles consisting of current events and international news are often carried over to inside pages. Subsequent sections are: Local News, Economics and Business, Culture (if included), and Sports. Foreign Arab news and other international news sections are usually located in the second half of the paper, followed by opinion articles, mainly on political topics.

Most newspapers focus on political news, the economy, and features, with lesser attention paid to cultural subjects. They usually cover urban areas more than rural areas. All newspapers run opinion pages analyzing newsworthy events and issues. Most Lebanese newspapers devote the last page to news stories about celebrities as well as to peculiar human-interest news.

There are several foreign-language newspapers printed in Lebanon that have relatively large audiences and are quite influential. The French-language *l'Orient le Jour* is very influential among French-educated Lebanese. Armenian and English newspapers are less important. Armenian newspapers circulate among the relatively large Armenian community in the country, where the Armenian language is almost exclusively spoken. The English-language newspapers circulate mainly among the foreign community; unlike the French-language newspapers, they are mainly targeted at visiting readers. Whereas the French-language newspapers do not differ very much in content from the Arabic language newspapers, the English language newspapers usually include more foreign news—particularly USA news—as well as more entertainment.

Stories about violent crimes are quite rare. Nudity and profanity are not published because Lebanese journalists and the culture as a whole consider such material to be immoral.

Radio Form in Lebanon

In Lebanon, radio program listings generally are not published in newspapers or magazines. Radio programs on commercial stations usually begin at exactly the top of the hour, or on the half hour.

Commercial radio stations are much more prevalent than the official government radio station. When scanning the FM band, listeners are literally sixteen times as likely to come across a commercial station as the official government radio station. On commercial Lebanese radio stations, advertising minutage typically ranges anywhere from one to twelve minutes per half hour. The official government radio station only airs administrative announcements (e.g., procedures for passport renewal, due dates for paying telephone bills, introduction of a new service by a government agency, announcement of bids for public-works projects).

There are many foreign-language radio stations broadcasting from within Lebanon. When scanning the FM band, a radio listener is equally likely to come across a foreign-language (English or French) station as an Arabic-language station.

Radio hosts often spend more time talking than playing songs. Hosts on music stations regularly speak a mixture of Arabic, French, and/or English. For example, hosts often introduce songs in Arabic, French, English, and sometimes even other languages such as Italian. Usually, hosts are men who have a very energetic speaking style and who use light humor when interacting with the listeners. Listeners routinely call in to request songs and to chat with the host about personal interests such as dinner plans, hobbies, and interesting movies.

Radio Formats in Lebanon

Radio stations in Lebanon are licensed to broadcast according to two general formats: political and nonpolitical. Nonpolitical stations broadcast mainly music and entertainment programs, often consisting of listener call-ins and social advice provided by amateurs and nonprofessionals. For example, RML airs a program in which listeners call in to seek advice about personal and professional problems they face, such as quarrels between lovers, disagreements at work with the boss, and disloyalty to friends. The host is often a layperson without professional credentials in psychology. There are also some radio stations that play classical music, which includes but is not limited to orchestral and baroque music, and opera.

Political radio stations, on the other hand, are the only type of station permitted to broadcast news and political programs. For the most part, programming on political radio stations focuses on local Lebanese politics in the form of news—commentaries as well as talk shows. Contrasting political opinions are commonly found across Lebanese radio stations. For example, one program may criticize the policies of Syria, while another supports them. However, no political program is pro-Israel. Political stations also broadcast some programs dubiously portrayed as being in the public interest, such as horoscope and for-tune-telling programs.

In Lebanon, there are at least two themes that are distinctive to radio. One theme is "three-language" programming, wherein some stations specialize in English songs, some in French songs, some exclusively in Arabic songs, and some (like *PAX FM*) in songs of all three languages. The talk shows on these stations, however, are almost always in Arabic. A second distinctive theme is "religious worship" programming. For example, *Sawt el Nour* (*The Voice of Enlightenment*) focuses on the Islamic religion by airing talk shows in Islam as well as Islamic religious songs. *Sawt el Mahaba* (there is no direct English transla-tion for the Arabic word of "mahaba"; the closest translation would be "love and caring") focuses on the Christian religion by airing Christian prayers and songs.

Television Form in Lebanon

Television listings are published in most daily newspapers and weekly magazines. Among the leading daily newspapers that present television listings are *as-Safir* and *an-Nahar*. Most newspapers and magazines present just the titles of programs and the times that they air. *As-Safir* newspaper runs a page entitled "*Voice and Picture*," to discuss selected local and Arab radio and television programs.

Television programs on all channels are normally scheduled to start and end exactly on the hour, half hour, or quarter of the hour, but they often start and end late, which is related to the fluid sense of time that exists in Lebanon, as discussed in Chapter 4. In Lebanon, television program segments vary in length although they are usually scheduled to run in fifteen-minute increments (:30, :60, :75, :90, etc.). All television programs—on both terrestrial and cable/satellite channels—are introduced by announcers (usually females), who provide background information about the program to follow. The introduction is then followed by a segment of advertisements and promotions for upcoming shows that vary in length according to the season and the time of the broadcast. Though the audiovisual law (discussed in Chapter 6) stipulates that "advertisements are to be aired between programs and during programs, provided that the unity and value of the programs are intact, and in a manner not harmful to the owner's literary and artistic rights," this regulation is not usually followed. For example, advertising breaks often occur at climactic scenes of programs, and the number of these breaks is determined by the amount of advertising available. Similarly, during talk shows, the host often introduces an advertising break, but then allows guests to carry on the discussion for another five to ten minutes before ads are aired. During big holiday seasons when viewership is higher (mainly Christmas, Ramadan, and Easter), advertising often accounts for more minutes than regular programming. Thus, some half-hour programs may include up to twenty minutes of advertisements. Table 9.7 shows sample television program listings in Lebanon.

Television Genres in Lebanon

Most television programs (on both the commercial stations and on the quasi-public station) are entertainment-based. Especially during prime-time evening hours, entertainment programs constitute the bulk of the listings. Of the cultural programs that are aired, most are presented in English or French, and are usually broadcast outside of evening hours. Similarly, there are few educational programs geared toward children, and those that have been imported from England, France, or the USA are presented in the given foreign language without Arabic subtitles.

The content of Lebanese television shows usually follows this sequence: Early morning is dominated mainly by cartoons and other shows for children. Late morning consists mainly of chatty news shows in which hosts discuss entertainment and politics. Morning news shows usually start around 0800 (8:00 AM) and finish around noon. Early morning news programs as a rule start on schedule as there is little advertising in the morning and they come after late-night, prerecorded programs. Although morning news shows may contain some political and educational news, most of their content is entertainment news covering subjects such as cooking, fashion, decorating, and wedding plans. Examples include *Alam el Sabah* (*Morning World*) on *Future TV*, and *Naharkon Said* (*Good Morning*) on *LBCI*. Afternoon consists mainly of sitcoms, soap operas, and game shows. The evening consists mainly of newscasts, game shows, political and social talk shows (for example, *Seera wa Infatahit*—"*Since the Subject was Raised*"—on *Future TV* or *Kalam el Nass* (*People's Talk*) on *LBCI*), plus parodies and foreign or local films, and documentaries. In Lebanon, programs vary from thirty minutes to three hours. Films are not very common.

One distinctive genre on television is political satire (in Lebanon commonly called *chansonnier*, borrowing French vernacular). Political-satire programs usually involve characters impersonating and making fun of politicians through costumes and mannerisms. Almost every terrestrial channel runs a weekly satire program in which comedians make fun of politicians and political events in the country. For example, *LBCI*'s show *Bas-mat Watan* has a double meaning in Arabic, depending on how one interprets the word *basmati*. If one views it as two words—*bas* and *mat*—then it can be understood as "when the nation dies." Or, if it is viewed as one word, *basmati*, then it will mean "the smiles of the nation."

A second distinctive genre on Lebanese television is the interview talk show, in which a host interviews a politician, a celebrity, a specialist, or a group of people about salient issues. Interviews are conducted in the television studio, in a foreign country where the host meets a person or group, or via satellite connection. Every television station has one or more of such shows weekly. Among the prominent talk shows are *LBCI*'s "*Kalam en-Nas*" (*The Talk of People*) and *Future TV's* "*Khaleek bil Bayt*" (*Stay at Home*).

TABLE 9.7 Sample Television Program Listings from Lebanon, January 6, 2005

TIME	TELE LIBAN	TIME	LBCI	TIME	FUTURE	TIME	TELE LUMIERE	TIME	ALMANAR	TIME	NEW TV
6:00pm	Lebanese Sitcom	6:00pm	Lebanese Sitcom	4:30pm	Lebanese Football	5:00pm	Lebanese Folklore Music	5:30pm	Kids Special	6:00pm	Health
6:30	Lebanese Theater	6:30	Star Academy 2	7:00	Lebanese Game Show: The Trap	7:00	Speech for Life	7:30	News	7:40	News
7:30	News	7:50	News	8:30	News	8:30	New Year's Eve (Rerun)	8:00	Documentary	8:30	A.M.
8:30	Lebanese Soap Opera	8:40	Star Academy 2	12:10am	Documentary: Arab Women Singers	12:10am	Rosario	9:30	Political Talk Show	10:00	Sports Summary
9:30	American Movie	11:00	Tele Auto	1:00	A.M. Tycus Political Commentary	1:00	The Mass	11:30	Political Commentary	11:00	Weathercast
11:00	Soap Opera	11:30	Naked Truth					12:30	News in French: Le Journal		
		12:00am	Star Academy 2					1:15	Koran		
		12:30	American Movie								

Source: Nabil Dajani.

And a third distinctive genre on television in Lebanon is the poor imitation of a foreign comedy from the West. In the process of television stations importing television sitcoms from the West, some stations have begun to produce their own local sitcoms. For example, *LBCI* airs *Marti wa Ana* (*My Wife and I*). This show has also been very popular in Saudi Arabia and many Gulf countries. Such sitcoms usually are inferior imitations of foreign comedies because of their weak scripting and acting and cheap production quality.

Although Lebanese television stations are notorious in the Arab world for portraying women in revealing attire, Arab audiences in Saudi Arabia jokingly refer to the Lebanese station LBCI as *ilbisi,* which in Arabic means "get dressed." Nudity is not tolerated. Pornographic and erotic programs are not permitted on terrestrial television. Foreign pornographic and erotic programs can be seen only on pay-cable channels after midnight; At the time of the writing of this book, Arabic pornographic programs did not exist. Violence is somewhat common on television in Lebanon—especially in programs targeted at teenagers and men, such as films and action dramas.

Internet Content

In Lebanon, web sites do not usually voluntarily restrict content. However, the Ministry of Post and Telecommunications and the Vice Police (an arm of the Internal Security Forces) require internet cafés to block users from accessing pornographic sites. In addition, the Vice Police have been known to pressure operators of internet cafés to block access to web sites hosting gay and lesbian content. Internet cafés typically provide a start-up page, with advertisements designed especially for the cafés.

COMPARATIVE SUMMARY

This chapter compared media content across the eight countries. Content is shaped by a media system as a result of various influences from other elements of a media system. Media content is that one element through which the other elements—cultural characteristics, philosophies for media systems, regulation, financing, accessibility, news reporting, imports/exports, and audiences—can be most comprehensively understood. Like the leaves on a tree, media content is the most noticeable element of a media system, and is thereby in the forefront of most people's experiences with media. Media content was defined in this chapter as an inseparable combination of both form and substance. Because the range of media content in a country is so immense, the chapter focused on distinctive themes in each country.

In terms of newspaper form, the following distinctive themes were observed. Countries with less visual newspapers included France and Ghana. Countries with moderately visual newspapers included China, Lebanon, and the USA. Countries with highly visual newspapers included México, Sweden, and the UK. Countries with low or medium-quality print included China, Ghana, Lebanon, México, and the USA. Countries with high-quality print include France, Sweden, and the UK. Countries with relatively little advertising in newspapers included France, Ghana, and Lebanon. Countries with moderate advertising in newspapers included México, Sweden, the UK, and China. The USA stood out from the other countries in terms of having newspapers with a large proportion of advertising.

In terms of national newspaper sections and orientations, the following distinctive themes were observed. The French press is very formal, and more national newspapers are to the political left than to the right. The French press often employs academic word choices. Big cities have newspapers subsidized by government funding to provide opposing political perspectives. The Swedish tabloids are highly sensational. The Swedish serious newspapers have vibrant debate pages. The UK press has a fairly equal number of national newspapers on the left, in the middle, and on the right. Almost all the newspapers take up and advocate causes. The UK tabloids have worldwide reputations for being very gossipy and vitriolic. The UK broadsheets are very detailed. The USA press pulls to the center but overall leans slightly to the left. The "prestige press" in the USA often protects the agenda of stories in the other newspapers. Big-city newspapers often focus on high drama, and small-town newspapers often focus on community events. The Mexican press is made up of many newspapers, leans slightly to the left, and frequently focuses on government corruption. The Chinese press is regulated to support Chinese communist/socialist government policy. Chinese national broadsheets carry less information overall than Chinese tabloids because government funding is the main source of revenue, but carry more political information. The Ghanaian national press leans toward supporting post-2000 governments. Most articles in Ghanaian newspapers cover politics. The Lebanese national press is fragmented in that individual newspapers lean to the left or the right based on the financing sources or ownership ties. Lebanese newspapers consistently publish opinions about domestic politics and international events.

In terms of the form of content on terrestrial radio, the following distinctive themes were observed. Public radio has a very high profile in the landscape of radio frequencies in the three European countries (France, Sweden, and the UK), as well as Ghana. Public radio has a moderate profile in the USA and in México, and a low profile in Lebanon. Government radio has a dominant profile in China. Private radio has a high profile in the USA, México, and Lebanon, a moderate profile in the Sweden, the UK, and Ghana, but does not exist in China. Radio content segments usually start and end on the half hour or hour on almost all stations in the USA, México, China, Ghana, and Lebanon, and on most of just the private broadcasters in France, Sweden, and the UK. In contrast, radio content segments on the public-service stations in France, Sweden, and the UK often start and end on the :05s. In Sweden, start and end times of radio content segments on public-service stations are sometimes so precise as to be on the :01s. Advertising occupies a significant proportion of programming on private radio stations in France, the UK, the USA, and México, as well as on public-service channels in France. Advertising occupies a moderate proportion of programming on private radio stations in Sweden, Ghana, and Lebanon, on government radio stations in China, and on public-service radio stations in Ghana.

In terms of content formats (substance) on terrestrial radio, the following distinctive themes were observed. The public radio services in France, the UK, and Sweden are divided into multiple networks, each one providing a format designed primarily to serve an age range. Each of these countries has a public-service radio network that plays pop-oriented music targeting a younger audience. In addition, Sweden has a public-service radio network that is designed for a Finnish-speaking or Finnish-heritage audience. France, the UK, and Sweden all have one or more public-service radio networks that regularly air educational and cultural programming—including theater, documentaries, intellectual discussion programs, and classical music. Similarly, the public radio networks in the USA are formatted mostly with cultural, arts, classical music, jazz music, and news programming. Unlike the other countries, the public radio stations in México are individually formatted with many different kinds of talk and music programming; in Ghana, with pop music, news and talk, as well as indigenous-language programming; and in Lebanon, with official government information. Government radio in China airs contemporary pop or rock music in the big cities, and cultural and talkback programs nationwide.

The private radio stations in each country have varying formats, with the exception of China. France collectively broadcasts wide plurality in terms of politics and music; Sweden broadcasts pop music, local news, and local culture; and the UK broadcasts mainly pop music and local news. The USA has narrow niche formats, which collectively cover a range of mostly contemporary music, as well as conservative talk shows. México's private radio stations cover a range of news and music, with an emphasis on indigenous Mexican musical styles; Ghana's are broadly formatted, and often include many types of music, as well as magazine and discussion programs; and Lebanon's private radio stations are divided between political formats, which include a lot of discussion and commentaries (mainly on affairs in the Arab world), and nonpolitical formats, which include a lot of pop music and advice programs.

In terms of the form of content on terrestrial television, the following distinctive themes were observed. National public television has a very high profile in the landscape of channel selections in the three European countries, as well as Ghana. Public television has a moderate profile in the USA and in Lebanon. Regional public television has a moderate profile in México. Government television has a dominant profile in China. Private television has a high profile in the USA, México, and Lebanon. Private television has a moderate profile in France, Sweden, the UK, and Ghana, but does not exist in China. Television shows usually start and end on the half hour or hour on almost all private and public stations in the USA, México, China, Ghana, and Lebanon. Television shows often start on the :05s and the :15s on private and public stations and channels in France, Sweden, the UK, and China. Start and end times of television programs are on the half hour or hour in the USA, México, Ghana, and Lebanon. Advertising occupies a significant proportion of the content on private television in the USA. Advertising occupies a moderate proportion of content on private and public television in France, and on private television in the UK, México, China, Ghana, and Lebanon. Advertising occupies a small proportion of content on private television in Sweden.

In terms of genres of content on terrestrial television, the following distinctive themes were observed. Public-service channels in France and Sweden air a lot of cultural programs. The BBC networks in the UK consistently air educational programs or entertainment programs with a learning emphasis. Private channels in these European countries consistently air entertainment-based programs. Documentaries are frequently aired on both private and public-service television in France, Sweden, and the UK, and are moderately aired on government television in China, and on private and public television in México. Television programming on most stations in the USA includes a lot of entertainment-oriented programs (dramas, sitcoms, and reality programs). Television in México frequently includes telenovelas. Television in China frequently includes melody dramas. Television programs in Ghana regularly include medical and social education programs and indigenous-oriented cultural programs, as well as political discussion programs. Television programs in Lebanon regularly include local music videos, discussion programs, foreign entertainment programs, and poor imitations of foreign comedies.

In terms of nudity and/or "profanity," the following observations were made. In France, female nudity is common in newspaper and television content, including advertising, but profanity is rare in any media content. In Sweden, female and male nudity are somewhat common in newspaper content and fairly common in television content, whereas profanity is common in radio and television content. In the UK, female nudity is very common in newspaper and television content, male nudity is occasional in newspaper and television content, and profanity is found regularly in newspaper, radio, and television content. In the USA, nudity is not found in newspapers (except for stories on art exhibits) or television, and profanity is not found in newspapers, radio, or television—though code words are used to imply profanity. In México, female nudity is common only in newspaper content covering art exhibitions, while profanity is not common in newspaper, radio, and television content. In China, nudity is not found in newspaper content and is prohibited in television content, and, similarly, profanity is not found in newspaper, radio, and television content. In Ghana and Lebanon, nudity and profanity are not found in newspaper, radio, and television content. In China and Lebanon, sexually oriented web sites are prohibited by law from being accessed in internet cafés.

In terms of violence, the following distinctive themes were observed. Violence in photos is somewhat common in newspapers in the USA (though not as close-up camera shots), as well as in México and Lebanon. Violence in photos is not common in newspapers in France, Sweden, the UK (except in photos depicting war), China or Ghana. Violent programming is very common on television in the USA, is fairly common on television in México and Lebanon, and is somewhat common on television in the UK and in France. violent content is rare on television in Sweden, and mostly consists of news coverage of war. Violent programming is prohibited on fictional television in China, except in choreographed martial-arts scenes.

CHAPTER 10

NEWS REPORTING

PRIMER QUESTIONS

1. What is news? How does news serve as a larger commentary on society?

2. In general, what are the most common types of news stories—for example, politics, crime, current events, and so on—covered by the newspapers, radio and television newscasts, and web sites that you access?

3. To what extent is the news content of newspapers, radio and television newscasts, and web sites that you access objective or biased?

4. To what extent is the news content of newspapers, radio and television newscasts, and web sites that you access entertaining versus serious?

5. To what extent does the news content of newspapers, radio and television newscasts, and web sites that you access exhibit depth or brevity?

When you read a newspaper, watch television news, listen to radio news, or link to news on the web, in effect you are dropping in on a kind of society-wide conversation about the country you are in, as well as other countries. When you are exposed to news in the media, you are invited to witness a multilevel discussion about what society believes is important or unimportant, dangerous or safe, wrong or right, and so on. These implicit and explicit evaluations of phenomena happening around you are presented on a continuous basis by the cumulative discourse of news reporting. Such societal commentary by news reporting takes place in newspaper content every single day, and in broadcast and internet content just about every second.

In Chapter 3, news reporting was likened to the "standout" leaves of a tree. Standout leaves are more noticeable than the other leaves of a tree because they are brighter, larger, shinier, or in some way more robust. Standout leaves can be examined to determine the general well-being of other parts of the tree, the whole tree, and to some extent the environment in which the tree grows. As Alan Albarran indicates in *Management of Electronic Media* (2002), news content makes a media system more visible than other kinds of content because, for most people, news reporting is the main source of information about national and international events.

Like other kinds of content, news reporting has been swept up by the winds of globalization. The *BBC World Service* from the UK is credited as the first organization to successfully distribute radio news twenty-four hours a day to mass audiences across the world. *CNN* from the USA is credited as doing the same in television news, ushering in other twenty-four-hour television news distributors such as the *BBC* (UK), *CCTV* (China) *Al Jazeera* (Qatar) and *FoxNews* (USA). In the realm of the internet, the *Guardian* (UK) in 2004 had the newspaper-based web site most frequently visited by people around the world (see Figure 10.1).

Global news distributors are constantly jockeying to position themselves as worldwide authorities on events that have international appeal. As discussed in Chapter 2 on Globalization, though these organizations deliver fairly standardized news content on the worldwide scale, they also deliver a significant amount of news content that is shaped individually for domestic markets. For example, CNN's news service CNN International is distributed primarily to countries outside of the USA, whereas CNN's Headline News is almost exclusively distributed inside the USA (see Figure 10.2). The CNN news programs that are seen in the USA often feature different reporters and stories from those seen on CNN news programs in other countries.

DEFINING NEWS REPORTING

News reporting is defined as the delivery of new information to mass audiences. There are many ways to classify news reporting, including hard news, breaking news, soft news, feature news, human interest news, entertainment news, business news, medical news, education news, technology news, sports news, culture news, travel news, and many, many other categories. News content in profit-making media tends to be packaged as a product designed to appeal to the largest possible audience. Full-fledged profit-making media run ads within the news content and does not have a strong organizational mission of serving the public. News reporting delivered by profit-making media tends to prioritize brief stories that capture the attention of the audience, but does not do much to increase the understanding of the audience. In contrast, news reporting delivered by public-service media tends to be designed as a service to provide the public with information in longer stories that are perceived to meet public needs. Full-fledged public-service media do not run ads and have a strong organizational mission to serve the general population.

FIGURE 10.1 *Web Site for* The Guardian

Source: © Guardian.

FIGURE 10.2   *CNN's Headline News, Distributed Primarily in the USA*
Source: Screen grab by Frank Kutch; permission courtesy of CNN.

The impact of news reporting on audience perceptions about a media system and the larger global environment can be observed at multiple levels. At one level, news has an impact on people's basic decision making as they go about the day. For example, people who hear a weather forecast on the radio about rain may end up canceling something they were going to do outdoors. At another level, news affects people's mind-sets as they experience nonnews events in life. For example, people who watch a television news report about a sexual predator may become more guarded in their interactions with unfamiliar people. At another level, government officials who read about other countries in a newspaper may pursue policies designed to address issues that were raised by that news story. And at another level, personnel in decision-making positions at news organizations may decide to cover an event mainly because other news organizations are covering the event.

Below, three dimensions of news reporting are identified that will be compared across the eight countries to provide the opportunity to assess fundamental differences in the way news is constructed across the eight countries.

BIAS VERSUS OBJECTIVITY IN NEWS REPORTING

One dimension of news reporting involves the degree to which the news content is objective or biased. This is somewhat of a misnomer, because there is no such thing as truly objective news, as many scholars have written—among them Davis Merrit in *Public Journalism and Public Life* (1998), Philip Meyer in *Ethical Journalism* (TK), Barrie Gunter in *Measuring Bias on Television* (1997), and Klaus Bruhn Jensen in "News as Ideology: Economic Statistics and Political Ritual in Television Network News" (1987). Rather, news reporting always presents a particular viewpoint that is situated within the cultural, political, and economic contexts of the country in which it operates.

At the core of the objectivity versus bias dimension is the degree to which a news organization is independent from outside financial or political influences on the organization's news content. The extent to which a news organization is independent depends on the degree to which its operations rely on other organizations to provide financing; whether the news organization is expected to generate profit; and whether the news organization has a charter or other governing document asserting its autonomy.

Taking into account the qualifying remarks stated above, the analysis in this chapter focuses on the degree to which news content is biased but leaves the impression that it is objective. This distinction can be observed in the amount of time or space devoted to the following:

Commentary: Reporting by individual media professionals and citizens that effectively editorialize an issue—reports that essentially appraise what is right or wrong.

Advocacy Journalism: Reporting that advocates a policy, position, belief, or action.

Meta Messages: Slogans, promotions, titles of programs and publications, word choices, and imagery that indicate whether the news organization perceives of its news reporting as having either a mission of objectivity or a mission that follows a bias.

Balance: Providing opposing viewpoints within a story, either between two stories that are juxtaposed or across stories appearing on successive days.

ENTERTAINMENT VERSUS SERIOUS NEWS REPORTING

A second dimension of news reporting involves the degree to which news is more entertaining or more serious. The rise of news as entertainment is related to the proliferation of cable and satellite television channels plus internet web sites, all of which compete intensely for audiences. One result is that news reporting is constantly in "breaking news" mode—that is, presenting news as urgent and developing. Important books that discuss adverse effects of aggressive competition for news audiences include: *News in the Global Sphere: A Study of CNN and Its Impact on Global Communication* (1997) by Ingrid Volkmer; *Global News* (2001) by Tony Silvia; *The Global Journalist* (2002) by Philip Seib; and *Breaking the News: How the Media Undermine American Democracy* (1996) by James Fallows.

The distinction between entertainment-oriented news and serious news is not meant to imply that news is either one or the other. However, the following principles can be laid out to identify predominantly entertaining news or predominantly serious news:

People: Entertainment-oriented news covers celebrities or scandals in the private lives of public figures; serious news covers politicians and ordinary people involved in events that are important to the general population.

Priority: Entertainment-oriented news presents dramatic or horrifying news (murders, sexual scandal) at the front of the content (the first page of a newspaper, the first story in a radio or television newscast, the first and biggest link on a web page), or as a constant theme of the overall news content; serious news presents news in order of priority and proportion according to its impact on people's lives.

Special Effects: Entertainment-oriented news makes more use of eye-catching and ear-catching special effects in photographs, graphics, and radio and television stage sets, thereby placing emphasis on the delivery of the news; serious news downplays special effects, thereby placing emphasis on the news itself.

DEPTH VERSUS BREVITY IN NEWS REPORTING

A third dimension of news reporting involves depth versus brevity of the information. Brief news reports can be thought of as superficial "headline" reporting, whereas in-depth news reports can be thought of as more substantial and therefore more meaningful. In general, longer news reports have more depth than shorter news reports. Similarly, news reports that are companion reports to other reports are thought of as providing more depth than single news reports. The following principles indicate depth or brevity in news reporting:

Length: The time length of a story on radio and television.
Space: The amount of space a story occupies in a newspaper or on a web site.
Companion Reports: Multiple reports in a single newspaper, web site, or radio or television newscast that address the newsworthy event.
Serializing: News reporting that includes more than one story on a news event on successive days.

NEWS REPORTING IN FRANCE

Bias versus Objectivity in Newspapers in France

In France, four out of five of the national newspapers are associated with individual political orientations—most of which are to the left side of the political spectrum. *L'Humanité* is considered to be a far-left communist newspaper. *Libération*, founded during a Parisien student revolution in 1968, is characterized as a left-wing intellectual newspaper. *Le Monde* (*The World*) is perceived of as a left-of-center "paper of record." *Le Canard Enchaîné* (*The Enchained Duck*) is perceived of as a left-wing paper that is derisive of politics as a whole. Only *Le Figaro* is perceived of as a right-wing newspaper.

In France, the national newspapers are known for generally practicing objectivity, but also for frequently crossing over into bias. *Le Figaro*, *Le Canard Enchaîné*, and *L'Humanité* carry metamessages, but none designates objectivity as a guiding criterion. Their respective metamessages, carried on their front pages, are "Without the Freedom of Criticism, There is No Way of Flattering Praise" (*Le Figaro*); "Satirical Newspaper" (*Le Canard Enchaîné*); and "The Newspaper of the French Communist Party" (*L'Humanité*). All of these statements invite readers to assume that the newspapers are not objective. *Le Monde* and *Le Figaro* carry two pages of clearly identified commentary and debate; the other newspapers tend to mix commentary into most of the pages. The commentary pages in *Le Monde* and *Le Figaro* usually come toward the middle of the newspaper. It is much more common to see columnist-opinion stories in French newspapers than it is to see letters-to-the-editor opinion pieces.

French newspapers are not known for actively engaging in campaigns to advocate positions on issues and policies that are perceived to impact French society. However, there are two general exceptions: stories that advocate more involvement in EU affairs, and court decisions that appear to contain an injustice. In both situations, French newspapers generally take a more investigative and campaigning approach than they normally do.

The bias that comes through in French newspapers generally is in line with the political orientations described in Chapter 10. For example, on August 24, the communist *L'Humanité* carried a story on its web site with the statement: "At the end of July, hundreds of néonazis met with impunity in the village of Hipsheim in the south of Strasbourg. Impotence of the authorities? Kindness?" More regularly, though, if there is bias, it is less obvious. For example, on the same date, *Le Figaro*—known as a right-wing newspaper—ran a front-page story with the headline "Bank Robberies in France Have Fallen by Half." This story contained no breaking news in terms of the release of a study's results by the police or the government, and instead was probably selected for the front page mainly because of *Le Figaro*'s support for law-and-order social policies. Similar editorial selections on the left side of the political spectrum can be found, though less so, in *Le Monde*.

Bias versus Objectivity in Radio and Television News in France   In France, television newscasts (and to a lesser extent radio newscasts) on both private and public channels are not known for being conservatively or liberally biased. Television and radio news in France generally aims at relative objectivity by balancing opinions and by refraining from commentary or advocacy journalism. However, television news—on both the public and the private broadcasters—is known for being somewhat acquiescent by avoiding aggressive questioning and criticism of government officials.

Entertainment versus Serious News in Newspapers in France

Most reporting in newspapers is very serious. The priority of stories generally is current events, politics, medicine and technology, EU news, and crime. Though scandal is also a theme in these subjects, generally the private indiscretions of people in the news are not as prominent as more weighty subjects. In terms of people, French newspapers often focus on government officials, artists, academics, and business executives. *Le Monde* and *Libération* (*Liberation*) are particularly well-known for focusing on academics and civil-servant administrators for news stories. For example, on August 24, 2004, *Libération* ran a lead story on its web site about an agreement between trade unions and organizations of surgeons. The story, which claimed that the agreement was a "revalorization" (earning more money) for the surgical profession, repeatedly quoted the Coordinator of Surgeons. Stories using literary or academic words such as *revalorization* and citing quotes from academics or artists are typical in the French national press.

Entertainment versus Serious News on Radio and Television in France

Radio news on commercial channels and on the Radio France networks tends to be serious with some entertainment-oriented qualities. For example on August 3, 2004, a 1000 (10:00 AM) newscast on the private pop-music station *Cherie FM* contained the following headlines: Prefect Serves Jailtime; Four French Detainees Released from Guantanamo Bay Military Base; American Soldier Holding a Leash on Iraqi Prisoner; Michael Moore Is Making a Film about Florida Vote Counts; 70 percent of Young People Believe That Getting Sun-tanned Is Okay. The stories listed show how even the entertainment-oriented stories have a serious angle to them.

On television, news reporting on both the France Television networks and the commercial broadcaster *TF1* tends to have more serious than entertaining qualities. Unlike other countries, where there are significant differences in the form and substance between the private and the public television broadcasters, in France the public broadcaster *France 2* and the private broadcaster *TF1* often have striking similarities to them, in terms of story selection, story length, and ads.

French television news stories focus on politics, crimes, and international events—especially those occurring within EU countries. French television news tends to be uncomplicated, with somewhat of a sleek look. Graphics are not used very much in television newscasts. One exception is the use of a map graphic to begin most stories, wherein the region or city where the story takes place is highlighted with a map graphic.

Depth versus Brevity of Reporting in Newspapers in France

It takes a lot of concentration to read and understand French national newspapers because of their intellectual depth, especially in the coverage of culture, medicine, politics, the environment, and history. That depth is largely achieved by elevated language and by companion reports within a single edition of a given newspaper. For example, on page 7 of the May 21, 2004, *Le Monde*, there were four articles about the 2005 national budget adopted by the government. The headline of the main article was: "The 2005 Budget Has Revived Rivalries in the Center of Government." The three companion article headlines were: "Mr. Sarkosy Replies to Mr. Strauss-Kahn"; "The Economy Sets Out Again but the Motors of Growth Remain Attached"; and "The Black Spot, It Is the Purchasing Capacity of Households." All of these articles revolved around the role of the 2005 budget in stimulating the French economy.

Often, the most detailed news reporting focuses on a scholar or artist, and brings into the discussion analyses by academics and cultural experts. For example, in the June 19, 2004, edition of *Libération* referenced on its web site, several articles focused on the legacy of the French philosopher Michel Foucault, who had died twenty years earlier. Separate articles examined: Foucault as an "archaeologist of knowledge"; the last days before he died; his stance against the death penalty; and his heritage. The group of articles on Foucault's heritage incorporated opinions from a lawyer, a psychoanalyst, philosophers, sociologists, historians, young people, and fellow travelers. The depth of analysis in these articles is shown in the following quote from a psychoanalyst:

> What should hold the attention of the psychoanalysts particularly today, is all the reflection of Foucault on the devices of monitoring and punishment of the capacity, the panoptical devices to the devices pan acoustic—the psychologization of all these devices which circulate in loop images and account for the lies and truths of the madness of the sex . . . and of the capacity.

Depth versus Brevity of Reporting on Radio and Television in France

Radio news stories are usually framed as either national or local news, but some stories are framed as European news or international news. Most radio stations in France carry news of some sort. News reports fifteen seconds and longer often include sound bites. The bulk of radio news is scheduled in the morning hours, though news also continues into the evening and late night. *France Info* carries the most news on domestic radio stations. *France Info* carries discussion programs and music (in the evening hours) that are interrupted by five-minute news flashes every twenty minutes.

The most common radio news report is the brief, three-minute flash, which can be heard on both public and private stations. Typically, this news flash is aired at the top of every hour; stories typically run ten to fifteen seconds long, with some stories running thirty seconds but rarely longer. The news flash format is usually as follows. Normally the first and second stories are regional French stories. Often they originate in Paris. Then comes an international story—often about an event involving the EU or the USA. Then the remaining two stories are usually feature stories centered in France.

Television news is broadcast mostly on *France 2, France 3,* and *TF1*. The main newscasts on *France 2* and *TF1* are aired at the same times, 1300 (1:00 PM) and at 2000 (8:00 PM). The newscasts are both forty minutes long. These observations again indicate how similar the public television newscasts and the private television newscasts are. Newscasts on *France 3* are aired at 0600 (6:00 AM), 1200 (12:00 PM), 1900 (7:00 PM), and 2245 (10:45 PM). The morning newscast on *France 3* is *Euronews*, a pan-European newscast, which is partly owned by *France 3,* as well as other European public-television organizations. The noontime newscast on *France 3* is forty minutes long and is regional, whereas the evening newscast is an hour long, and has regional news followed by national/international news. The newscasts on *France 2* and *TF1* are national/international, whereas the newscasts on *France 3* are regional. Ads are not aired within any newscasts on French television, but are aired before the newscast or between the newscast and the weather report.

In France, newscasts tend to have more breadth than depth because of the brevity of most stories. Most stories are between one and two minutes long, and are rarely longer than three minutes. Over the course of a forty-minute newscast, typically there are between twenty and twenty-five stories. The first news stories usually focus on current events and bad news. Often these stories deal with conflicts between politicians. Later in the newscast, common categories of stories include international events, animals, outdoor leisure activities, cultural and art festivals, and sports. Sports news usually comes almost at the end of the newscast. Sports segments are often shorter than in other countries. After the last news story, there are segments of ads and promotions, and then a more developed weather segment than the one prior to the beginning of the newscast. Figure 10.3 lists sample headlines for stories from the 1300 (1:00 PM) August 2, 2004, newscast on *France 2*. To further illustrate how the *France 2* and *TF1* newscasts are similar in terms of story content and story placement, the stories in the *France 2* newscast that are marked with an asterisk also were broadcast during *TF1's* 1300 (1:00 PM) newscast. These four stories, which appeared early in the *France 2* newscast, were the lead stories on *TF1*.

Preview of 4 Headlines
*X-Ray Doctor Who Was a Fake
3 Days of Intense Heat Addressed by the Minister of Health
*Shortage of Doctors Because They Are on Holiday
Pollution in Big Cities is Causing Breathing Problems
*4 People Killed by Disease Spread by Air Conditioning
*17 People Killed in Gas Explosion in Belgium
Regulations of Gas Pipes in France
Investigation of Explosion in Toulouse that Occurred 3 Years Ago
Probe from USA Going to Mercury
Bankrupt Tati Supermarket Chain May be Bought by Two
   Businessmen
Prefect Arrested on Corruption Charges
USA Pressures Sudan to Control Rebels
346 People Killed in Grocery Store Fire in Paraguay
Statue of Liberty in USA Open Again for First Time Since 9/11
Drought in South of France Causing Water Restrictions
More and More Animals in Cages at SPCA Each Summer
Iraqi Athletes at Olympics
French Footballers being Bought and Sold
Regatta in Spain
Holiday Activities in South of France
Fly Fishing as a Sport and a Philosophy
French Actress Who Just Died
Festival of Theatre
A French River (an installment of a series on French rivers)

FIGURE 10.3   *Sample Headlines from 1300 (1:00 PM) Newscast on France 2; August 2, 2004*
Source: Robert McKenzie.

Video/sound bites featuring either a witness to a news event or an expert are fairly common in television news reports. Very often, a story includes a bite from an average citizen. Bites are usually short, typically lasting around fifteen seconds. It is somewhat common in television news in France for a story to be followed by one other, related news report, especially if the first story occurs in another country but has implications for France. For example, in the August 2, 2004, *France 2* 13:00 (1:00 PM) newscast, a two-minute story on a natural-gas explosion in Belgium was followed by a brief story on regulations related to natural-gas distribution in France.

NEWS REPORTING IN SWEDEN

Bias versus Objectivity in Newspapers in Sweden

Sweden's national newspapers usually are associated with individual political orientations—most of them to the left side of the political spectrum. Of the major Stockholm-based newspapers, *Dagens Nyheter* (the *Daily News*) is known as being center-left; it is also generally considered to be Sweden's most prestigious newspaper. *Svenska Dagbladet* (the *Swedish*

Daily Sheet) is considered to be a center-right newspaper. *Aftonbladet* (*Evening Sheet*) is known for being to the left in regard to labor issues, and both *Expressen* (*The Express*) and *Kvällposten* (*The Evening Post*)—which are owned by the same company—are known for being center-right.

The national serious newspapers have moved away from representing political parties and toward striving for objectivity—though some political leanings remain. Of the morning publications, *Dagens Nyheter* is known as an independent newspaper with leanings toward the Social Democratic Party; *Svenska Dagbladet* has been known to lean toward supporting policies of political parties in opposition to the Social Democrats. Of the afternoon sensational tabloids, *Aftonbladet* tends to support policies of the Social Democratic Party, whereas *Expressen* and *Kvällposten* do not routinely demonstrate political-party biases. Swedish newspapers generally do not contain promotional metamessages on the front pages that indicate a mission to be objective.

Almost all newspapers in Sweden have a *Leder* (Leader) page, which prints a staff editorial that tries to convince readers of a certain point of view. Most Swedish newspapers also run letters from ordinary citizens seeking to offer opinions on government policy. For example, in the June 2, 2003, *Expressen*, there was a section containing several letters to the editor commenting on the government's policy of permitting modern windmills to be erected in the south of Sweden to produce electricity. The letters contrasted comments by some people saying that the windmills make the countryside ugly, with others saying that the windmills do not take away from the beauty of the countryside.

In addition, *Dagens Nyheter* and *Svenska Dagbladet* are known for running "debate pages" in which readers express opinions. The debate pages come early in the newspaper, on page 3 and 4. Articles on the debate pages can be written by ordinary citizens, but more commonly are written by politicians, business executives, and employees of the state. The debate pages serve as a kind of national dialogue on issues—often related to government policy—that are considered to be important to Swedish people. For example, on page 4 of the June 2, 2004, *Dagens Nyheter*, the education minister wrote an essay arguing against schools becoming bilingual. It is typical for the debate pages to contain articles by different writers that provide a running debate continuing for several days or even weeks.

Swedish newspapers are known for actively framing stories around two subject matters that relate to socialism: One has to do with the proper role of a "welfare state"—that is, a society in which the government has the duty and the right to tax the citizenry to meet humanitarian needs of the general population (e.g., health care, access to a clean environment, protection of children, providing for the elderly). For example, in the August 5, 2004, *Svenska Dagbladet* there was a front-page story with the headline "Foreign Office to Stop Deporting Children." This story focused on how the government was reversing its policy of deporting unlawful immigrants back to their countries of origin, because it was leading to children being deported back to difficult living conditions in southern Iraq. Though Swedish newspapers differ in the degree of support for the welfare state, much of their news coverage uses language that discusses societal problems in a way that implicitly supports the welfare state but questions how much power and reach it should have.

A second subject matter typically covered by Swedish newspapers that relates to a socialist orientation involves injustices against humanity and the environment. Across Swedish newspapers, there is a strong tendency to publish stories and photographs that expose conditions such as famine, starvation, war, water and soil pollution, litter, people without homes, prison conditions, and cruelty to animals. These stories are commonly placed on the front page and are lengthy. For example, in the June 2, 2003, regional newspaper *Sydsvenska Dagbladet* (the *South Sweden Daily Sheet*), there was a front-page story on an oil tanker that sunk off the south coast of Sweden and spilled 66,000 tons of oil into the sea. The article contained a color photograph of the tanker sinking, which took up a quarter of the front page. The text focused on the environmental damage, and continued onto page 2.

Bias versus Objectivity in Radio and Television News in Sweden

Television and radio newscasts are not known for being conservatively or liberally biased. Television and radio news in Sweden generally aims at relative objectivity by balancing opinions and by refraining from commentary or advocacy journalism. However, largely due to the laws that permit citizens (including journalists) to have access to receipts documenting how government officials spend tax dollars (see Chapter 4), television news on both the public channels and the private channel is known for aggressively investigating officials in regard to potentially improper expenditures.

Entertainment versus Serious News in Newspapers in Sweden

In Sweden, most reporting in the morning newspapers is serious. The priority of stories generally is people's lives, politics (especially articles focusing attention on the role of the welfare state), culture, environment, immigration issues, and EU news. Much of the coverage in Swedish newspapers uses a feature-story approach (rather than a hard-news approach) and revolves around two common themes: culture and providing assistance to people in need. As an example of culture's importance, four out of the nine stories on the front page of the August 5, 2004, *Dagens Nyheter* were continued inside the newspaper in the Culture section. One was headlined "Japan, Japan, All Over Stockholm," and was about a Japanese art exhibit in Stockholm. On the same front page, there was a feature story with the headline "All People Remember in Front of the Camera." This story, which was accompanied by a quarter-page color photo on the front page, as well as another quarter-page color photo on page 7 where the story was continued, was about a government social worker helping elderly people to feel valuable to society by recording video interviews with them so they can talk about their lives. This activity was described as being good for the self-esteem of elderly people, which in turn helps them maintain a high quality of life.

In Swedish newspapers, often there is a vivid openness and directness with which serious subjects are covered, especially when it comes to issues related to the human body. For example, the front page of the June 2, 2003, regional newspaper *Skånska Dagbladet* (Skånska is a region in south Sweden) included a story about a couple having a baby through the cesarean-section birthing technique. The story reported:

> At 9.50 PM on the Friday of May 23, little "somersault" made his entrance by a planned cesarean section. For his parents Eva Toumainen and Jörgen Pedersen, it's a dazed experience. Eva does the CS with spinal anaesthetics, and she is awake during the operation while Jörgen is standing beside her.

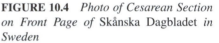

FIGURE 10.4 *Photo of Cesarean Section on Front Page of* Skånska Dagbladet *in Sweden*

Source: Photo by Eva-Lisa Svensson; permission by Skånska Dagbladet.

The anxiety he feels during the operation is transformed to pure happiness as his son arrives. At the maternal clinic in Lund the proportion of CS has been doubled the last 15 years. The reason is that more risks are discovered per birth with the technology of today, but also due to more women asking for a CS out of fear of a normal delivery.

Accompanying the story was a graphic photograph of the baby's foot coming out of the mother's womb during the cesarean section (Figure 10.4).

In the Swedish afternoon sensational tabloids, most of the news is not about personal misadventures of celebrities unless an illegality has been committed. Rather, news usually involves a crime or a tragic accident. For example, on pages 10 and 11 of the June 2, 2003, *Kvällposten,* there was a story about a man driving a car that hit a fifty-four-year-old woman pedestrian and then crashed into a house. In the same issue, there was a story about a naked man in Gothenburg who tried to blow up a car (p. 20).

In terms of people, both Swedish broadsheets and sensational tabloids tend to focus on government officials, political-party officials, civil servants, artists, citizens, and foreign politicians. Very often the news is about a government policy that is not working. For example, in *Kvällposten,* there was a story with the headline "One Shot in the Air Kills the Chances of Going to the Olympics." The story criticized claims that a new law in Sweden further restricts the ownership of guns, resulting in the ionic outcome that it is now more difficult to use guns to start a race in track and field competitions. The story stated:

> This country's target shooters and hunters is not a group of problem makers and only a small number of this country's arms owners commit crimes against keeping arms. Percentage

wise, more cops commit crimes of keeping arms than legal weapon owners every year. Every time there's a change in the law of owning and keeping a weapon the focus is on the hunters and target shooters. The last change affected the hunters negatively. The tactics of the Swedish government have been to make it even harder for hunters and target shooters and intermittently to weaken the opinions of these groups. (Aug. 5, 2004, p. 4)

Entertainment versus Serious News on Radio and Television in Sweden

In Sweden, radio news on the public-service channels is usually serious. For example, the headlines from an August 8, 2004, newscast on *P3* were: Inmates Escape from Prison; An Accident at Nuclear Plant; Insurgents Attacking in Iraq; Saving Money on Insurance. Other examples of serious news on public-service radio include Culture News on *P1* and Children's News on *P4*.

Television news reporting on both the SVT News Channels and the commercial *TV 4* tends to have more serious than entertaining qualities. *TV 4* is considered to be more informal than *SVT 1* and *SVT 2,* and will sometimes include funny comments in the graphic showing the name of a reporter or witness. For example, if there is a story about a motorcyclist, the graphic may say "[Firstname] [Lastname], Proud Motorcycle Owner." Such jokes are always lighthearted and not degrading.

In general, Swedish television news stories tend to focus on accidents, crime, social conditions, and international events—especially those focusing on humanitarian crises. As an example of news on social conditions, the 2100 (9:00 PM) news on August 25, 2004, *SVT 2* included a story on women committing more violent crimes than ever before. As an example of humanitarian crisis, the 2000 (8:00 PM) news on *TV 4* included a story on famine and disease in Chad.

Sets for *SVT* television news in Sweden tend to have a nature theme and sets for both *SVT* and *TV 4* use warm lights to illuminate parts of the set. Figure 10.5 shows the set for a newscast on SVT, which uses a flowerlike logo.

Graphics are not used very much in Swedish television newscasts. Stories filed from the field often include camera shots panning across landscapes, lakes, seas, forests, and flowers.

Depth versus Brevity of Reporting in Newspapers in Sweden

Swedish morning newspapers are known for providing in-depth feature news (as opposed to hard news) covering subjects relating to culture (especially art, music, and handicrafts), the social welfare state, party politics, the human body, humanitarian crises, and the environment. Articles on newsworthy events fitting into these categories usually involve extensive analysis. Typically, news reports on the front page are not keyed to several companion reports inside the paper. However, front-page news stories are typically continued to specific sections inside the newspaper such as Culture, Family, and Economy.

Much of the depth in Swedish morning newspapers revolves around the debate pages. For example, in the August 5, 2004, *Svenska Dagbladet*, a conservative paper by Swedish standards, there was a newspaper editorial on the ineffectiveness of opposition

FIGURE 10.5   *Television Set for* SVT 1 *News in Sweden*
Source: SVT Bild.

conservative parties to challenge the policies of the majority government party, the Social Democrats. The editorial stated that the leader of the Liberal Party (the leading opposition party) is "not helping opposing parties to unite against the Social Democrats. . . . The right-wing parties shouldn't let the best be the enemy of the good" (p. 4). Below this editorial was a section called Reply, which contained three opinion pieces responding to articles on the business climate in Sweden that were published in a previous edition of *Svenska Dagbladet*. The opinion pieces were authored by: a company president, the chairman for a worker's unit of a union for administrators, and the former leader of the Christian Democrats (an opposition party). The latter's piece had the headline, "The Parties Have to Heal Together." In-depth discussions about party politics and issues affected by the scope of a welfare state (such as the business climate in Sweden) are commonly centered on the debate pages of Swedish newspapers.

The sensational afternoon tabloid newspapers in Sweden are known for providing depth in reporting about dramatic crimes and accidents. Often the tabloids will devote multiple pages covering such issues, using text, graphics, and photographs. For example, the August 5, 2004, *Expressen* covered a story involving an escape from prison by three inmates—which followed another prison escape a few weeks earlier. *Expressen* ran the story on the front page, and then starting on page 8 ran another fourteen consecutive pages of stories on the prison break. The stories covered the design of the prison, the failures by prison security, the failures by the government, police action, what the men were in prison for, how they made their escape, and people who knew the prisoners. The stories included detailed graphics showing the layout of the prison, and multiple color photographs—many of them taking up half to three-fourths of a page. Similarly, the August 5, 2004, *Kvällposten* covered this news event with a front-page story and twelve additional pages inside the newspaper; *Aftonbladet* ran a front-page story and eleven additional pages of coverage.

The sensational afternoon tabloids in Sweden are also known for providing detailed coverage of sexuality issues. Even though such stories in the tabloids will often have a sensational orientation, usually there is also a serious educational component. For example, on page 9 of the June 2, 2003, *Kvällposten*, an article reported that Swedish model Victoria Silvstedt had sex with another woman. Included with this article was a section speculating about how many lesbians there are in Sweden, and what percentage of females have had lesbian sex. Also included in this story were the results of a survey—"Is It Okay to Have Sex with the Same Gender?"—posed to five people ranging in age from twenty-two to thirty-one. Issues such as this one relating to the human body and sexuality are covered routinely in Swedish newspapers with openness and directness.

Depth versus Brevity of Reporting on Radio and Television in Sweden

In Sweden, most radio stations carry news of some sort. Radio news is continuous throughout the day, though reports in the morning and late afternoon hours are longer. News reports fifteen seconds and longer often include sound bites.

The most common news report is the three-minute bulletin, which can be heard on both public and private radio stations. Typically, the bulletin is aired at the top of every hour across the twenty-four-hour day. Stories typically run five to fifteen seconds; fewer stories are thirty seconds or longer. Often, the bulletin sounds like a reading of headlines.

The format of the three-minute bulletin is usually as follows. Normally, the first two or three stories are current events from anywhere in Sweden. Then come international stories from anywhere in the world. Then the remaining stories are feature stories centered in Sweden. National news that is broadcast on *P1, P2, P3,* and *P4* National is provided by Swedish Radio's Ekot (translated "Echo") news service.

Television news is aired on the public broadcasters *SVT 1* and *SVT 2,* as well as the private commercial broadcaster *TV 4.* Between the two public broadcasters, the more substantial newscasts are a twenty-minute newscast on *SVT 1* at 1930 (7:30 PM), and a thirty-five-minute newscast at 2300 (11:00 PM). There are two fifteen-minute newscasts on *SVT 2,* at 1800 (6:00 PM) and 2100 (9:00 PM). On the commercial broadcaster *TV 4,* the main newscasts are a twenty-four-minute newscast at 1830 (6:30 PM) and a fifteen-minute newscast at 2200 (10:00 PM).

News reporting on all television channels generally does not follow a set format. National news stories can come in the first part of the newscast, with international stories coming later in the newscast, or vice versa. News stories at any point in the newscast can range from twenty seconds to four minutes. Thus, newscasts can have either breadth or depth, depending on the particular newscast. Because of the variance in story length, it is difficult to provide an accurate figure for the average number of stories per newscast.

Similarly, hard-news stories as well as feature-news stories can appear almost anywhere in the newscast—with the exception of the first three stories, which are usually current-events stories. It is very common for newscasts to include at least one story on human rights, and at least one story on a person enjoying an aspect of nature. Sports and weather news usually come toward the end of the newscast. Both *SVT* and *TV 4* run separate economic news programs after the regular news programs. In addition, SVT 1 and SVT 2 run a Culture News program that relates only to culture. The public broadcasters tend to do more economy than sports news, whereas the private broadcaster *TV 4* tends to do more sports than economy news. Sports news usually comes almost at the end of the newscast. On the commercial broadcaster, there is an advertising break between the newscast and the weather report. Figure 10.6 lists sample headlines for stories from the August 25, 2004, *SVT 2* 2100 (9:00 PM) newscast.

Many television news stories include a segment in which a reporter interviews a witness to a news event on camera—usually a regular citizen who witnessed a news event or who has an opinion on a news event. Sound bites for a typical story can be extended, typically lasting thirty to forty-five seconds. It is common in television news in Sweden for at least one story to be followed by a second, related news report. For example, in an August 7, 2004, newscast, a story on parachuters on an airplane that crashed was followed by a story about a previous airplane accident that had not yet been solved.

Preview of Three Stories with Video
Airplane Crash in Russia a Potential Terrorist Act
A Look at Russian Flight Safety
Terrorists in Chechnya and Their Previous Actions
Olympics in Athens
Military Report on Violated Human Rights at American Prison in Iraq
People Walking to Mosque in Holy Town in Iraq
Margaret Thatcher's Son Arrested for Attempting to Help a Coup Bring Down a
   Government in Equitorial Guinea
Swedish Air Department Laying Off People
47,000 Chickens Put Down Due to Salmonella Disease
Women Committing More Violent Crimes than Before
France has New Hot Shot in Politics: Finance Minister
Swedish Government Sends 6 Million Kronors to Needy Countries to Develop Jobs
Volvo Returns Big Profits to Ford
Saab Automaker Has to Lay Off Employees
Swedes Borrowing More and More Money to Buy Real Estate
Stock Market Up
Interest Rate and Currency Exchange Rate Report
American Stock Market Up
Weather
Repeat of Main News Stories
Sports Scores

FIGURE 10.6   *Sample Headlines from 2100 (9:00 PM) Newscast on* SVT 2 *in Sweden; August 25, 2004.*

Source: Robert McKenzie.

NEWS REPORTING IN THE UK

Bias versus Objectivity in Newspapers in the UK

In the UK, most of the national newspapers are associated with individual political orientations. Of the broadsheets, the *Times* is generally perceived as an establishment-oriented newspaper supporting whichever government is in power; the *Telegraph* as a right-wing newspaper advocating free-market policies; the *Guardian* as a left-wing newspaper advocating socialist policies; the *Independent* as a politically independent but economically and socially liberal newspaper that advocates for the environment and against war; and the *Financial Times* as a paper that advocates pro-business positions. Of the sensational tabloids, the *Sun* and the *Daily Star* are generally perceived as gossip newspapers often focusing on sexual escapades of famous people; the *Daily Mirror* as a newspaper focusing on working-class concerns; the *Daily Express* as a paper that catches public personalities "in the act"; and the *Daily Mail* as a conservative paper focusing on the lives of members of the royal family.

To gain insight into how the newspapers in the UK are perceived to have distinct personalities, it is instructive to consult a well-known saying that was originally used on the television show *Yes, Minister,* but that also appears in a tongue-in-cheek reference source called *United Kingdom English for the American Novice*. The saying goes:

The *Times* is read by the people who run the country.

The *Daily Mirror* is read by the people who think they run the country.

The *Guardian* is read by the people who think they ought to run the country.

The *Daily Mail* is read by the wives of the people who own the country.

The *Financial Times* is read by the people who own the country.

The *Daily Express* is read by the people who think that the country ought to be run as it used to be.

The *Daily Telegraph* is read by the people who think the country still is run as it used to be.

And the *Sun* is read by people who don't care who runs the country as long as she has big tits.

In the UK, most national newspapers—particularly the London tabloids—are known for being openly biased. Generally, UK newspapers do not contain promotional metamessages indicating that they are unbiased or that they aim toward objectivity. In terms of commentary, both the tabloids and the serious newspapers normally devote several pages to opinions by regular columnists. The insert sections such as T2 in the *Times* and G2 in the *Guardian*, which run feature stories, are comprised largely of opinion stories. It is more common to see columnist-opinion stories in UK newspapers than it is to see letters-to-the-editor opinion pieces.

The bias of UK newspapers appears not only in the editorial sections toward the back of the newspaper—often referred to as "Comment and Analysis"—but also in hard-news stories closer to the front of the newspaper. Typically, the bias is manifested in stinging rebukes of existing government policies or the conduct of private citizens, companies, and celebrities.

In the tabloids, bias often appears in both the headline and the body of a story. For example, in the June 11, 2003, *Daily Express*, a bolded headline on the front page stated: "Mortgage Upheaval on the Way." The story body then explained that "Monthly mortgage repayments could double as the Government prepares to take Britain into the Euro, leading housing experts warned last night." This kind of overt bias, which essentially argues against a government (domestic or foreign) position, is typical of UK tabloids. Very often, the tabloids will take up a daily campaign on the front pages to urge the government to follow a particular course of action. Such a campaign might run for several weeks, before giving way to another campaign.

In the serious broadsheets in the UK, bias is less overt but still pervasive. Often the bias appears over the course of a series of quotes from officials that cumulatively argue against or in favor of a position. For example, the March 4, 2004, *Independent* ran a story on a former executive of a television company receiving a severance package that included a "whopping 15.1 million" (in GBP). The story included the following: "A Department of Trade and Industry Spokesman said the Government had decided last week not to act on fat-cat payoffs because consultations found the move would be unwelcome" (p. 3). Use of the phrase *fat cat* demonstrates a common journalistic convention in the UK that it is acceptable for writers to show displeasure. Moreover, there were no opposing viewpoints in this story provided either in quotes or in the author's own writing to counter the general theme that the executive took an inappropriate payoff. This implication was also presented in a second article in the Business section, in which the writer observed that a comment on the severance package by another of the television company directors was "an insultingly brief and completely inadequate account of what looks like one of the worst cases of executive excess yet to grace these shores" (p. 39). This kind of bias, using words of strong condemnation, is common in UK newspapers.

Most newspapers—broadsheets and sensational tabloids alike—are known for printing advocacy content. This kind of content—in contrast to objective content—serializes an opinion, usually in front-page stories day after day until the given issue is replaced by another opinion serializing a different issue in successive newspaper articles. The advocacy content often appears on the front pages of the newspapers (in addition to the editorial pages). For example, in the summer of 2003, both the *Daily Mail* (a tabloid) and the *Telegraph* (a broadsheet) took up the issue of whether the UK should adopt the Euro as its monetary currency, in response to the prime minister's consideration of whether the issue should be put to citizens in a referendum. In front-page headlines for several days in a row, both newspapers campaigned against the UK adopting the Euro currency. The *Daily Mail* even held its own self-styled referendum in which its readers could register a vote with the newspaper on the issue.

Bias versus Objectivity in Radio and Television News in the UK

In the UK, television newscasts and, to a lesser extent, radio newscasts—on both commercial and BBC channels—are not known for being biased. Television and radio news in the UK generally aims at relative objectivity by balancing opinions and by refraining from commentary or advocacy journalism.

Entertainment versus Serious News in Newspapers in the UK

Most news reporting in London tabloids is entertainment oriented, though serious news is also a staple of the reporting. Scandal and crime generally take priority. In terms of people, the tabloids tend to focus on public officials and celebrities, very often when they are in trouble because they have behaved badly; the *Sun* and the *Daily Mirror* in particular run these kinds of stories. The *Daily Mail* centers many of its stories on members of the royal family. These stories generally are not as harsh in exposing or commenting on the private lives of royals compared to stories about other celebrities. For example, a story in the June 15, 2003, *Daily Mail* is about "Prince William falling in love with a girl he met in Kenya" (p. 3). Such a story having to do with a celebrity would likely include more speculation about their sexual escapades. The tabloids also focus on crime—especially murders and arrests—but celebrity scandal tends to be prized over crime news. When crime is reported, often the wording makes the crime look particularly silly, as in a *Mail on Sunday*'s June 15, 2003, headline: "Shot dead . . . in row over a privet hedge" (p. 5).

In contrast, the broadsheets in the UK focus almost exclusively on serious news. Very often, politicians and business executives are covered. The priority of stories tends to favor policy rather than crime and scandal. Even if an entertainer is discussed in a serious broadsheet, the story tends to move toward an intellectual analysis of how the person embodies entertainers as a group, rather than on more titillating information about an individual entertainer.

The tabloids in the UK are mostly about entertainment. One nickname for the tabloids commonly used is "red tops" because of the bright red bar across the top of the front page. In scandalous reports, it is common for color photos depicting celebrities in awkward poses to take up anywhere from one-fourth to three-fourths of a page. For example, the *Sun*'s December 3, 2002, a story on Oasis member Liam Gallagher's "brawl at a bar" contained three photos of him looking frazzled and being restrained by friends (p. 5).

Entertainment versus Serious News on Radio and Television in the UK

Radio news on commercial channels displays more entertaining qualities than news on most of the BBC radio networks. Lead stories on both commercial channels and the BBC radio networks typically focus on politics and crime. Commercial radio tends to focus more on dramatic scandal, as exhibited in the third story of a *Southern Radio* newscast on June 13, 2003: "Too explicit: A religious group hits out at sex lessons in East Sussex, and Brighton and Hove." Soundwise, commercial radio news often enhances the entertainment orientation with a music soundtrack playing underneath the announcer's voice during news reports. Of the BBC networks, news on *Radio 1* (the contemporary channel) has less of an entertaining feel to it than the commercial networks, but a much more entertaining feel to it than the other BBC channels.

Television news on both the BBC and the commercial channels tends to have more serious than entertaining qualities. Lead stories focus on politics and crimes, and graphics tend to be static rather than mobile. One exception is the satellite broadcaster Sky News, which constantly runs a bright red banner across the bottom of the screen, with text announcing news alerts. Graphics on Sky News are fast-moving, and are often accompanied by searing sound effects.

Depth versus Brevity of Reporting in Newspapers in the UK

UK broadsheets are known for providing in-depth news reporting in terms of elevated vocabulary, historical background, detail, statistics, quotes, context, and especially analysis.

For example, a June 11, 2003, front-page article in the *Independent* reported on five hundred lost artworks painted by J. M. W. Turner, one of Britain's most "important painters." This article stated how many Turner works were discovered, how many were watercolors, how many were pencil drawings, how many works remain missing, the time period in which Turner painted, the age of Turner when he painted a particularly famous piece, and other information.

Typically, news reports on the front page are keyed to several companion reports inside the newspaper. For example, the June 11, 2003, *Times* ran a front-page story on government ministers being "given the free rein to go out and make the case for the euro." Below the story, five headlines of stories related to this story were listed, along with corresponding page numbers. The headlines were:

Gear change, page 13 (Politics pages)
Simon Jenkins, page 20 (Commentary pages)
Leading article and Letters, page 21 (Letters to the Editor page)
Trade gap, page 23 (Business section)
Mary Ann Sieghart, T2 (Insert section)

Detail is also provided in UK broadsheets in terms of titles of reporters. For example, stories in the *Daily Telegraph* on June 11, 2003, included the following titles: Political Editor, Chief Political Correspondent, Art Sales Correspondent, Education Editor, Media Editor, Social Affairs Correspondent, Transport Correspondent, and Environment Editor.

Tabloids in the UK are known for some depth as well. The *Daily Mail* is better known for providing depth in serious news than the other tabloids, though all tabloids in the UK cover serious news in addition to entertainment-oriented news. Frequently, tabloids will serialize an issue on the front pages across several days or even weeks. In the summer of 2003, for example, it was common to see photos in the tabloids of football star David Beckham along with a news report on a weekly and sometimes daily basis. Some depth is also often provided in tabloid stories through quotes and historical context. For example, a June 11, 2003, story on page 2 of the *Daily Mirror* reported on the possibility of Beckham being traded from an English club to a different club in another country. This story quotes six sources. A table providing a chronology of Beckham's football career from 1991 to 2003 was also included in the story.

Depth versus Brevity of Reporting on Radio and Television in the UK

In the UK, radio news reports commonly focus on local, national, European, and international news. News reports fifteen seconds and longer often include sound bites. One category of news that stands out on radio (as well as television) is weather news, because the weather in the UK can be volatile. The bulk of radio news is scheduled in the morning hours, though news also continues into the evening and late night. Almost all radio stations carry radio news. BBC broadcaster *Radio 5 Live* and commercial broadcaster *LBC* (in the London area) offer programming that is primarily news/talk oriented; *Radio 5 Live* is broadcast nationally. The BBC's *World Service,* aimed at other countries, runs news twenty-four hours a day.

The most common news report is the three-minute bulletin, which is aired on both commercial and BBC local stations. Typically, bulletins are aired half hourly during morning and afternoon drive times, and hourly during lunchtime. Stories during the three-minute bulletins typically run ten or fifteen seconds long, though a few are thirty seconds. Rarely are stories longer than thirty seconds.

The format of the three-minute bulletin is usually as follows. Prior to the start of the newscast, there is usually a weather segment that typically lasts sixty seconds. Weather news is normally presented as a stand-alone segment separate and apart from a regular newscast. Within the regular newscast, the first two stories are usually national news stories. The remaining stories normally are local news stories. The three-minute bulletin usually ends with a traffic report.

On the BBC national channels, radio news is frequent and has depth. Most news is national, and incorporates sports news at the end of the newscast.

Television news is scheduled on most of the television channels three times a day, though collectively these times are somewhat staggered throughout the broadcast day. Morning newscasts are normally brief. Newscasts have more depth in the afternoon and evening. Most newscasts are no longer than a half hour. Most newscasts are national and international in scope. The exception is news on *ITV,* which is formatted with regional programming. All newscasts on the commercial channels are uninterrupted by advertising.

Television news on the commercial channels is broadcast throughout the day. For example, *Channel 4*'s first, thirty-minute newscast is at noon; the second and final newscast airs at 1900 (7:00 PM) for fifty-five minutes. *Channel 5* airs three 30-minute newscasts beginning at 0600 (6:00 AM). *ITV* has four half-hour newscasts.

On the two BBC channels, television news differs significantly. News on *BBC1* has depth, whereas news on *BBC2* is brief (mainly the headlines). On *BBC1*, for example, the first newscast begins at 0600 (6:00 AM) and continues for three hours. Regional/local news is run at :25 and :55 on the hour during this newscast. The next newscast is national/international news at 13:00 (1:00 PM) for half an hour, then a local newscast at 13:30 (1:30 PM) for half an hour. The next newscast is national/international news at 18:00 (6:00 PM) for half an hour, followed by regional news at 18:30 (6:30 PM) for half an hour. The final newscast is national/international news at 22:00 (10:00 PM) for 25 minutes, then followed by local news for 5 minutes. On *BBC2*, five-minute newscasts air national/international or regional news throughout the day. The next newscast is national/international and airs at 15:20 (3:20 PM) for 5 minutes. The final newscast is regional news and airs at 15:25 (3:25 PM) for 5 minutes. Figure 10.7 lists sample headlines for stories from the 1900 (7:00 PM) *Channel 4* newscast on July 28, 2004.

In addition to newscasts on the terrestrial channels, there are two UK channels on cable/satellite that carry news twenty-four hours a day. One is News Corporation's *Sky News,* and the other is *BBC News 24*.

News-report lengths can differ widely on television news in the UK. A lead story can run more than five minutes. Subsequent stories typically can range from twenty seconds to

Preview of Top 3 Stories
Scientists at Southampton University Unveil First Test for Undetectable DMG
American Military Tactic on Iraq
Suicide Bombers Step It Up in Iraq
Oxford Research Laboratory Will Consider Moving Scientists Abroad
Will Europe Notice a Difference If John Kerry Took Over for Bush
Catching the Cheats in Athens
Iraq: More than 70 Killed in Car Bomb
The Kerry Campaign—Are Kerry and Bush Really Different?
Animal Rights and New Oxford Laboratory—Construction Company Pulls Out
Recap of Headlines
Advertising Break (1 min)
Recap of Headlines
New Dope Test—Catching Cheats in Athens
Iraq: More than 70 Killed in Car Bomb
The Kerry Campaign—The Pros and Cons
Animal Extremists Threat and Construction Company Bails Out of Contract with
    Oxford University
Afghanistan No Longer Safe for MIS—Afghans Lose Medical Assistance
Iraqi Family with Six Dead Launch Legal Test Case Against Unlawful Killing
Teenage Boy Faces Life in Prison after Admitting to Murder
British Airways will Decide whether or not to Strike Over Pay Dispute
Economic Reports
Weather Reports
Man Sentenced to Life for Murdering Cell Mate
Sven Silence: Denied Affair with Secretary
Democratic Convention—Will Edwards Strength Help Kerry Win?

FIGURE 10.7   *Sample Headlines from 1900 (7:00 PM) Newscast on* Channel 4 *in the UK; July 28,*
2004.

Source: Robert McKenzie.

two minutes. Generally, news reports on *BBC1* are longer than news reports on the other channels. Video/sound bites containing parts of newsmaker speeches are fairly common in television news reports, and can run up to thirty seconds. Sometimes multiple sound bites from the same source (usually a political figure) are used in the same story. And, often, video/sound bites of more than one person are used in a story.

In the UK, it is very common for a television news story to be followed by one or two other related news reports. The first story normally focuses primarily on the facts of the news event, whereas subsequent stories focus more on analysis. It is also common for the lead story to be followed by a live interview with an analyst who comments on events described in the story. For example, on April 28, 2003, *Channel 4* aired a story on a press conference by the prime minister in which he announced a new government plan to reform education funding. This story was followed by a segment in which the anchor conducted a live interview by satellite with the Shadow (minority party) Education Secretary; then the anchor conducted a live interview with the government's Education Minister in the television studio. Such interviews are often characterized by hard questioning of guests and aggressive challenges to their positions, in both tone and content.

NEWS REPORTING IN THE USA

Bias versus Objectivity in Newspapers in the USA

In the USA, almost all newspapers (and radio and television newscasts as well) are known for expressing a goal of practicing objectivity. This does not prevent newspapers from being perceived as leaning to the left or the right. But generally, even newspapers that are perceived as leaning to the left or to the right make attempts to achieve objectivity by providing "both sides" to an issue. Typically, a story will begin with a proposed policy, and then present opposing viewpoints on the policy. For example, the November 13, 2004, *Washington Times* ran a story on the front page with the headline, "Hatch joins Kennedy to Push Hate-Crimes Bill." The first two paragraphs of the story were as follows:

> A new "hate-crimes" proposal supported by Democrats and key Senate Republicans, including Sen. Orrin G. Hatch of Utah, would vastly expand the federal government's power to prosecute such crimes committed anywhere in the country.
> Opponents of one of the most contentious provisions—inclusion of "sexual orientation" as protected category—"have got to grow up," Mr. Hatch said earlier in the negotiations.

This kind of sentence construction using the words of opponents, in which two sides of a story are presented, is typical of newspaper (and radio and television) stories in the USA.

In terms of metamessages, only the *New York Times* runs a front-page message that promotes one particular ideal of objectivity. The message, "All the News That's Fit to Print," implies that no story is out-of-bounds, and therefore that the newspaper does not apply a political agenda to story selection. *USA Today* runs a metamessage, calling itself "The Nation's Newspaper." The *Wall Street Journal* does not run a metamessage.

However, in newspapers in the USA (as well as in radio and television news), there is one regular bias that in essence dismisses socialism and communism as distasteful ideologies. For example, a September 15, 2004, Associated Press story that ran in newspapers across the country reported on Hurricane Ivan and the "heavy flooding" it caused in Cuba. The story reported that "Cuba's tobacco crop was safe," and that "tobacco is the communist-run island's third largest export." The mentioning of communism in the context of a disaster story wherein a harmful crop (tobacco) is grown, invites the reader to link the political ideology to the bad news and immoral behavior. The mention of "communist" in this kind of disaster-story is not normally balanced by mentioning "capitalist" in similar stories occurring in the USA or in other market-based economies.

This antisocialism and anticommunism bias is also very common in quotes that are selected for hard news stories. Often, such news reports with this bias will cover a speech by a politician in which socialism is talked about in a way that identifies it as being obviously undesirable. For example, a May 13, 2004, front-page article by David Pierce in a local newspaper in Pennsylvania (the *Pocono Record*) reported on a county commissioner meeting involving a discussion about rising taxes due to population growth. The report stated:

> Commissioner Bob Nothstein said growth is the inevitable consequence of the Poconos [a region in the state of Pennsylvania] being so close to metropolitan New York. But not all growth is bad, he said, and it's important to strike a balance that results in orderly growth.

"The United States of America was built on free enterprise," he said. "America was not formulated on socialism. America was not formulated on communism." (pp. A1–A2)

Typically, this convention of journalistic bias, which presents a newsmaker's criticism of a policy by calling the policy socialized (or socialist), is unanswered by a counteropinion in the story. Such criticisms typically stop short of explaining the demerits of a socialized policy, thus implying that the policy is automatically wrong because it is socialist or communist.

Another, related bias involves statements that describe the USA as being the greatest or most-envied nation in the world. For example, an article in the July 3, 2004, *Courier Journal* from Kentucky ran a columnist editorial with the headline: "One Great Nation, Despite Its Flaws." The editorial began with the sentence: "Today, class, some letters, comments and large thoughts as we all begin to celebrate the birthday of the greatest nation in the history of the world by complaining about the price of gasoline." These kinds of matter-of-fact statements about the "greatness" of the USA are fairly common in columnist articles and letters to the editor. Often, such articles discuss "freedom," "democracy," or "economic opportunity" in support of the claim that the USA is the greatest nation.

In the USA, most newspapers run commentary on two pages, usually toward the end of the first section. Typically these pages consist of an editorial by the newspaper, opinion pieces by weekly syndicated or regular columnists, and letters to the editor from citizens. It is very common to see all three types of commentary in US newspapers. The *New York Times* editorial has a particularly high status in the second-wave news circulation, as excerpts of the editorials are subsequently widely discussed on politically oriented talk shows on both radio and television, and excerpted or covered in other newspapers.

USA newspapers are not known for actively engaging in campaigns to directly advocate positions on issues and policies that are perceived to affect USA society. More commonly, USA newspapers report opinion polls on attitudes by citizens toward policies, leaving it to policy makers to decide whether the polls warrant further action. For example, the December 22, 2004, *Las Vegas Review-Journal* ran an AP Story on page 11A with the headline: "Most in the U.S. Confident About Drugs." This story reported a poll showing that most Americans felt confident about the safety of prescription drugs "at a time when several popular medications have been linked to increased risk of heart attack and stroke." The newspaper story in itself did not editorialize about whether new procedures should or should not be considered to change the approval process for prescription drugs. Rather, the story reported the poll and then followed up with contrasting quoted opinions from politicians and political advisors regarding whether the approval process should be changed.

Bias versus Objectivity in Radio and Television News in the USA

Radio and television newscasts are not known for being politically biased. Radio and television news generally aims at objectivity by balancing opinions and by refraining from political commentary or advocacy journalism as part of a regular newscast. Usually, radio and television reports include "two sides" to controversial issues to achieve balance, which is seen as a central component of objectivity.

Entertainment versus Serious News in Newspapers in the USA

Most reporting in newspapers is serious, though many newspapers—for example, *USA Today*—also run entertainment-oriented sections or pages. The priority of stories generally is current events, crime, local news, business news, and sports. The big-city newspapers also usually run sections on Metro, Culture/The Arts, House and Home, and Food. Generally, private indiscretions of people in the news are not as prominent in news reporting about more substantive events. In terms of people, USA newspapers tend to focus on government officials, famous people, sports figures, successful businessmen and women, and military officers. Very often the news is about elected politicians and other government officials. Most often, the leading stories involve current events happening within the USA.

Entertainment versus Serious News in Radio and Television in the USA

Radio news on commercial channels tends to be serious with a lot of entertainment-oriented qualities. For example, often the first two-thirds of a radio station's newscast covers serious stories, and the last third covers sports, weather, and entertainment. Many local and syndicated radio newscasts are integrated into a talk show or music show in an entertaining way, wherein the host and the news announcer exchange pleasantries and jokes before the news announcer begins the newscast. Sometimes, the host will even interrupt a newscaster's story to make a joke. In the USA, musical introductions to radio news programs tend to be pulsating and dramatic. On the noncommercial broadcaster NPR, the tone of news coverage is more subdued and slower-paced.

Television news reporting on commercial stations has many entertaining qualities. Musical introductions to network newscasts and local newscasts typically have a dramatic "fanfare" quality centered on trumpets and bass guitar, which communicate a sense of urgency. USA television news tends to be modern and colorful, with multiple television sets visible in the background. Some anchors—for example, on NBC's broadcast and cable networks—stand in front of virtual backgrounds displaying graphics, video, and still shots. Often, there is a lot of motion on the television screen during newscasts, created by crawling text, rolling video, high-tech animation, and flashy graphics used to illustrate stories as well as provide transitions between camera shots. *FoxNews* is known for using searing sound effects as graphics are presented. On noncommercial PBS newscasts, however, the set is somewhat bland, and graphics are not used very often.

Depth versus Brevity of Reporting in Newspapers in the USA

The prestige and big-city newspapers in the USA are known for providing some depth to big current-events stories, by carrying over stories from the front page to inside pages, and by providing companion stories on inside pages. However, USA newspapers are better known for providing more breadth than depth to news stories, due to a tendency toward large number of stories per newspaper, rather than fewer stories with greater word counts. *USA Today* in particular is known as a newspaper of headlines and news-event summaries. Small-town newspapers are not known for achieving much depth because of a commonly applied journalistic practice of writing to a "5th-grade reading level," which is pursued to make the newspaper understandable to as many people as possible and achieve the largest audience possible.

Two subject areas are consistently covered with a lot of depth in most USA newspapers. One area is public-opinion polls on a variety of subjects generally questioning people "how things are going in the country." Three common subject areas targeted by polling include opinions about political figures (such as job-approval ratings, or general favorable/unfavorable ratings), USA foreign policy, and the economy (such as consumer confidence, or whether people plan to spend more or less money during the upcoming year on "big-ticket" items). The statistics presented in newspaper stories reporting these polls fit in with a general theme that characterizes newspaper journalism in the USA—that is the common use of numbers to describe newsworthy events.

A second subject area commonly covered in USA newspapers is business and economic news. The *Wall Street Journal* is particularly known for specializing in this kind of news. Within the general area of business and economic news, most newspapers provide in-depth consumer reports. This news includes a wide range of information generally geared toward reporting on new products and services, manufacturers' recalls, and popular brands that Americans are purchasing.

It is very common to see essentially the same story—attributed to the AP newswire— in hundreds of local newspapers across the USA on any given day. For instance, on December 29, 2004, an AP-cited story on the death of author and activist Susan Sontag ran in the *Sun* (San Bernardino, California), the *Charlotte Observer* (North Carolina), the *Morning Call* (Allentown, Pennsylvania), and *USA Today*—as well as hundreds of other newspapers across the USA. Out of the four newspapers mentioned, three contained articles discussing one of Sontag's books, *On Photography* (the *Charlotte Observer* did not discuss that book). All four newspapers carried articles commenting on Sontag's observations about the relationship between the photograph and the viewer of the photograph. Two of the newspapers carried articles using the exact same Sontag quote: "Pictures sometimes distance viewers from the subject matter." This kind of homogeneity in news stories in the USA—particularly in news constructed from AP stories—is very common not only in newspapers but also in radio newscasts.

In-depth international news is not usually found in most USA newspapers (notable exceptions include the *New York Times* and the *Christian Science Monitor*), especially small-town newspapers. Newspaper stories on other countries are often a single paragraph placed toward the middle of the newspaper in a column that runs four to six of these one-paragraph international stories. In addition, most international news stories in newspapers amout to "bad news" stories, involving such themes as natural disasters, armed conflicts, disease outbreaks, human tragedy, and other unseemly subjects. For example, the front page of the December 29, 2004, *Los Angeles Times* included the following headlines and subheadlines on events in foreign countries:

Tsunami Death Toll Hits 60,000 (in Asia Pacific); —Survivors Scramble for Food; Small Aid Shipments Reach Hardest-Hit Nations

Getting an Education in Jihad—Infuriated by the U.S.-led 'Crusade' in Iraq, a Lebanese Teacher Left his Country and Steady Job Intending to Die for the Insurgency

Father's Grip No Match for Wave—Hundreds of Children in a Southern Indian City were Killed, Unable to Fight the Torrent

Pledges of Help [To Countries in Asia Hit by Tsunami] Grow with Problems—More than $120 Million is Promised; Damage, War and Other Obstacles Slow Delivery of Relief

Five Roadblocks to Peace—Staking Their Claim to a 'Greater Israel'
Economic Fallout—Island Tourism Takes a Big Hit
Disease—Water Is a Bigger Health Risk than Corpses
Death of a Prince—Thai Royal Grew up in San Diego

Similarly, international stories often portray other countries as having problems that implicitly are not present in the USA. For example, two front-page stories in the October 2, 2003, *New York Times* reported on labor practices in China. The headline for one story was "Vague Call in China for More Democracy." This story began: "President Hu Jintao has made a vague but insistent call for more democracy in his country on the eve of the country's National Day, raising expectations that he may support introducing greater pluralism in the one-party state." The article then went on to analyze the situation as follows: "Chinese leaders promote the concept of democracy mainly as a way of enhancing the credibility of the Communist Party and fighting corruption by low- and middle-ranking officials. Mr. Hu almost certainly does not plan to push Western-style democracy."

Next to this story was another story with the headline, "Chinese Girls' Toil Brings Pain, Not Riches." This story discusses how Chinese girls working in factories making products such as false eyelashes receive much lower pay and poorer working conditions than they were promised. However, the story did not discuss the integral role of consumers in the USA and other countries in purchasing Chinese-made products.

Both of these stories, taken together, illustrate a common theme in international coverage in USA newspapers (and radio and television newscasts)—namely, that many foreign countries are portrayed as having problems that implicitly could be corrected by adopting USA-style democracy and capitalism. Moreover, the problems discussed in newspaper stories often exclude basic background information on the foreign country (for example, defining and explaining what China's "National Day" is), criticisms of similar practices in the USA; and comments on how policies in the USA are related to the identified problems in the foreign country.

Depth versus Brevity of Reporting on Radio and Television in the USA

Not all radio stations in the USA carry news. The stations that usually carry news include big-city, talk, small-town, top-40, and NPR stations. Other, mainly music-oriented stations may or may not carry news. Almost every big city has at least one radio station that carries news twenty-four hours. Most radio news stories are local. International news stories are more prominent on network newscasts carried by affiliates, but these newscasts are also focused primarily on domestic news. A radio news story on commercial stations typically is fifteen to thirty seconds, and includes a five- to ten-second sound bite. Often, the sound bite cuts off the end of a person's sentence. The bulk of radio news is scheduled in a five- to ten-minute block at the top of the hour during morning drive from 0600 to 1000 (6:00 AM–10 AM), though news also commonly airs at the top of the hour during evening drive from 1500 to 1900 (3:00 PM–7:00 PM). A typical schedule at small and medium-market stations is for a five-minute block of local/regional news to be aired, followed by a block of five-minute network news. Here are the headlines of stories that aired on December 9, 2004, on *WSBG*, a small-town radio station in Pennsylvania:

> Icy Conditions on Roads
> Fund Established for Family Whose House Burned Down
> Co-Owner of a Public Relations Firm Approached by Political Party to Run for Office
> Shooting in an Ohio Nightclub
> Usher Won 11 Billboard Music Awards
> Last Month's Unemployment Filings Show an Increase
> No New Talks between New Jersey Power Company and Electrical Workers
> Sports Scores (University, High School, Professional)
> Baseball Team Signs a Pitcher
> Weather (sponsored by Blue Ridge Digital Cable Provider)

In the USA, national public radio stations usually carry more extensive news. The NPR morning news program *Morning Edition* runs for one hour, and the afternoon news program *All Things Considered* runs for one and a half hours. News reports on these programs typically can run up to ten minutes and usually include follow-up discussions with experts in the studio or by phone.

Almost all terrestrial commercial television stations—both network affiliates and independents—carry news. Often, affiliates and independents run a one-hour local news program at noon, three consecutive half-hour news programs beginning at 1700 (5:00 PM)—wherein the first newscasts concentrate on local news while the latter newscasts concentrate more on national news—and a one-hour local news program either at 2200 (10:00 PM) or 2300 (11:00 PM). Affiliates also usually carry a two-hour network news program at 0700 (7:00 AM), and a half-hour news program at 1830 (6:30 PM). Stations that are members of noncommercial PBS usually only run the network's one-hour news program at 1800 (6:00 PM). Most newscasts focus on local and regional news. National and international news on terrestrial television is normally a staple only on the 1830 (6:30 PM) commercial network newscasts and the 1800 (6:00 PM) PBS newscast.

In addition to terrestrial television news, several cable channels carry news programs during morning, midday, and evening hours. These channels include CNN, Headline News, MSNBC, CNBC, FoxNews, and local cable channels.

Local news programs on commercial affiliates and independents usually follow a similar format. Most stories are one minute or less, and are rarely longer than three minutes. Several stories are usually around fifteen seconds. Usually a newscast begins with a story involving a crime or another kind of tragedy. Fires and murders are common lead stories. For example, the headlines for the three lead stories on the 1700 (5:00 PM) newscast on January 2, 2005, on ABC-affiliate WNEP were: A Fire Kills Two Young Boys; A Fire Destroys Row Homes; Two Bank Robberies Occurred Within a Couple Hours of Each Other. After the lead stories, the subsequent stories usually deal with local current events. Sports stories and weather forecasts usually come about two-thirds of the way through a newscast. Weather is often "teased" at several points in between news stories, wherein anchors indicate to viewers that something investing may be happening with the weather, and that they should stay tuned. Often near the end of a newscast, a human-interest news story is aired. For example, a January 20, 2005, next-to-last story of a *WBRE* newscast in Scranton, Pennsylvania, was about a teacher organizing a "mathathon" for second-grade students to compete at solving fifty math problems to raise money for victims of tsunamis that hit the South Pacific three weeks earlier.

The formats of commercial network news programs are also fairly standard. Most stories are right around three minutes long. Rarely are stories longer than five minutes. Usually there are three or four advertising and promotional breaks (for upcoming programs), totaling up to twelve minutes. Over the course of a half-hour newscast, typically there are nine or ten stories. Most stories focus on national current events. Stories also often focus on health-related issues such as breakouts of diseases, new drugs, drug recalls, and on tragedies. Sports and weather news is not usually covered on the network news programs. In television news in the USA, there is a lot of "teasing" where, prior to an advertising break, the anchor promotes an exciting, important, or surprising story that is coming up later in the broadcast. This kind of story may be teased several times during a newscast before the story is actually aired. Figure 10.8 lists sample headlines of stories on an ABC evening newscast. Overall, television newscasts in the USA tend to have greater breadth than depth because of the brevity of most stories, due largely to substantial advertising minutage.

The format of news on noncommercial PBS is different from the commercial stations and networks, and has much more depth. Stories are longer, and typically run around fifteen minutes. Over the course of the hour-long newscast, there may be four or five news stories. Most include an anchor introducing a story, followed by the report, then followed by a panel discussion between a PBS anchor and one or more experts in the studio or via satellite link.

Video/sound bites containing a witness's account of a news event or an expert's commentary are very common in television news reports. Bites are usually short, typically

---

Advertisements
Previews of 5 Stories
President Submits Budget to Congress
Defense Budget
Agriculture Budget
Two Large Attacks in Iraq
Secretary of State Leaves the Middle East
New Palestinian Leadership Making Efforts to Change Status Quo
Vatican Says it Could be Several More Days before Pope Leaves Hospital
Promos for 3 Upcoming Stories
Advertisements
Conviction in Sexual Abuse Case Involving Catholic Priest
Debut of a Super Computer Chip
Rising Costs of Prescription Drugs Leading Americans to Order Drugs from Canada
Promo for Upcoming Story
Advertisements
Cable TV Companies Airing Porn Yet Donating Money to Candidates for Moral Values
Promo for Upcoming Story
Advertisements
British Woman Sails Around the World Solo
Advertisements

FIGURE 10.8   *Sample Headlines from 1830 (6:30 PM) Newscast on ABC World News Tonight in the USA; February 7, 2005*

Source: Robert McKenzie.

lasting from five to fifteen seconds. Often, the bite is edited in such a way as to chop off the ending of a person's sentence to keep the bite as short as possible. It is somewhat common in television news in the USA for the lead story to be followed by another related news report.

NEWS REPORTING IN MÉXICO

Bias versus Objectivity in Newspapers in México

In México, most national newspapers are known for striving for objectivity, which comes from an emerging general outlook of most newspapers not to flatly support or oppose a political party. But Mexican newspapers are also known for exhibiting contradictory biases that are an outgrowth of a clash between traditional conventions of journalism and newly found press freedoms. Since the 2000 election, there has been a surge of bottled-up criticism of the federal government that probably has greater invective than if there had been a long-standing tradition of critical journalism. Such criticism has been strengthened also by the 2002 federal law, Freedom of Access to Information, which allows citizens and journalists for the first time to access federal records pertaining to the public interest. It remains to be seen whether the hypercriticism of government will be moderated over time.

However, the sensational criticism of the government conflicts with a second bias in Mexican newspapers: the reluctance to criticize governments—particularly state governments—and the tendency to print unedited press releases from the government. Both of these attributes are an outgrowth of the reliance of newspapers on revenue from government-financed advertising insertions.

It may seem contradictory that these two biases—the tendency to sensationalize criticism of the government, and the tendency to refrain from criticizing government—can coexist in Mexican journalism. However, two examples from the November 14, 2004, *La Jornada* (*The Day*) illustrate these two opposing biases. One article supportive of the government ran on page 12 with the headline: "Reducing Seats in the Government Has Resources Going Towards Productive Investments." This article reports on comments that President Vicente Fox made the radio regarding achievements of his administration. In a subheadline, the article states: "The Best Years are Coming in the Two Years Left of the Fox Administration." But a second article that was critical of the government ran with the headline: "Siege to Inform and Lack of Freedom of Expression Constitutes Foxism" (a play on words using the name of the then president). The article states, "The Mexican academy of human rights denounces that the present government favors the concentration of assets of communication, impunity in the aggressions to the freedom of press, and the excessive use of the laws to inhibit the freedom of expression" (p. 17).

In México, some of the national newspapers follow a political bias. *La Prensa* is known for covering crime stories using vivid descriptions and photos of people who have been injured or killed, without a political orientation. For example, it would be typical in *La Prensa* for a story to describe in detail how a victim's arm was cut off in a robbery. *El Grafíco* (*The Graphic*) is known for being apolitical, and for being sensationalist, though not as much as *La Prensa*. *La Jornada* has been known as a leftwing intellectual and workers' newspaper that often criticizes Mexican government as being corrupt, and foreign policies of the USA as being imperialistic. *La Jornada* also frequently portrays government policies of socialist Cuba as positive. *El Financiero* (*The Financial Report*) is known for covering the economy, finance, and trade. *El Financiero* has a reputation of being politically independent (it will criticize both the left and the right), but on the editorial pages tends to lean slightly to the left. Part of the reason for this reputation for independence is that *El Financiero* caps government-paid insertions at 30 percent of revenue, which is assumed to be less than other national newspapers. *Reforma* is commonly thought of as the most "important" newspaper, in part because of its reputation for insisting on professional journalism and ethical conduct from its reporters, but also because of its impact on government policies and public opinion. *Reforma* is known for being a very serious newspaper, and for being politically independent overall, though the editorial pages lean to the right. *Reforma* tends to cover stories supportive of private enterprise and market forces. *El Universal* is known as a left-of-center paper that also generally supports the status quo. *Crónica* is known for being a right-wing newspaper criticizing socialist policies. *ESTO* is known for almost exclusively covering sports and show business, without a political orientation.

In México, most newspapers run clearly identified commentary pages. The placement of the commentary in newspapers varies, though commentary does not usually appear on the front page of any of the newspapers. *La Crónica* and *La Jornada* typically run commentaries on page 2, *La Reforma* on pages 16 and 17, and *El Universal* on three pages beginning on page A31. *Milenio*, *El Heraldo*, and *Excelsior* do not have commentary pages. Across Mexican newspapers, commentaries are written by a wide range of people. In *La Jornada,* commentaries tend to be written by citizens. However, in *El Universal*, commentaries tend to be written by experts—including political analysts, academics, directors, elected officials, and party leaders. Such commentaries and opinion articles often discuss from an academic point of view the political and social progress that México is, or is not, making. For example, in the November 16, 2004, *El Universal* on page A32, an article by a political analyst appeared with the headline "Mexican Revolution." The writer argued that the Mexican Revolution is still alive and is playing an important role in México, and that México needs to form a new constitution and use the USA as a guide to better the country.

Often, as already indicated, newspaper commentaries are directed at, or allude to, issues related to the USA. For example, a story in the November 14, 2004, edition of *Milenio,* which was analyzing the 2004 USA presidential elections, ran a story stating:

> One knows the boys who voted for George W. Bush: Neither the eternal War in Iraq nor the economic crisis nor the increase of unemployment. . . . If George W. Bush were reelected, it is because for many in the USA there is a series of untouchable things: Its weapons, its faith, to restrain abortion, and that homosexuals do not marry. (p. 30)

Commentaries are also often directed at the decisions of the federal government or the local municipal government. For example, on November 14, 2004, *La Jornada* ran a letter to the editor with the headline: "Refusing the Construction of Wal-Mart in Teotihuacán" [place where ancient pyramids are located]:

> The government is responsible for the defense of culture and the conservation of the Mexican history of Patrimony. It is hard for citizens to believe that the government is allowing the construction of a Wal-Mart in the heart of Teotihuacán, México. (p. 2)

Bias versus Objectivity in Radio and Television News in México

Private television and radio newscasts are known for having fairly regular bias insofar as it is very common within a factually based news report for the reporter to state his or her personal opinion. In the past, reporter commentary was generally praiseworthy of government policies and actions. Since 2000, though, broadcast news reporting has been more critical of government policies, though the criticism tends not to be very harsh. However, reporter commentary is a regular feature in a newscast that is dominated by hard-news reporting. For example, Televisa regularly includes a reporter editorial toward the end of the newscast called "The Opinion of Carlos Monsiváis." As another example of the prevalence of commentary, in a November 12, 2004, news report covering the death of Palestinian leader Yassar Arafat on the all-news radio station *Monitor* in México City, an anchor commented that "Bush [George W.] and Rabin [former Israeli prime minister Yitzhak Rabin, who was assassinated] must be happy and dancing with joy now that Arafat is gone." Similarly, during the 2300 (11:00 PM) newscast on Azteca television, about halfway through the report on Arafat's death, the reporter commented: "Now this is important to world affairs. It's much more important than the stupid stories on government corruption in México City." Much of the bias in radio and television news reporting—such as that in the preceding example—centers on a long-running antagonism between México City (where the federal government is located), and the individual states, or the country at large.

In addition to this kind of bias, there is also a tradition of radio and television news programming exercising self-restraint that keeps from harshly criticizing government institutions. Though government institutions are targeted, the criticism stops short of personally attacking elected officials and government institutions. For example, in a December 12, 2003, report aired on Contacto News networked stations in the state of Veracruz, an anchor stated: "The government does not keep its word. They say one thing and always do something else. It is important for the government to have good credibility, and for people we trust to run the government." This kind of criticism—which is strong but also restrained in that it does not identify any specific government officials and does not engage in name-calling—is an outgrowth of strict licensing procedures that guarantee broadcasting time for the government and prohibit broadcasters from personally attacking government institutions (see Chapter 6).

Entertainment versus Serious News in Newspapers in México

In México, most of the news reporting in the newspapers is serious, though entertainment is commonly reported on as well. Even the two national sensational tabloids—*La Prensa* and *El Gráfico*—have mostly serious news, though they cover entertainment news as well. The priority of stories in newspapers in México generally is current events, government activity, and crime. And, as mentioned earlier, most newspapers in México cover sports. Also, in entertainment news, radio and television stars from the USA as well as from México are regularly covered. The subject areas range from breakups to Oscar nominations to the latest "victims" of paparazzi. For example, pages E2 and E4 of the Entertainment section of the November 16, 2004, *El Universal* contained the following stories on USA celebrities: The breakup of actors Goldie Hawn and Kurt Russell; actor John Travolta's secrets to a successful marriage; and Tim Allen's "must-see" Christmas movie. Similarly, in the November 16, 2004, *La Reforma,* the "People" section ran an almost-full-page cover article on Tom Hanks and a movie he was appearing in, *The Polar Express.* The remainder of the cover page was made up of a smaller article reporting the end of the three-year marriage between Mexican singers Ninel Conde and Jose Manuel Figueroa.

Entertainment-Oriented versus Serious News in Radio and Television in México

In México, news on both the private and the state-funded stations tends to have a serious orientation that focuses heavily on politics, current events (often international, and often about the USA), and health. For example, a January 27, 2004, newscast on private broadcaster Hechos 7 (roughly translated as "things happening") on Azateca Television contained the following headlines: tornadoes in Hawaii; freezing temperatures in the USA; the engagement of the Princess of Spain; and the power of horseback riding for children who have muscular disorders and mental illnesses. There were no entertainment stories in the newscast.

The look of television news in México is similar to that of the USA. One difference is that anchors tend to have a more expressive style of presentation, using more pronounced eye and eyebrow movements, as well as head, hand, and mouth movements. On radio, sound bites from the field are sometimes difficult to hear because of equipment deficiencies.

Depth versus Brevity of Reporting in Newspapers in México

In México, there are sensational tabloids (*La Prensa* and the *El Graphíco*) and serious tabloids (*Economist, Milenio, La Jornada, Cronica*), plus a sports and celebrity tabloid (*ESTO*). The sensational tabloid newspapers in México are known for covering crimes—particularly violent crimes such as murder, robberies, and rapes. Often the coverage links the crimes to illegal drugs. *La Prensa* is especially known for focusing on death, as illustrated by the November 13, 2004, headlines on pages 24 and 25: "A Young Person when Hitting Herself against a Concrete Barrier Passes Away"; "He Killed the Man's Mistress while Sleeping with his Wife"; "The Psychopath Recounts How He Violated and Killed Jessica, a Youngster Found without Life in Topilejo"; and "She Died outside the American Embassy." In addition, coverage of crimes in Mexican tabloid newspapers is often very detailed. For example, in the November 16, 2004, edition of *La Prensa,* an article with the headline, "They Killed Albañil," contained this description:

> While looking around to leave, they discovered on asphalt and in front of the house marked with number 119, on the street Pachicalo, in the District of Iztapalapa, a man's body lying and bathed in blood. When paramedics arrived and reviewed the body, they found a bullet inlaid in his left side. (p. 26)

Most newspapers in México—but particularly the serious tabloids and the broadsheets—are known for providing detailed coverage of politics. Many dimensions of politics are regularly covered, including party conferences, strategies by political parties to win elections, elections, speeches by politicians, policy announcements, legislation, reports by government officials, and conflicts between politicians. *Reforma* has a Sunday magazine insert, "In Focus," which is well known for covering politicians and the government. Similarly, *El Universal* has a Sunday magazine insert, Bucarelli, which also covers politics. Moreover, often there is a tone to the coverage of politics and to journalism in general that can be described as enthusiastic about the changes coming to México and idealistic about the role of journalism in reporting the changes. For example, consider the idealism in the following mission statements of the government-funded SNN (National System of News) network, which supplies news to the IMER radio stations:

> We offer culture, education, information, services and entertainment with the purpose of taking care of the democratic, social and cultural necessities of the population. We are independent of commercial and partisan interests. We are governed by our own code of ethics. We contribute to the projection of the image of México in the world and serve as bond with Mexican communities.
>
> Impartiality, veracity, integrity, independence are our axes of work because we are not federal government nor state government spokespeople but servants of society.
>
> Unlike the commercial radio, we have an immense freedom to project a healthy journalistic work; without the force to sell; without the censorship of enterprise interests allied to dark phobias.
>
> We want an unforeseeable journalism as it is in the course of our mortal lives; a susceptible journalism of surprises and findings; of lucks and misfortune; a woven journalism of events that occurred and that can occur; a journalism without the shroud of the commercial interests; a journalism-art, near its prime sister the literary narrative; a journalism of bold flights and time always confirming the note—like our loves. . . .

One dimension of depth that is often included in Mexican newspapers is alleged misdeeds of government officials or associates of government officials. The word *corruption* is regularly used in such articles. Such coverage usually focuses on the various parties that are responding to the allegations of corruption, including those who are making the allegations and those who are defending themselves against the allegations. Often the corruption revolves around the misuse of money—usually the way money has been spent by the government, or the use of money to bribe a person, or the extortion of money from a government official to prevent potentially embarrassing information from being made public. For example, on the front page and then continued on page A9 of the November 14, 2004, *El Universal,* a story ran under the headline: "Bejarano Looks to Cover Corruption in the GDF [Government of the Federal District]." The story was about the president of México dismissing charges by an ex-deputy of the PRD (the party in power at the time in the Federal District of México City), René Bejarano Martinez, that the president's government had misspent government funds. In the article, the president claims that Bejarano was resorting to lies to conceal "the extended corruption that exists within the Government of the Federal District." The article reported that the president of México denied Bejarano's claim that the president's daughter, Anna Christina Fox, had relations with an Argentinean industrialist, and charged Bejarano with "trying to involve the President's family in acts of corruption" to divert attention from corruption in the government of México City. Accompanying this story was a vivid photograph of Bejarano in a cell behind prison bars for accepting "wads of money" from an Argentinean industrialist who owned several construction companies that had completed public-works projects for México City. This story not only points out the level of drama and intrigue that often permeates allegations of corruption in news reporting about Mexican government, but also the antagonism between the federal government and the government of México City discussed earlier.

The broadsheets are also known for extensively covering issues having to do with economic, social, political, and infrastructure development in México. Many articles have an underlying tone that things are either improving in México, or getting worse. Often, articles on infrastructure development compare México to other countries. For example, in the online January 12, 2005, *Reforma,* a lead article with the headline "Attractive México Loses," stated that "in the last 10 years, México lost 2 percentage points of total of IED (International Investment) in the world, whereas Brazil and countries of Asia elevated their participation." Another example of development-related news is the following December 8, 2003, *El Sol de México* headline, "The Present SEP Academic Evaluations of Schools in the City of México, and Thousands of New Jobs are Generated in BCS in 2003" (p. 3).

Mexican national broadsheets are known for providing a lot of international coverage, especially coverage of the USA. Typically, about 20 to 30 percent of Mexican newspaper coverage focuses on international events.

All Mexican newspapers are known for providing regular and detailed coverage of religion. For example, the main headline in the December 8, 2003, *El Sol de México* was: "The Church Refuses to Legitimize Gay Unions." This headline is then found as the main story as well on the cover of the City section. Then, on page 4 of the City section the headline stated: "Cardinal Norberto Rivera Carrera Criticizes the Race of Parties to Approve Laws." This sequence of stories illustrates also that big stories on the front pages of Mexican newspapers are sometimes keyed to companion reports inside the newspaper.

Depth versus Brevity of Reporting on Radio and Television in México

Most radio stations carry news, and most newscasts contain local, national, and sometimes international news. International news tends to focus on the USA more than Central America or South America. Most radio reports typically range from one minute to one and a half minutes, though longer news reports of up to five or even ten minutes are also commonly heard. Within the longer news reports, sound bites can be heard that are three or four minutes long. On IMER radio stations, three different SNN news programs are broadcast daily. The "informative" news program consists of a three-minute capsule airing at 0557 (5:57 AM), 1157 (11:57 AM), 1657 (4:57 PM), and 2157 (9:57 PM). Stories in these capsules can range from fifteen seconds to one minute.

Political and local news stand out on Mexican radio. For example, during the week of January 5 through January 11, 2005, 104.1 FM on Cadena Radio Uno broadcast the following headlines on the *Al Aire* [roughly translated as "the air"] program: Fox, the Unjust One; The Policy of Avestruz (Ostrich); The Narcotics . . . Cold Terror . . . Hot Violence; Fox Against the Congress; and The Dead of the Week (obituaries).

In México, the main radio news reports are aired between 0600 (6:00 AM) to 1000 (10:00 AM). Many stations run three to four hours of news during this time block. Outside of this time block, most stations air two-minute newscasts at the top of the hour, until 1800 (6 PM) to 2000 (8 PM) a second time block in which many stations air newscasts (but not as much as during the morning time block). The format of the two-minute newscast is fairly loose. News in all three major categories (local, national, international) can be heard in any order. Normally, a weather forecast is delivered at the end of the report. Two AM stations in México City are well known for extensive news coverage. One is Radio Net (translated in English as Radio Red), with the call letters XERED, which airs the program *Monitor,* specializing in analysis of business news, advice on improving family relationships, and information on religions of the world. The other is Format 21 (XERC), which specializes in México City news and international news. On Format 21, the top news stories are announced every twenty minutes in between mainly discussion-oriented programs on a wide range of serious subjects such as health, cinematography, culture, politics, and the economy.

In México, national television news is scheduled in the afternoon and evening. On *Channel 2* (Televisa), half-hour newscasts are aired at 1430 (2:30 PM) and at 2230 (10:30 PM), and sports news at 2300 (11:00 PM). On *Channel 4* (Televisa), a one-hour newscast is aired at 1500 (3:00 PM). On *Channel 9* (Televisa), a one-hour newscast airs at 2000 (8:00 PM). On *Channel 7* (Azteca), a half-hour newscast airs at 2100 (9:00 PM) on *Channel 13* (Azteca), a one-hour newscast airs at 1500 (3:00 PM), and a half-hour newscast airs at 2200 (10:00 PM).

News formats on commercial and public newscasts are similar in basic format, but have major differences in the lengths of stories. Whereas public-station newscasts such as *RTV* tend to have four top headlines, private-station newscasts such as Azteca can have as many as nine top headlines. Azteca and Televisa newscasts are one hour long, and public television newscasts are usually thirty minutes. During an hour-long newscast on a private station, there can be two or three advertising breaks, each lasting about two minutes.

News on private networks focuses primarily on national news (mainly political news) and international news. Often, when reports cover international news, a video clip containing a foreign language being spoken is accompanied by Spanish translations in text displayed at the bottom of the television screen. Opening stories on private networks can run up to ten minutes. In contrast, news on public stations focus primarily on local and regional news. But opening stories on public stations can also run eight to ten minutes long, while the rest of the stories typically run a few minutes each. However, newscasts on both news stations regularly include stories from the USA. Figure 10.9 lists sample headlines from a newscast on the private network Televisa.

Video/sound bites containing parts of a witness's testimony on a news event or comments from an expert are fairly common in television news reports. Stories often include bites from politicians, experts, and average citizens. Bites typically last around thirty seconds. It is common on television news in México for the lead story, especially if it is about politics, to be followed by one or two other related political news reports. For other news stories, related sequential news reports are not so common.

NEWS REPORTING IN CHINA

Bias versus Objectivity in Newspapers in China

In China, newspapers are considered openly biased toward the central government and the Communist Party. Although many newspapers have adopted a market orientation, they remain within tightly regulated confines, acting as propaganda organs that serve the interests of the government and the Party. For example, when newspapers deviated from government guidelines on news reporting in 2002, authorities responded with a directive that stated: "No

Preview of Headlines
Two Boys Trapped in Underground Hole
PRD Representative Speaks
Alcaldia's Government Party Results
Tamaulipa's Government Party Results
Michoacan Government Party Results
Preview of Upcoming Headlines
PRI Representatives and the Presidential Election
Sinaloa Government Party Results
Tlaxcala Government Party Results
Government Secretary and Economic Issues
Presidential Commission Deputies Convention
President Fox Speaks on Economics, Politics, and Society
UNAM Gives Five Publication Prizes
PAN Representative Tells Truth on Lies and Corruption within the Government
Preview of Upcoming Headlines
Discussion of Murdering PRD's Ramón Martin Caught on Video
Presidential Commission Deputies Convention
Advertising Break
The Opinion of Carlos Monsivaís
Joaquin López Doriga Speaks with PRD Coordinator

FIGURE 10.9   *Sample Headlines from 2230 (10:30 PM) Newscast on Televisa on Channel 2 in México; November 15, 2004*

Source: Robert McKenzie.

matter how objective and balanced the story is, the reporting is no good if it disrupts social stability. It is absolutely unacceptable for the general public, to seek explanations and settlements from the government based on what is reported." In 2003, news organizations were instructed by the Communist Party's Central Publicity Work Conference to "speak the truth on approved topics," but "not to cover protests and other social unrest." Accordingly, Chinese newspapers have struggled with issues of independence and autonomy, which has increased self-censorship in news reporting.

National broadsheet newspapers directly controlled and funded by the government and the Party such as *Renmin Ribao (People's Daily), Guangming Ribao (Guangming Daily)*, and *Zhongguo Qingnian Bao (China Youth Daily)* openly support the decisions and actions of the government and the Party. For example, in the August 4, 2004, *Renmin Ribao*, an editorial on the front page advocated that all people, including officials at all levels, should integrate their ideas to "unanimously support the macro-regulation policy" introduced by the central government in June 2003. The article called for people to understand the importance of the policy, and to "bravely sacrifice their personal or partial interests for the whole interest of the country and the people." Following this announcement, other national broadsheets wrote similar stories supporting the government's position. For example, on August 8, 2004, *Guangming Ribao* published a commentary with the headline: "The facts prove macro-regulation policy correct and effective." The article used a series of economic statistics to show the effectiveness of the policy, and concluded that: "Currently we need to fully understand the difficulty and complexity of conducting macro-regulation policy. We must make sufficient preparation for the coming challenges in the process of launching the macro-regulation policy" (p. 4).

This kind of overt bias, which faithfully supports the government and the Party leaders' opinions and viewpoints, is typical of China's broadsheets. Such bias is typically linked to a current campaign by the government, and urges Chinese people to follow or cease courses of action.

In contrast, broadsheet newspapers generally have more flexibility in reporting economic or social issues, such as the conduct of private companies and prominent individuals. These commentaries often initiate extensive debates among readers, and raise a variety of opinions. For example, *Zhongguo Qingnian Bao* openly voices criticism of negative social issues relating to corruption and abuse of power. In the June 9, 2004, column "Ice Point" (*Bing Dian*), the newspaper called on local government officials to take responsibility for the polluted Huai River. The article said local officials had failed to adequately implement an environmental protection initiative for the Huai River, despite spending 60 billion RMB (8 billion USD) over ten years (p. 3). The column demanded that officials explain to the public why the project had failed. This type of limited advocacy reporting is supported by the central government as a strategy to weed out lower-level corruption and abuse of power.

In city-based tabloid newspapers, bias is less overt but still pervasive. Like the broadsheets, these tabloids are given more flexibility and autonomy in reporting social justice issues, but have much less freedom to directly criticize the central government and the Party. For example, in the August 14, 2004, *Xinwen Chenbao (News Morning)* on page A2, a story focused on four "wrong behaviors" of local government agencies and institutes. These behaviors related to abuse of power in real-estate construction, overcharging of tuition fees by some public middle and high schools, corruption by state-owned medical companies, and delays by state-owned enterprises in paying rural workers. In the same publication, *Xinwen Chenbao* praised the government's effort in controlling traffic noise.

Bias versus Objectivity in Radio and Television News in China

In China, television and radio newscasts on both national and city stations are known for bias because of tight government controls over news and opinions. Like newspapers, television and radio news in China delivers advocacy journalism and commentary that favors the opinions, viewpoints, or campaigns of the government and the Party. For example, on August 19, 2004, on *CCTV 1,* the lead news story focused on the rapid economic growth in the west of China, which was attributed to the government's policy of macroregulation. The report outlined how this achievement in the west demonstrated the effectiveness of the government's macroregulation policy. There is little or no leeway for objective reporting on political issues unless the coverage relates to local government corruption or abuse of power. However, news reporting on economic and social justice issues that adversely affect people's daily lives has become common.

Entertainment versus Serious News in Newspapers in China

In China, most of the news reporting in tabloids relates to entertainment. In terms of people, tabloids focus predominantly on personalities and celebrities. Other prominent coverage relates to crime stories. For example, on August 14, 2004, the Shanghai-based *Qingnian Bao (Youth Daily)* led the front page with coverage of Chinese Olympians who were promising to win golden medals in shooting, diving, weight-lifting, and swimming. However, this celebrity coverage was balanced with social-justice news on the front page, which focused on twenty-six new medical shops in Shanghai, which ostensibly would provide more facilities to Shanghai citizens. Then, on page 2, there was a story about former leader Deng Xiaoping's bronze sculpture, which was erected in Deng's hometown in memory for his centennial.

In contrast, China's national broadsheets prioritize reporting on political figures. For example, the August 14, 2004, *Renmin Ribao* ran the story on Deng Xiaoping's bronze sculpture as the lead story. The coverage included a large color photograph of President Hu Jintao unveiling the sculpture in Deng's hometown of Guangan in the Sichuan Province. The story told of how another former leader, Jiang Zemin, had provided a handwritten dedication to the sculpture.

Entertainment versus Serious News in Radio and Television in China

In China, radio and television news is predominantly serious with few entertaining qualities. Lead news stories on the national broadcaster *China Central Radio* (*CCR*) focus predominantly on domestic politics, economics, and social issues. However, the commercially oriented city radio stations tend to include more sensationalist stories on personalities and celebrities in their news broadcasts to gain audience support and advertising revenue to fund their operations.

Television news reporting on the China Central Television channels as well as city or provincial channels is predominantly serious. Commercialization has led them to become somewhat more colorful. Still, a government directive in 2004 instructed *CCTV* anchors to dress more conservatively to match the "serious" nature of news in China. Thus, graphics tend to be simple and static.

Depth versus Brevity of Reporting in Newspapers in China

Since the major function of the national broadsheets is to promote nationwide policies and actions of the government and the Party, broadsheets generally do not cover sensational stories. And because national broadsheets depend on financial support from the government and the Party rather than advertisers and subscription fees, they have fewer pages than tabloids. This situation provides tabloids with a platform for more in-depth reporting on some topics compared to national broadsheets—except when the government or the Party initiates propaganda campaigns on selected issues, or when national events, such as the opening of People's Congress or the National Day ceremony, dominate news coverage.

Tabloids normally devote the most space to reports on sensational events. For example, on August 14, 2004, pages A15 and A16 in *Xinwen Chenbao* were allocated for reports on alleged drug taking by two Greek athletes on the eve of the 2004 Athens Olympic Games. Three *Xinwen Chenbao* journalists, who were sent to Athens to cover the Olympics Games, contributed a lead story, which ran with a half-page color photograph and four companion stories. The lead story focused on the Greek athletes who failed to take the mandatory drug tests asked for by the Medical Committee of the International Olympic

Committee (IOC). Another story listed an hour-by-hour timetable of events in the two days of testing from August 12–13. A third story reported on the official responses by the Greek media. A fourth story covered how one of the three journalists had sneaked into a hospital where the two runners were taking the on-the-spot drug tests. And a final story focused on the press conference by IOC members.

Depth versus Brevity of Reporting on Radio and Television in China

In China, most radio news broadcasts are local or national, with the remaining time allocated to international news relevant to China's standing in the world relative to economics or politics. On average, two-thirds of the broadcasting time is devoted to domestic news, while international news takes up one-third of the broadcasting. *CCR* reports mostly on national political and economic news. However, there are exceptions to this situation when major events relevant to China dominate international news. For example, in an August 15, 2004, newscast, *CCR*'s main news program, *Baozhi Zhaiyao,* presented a two-minute lead story on a construction project launched in the western Chinese province of Fujian. The news anchor introduced the background of the project, while an on-the-spot reporter described the project in detail. The story cited three informants. However, the majority of time was allocated to in-depth reports on the Athens Olympics Games, with five stories running over five minutes. The reports covered a press conference of the Chinese Olympic Delegation, the latest game results, the timetable of incoming games, and activities held in the hometown of one of the Chinese gold medalists. This in-depth coverage of international news is rare in China, though the Olympic Games is considered important because of the 2008 Olympics in Beijing.

Local city and provincial radio stations are also required to report the key national political or economic news items, but they generally carry more local or localized news reports to cater both to audience tastes and to advertisers. Often local radio stations provide a localized "impact" report that complements the leading national news stories they are required to broadcast. City radio stations also carry more service-based news reports. One category of news that is becoming more popular on radio is traffic reports, because of the reliance on public transportation such as taxis and the growth of private ownership of cars.

In China, radio news broadcasts run from fifteen to thirty minutes, depending on the time of day or night. Typically, radio news is broadcast throughout the day, starting on the hour or half-hour. Stories typically run for one to two minutes on CCR with local radio stations broadcasting shorter stories of around thirty seconds.

Within the regular local on-the-hour newscasts, the first two stories are national political or economic news stories, focusing mostly on government or Party policies or announcements. The remaining stories are local or localized stories catering to audience tastes. Main newscasts typically end with weather and a brief traffic report. Briefer news updates feature only headlines, weather, and traffic reports.

In China, television news is generally scheduled on most channels at least four times a day, though collectively these times are somewhat staggered throughout these periods and the news focus varies considerably depending on the channel. Longer news broadcasts of thirty minutes occur at 1830 (6:30 PM) to 2000 (8:00 PM) and at 1900 (7:00 PM) to 2100 (9:00 PM)—the "golden period"—on both national broadcaster *China Central Television*

(CCTV) and provincial and city television stations. Lunchtime and late night news broadcasts, which typically commence between 1100 (11:00 AM) and 1200 (12:00 PM) and at 2200 (10:00 PM), are shorter in duration and provide news updates on key events covered in earlier newscasts. Most newscasts are predominantly national in scope, with relevant international news focusing on issues related to China's position in the world, usually featuring political or financial news from the USA.

The main news channel is *CCTV-1* (Comprehensive), which broadcasts news thirteen times a day. From morning to evening, domestic and international news is aired, including a series of in-depth reports on key national news events at 7 PM, which is the most popular program serving as the official source of information for viewers around China. *CCTV-2* (Economy, Life, and Services) specializes in domestic and international economic and finance news, focusing on stocks, securities, and new economy issues. The channel's main role is education, helping Chinese viewers to learn more about market economy activities and trends. *CCTV-4* (International) specializes in news reports that serve residents in Hong Kong, Macao, Taiwan, and internationally with cooperative ties established with foreign media outlets in the USA, Europe, Singapore, and Australia. *CCTV-4* rotates its news reports three times a day. *CCTV-5* (Sports) broadcasts frequent news reports on domestic and international sports throughout its sixteen-hour-a-day broadcasting schedule. *CCTV-7* covers both military and agriculture news. *CCTV-9* International's news service focuses mostly on around-the-clock rolling news, business news (including international financial activities and market trends), and *Worldwide Watch,* which provides in-depth news feature stories on key international events relevant to China. The channel's rolling news service begins at 0600 (6:00 AM) with news updates and *Biz China,* which focuses specifically on business news. These news updates are broadcast periodically throughout the day, typically scheduled every two hours. The news feature program *Worldwide Watch* is broadcast at 0800 (8:00 AM) and again at 1900 (7:00 PM). *CCTV-9's* first main news broadcast is scheduled at noon and runs for thirty minutes. Next are newscasts at 1300 (1:00 PM), 1700 (5:00 PM), 2100 (9:00 PM), 0000 (12:00 AM), and 0400 (4:00 AM). CCTV also launched a twenty-four-hour national news channel in 2004. The channel focuses predominantly on domestic political and economic news, but also includes relevant international news events. Figure 10.10 lists sample headlines for stories from a September 26, 2004, newscast at 1900 (7:00 PM) on *CCTV-1.*

In addition to the satellite national broadcaster, China has an array of provincial and city terrestrial and cable television stations that incorporate news broadcasts into their daily program schedule. Each station carries coverage of domestic news (about two-thirds of the broadcast) and international news (about one-third of the broadcast) events. Content varies considerably, though news broadcasts on these television stations generally follow the guidelines of featuring national political and economic news as lead stories, and then providing localized or local stories to address specific audience tastes. Newscasts run for either thirty minutes or fifteen minutes for news updates, which appear more frequently throughout the programming day.

In China, lead news reports focus predominantly on national politics, government policies, important political figures attending meetings, political events, or foreign delegations. Other common categories include: economic news, Greater China news (Hong Kong, Macao, and Taiwan), social news such as crime and the environment, and international news. Sports news usually comes at the end of the broadcast and before the weather report.

Decision by CCP's Central Committee to Strengthen Administration Ability
Publication and Distribution of Learning Materials on CCP's Recent Decisions
President Hu Jintao Attends Music Play of "A Soldier's Diary"
Premier Wen Jianbao Finishes Visits to Kyrgyz and Russia, Returns Home
Jia Qinglin Stresses Science and Technology as Crucial to Strengthen the Party's
    Administration Ability
Seminar in Memory of the "Tenth Anniversary of the Establishment of Chinese Religion
    Peace Committee"
Daqing: "A Conversion of a Resourceful City" under the Guidance of Scientific
    Development
Chinese Disabled Swimming Team Wins Gold Medals at the Athens Olympics on
    September 25
Results of the Selection of "Top 10 Favorite Policemen" Released
Zhou Yongkang, Minister of Public Security, Reiterates "People's Policemen" Should Love
    the People; A Seminar of the Selection of "Top 10 Favorite Policemen"
Central Committee of Zhigong Party Is Active in Environmental Protection
Luoyang: Government Officials Came to Solve People's Problems
Domestic News Briefing
Continuous Attacks in Iraq; Dozens of Civilians Killed or Injured within One Day
International News Briefing

FIGURE 10.10 *Sample Headlines from 1900 (7:00 PM) Newscast on* CCTV-1 *in China; September 26, 2004*

Source: Lu Jia.

News report lengths vary considerably on television in China. A lead story can run from two to three minutes. Subsequent stories can run from thirty seconds to three minutes. Video/sound bites typically run twenty–thirty seconds for citizens, and up to one minute for high-ranking government officials. In reports on an international story with a foreign spokesperson, the viewer can hear both the speaker's native language in the background and a Chinese translation by the anchor or reporter. The main news story generally focuses on the facts as issued by the government or Party's news release. At provincial or city television stations, reports are sometimes followed by comments from local government officials supporting the government's policies, directives, or campaigns. It is common for a big story on a major historical event in China's Communist history to dominate a newscast. Such segments normally include extended historical footage to remind people of the event or person, followed by current footage of key political figures commemorating the event, person, or date. Rarely do newscasts use live footage or interviews, as content needs to be vetted and censored if necessary before broadcasting. The exception to this situation is when the Chinese president or a prominent political leader addresses the nation. For example, on August 14, 2004, *CCTV-1* aired an extended story on the celebrations of the centennial birth date of former leader Deng Xiaoping. News reports showed extensive coverage of Deng meeting people and international dignitaries during his leadership of China throughout the 1980s and early 1990s.

NEWS REPORTING IN GHANA

Bias versus Objectivity in Newspapers in Ghana

In Ghana, most national newspapers are known for striving toward objectivity but retaining biases that were historically present prior to the relative government stability that was achieved after the 1992 Constitution. Many of the newspapers carry a metamessage on the front page implying that objectivity is not as important as truth or independence—for example, *The Evening News* ("Truth Well Told"), *People and Places* ("We Report Nothing but the Truth"), *The Chronicle* ("The True Independent"), and the *Daily Guide* ("An Independent Newspaper"). The use of the words *true*, *truth*, and *independent* is largely a reaction to a widely held perception that during previous military dictatorships, state-operated media used the word *objective* to describe the news that was delivered, when in fact the news was often government propaganda.

Both the state-owned newspapers and the private newspapers normally devote one or two pages to commentary, either as an editorial by the newspaper, as commentary by newspaper writers, or as letters to the editor. The most common type of commentary is the editorial, which for most newspapers appears on page 2 as a vertical column on the left-hand side of the page. (The *Daily Graphic* puts its editorial on page 7.) It is also typical to see editorial-type comments outside of Editorial sections of the newspaper. For example, in the May 20, 2004, *Ghanaian Times*, a headline in the Foreign News Section read: "States Should Observe Int. Humanitarian Law" (p. 2). Not all newspapers run letters to the editor, or commentaries by staff writers.

Most of the bias in newspapers in Ghana is subtle. As indicated in Chapter 9, the majority of bias in Ghanaian newspapers can be categorized either as being supportive of the governments in power since the 2000 elections, or against the governments in power from the years 1992–2000. The bias against the pre-2000 governments is largely a carryover from a time period in which the "privates" were agitating strongly against alleged civil-rights abuses by those governments. A more contemporary bias in these newspapers involves reporting on misdeeds of former government officials. For example, in the May 20, 2004, *Statesman*, a front-page article comments:

> When in the last year of the NDC regime [in power from 1992–2000], the Government, with Prof John Evans Atta Mills heading the Economic Management Team, refused to listen to its own counsel and chose not to adjust upwards the pump price of fuel, it resulted in a Tema Oil Refinery debt of about $250 million.

This kind of bias does not present as stinging criticism, but rather an emerging confidence to moderately criticize the activities of pre-2000 government officials while they were in office.

In contrast, the predominant bias of the state-owned newspapers leans toward implied support of government policies—regardless of who is in power—or toward the routine coverage of government policies using quotes exclusively from government spokespeople. For example, in the May 17, 2004, edition of the *Daily Graphic*, a front-page article reported on an agreement signed between the Ghanaian government and a USA firm to conduct oil exploration in a region of Ghana. In the article, the only quotes and para-phrases reported were attributed to the government's Deputy Minister of Energy.

Bias versus Objectivity in Radio and Television News in Ghana

In Ghana, private radio and television newscasts did not exist until 1995. In the ensuing years, private radio and television newscasts have not generally been known for being biased; rather, private television and radio news aims for relative objectivity by balancing opinions and by refraining from commentary or advocacy journalism.

In contrast, the state-owned *GTV* has had a history of serving as a virtual mouthpiece for government initiatives. This reputation began to recede after 2000 as it incorporated more stories that were critical of government. However, like the state-owned newspapers, the criticism is not known for being harsh, and is normally outweighed by stories implicitly supporting government activities.

Entertainment versus Serious News in Newspapers in Ghana

In Ghana, most news reporting in the newspapers is serious. There are no daily newspapers focused primarily on entertainment news—only two weekly newspapers: *Graphic Showbiz* and *P&P* (People and Places). The overwhelming subject covered by most newspaper stories is politics. Most stories in the private newspapers focus either on new government policies or on criticisms of policies and activities of people in the public eye. The criticisms normally are less about alleged illegality and more about alleged impropriety. In terms of people, Ghanaian newspapers tend to focus on politicians—present and former—and religious leaders. For example, a May 20, 2004, story on the first page of the *Ghanaian Times* Regional Diary insert leads with "Pastor Accused of Receiving Stolen Money . . . insists it was a 'thank you gift.'" Like this story, very often the news in Ghanaian newspapers is about people formerly in the public eye who in retrospect were involved in the potential mismanagement of money. Across the private newspapers, criticism can be strong but is not usually scathing.

In contrast, the state-owned newspapers prefer to focus on reporting government activities with implicit support for the activities as discussed earlier. Articles frequently report on policies and initiatives of government officials. For example, a May 17, 2004, article in the *Daily Graphic*, "Don't Use Foreign Labels," reported that the Minister of State in charge of Trade, Industry and President's Special Initiatives "warned" local industries not to use foreign labels on their products because it makes it "difficult for the government to collect data on local manufacturers" (p. 3). Often stories in the state-owned press are formed around information provided by government officials or by the Ministry of Information.

Exemplifying the serious orientation of newspapers in Ghana, the typical layout of newspapers tends to be dominated by black-and-white text. Though photos frequently accompany stories, the photos tend to be of people in natural settings, as opposed to staged portraits. Typical examples include long shots of people standing in front of microphones or people sitting in chairs behind desks.

Entertainment versus Serious News on Radio and Television in Ghana

In Ghana, news on both state-owned and privately owned stations tends to have a serious orientation. Lead stories focus on current events, politics, and developing democracy. For example, the lead story on a May 20, 2004, radio newscast on *Joy FM* focused on comments by the Public Affairs Director of the Electoral Commission. Most of his comments, spoken in an indigenous language, were about how the upcoming national elections would be conducted to achieve fairness. This story was then followed by a story about a delegation from the USA who met with Ghanaian media organizations to discuss guidelines for achieving fair coverage of the upcoming elections. Similarly, on a May 18, 2004, newscast on *GTV,* all the stories were about current events and politics. Examples included a story about Ghana submitting to peer review by other African countries; a sixth annual conference of a Muslim delegation; a chief talking about tolerance of others' beliefs; and the Ministry of Manpower training families in modern farming techniques. No stories were about entertainers.

Underlining the serious orientation of radio and television news is the style of presentation. On television, sets and graphics are minimal and tend to be static. Anchors deliver copy in a somewhat subdued tone with little body or facial movement, except for a large smile at the end of the newscast. On radio, music is not played underneath news reporting. Sound bites from the field are often difficult to hear because of equipment deficiencies.

Depth versus Brevity of Reporting in Newspapers in Ghana

The state-owned newspapers in Ghana are known for providing more depth to their news reporting than most of the private newspapers. The state-owned newspapers have many more pages than the private newspapers, some of which have a total length of six to eight pages.

Typically, news reports on the front pages are stand-alone reports that are not keyed to companion reports inside the newspaper. It is a hallmark of Ghanaian newspapers that stories of all types appear on opposing pages. For example, on pages 4 and 5 of the May 20, 2004, *Chronicle,* the following stories appeared: "The War on Filth—A Nine-Day Wonder" (the newspaper's editorial—about litter); "Chiefs Warned About Politicians' Fat Envelopes"; "28 Varsity Students Honored"; "More Torture Tales at NRC" (National Reconciliation Commission); "Constituency Chairman Backs Ms. Churcher?" (a candidate for the New Patriotic Party); and "NPP Leadership Warned." In addition to these stories, the only other material on these pages included an advertisement for someone seeking a house-painting job and a public-service message with this wording: "Procure a condom before you go in for sex—life is precious and worth living—AIDS is real."

State-owned newspapers are known for having more comprehensive news than private newspapers, but neither are known for in-depth reporting. Newspapers achieve some depth in political news, not necessarily through extensive research and quotes or paraphrases from experts, but rather through analyses and speculation about deeper motives behind public actions—and that there may be wrongdoing or incompetence involved. For example, in the May 14, 2004, *Ghana Palaver*, a front-page article reported several activities that it speculated might be leading the president to "dump" the sitting vice president when the party runs for re-election. The article cited quotes by a "party insider," and speeches by another party member indicating that the person was vying for the vice president's position.

Depth versus Brevity of Reporting on Radio and Television in Ghana

Most radio stations carry news in Ghana. Radio newscasts usually contain international, national, and local news. Prioritizing news is related more to what is considered to be newsworthy than whether local news should come before national news, and whether national news should come before international news. News related to neighboring West African countries tends to be grouped together under international news, which includes news from anywhere in the world. However, there are many briefer newscasts that focus on local news. News reports typically run about one minute, though longer news reports of five or even ten minutes are commonly heard; these reports can include three- or four-minute sound bites. Three categories of news that stand out on radio are political news, public health news (often related to AIDS), and African news in indigenous languages.

Radio news is scheduled across most of the day and can be heard at the top of most hours until 2200 (10 PM). The most common news report is the brief bulletin that ranges from three to five minutes (this segment typically does not have a set time), which can be heard on both the state-owned GBC networks and the local commercial radio stations. Bulletin stories typically run ten or fifteen seconds long and are loosely formatted. News in all three major categories (local, national, international) can be heard in any order. Normally, a weather forecast is delivered at the end of the report. Aside from the bulletins, typically there are major newscasts lasting thirty minutes or one hour at 0600 (6:00 AM), 0700 (7:00 AM), 1200 (12:00 PM), 1300 (1:00 PM), and 1800 (6:00 PM).

Straight television news is scheduled for the afternoon and evening. On *GTV*, news is aired at 1400 (2:00 PM), 1900 (7:00 PM), and 2230 (10:30 PM). On *TV3*, news is aired at 1200 (12:00 noon), 1820 (6:20 PM), and 2230 (10:30 PM). On *TV Africa*, news is aired at 1930 (7:30 PM) and 2230 (10:30 PM). On *Metro TV*, news is aired at 1300 (1:00 PM) and 2100 (9:00 PM). In addition to these news programs, foreign news-carriers also broadcast on Ghanaian television. These carriers include the BBC, CNN, and DW-TV (from Germany), all of which have one or two newscasts across one or two of the television channels in Ghana. The afternoon and late evening newscasts are half an hour. The evening newscasts are one hour. Most newscasts are national and international in scope. All newscasts—including those on *GTV*—contain conventional advertising as well as paid announcements (discussed in Chapter 9).

News reports early in the newscast for both the *GTV* and the private stations focus on national news (mostly politics). Other common categories of news reports include speeches by chiefs, evaluations of Ghana's finances and foreign-loan programs, announcements from ministries, improvements in the country's infrastructure, and the exchange rate between the Ghanaian Cedi versus the USDollar and the Euro. Figure 10.11 lists sample headlines for stories from the May 18, 2004, 1830 (6:30 PM) newscast on *TV3*.

Newscasts on both the *GTV* and the private television stations typically include a sizable number of international stories, which are not usually predicated on originating from a particular region of the world. For example, a May 18, 2004, *GTV* newscast included the following stories back-to-back: "Gandhi will not be India's Next Prime Minister"; "Nigerian State of Emergency"; "Honduran Jail Killings"; and "Rwanda's former President Accused of Compromising State Security." Sports news usually comes almost at the end of a newscast.

Preview of 2 Stories
Labor Ward of Hospital Closing Down?
Local Exporters Meeting in Accra to Boost Exports
Ministry of Land and Forestry Announces Conservation Plans
Monitors of Trust Fund
Advertising Break
Currency Exchange Rates of Cedi Against the USDollar and the Euro
Advertising Break
Chairman of Human Rights Committee Speech
Ghanaian Woman Recognized by Award for Helping People
India's Ghandi Declines to Assume Presidency
Weather Reports
Sports: Drug Testing
Summary of Headlines
Paid Announcements

FIGURE 10.11   *Sample Headlines from 1830 (6:30 PM) newscast on TV 3 in Ghana; May 18, 2004*
Source: Robert McKenzie.

News report lengths differ between the *GTV* and the private stations. Generally, news reports on *GTV* are longer than news reports on the other channels. Several news reports on the *GTV* can run for four or five minutes. On the private stations, news reports are usually two or three minutes long. Usually, there are three advertising breaks per half hour on both the *GTV* and the private stations. Video/sound bites containing parts of newsmakers' speeches are fairly common in television news reports. Video/sound bites are usually extended and often run up to one minute or more. Often, bites of more than one person are used in a story. Live interviews are not very common on television news in Ghana. Most of the newscast revolves around the anchor announcing news stories.

NEWS REPORTING IN LEBANON

Bias versus Objectivity in Newspapers in Lebanon

In Lebanon, most newspapers have political biases that come through clearly in the news coverage, as well as editorials and features. *An-Nahar* (*The Day*) tends to be a right-of-center newspaper that opposes all governments. *An-Nahar* focuses mainly on Lebanese political news, particularly those of the political opposition to government, but also covers economic and social events as well as sports. It is widely read by Christians and university students in and around Beirut. *As-Safir* (*The Ambassador*) is a left-of-center newspaper that concentrates on Lebanese political news from an Arab nationalist point of view. Its motto is "the voice of the voiceless" and it claims to be "the newspaper of Lebanon in the Arab nation and the Arab nation in Lebanon." *As-Safir* is strong on local political news, political background features and articles, as well as cultural news, and usually appeals to Arab nationalist and leftist intellectuals, as well as to Shiite Muslims. The French-language *l'Orient le Jour*s (*The Orient The Day*—a merger of two newspapers) is a right-wing newspaper with strong editorials on current political issues, usually having to do with relations with the West, and is geared toward French-educated, intellectual Lebanese. *Al-Balad* is a right-of-center newspaper that usually reports the news from a USA political perspective. *Al-Balad* is financed by a wealthy Kuwaiti group (called al-Khurafi) that in 2004 launched an aggressive subscription campaign, selling the newspaper for one fourth of its listed price and offering new subscribers the opportunity to win several luxury German cars. *Ad-Diyar* (*The Homeland*) has been known for defying powerful political and militia bosses in Lebanon. *Al-Anwar* (*The Lights*) was founded in 1950 to champion the cause of "Nasserism" (after the former Egyptian President Gamal Abdel Nasser) in Lebanon and the Arab world.

Because of their tendency to mix news with opinions, local newspapers are often called "views papers." Opinions are manifested in several areas. First, each newspaper tends to represent or support one or more sectarian or ethnic authority or group. Because of the mixed system of authority in which sectarian and ethnic leaders have a great deal of political authority, the Lebanese news media, including newspapers, generally tend to oppose the government in their news reports. This does not mean that the Lebanese press acts as a "watchdog" to safeguard the public interest. Rather, opposition to the government is usually in the form of supporting another authority, or possibly several other authorities, which are politically active in Lebanese politics. Such authorities can also include foreign powers such as the USA, Syria, Kuwait, Libya, and other Arab and foreign governments. Second, as Nabil Dajani discusses in *The Vigilant Press* (1989), the extreme politicization of Lebanese society has contributed to a bias in news reports that focuses on political events at the expense of news concerning the average citizen—such as spiraling prices, deteriorating economic conditions, and regular power failures. As a consequence, labor and business news stories typically receive heavy coverage because such news is linked to bankers, industrialists, and merchants. Similarly, rural areas are rarely mentioned in the Lebanese news reports.

Lebanese newspapers usually do not contain metamessages implying objectivity. (*Al-Balad* states that it is "a comprehensive daily political paper.") All of the Arabic-language newspapers in Lebanon run their leading editorials on the front page. For example, during the 2004 campaign for president in Lebanon, *as-Safir* on October 21, 2004, ran a seven-column editorial by its publisher, arguing against re-electing Lebanese President Emile Lahhoud. The sarcastic title of the editorial was: "On the Road: Emile Lahhoud the Second, the Conqueror of the World."

As is the case in France, it is much more common to see columnist-opinions in Lebanese newspapers than letters-to-the-editor expressing opinion, which are scarce. Readers rarely send opinion letters because they usually only read newspapers that reflect their own political orientations.

Lebanese newspapers frequently engage in campaigns to advocate positions on issues and policies that represent the power groups behind these papers. For example, when former prime minister Rafik Hariri in 1998 did not succeed in forming the first government under the then-newly elected Emile Lahhoud, his newspaper, *al-Mustakbal,* launched a fierce campaign against the prime minister who replaced him, Salim el-Hoss. During this time period, hardly a day would pass without *al-Mustakbal* running articles strongly criticizing el-Hoss and his cabinet members. Still, investigative reporting is largely absent in the Lebanese media, primarily because of a lack of trained investigative journalists, plus an unwillingness of media outlets to assign reporters to this kind of beat.

Bias versus Objectivity in Radio and Television News in Lebanon

In Lebanon, radio and television newscasts on both private and public channels are widely perceived as biased. As in the case for newspapers, both radio and television news in Lebanon often represent the points of view of the subsidizing authorities: On radio, *Voix du Liban* (*Voice of Lebanon*) is perceived as a right-wing station advocating opposition to Syrian influences in Lebanon; *Saout al Shaab* (*Voice of the People*) is perceived as a left-wing station advocating resistance against Israel and calling for social reform; and *Radio Orient* is owned by a former prime minister and is known as a right-of-center station advocating a Saudi outlook on the affairs of Lebanon and the region. On television, certain stations are known for representing particular political views: *Future TV*—pro-Saudi former Prime Minister Rafik Hariri; *LBCI*—the Maronite Patriarch and his political supporters; *NBN*—the pro-Syrian Speaker of the House, Nabih Birri; *al-Manar*—Lebanese resistance against Israel; and state-financed public station *Tele Liban*—official government positions such as decisions on administrative appointments and budgetary expenses. For all Lebanese mass media, including radio and television, news is known for being compliant insofar as it avoids questioning and criticizing sectarian and religious authorities, as well as power groups that subsidize these authorities.

Entertainment versus Serious News in Newspapers in Lebanon

In Lebanon, reporting in newspapers is usually very serious. Most news stories cover politics, labor, the military, and business. Subjects dealing with social services are less frequent. By far, most newspaper stories cover labor and business news related to merchants, industrialists, and business owners. Political crimes are almost absent from the Lebanese press but civil crimes are not. Stories dealing with the environment and student matters are quite scarce. About half the newspapers' news coverage focuses on Beirut, and just over 10 percent on rural areas. For example, the November 25, 2004, issue of *as-Safir* had twenty pages of stories, but only three included rural news items, identified by these headlines: "The meeting of notables of Bint Jbeil [a village in south Lebanon] with the Minister of Economy to request the reduction of the price of fuel"; "A new plan to move the graveyards of the burial places of the town of Tyre"; and "The Mayor of Souk el-Gharb [a summer resort] calls for administrative decentralization."

Entertainment versus Serious News in Radio and Television in Lebanon

In Lebanon, almost all radio news programs are brief but serious. For example, on November 15, 2004, an 1800 (6:00 PM) newscast on the private station *ash-Shark* contained the following major headlines: "Two weeks after the election of Bush, Powell and three other ministers resign"; "Nabil Sha'th (Foreign Minister of the Palestinian Authority) announces that Powell will visit the West Bank and possibly Gaza"; "Reduced airline ticket prices for the Lebanese escaping from Abidjan"; "Europeans satisfied with the transfer of power in Palestine"; "Shooting in the tent of Mahmoud Abbas in Gaza"; "President Lahhoud stresses the importance of the rehabilitation of prisoners in Lebanon."

Similarly, television news reporting in Lebanon is mostly serious, until near the end when it finishes with an entertainment-oriented news item followed by a brief sports recap and then a weathercast. Two channels—*Future TV* and *New TV*—conclude their newscast with a political cartoon. For example, *New TV*'s cartoon on its Thursday, November 25, 2004, news program dealt with the topic of the withdrawal of the Syrian forces from Lebanon. The heading for the cartoon read: "[Deputy] Nasser Kandil says 'Expect a sudden Syrian withdrawal.'" At the time of publication, Deputy Kandil was a pro-Syrian member of the Lebanese parliament and his name in Arabic means *lantern*. The cartoon shows two Lebanese people conversing. The first asks: "How did he know the Syrians will go?" The other replies: "Maybe because of the lack of fuel."

Lebanese television news stories often focus on local politics, Arab developments, and international events—especially those relevant to the Arab world. For example, the November 15, 2004, newscast at 1945 (7:45 PM) on *New TV* included following the head-lines: "America Admits Fierce Fighting in Falluja"; "Colin Powell Resigns and Will Visit the West Bank"; "Continued Palestinian Meetings to Deal with the Shooting Incident in Gaza"; "Iran Temporarily Suspends Production of Enriched Uranium"; and "Chocolates as Far as One's Eyes Can See."

There are not many colors used in the background or in the anchors' clothes on television news in Lebanon. As in France, a news story often begins with a map of a country and the region or city highlighted where the story takes place.

Depth versus Brevity of Reporting in Newspapers in Lebanon

Most newspapers in Lebanon run regular, specialized pages that provide news and feature stories about cultural subjects as well as specialized pages dealing with sports events and with economic matters. The economic page normally provides the currency exchange rates as well as reports about local and international financial situations. In most newspapers, sports news and feature stories cover more than one page. All newspapers run opinion pages with serious articles analyzing newsworthy events and issues. Several newspapers also run a page or more of entertainment features such as crossword puzzles.

Lebanese newspapers usually follow the same order of news presentation: first, they devote the front page to major news developments with editorials. News reports on the front page are then continued inside the paper on pages that generally are devoted also to a mix of local, Arab, and international news events. Pages 2 and 3 are devoted exclusively to important local political news. The last page usually contains human-interest stories and the political cartoon, if any. All newspapers typically print a box on page 2 in the top left column that includes brief "tips" about administrative news. For example, the December 9, 2004, edition of *an-Nahar* on page 2 ran the tip: "The government is trying to accomplish whatever it can of reform and to improve the living conditions of people so as to invest this in the forthcoming parliamentary elections in favor of candidates that support it." Local administrative news, selections of items from the police records for the previous day, and other local news occupy several pages. This is followed by economic news that usually reports about the state of the Lebanese currency, of local stocks, foreign currency exchange rates, values, and other local economic developments. Sports news comes next, and usually occupies one to four pages, beginning with local sports and ending with foreign sports. For example, in the December 6, 2004, edition of *as-Safir*, there were four pages of sports. Page 8 and most of page 9 were devoted to eight sports articles, each reporting on a football (soccer) match between local teams. Page 9 also included an article about the election of a new national basketball committee and another about preparations of the Lebanese athletes for a forthcoming Arab Olympics. Then, page 10 reported results of the previous day's football games in the leagues of twelve European countries. Results from the football leagues in each country were also reported. Page 11 included four sports news reports, with the following headlines: "Spain Captures the Davis Cup for the Second Time"; "Two Surprises in the First Round of the Asian Chess Championship"; "Competition Continues between San Antonio and Seattle in the American Basketball Championship"; and "Lasi and Castio Maintain their Titles in the World Boxing Championship."

The two sports games that get extensive coverage by Lebanese newspapers are basketball and football (soccer). European and Latin American football leagues are covered extensively. Basketball games—particularly games from the National Basketball Association (NBA) in the USA—are also covered at length, but not with as much detail as football (soccer) coverage.

Arab and international news are usually presented on the inside pages. The location of these foreign news events depends on the number of pages of the newspaper. Most newspapers devote one page or more to editorial comments of leading international newspapers. Some newspapers, such as *as-Safir* and *an-Nahar*, regularly devote a whole page to translations of editorial comments by Israeli newspapers. *An-Nahar* and *as-Safir* devote one page to lengthy articles by intellectuals and professionals. Some of these articles are sometimes printed in several installments.

Depth versus Brevity of Reporting on Radio and Television in Lebanon

In Lebanon, radio news stories are national, Arab, or international. However, not all radio stations carry news because audiovisual regulations in Lebanon restrict broadcasting of news to certain stations. The rest can broadcast only music and other entertainment programs. Usually radio news is scheduled either on the hour or just in the morning, noon, evening, and night. When news breaks, all stations stop their regularly scheduled programs with a special musical introduction understood as a "flash." Other than *ash-Shark Radio,* which runs a fifteen- to sixty-minute newscast on the hour (depending on the time of the day), there is no station that carries news twenty-four hours a day.

The official radio station, *Radio Lebanon,* broadcasts news on the hour as well as music and cultural programs. Its news service usually features official government news. For example, an official dinner party hosted by the president or a senior government official typically takes precedence over other news. *Radio Lebanon* has an agreement with the French government to broadcast French cultural programs that are prepared by French media production companies. These programs typically focus on French cultural issues such as reviews of recently published French literary books.

In Lebanon, there are three types of radio newscasts: a thirty-minute newscast (sometimes stretching longer), a three- to five-minute news brief, and a news flash that breaks important news developments. Breaking news events usually include major political or military developments or a natural disaster.

The format of the regular newscast is usually as follows. Normally the first news stories are those dealing with the most important local or Arab news developments, unless an international news event is quite major. However, the bulk of the news is local, often originating in Beirut. Arab news, particularly news about the occupied Palestinian territories and Iraq, usually is given prominence in every newscast. The length of radio news stories varies with the topic. Normally, however, a radio news story lasts between one and three minutes.

The main television news is broadcast in the evening by all television channels. *NBN* and *Tele Liban* air their main newscasts at 1900 (7:00 PM) in the evening. *Al-Manar* follows at 1930 (7:30 PM), then *New TV* at 1945 (7:45 PM), then both *LBCI* and *Future TV* at 2000 (8:00 PM). All television stations air afternoon newscasts and a few (*al-Manar, NBN,* and *New TV*) have late-night newscasts. The length of newscasts varies every night. They usually last between thirty minutes and one hour, depending on the volume of news that is of interest to the gatekeepers. News flashes interrupt programs when there are important news developments. These are introduced with a sirenlike sound and the words "News Brief." An anchorperson then presents the news brief.

Though major news events presented are usually similar on all television stations, there is some variation, mainly in the order of new stories across each station. For example, on December 6, 2004, *Future TV* led with a story about a Lebanese politician being shot at with a gun (the politician was also a major political supporter of the station). At the end of the report it was mentioned that police denied the claim. *Al-Manar* led with a report that French authorities were recommending that the station be banned from French cable systems because of its continued criticism of Israel. *LBCI* led with a report about a strong political statement by the Maronite Patriarch that was critical of the government. *NBN* and *Tele Liban* led with a report about a statement by the Minister of Justice supporting the government's handling of an investigation involving an opposition leader.

News reporting on all television channels usually follows a similar format. News stories are often either introduced or followed by a brief editorial commentary provided by the anchor. For example, the *LBCI* 2000 (8:00 PM) newscast on November 24, 2004, opened as follows: "The confrontation between the [government] supporters and the opposition has moved to the streets with the call for [a pro-government] demonstration next week. The demonstration comes as a challenge before the general parliamentary elections. The confrontation also moved to unresolved issues: the rationing of electricity and the increase in the price of fuel: "The government has set a fixed price for the fuel, but did this become effective? And was the law applied?" That introduction was then followed by interviews with a number of opposition leaders who criticized government policies.

Television news stories in Lebanon tend to range between one and two minutes long. Often the newscast may include an official or an expert who answers questions by the anchor about certain news developments. The bulk of television news in Lebanon transitions from news about Lebanon to news about the Arab world, unless there is a major international news event. As in the case of radio news, almost every television newscast tends to include reports about developments in the Palestinian-occupied territories and Iraq. Cultural and sports news usually come almost at the end of the newscast.

Government Officials Talk Politics
Weather Forecast
Visit of a Senior UN Official to Lebanon
Lebanese Speaker of the Parliament Visits France and Makes Pro-Government
    Statements
Issues Facing the New Government
The Palestinian Rights of Return to their Homeland
Forthcoming Lebanese Parliamentary Elections
Visit of Government Officials to Political Prisoner
Meeting of President Lahhoud with Foreign and Local Officials
Protocol Visit by French Ambassador to Lebanese President
Syrians Withdrawing from Lebanon
Improving Security in Lebanon
Civil Crime
Teachers Protest Low Wages
Protest Against High Fuel Prices
Poverty in the North
News from Around the World
Weather Forecast

FIGURE 10.12 *Sample Headlines from 2000 (8:00 PM) Newscast on LBCI in Lebanon; November 28, 2004*

Source: Robert McKenzie.

In Lebanon, it is very common to have several advertising breaks in a single newscast. The number of these breaks depends mainly on the volume of ads sold. Then the newscast resumes with the anchor presenting the news reports. After the last news story, there are ads and promotional segments, and then a weather report. Figure 10.12 lists sample headlines for stories from the 2000 (8:00 PM) newscast on *LBCI*.

In Lebanon, video/sound bites containing a witness's account of a news event or an expert's commentary are common in television news reports. Very often, a story includes sound bites from average citizens who have been approached in the street by the reporter; such bites can last a couple of minutes.

COMPARATIVE SUMMARY

This chapter compared news reporting across the eight countries. News reporting was likened to the standout leaves on a tree, because these differentiated leaves provide insight about the general welfare of the tree. Similarly, news reporting is the standout content that provides a kind of society-wide conversation about a media system and the country in which it operates.

One dimension in news reporting across the eight countries is the bias versus objectivity dimension. Biases in French news gravitate toward promoting culture and French national interests. Biases in Swedish news gravitate toward Scandinavia, and the welfare state, international humanitarian crises. Biases in UK news gravitate toward individual positions of advocacy taken up by individual media organizations. Biases in USA news gravitate toward criticizing communism and socialism, and promoting the USA as having the ideal political and economic system. Biases in Mexican news gravitate toward individual reporter perspectives, and toward losing patience with conflicts between the federal government and the country. Biases in Chinese news gravitate toward supporting government policies and opinions of party leaders, promoting Chinese culture around the world, and criticizing negative aspects of capitalism and Western influences. Biases in Ghanaian news gravitate toward criticizing past dictatorships and toward backing off strong criticisms of its democratic governments out of concern that such criticism may retard progress. And biases in Lebanese news gravitate toward fragmented political orientations related to financial backers of the news outlets. To a great extent, news bias in a media system is a function of the prevailing ideologies within the given country.

A second dimension is the serious versus entertainment dimension in newspapers. France has very serious newspapers and no national entertainment tabloids. France also has a national satirical newspaper using cartoons, and a national communist newspaper. Sweden has serious national broadsheets and sensationalist serious tabloids. The UK has a large number of national newspapers equally divided between serious broadsheets and sensationalist tabloids—two of which focus on outrage and sexual indiscretion. The USA has a serious "prestige press," a national newspaper that has a similar form to television, and big-city and local newspapers—all of which focus on politics and crime. México has a large selection of serious national broadsheets and tabloids, as well as sensationalist tabloids, often focusing on bodily harm, and a sports tabloid. China and Lebanon have serious national broadsheets, whereas China has only entertainment-oriented tabloids. And Ghana has two very serious national broadsheets and several serious national tabloids.

And a third dimension is depth versus brevity. In France, newspapers provide in-depth political and academic reporting, and radio news provides in-depth political-issues news, but television news provides more breadth than depth. In Sweden, newspapers provide in-depth reporting on political issues primarily through debate pages, whereas radio news provides in-depth reporting about nature through discussion programs, and television news provides in-depth news on humanitarian issues. In the UK, newspapers, radio news, and television news provide in-depth analyses of just about any issues—particularly world affairs. In the USA, newspapers provide in-depth reporting on business and consumer news, but radio and television news provides more breadth than depth. In México, newspapers provide in-depth reporting on political news, government-achievement news, and news about the USA, whereas radio provides in-depth reporting about politics and developmental progress through discussion programs, but television news provides more breadth than depth. In China, tabloids have more depth than government-funded broadsheets because of the sensational news component (an interesting twist—broadsheets in other countries usually have more depth); radio and television news have depth in domestic political news as well as world news related to China's economic growth. In Ghana, newspapers provide limited depth about political issues, democracy, and infrastructure development, whereas Ghanaian radio news provides in-depth news about world affairs, and television news provides in-depth news about whatever is being covered. In Lebanon, newspapers provide in-depth reporting about local and Arab political and economic issues; radio and television news provides in-depth political commentaries, especially related to issues involving Arab affairs.

CHAPTER 11

MEDIA IMPORTS AND EXPORTS

PRIMER QUESTIONS

1. How common is it to see foreign newspapers in the country where you are living? From what countries does the newspaper content tend to originate? Do these countries border your country? Do these countries share the same language as your country?

2. How common is it to hear foreign radio content—either individual songs or radio stations—in the country where you are living? From what countries does the radio content tend to originate? Do these countries border your country? Do these countries share the same language as your country?

3. How common is it to see foreign television content—either individual programs or television channels—in the country where you are living? From what countries does the television content tend to originate? Do these countries border your country? Do these countries share the same language as your country?

4. How common is it for domestic media content based in the country in which you are living to focus on foreign countries?

5. What are some factors that influence whether a country imports media content from other countries? What are some factors that influence whether a country exports media content to other countries? What are some consequences for countries that do not import very much foreign media content?

Think about how many foreign newspapers, foreign radio programs, foreign television shows, and foreign web sites are available in the country in which you are living. Some countries are big media importers—that is, they receive a lot of media content that originates from other countries. Other countries are small media importers—that is, they do not receive very much media content from other countries. Now think about whether the foreign media content that is accessible in your country generally tends to be more prevalent in newspapers, radio programming, or television programming. Some countries receive a broad range of media—newspapers, radio, television, internet, and film—from other countries. Other countries receive only selected media outlets—such as television and internet—from other countries. But as Jeremy Tunstall discussed in *The Media Are American*, almost all countries across the world receive lots of media imports from the USA. To put it another way, the USA is by far the most prolific media exporter in the world.

Speaking of exports, think about the types of media content that leave your country and end up in other countries. Now think about the main countries where that exported media content goes. And then think about the images of your country that are represented in the content being exported. As I discuss in "Images of the US as Perceived by US Students in France," a chapter in *Images of the U.S. Around the World* (1999, edited by Yahya Kamalipour), media content that leaves one country and arrives in other countries serves as a kind of ambassador for the originating country. That is, the exported media content rhetorically invites people in other countries who are exposed to the content to gain impressions about your country—what the people look like, how people act in certain situations, what issues people consider as important or unimportant, and so on. In essence, exported media content encourages foreign audiences—particularly people with little direct experience in the exporting country—to gain some fairly definitive first impression about the culture of the originating country.

In Chapter 3, media imports and exports were likened to the seeds on a tree. When seeds fall from a tree, they have the chance to spring up in other locations. Because of wind, birds, and other passersby, seeds get transported away from the tree—sometimes far away. If the short-term environmental conditions are favorable in the new location, the seed may then germinate. If the long-term conditions are favorable, the seed may grow into a tree (or a full-fledged media system). However, if the environmental conditions are adverse to what the seed requires, then the seed's existence may be short-lived. Similarly, media content is carried away to locations far away from the media system that originated the content. If the conditions are favorable in the new location, the content may grow into its own full-fledged media system cultivated by local cultural characteristics, philosophies for media operations, regulation, financing, and accessibility.

Moreover, trees that undergo a regular interchange with their immediate and distant environments generally tend to flourish compared to trees that live in insulated environments. Similarly, media systems that do not experience interchange with media systems from other environments are susceptible to stagnancy because there are not enough ingredients from the outside world to keep the media system fresh. In contrast, media systems that experience regular interchange with other environments are exposed to a kind of cross-pollination of ideas, which nourishes and promotes new growth in the media system.

FACTORS INFLUENCING THE EXPORTING OF MEDIA CONTENT

Some media content is purposefully exported to reach targeted audiences in other countries. Other media content is sort of accidentally exported because it spills over the border from one country to another.

Newspapers are mostly exported either by printing the papers at printing plants abroad or by physically transporting the papers via airplanes, trucks, trains, cars, and bicycles—expensive processes that are not usually undertaken unless there is a large enough readership that awaits the delivered newspapers. Plus, because newspapers have to travel a long distance, by the time they arrive, the news they carry may be relatively old. These two conditions typically lead to a pattern whereby newspaper hard copies are primarily exported to other countries mainly for expatriates or vacationing readers.

Of course, newspaper web site content is often exported anywhere there is internet access. However, it is important to make important distinctions between a hard-copy version of a newspaper and its online version. One difference is that the online version of a newspaper can have fewer or more articles than the hard copy, and can update its articles several times a day, whereas hard copy usually comes out once a day. Another difference is that the reading experience for the online version involves clicking and scrolling through links and pages, whereas reading the hard copy involves turning and pulling out sections and pages. These differences warrant treating online newspapers as being fundamentally different from hard-copy newspapers when discussing imports and exports.

Radio is mostly exported by terrestrial broadcast, which for AM, FM, and medium wave is limited by distances the radio signal can cover. Shortwave radio can be picked up almost anywhere in the world, depending on weather conditions, how many other short-wave broadcasters are crowding the airwaves at the same time, and whether it is day or night. AM and FM radio can be picked up within shorter, mostly local distances from a radio transmitter. Radio content is increasingly distributed by the internet through webcasting and podcasting, where the technology is available. This set of conditions typically leads to a pattern whereby foreign radio content spills across country borders, is accessed over the internet by expatriates and vacationers, or appears as foreign songs aired on a home country's radio station.

Television is mostly exported by satellite and cable distribution systems. In most countries, people have either satellite or cable, so their ability to access foreign television content is determined by the selection of channels provided by the cable or satellite service provider. Usually, a domestic cable or satellite service provider will not seek to downlink a foreign channel unless a large enough audience is expected for it. Often, it is more viable for a broadcaster or cable or satellite service provider to purchase the rights to television series from foreign countries that can be delivered by a television channel already offered by the provider. This set of conditions typically leads to a pattern whereby foreign television content is exported to countries simply where there is perceived to be a strong demand for it.

The internet is exported by a range of technologies including phone lines, fiber optics, coaxial cable, and wireless satellite. Any web pages can be accessed if a user has access to the internet, basically according to whether a user has current-enough software and hardware, and an internet service provider that does not restrict the accessible content. This set of conditions leads to a pattern whereby internet content is exported to all countries, but is accessed only by people who know it is available, and who seek it out.

Ethnocentric, Exocentric, and Worldcentric Countries

The discussion on information flow in Chapter 2 introduced several reasons why some countries exchange—or do not exchange—a lot of media content with other countries. Some reasons that countries exchange media content with other countries are: They are geographically close to each other—especially countries that border a lot of other countries; they share a common language; and they have a common history with each other—for example, wars between the countries, or immigration between the countries. In essence, each country has a unique set of relations with other countries across the world which determine how robust the exchange of content between two given countries will be.

However, the exchange of media content between two countries is rarely bidirectional (going equally between two countries). As Chapter 2 discussed, some countries do not import very much foreign media content—that is, they are **ethnocentric.** Ethnocentric countries are often geographically isolated and have their own economically vibrant media industries. Foreign media content that makes it into some ethnocentric countries often gets modified to suit the importing country's audience tastes and expectations—as when the dialogue portion of the content gets translated into the importing country's first language, or when the content structure is imitated with domestically produced content that follows the general structure of the foreign content. For example, the reality television show *Big Brother* is produced in the Netherlands (where the show originated), as well the UK, the USA, and other countries. In each country, the show uses different characters performing different tasks, but at the same time follows a similar structure—such as incorporating a big-brother voice, eliminating contestants one by one, and positioning the beds in the same room so the contestants sleep next to each other.

Other countries tend to be big importers of media content—that is, they are **exocentric.** These countries tend to be smaller countries with comparatively smaller populations. Some, but certainly not all, are economically disadvantaged and have underdeveloped domestic media industries. Often, these countries are trying to broaden their radio offerings or fill their television schedules, and it is cheaper and more feasible logistically for them to do so with imported media content. Exocentric countries that produce very little domestic content are susceptible to patterns of cultural imperialism discussed in Chapter 2 on Globalization.

Still other countries tend to be both big exporters of media content and big importers of media content—that is, they are **worldcentric.** These countries tend to be smaller but have vibrant domestic media industries, and are in close proximity to multiple countries that have their own vibrant media industries. Some worldcentric countries have populations of people who speak multiple languages, and are therefore more interested in foreign media content. Other worldcentric countries are former imperial countries that have histories of trade with many foreign countries. Still other worldcentric countries bring in foreign media content— particularly television content—because it is cheaper than domestically produced content.

From a rhetorical perspective, the extent to which a country imports media content and exports media content has profound implications for the country's media system and for many of the people who live in the country. Worldcentric and exocentric countries that import a lot of media content tend to have a more open—one could say organic—media system. An organic media system is one that thrives on an exchange of ideas with other media systems. Because people in these kinds of countries have access to a lot of imported media, they often are led to access a wide array of ideas coming from other parts of the world. Consequently, people who live in more worldcentric and exocentric countries are invited to become aware of how their perceptions are influenced by the country in which they live, because those perceptions are juxtaposed with perceptions of other countries as represented in imported media content. In essence, people who live in countries that import a lot of media content have a broader and more tangible conception of the world.

In contrast, ethnocentric countries that import little media content have a more closed—one could say sterile—media system. People who live in ethnocentric countries who do not make a deliberate effort to access foreign media, or who do not travel to other countries, or who do not interact with people from other countries, tend to be exposed on a regular basis to parochial ideas—that is, ideas that circulate mainly within a localized range, ideas that have a narrow range of differences or innovation, and ideas that focus mainly on the given country. Thus, some people who live in ethnocentric countries have a more difficult time conceptualizing the world as a whole or as a tangible entity. Sometimes people in ethnocentric countries tend to conceptualize the world as a two-part entity consisting of the home country versus the rest of the world. This very basic and somewhat primitive outlook in turn can bring on cultural myopia (discussed in Chapter 1), in which a person's conception of the foreground of the home country is clear, whereas the background of the rest of the world is blurry. Viewed through cultural myopia, certain dimensions of the home country ironically remain hidden because the home country takes on a greater proportion in size and importance than it actually has in relation to the size and importance of other countries in the world. Such a conceptual blur shows up when people talk about a foreign country in ways that stereotype an entire region. A hypothetical example is when a person who is talking about Holland is joined by another person who comments falsely that prostitution is legal "over there in Europe" (thereby conceptualizing Holland as representative of all countries in Europe). Use of the phrase *over there* in this kind of context usually indicates that a person conceives of foreign countries as a vast, indefinable perceptual space that can only be conceptualized as "not here." It is as if only the home country has definition and realism, but beyond its borders lies a big perceptual blank.

FRANCE'S MEDIA IMPORTS

Newspaper Imports into France

In almost all parts of France—not just Paris—it is common to see foreign newspapers sold in the *bureau du tabac* with the yellow diamond outside (see Figure 8.1). Most foreign newspapers are from other European countries (mainly border countries), but newspapers from Arab countries and the USA are also sold. Imported newspapers that can be found fairly easily across France include: Germany's *Die Welt* (the *World*), *Frankfurter Rundschau* (*Frankfurter Review*), and *Frankfurter Allgemaine* (*Frankfurter General*); Holland's *Volksrant* (the *Paper of the People*); the UK's *Guardian*, *Telegraph*, *Financial Times*, *Times* (London), *Express*, and *Sun*; the USA's *USA Today*, *Wall Street Journal Europe*, and *International-Herald Tribune* (published by the *New York Times* but distributed outside of the USA in Paris and other European cities); and Spain's *El Pais* (*The Nation*). In terms of foreign newswires that are cited in newspaper reports, is somewhat common to see AP and Reuters (from the UK) attributed.

Radio Imports into France

Along the borders of France, it is easy to hear radio stations from neighboring countries. It is possible to listen to English-speaking radio stations from the UK on the west coastline of France. On French radio, it is very common to hear English-speaking songs, even considering the quota system required by CSA regulations (see Chapter 6). Both USA and UK songs can usually be heard a few times an hour. It is also somewhat common to hear Arab music in the south of France and in Paris on stations formatted with Arabic music. Another kind of radio import that can be heard in France, as well as in other countries around the world, is the USA-based formula for commercial radio with fast-talking deejays cracking jokes, playing songs, and running contests for prizes.

Television Imports into France

In France, it is very common to see television imported from the USA—where the majority of programs come from—as well as the UK and Germany. Usually, but not always, imported television programs aired on French television have the original language edited out, and French voices dubbed in by French actors. This is a combined result of CSA regulations governing French-language quotas (see Chapter 6), as well as the government's commitment to funding the translation of programs, and a general preference by French people not to have to read subtitles while watching television.

Television programs are commonly imported and then aired by French television broadcasters (see Table 9.1). Most imported television programs are run as a syndicated series that ran in the exporting country during the previous season. All the French national television channels—the public channels *France 2, France 3,* and *France 5,* as well as the private channels *TF1,* C*anal+*, and *M6*—broadcast imported programs, mostly during evening hours. Films from the USA are a constant during the evening hours. Other commonly imported USA program genres include cartoons, sitcoms, dramas, films, and *CNN* news. Commonly imported UK program genres include sitcoms, dramas, films, and—on satellite or cable—BBC news. *France 5,* which splits time with *Arte* on a shared television channel, features a lot of documentaries and films imported from Germany.

In France, the typical listing of basic cable/satellite channels includes a lot of channels based in the USA. Examples include *TCM, National Geographic, Disney,* and *CNN.* In addition, the typical channel listing usually includes *Euronews* and *Eurosport* based in Europe, *RTL+* based in Germany, *RTL9* based in Luxembourg, and the French-language (Francophone) *TV5,* which is funded by governments of four countries: France, Belgium, Switzerland, and Canada (separate funding is also provided by the government of the Canadian province Québec).

Content Internal to France That Focuses on the Outside World

Much of the content in French newspapers, radio shows (including radio news), and television programs (including television news) focuses on subjects having to do with the French DOM-TOMS (described in Chapter 4 on Cultural Characteristics). *Le Monde* and *Le Figaro* newspapers cover foreign news extensively. Many magazine programs on television (as discussed in Chapter 9 on Media Content) focus on a range of subjects—including travel, history, animals, economy, politics, and societal facts—in foreign countries.

FRANCE'S MEDIA EXPORTS

Newspaper Exports from France

In French-speaking countries (former colonies and DOM-TOMs), it is fairly easy to find *Le Monde* and *Le Figaro* in major cities. In countries that border France, it is fairly easy to find *Le Monde, Le Figaro,* and *Libération.* Outside of these examples, French newspapers are not widely exported to many other countries. However, all of the national daily newspapers and many of the regional and local newspapers have web sites that can be viewed from anywhere in the world where there is internet access.

Radio Exports from France

Within French-speaking countries, it is somewhat common to hear radio songs from France. Outside of French-speaking countries, it is not common to hear radio songs from France. Radio France International (*RFI*) is exported around the world via the internet and short wave.

Television Exports from France

It is common to see television programs of all genres in French-language countries. Often the exported programs have already run on French television and are one or more years old.

SWEDEN'S MEDIA IMPORTS

Newspaper Imports into Sweden

In most parts of Sweden, it is common to see mainly Swedish newspapers sold in press bureaus. Around the perimeter of Sweden, it is somewhat common in press bureaus to see newspapers from the other Scandinavian countries (Norway, Denmark, Finland), as well as from Germany. In the big cities, it is fairly easy to find newspapers from Europe, the USA, and the Middle East. The most common imported newspapers that can be found in the big cities include: Denmark's *Berlingske Tiderne* (*Berlinkse Times*); Norway's *Afternposten* (*Evening Post*); Finland's *Helsingin Sanomat* (*Helsinki Messages*) and *Hufvudstadsbladet* (*Capital Paper*); Germany's *Die Welt* (the *World*), *Frankfurter Rundschau* (Review), and *Frankfurter Allgemaine*; the UK's *Guardian*, *Telegraph*, *Financial Times*, and *Times* (London); and the USA's *USA Today*, *Wall Street Journal Europe*, and *International-Herald Tribune* (published by the *New York Times* but printed in Stockholm and in other European cities). The most common newswire attributed is the domestic TT (Newspaper's Telegram Bureau), but it is also common to see a joint attribution between TT and either Reuters or AFP.

Radio Imports into Sweden

In the south of Sweden, it is easy to hear radio stations from Denmark. It is easy across Sweden to find Finnish-language programming on *P7*. It is not very easy in Sweden to find English-speaking radio stations, but there is a fair amount of English-language programming on Swedish radio in the form of guests who speak English and Swedish on-air personalities who make intermittent comments in English. In the west of Sweden, it is easy to hear radio stations from Norway. On Swedish radio across the country, it is very common to hear Danish, Norwegian, and English-language songs, mostly from the USA and UK, and also performed by Swedish artists who sing in English. On the east side of Sweden, it is common to hear Finnish-language programs on the public-service Swedish Radio channels (as discussed in Chapter 8). Another kind of radio import that can be heard in Sweden, as well as in other countries around the world, is the USA-based formula for commercial radio with fast-talking deejays cracking jokes, playing songs, and running contests for prizes.

Television Imports into Sweden

In Sweden it is very common to see television imported from the UK and the USA—where the majority of programs come from—as well as Denmark (See Table 9.2). It is somewhat common to see programs from Germany. As described in Chapter 4 on Cultural Characteristics (see Figure 4.2), imported programs aired on Swedish television almost always are in the originating language, with Swedish translation provided in a black bar at the bottom of the television screen. This is possible because of the high proportion of Swedes who speak English.

Television programs are commonly imported and then aired by Swedish television broadcasters. Most programs are a syndicated series that ran in the exporting country during the previous season. All the Swedish national television channels—the public broadcasters *SVT 1* and *SVT 2*, as well as the private broadcaster *TF 1*—air imported television programs, mostly during evening hours. Films from the USA and to a lesser extent the UK are a constant in evening hours. Other common USA programs include cartoons, sitcoms, dramas, soap operas, talk shows, films, and CNN news. Other common UK programs include sitcoms, crime dramas, films, nature documentaries, and—on satellite or cable—BBC news. Programs from Denmark include television movies and dramas.

The typical listing of basic cable/satellite channels includes a balanced mix of domestic channels versus channels based in many other countries. Examples of foreign channels include *TV 2 Norge* (Norway), *NRK 2* and *TV 2 Zulu* (Denmark), *TV Finland* and *Nelonen* (Finland), *Canal+*, *Film1,* and *France 5* (France), *MDR* and *Deutsche Welle* (Germany), *RAI Uno* and *Rai Due* (Italy), *TV Chile* (Chile), *TV Polonia* (Poland), *BBC Food* and *Sky News* (UK), *VH-1* and the *Cartoon Network* (USA), and Francophone *TV5*.

Content Internal to Sweden That Focuses on the Outside World

Content in all Swedish media—newspapers, radio shows (including radio news), and television programs (including television news)—routinely focuses on the outside world. In newspapers, articles often focus on events happening in other countries, regardless of where they are. As described in Chapter 10, news reports on foreign countries frequently center on a theme of humanitarian problems. In the electronic media, discussions on both news programs and nonnews programs often focus on what is happening in other countries. For example, a popular-music station may comment that a song that is about to be played just reached number one in the UK. In addition, many television documentaries focus on cultural forms in other countries. One cultural form that is commonly explored in Swedish documentaries is foreign music. For example, in the summer of 2003, *TV4* broadcast a documentary on the history of blues music in the USA.

SWEDEN'S MEDIA EXPORTS

Newspaper Exports from Sweden

Swedish newspapers are difficult to find outside of fairly limited locations including other Scandinavian countries, Germany, and selected holiday destinations in the Mediterranean such as the Spanish island Majorca and the Spanish Canary Islands. Within these areas, it is possible to find the serious newspapers *Svenska Dagbladet* and *Dagens Nyheter,* as well as the sensational tabloids *Aftonbladet, Expressen,* and the *Kvällposten.* However, all of the national daily newspapers and many regional and local newspapers have web sites that can be viewed from anywhere in the world where there is internet access.

Radio Exports from Sweden

Similarly, Swedish radio is difficult to find outside of the other Scandinavian countries (Norway, Denmark, and Finland). The exception is *P6,* which can be accessed by satellite and the internet throughout the world. Just across the borders in these countries, it is fairly easy to pick up Swedish radio. Also, domestic stations within the other Scandinavian countries regularly broadcast Swedish songs.

Television Exports from Sweden

Outside of the other Scandinavian countries, it is difficult to find Swedish television programs. In the Scandinavian countries, it is common to see Swedish television programs from almost all genres.

THE UK'S MEDIA IMPORTS

Newspaper Imports into the UK

In most parts of the UK, it common to see foreign newspapers sold in newsagents. Most foreign newspapers are from the European countries France and Germany. Some newsagents also carry newspapers from the USA. In London, it is common for newsagents to carry newspapers from Spain, the Middle East, and Asia. The most common imported newspapers that can be found in newsagents include: France's *Le Monde* and *Le Figaro,* Germany's *Frankfurt Allgemaine* and *Die Welt,* and the USA's *USA Today* and *Wall Street Journal Europe* (published by the *New York Times* but printed in Paris and other European cities). The foreign newswires AP (USA) and AFP (France) are also commonly cited.

Radio Imports into the UK

On the southeast coast of the UK, it is somewhat easy to hear radio stations from France. Some UK on-air personalities will very occasionally use short French phrases in their conversations such as *c'est la vie* ("That's life"), but generally foreign languages are not heard on radio in the UK.

Television Imports into the UK

In the UK it is very common to see television imported from the USA (see Figure 9.7). This is mainly because the USA and the UK share the same language, but also because of the shared ancestry and the economic relationships between businesses and governments in both countries, as well as shared military operations. Consequently, television content from the USA can be seen regularly at any hour of the day.

USA television programs are commonly imported and then aired by UK television broadcasters. Most programs are run as a syndicated series that ran in the exporting country during the previous season, or have aired a few weeks earlier. All the UK national television channels air imported television programs. In the mornings, the BBC channels tend to run *PBS* cartoons from the USA; the private commercial channels—*ITV, Channel 4, Five*—run cartoons that were previously run on USA commercial stations, as well as dramas and comedies that were aired from the 1960s through the 1990s. In the evenings, all channels (except the BBC, which tends to air UK programs exclusively) regularly air PSA films, made-for-television movies, dramas, detective shows, and sitcoms. On UK cable and satellite channels, many USA programs of all genres—for example, talk shows like *Oprah*—run on channels also running UK-based content. On cable/satellite channels, there is also a wide variety of news programs from commercial networks in the USA, including CNN, CBS Evening News, Fox News, MSNBC News, NBC's *Meet the Press,* and many others. There is also Al Jazeera from Qatar and Star News (from the parent company, News Corporation) from Asia.

In the UK, the typical listing of basic cable/satellite channels includes many US-based channels, and some European and Arab channels. USA-based channels include *Boomerang, Fox Kids*, *CNBC*, *CNN*, and many others. European channels include: *Deutsche Welle* (Germany), *TVEi* (Spain), and *Euronews* and *Eurosport*. There is also *CCTV* and *PCNE* (China), *Sony TV* and *Star Plus* (Asia), *Abu Dhabi TV* (Abu Dhabi), *Zee Music* (India), *South African TV* (South Africa), and the Francophone *TV5*.

Content Internal to the UK That Focuses on the Outside World

A significant portion of the content in UK media—newspapers, radio shows (including radio news), and television programs (including television news)—focuses on the outside world, with special emphasis given to former colonies, Europe, and especially the USA. In newspapers, articles often focus on events happening in other countries in these regions. In the electronic media, discussions on news programs often focus at great length on other countries, as discussed in Chapter 10 on News Reporting. In addition, nonnews programs often take place in other countries. For example, the popular travel-show genre, which includes many different kinds of television series—usually involving people from the UK visiting other countries to purchase real estate—is set in locations all over France and Spain. In addition, many UK television documentaries focus on life in other countries, present and past. For example, on June 16, 2003, *Channel 4* aired a documentary on the Tubu, an "exclusively female caravan train" that treks from "oasis to oasis" in the Sahara Desert.

THE UK'S MEDIA EXPORTS

Newspaper Exports from the UK

UK newspapers are commonly found in other European countries, in countries that were formerly UK colonies, and in southern Italian, French, and Spanish destinations along the Mediterranean Sea where people from the UK go on holiday. It is fairly easy to find several broadsheets and tabloids from the UK in all these areas. The broadsheets that are commonly found include: the *Guardian*, the *Telegraph*, the *Times*, the *Financial Times*, and to a lesser extent the *Independent*. The tabloids that are commonly found include: the *Daily Mail*, the *Sun*, and the *Mirror*. In addition, all the national daily newspapers and many regional and local newspapers have web sites.

Radio Exports from the UK

Domestic UK radio is difficult to find outside of the UK, except where France borders the English Channel (also known as the French Sleeve). In contrast, the international *BBC World Service* can be accessed by terrestrial or short wave in even remote areas of most regions of the world, including Latin America, Asia, Africa, North America, and the Caribbean. In addition, many UK radio stations—including the BBC channels as well as private stations—can be listened to on the web. Also, many pop songs by UK-based artists can be heard on radio stations in countries across the world.

Television Exports from the UK

UK television programs and films can be found in many parts of the world. In former UK colonies, many genres of UK television shows from both the public television channels and the commercial channels can be seen, including dramas, comedies, documentaries, television films, cinema films, and children's shows. The BBC's exported satellite channel is often included in the listings of other countries cable/satellite offerings, and typically airs "classic" sitcoms, dramas, soap operas—many of which may be up to twenty years old—as well as news. In developing countries, BBC series and programs are commonly aired by commercial television broadcasters. In the USA, BBC series appear frequently on the PBS television network, and sometimes are aired on cable/satellite channels. To a lesser extent, television series from commercial UK television broadcasters can be seen on cable/satellite channels in the USA. Also, UK actors often have parts on USA television shows.

THE USA'S MEDIA IMPORTS

Newspaper Imports into the USA

In most parts of the USA, it is very difficult to find foreign newspapers at convenience stores or even regular newsagents. Canadian and Mexican newspapers can be found at towns only very close to the border of either Canada or México. Some foreign newspapers can be found at sparsely located big-city newsagents specializing in foreign newspapers and magazines, at big-city hotels where foreign visitors frequently stay, or at newsagents in first- and second-generation ethnic communities. These newspapers generally include the UK's *Daily Mail*; Canada's *Globe and Mail*; México's *El Universal*, *Reforma*, and *La Prensa*; and France's *Le Monde* and *Le Figaro*. Some small-town newsagents carry an international edition of the UK's *Financial Times*. In addition, domestic Spanish-language newspapers are usually available in ethnic communities with concentrated populations of Spanish speakers primarily from México, but also from Caribbean islands, Central American countries, and to a lesser extent South American countries. Examples include *El Diario la Prensa* in New York

City; *El Nuevo Herald* from Miami, Florida; and *La Opinion* from Los Angeles, California. However, even considering these examples, the vast majority of the USA has little or no access to foreign newspapers. In terms of newswires, it is rare to see Reuters, the AFP, or other foreign newswires cited in stories in most newspapers in the USA (the *New York Times* tends to be an exception). In big-city newspapers, Reuters and AFP are occasionally attributed for photographs accompanying international stories.

Radio Imports into the USA

There is not much imported radio content in the USA. On the northern border of the USA, Canadian radio content is fairly common to hear, and along the southern border, Mexican radio content is fairly easy to pick up. Along the eastern and southern coast of Florida, Cuban radio can be tuned in. And throughout the USA in communities with high concentrations of Spanish-speaking inhabitants, Latino radio (radio from Spanish-speaking countries in Central America, South America, and islands in the Caribbean) is available. In addition, foreign musicians (mainly from the UK and sometimes from Canada) are commonly heard on the radio. Other radio content that is regularly imported and distributed widely is found in BBC World Service news reports carried on NPR. But even considering the imports mentioned here, the vast majority of content that airs on USA radio is home-produced programming.

Television Imports into the USA

It is quite rare to see terrestrial television imported from other countries in the USA. (see Table 9.3). There are many reasons for this, but two important interlocking ones are that (1) large enough audiences have not yet developed a taste for foreign television content, and (2) the general audience has not been exposed to many foreign television channels to see what kind of content exists on a worldwide or even regional scale. Thus, most media suppliers, including television cable and satellite service providers, supply USA-based content to a USA-based audience.

Still, there are isolated examples of foreign content made available on terrestrial television in the USA. Some classic UK comedies and documentaries from the BBC are aired on PBS stations or on more educationally inclined cable channels such as *The Learning Channel* (*TLC*), or *C-Span*. Similarly, some Canadian news programs and comedies, usually produced by the public-service Canadian Broadcasting Company (CBC), are aired on PBS stations. In addition, there are many actors and some reporters from the UK and Canada who have roles in television content. Plus, some television stations located in Spanish-language communities air Spanish-language news and telenovelas in conjunction with English-language programs. Also, some television stations affiliated with Azteca from México, which are located in cities with large Spanish-speaking communities such as Los Angeles, San Francisco, Reno (Nevada), and Houston (Texas), exclusively carry Spanish-language programs including news, entertainment, sports, and telenovelas.

In the USA typical listings of basic cable/satellite channels include very few foreign channels or even channels with foreign programming. Typically, there are only two bonafide foreign channels that are commonly found in the basic cable/satellite channel listings: *Telemundo,* based in México, and *BBC America,* based in the UK. Additionally there is usually one quasi-foreign channel: Spanish-language *Univision,* based in the USA. Foreign channels can be accessed, but usually only as part of a premium cable or satellite package. These channels tend to be from countries in the Middle East and Asia. European channels in general are not easy to access by cable or satellite. In upgraded cable and satellite packages, it is possible to receive some foreign channels such as the *BBC* and *Sky Sports* (UK), *Deutsche Welle* (Germany), *France 2*, *RAI International* (Italy), *NHK* (Japan), *CBC* (Canada), *Jadeworld* and *CCTV-9* (China), *Star Plus* (Southeast Asia), *Al Jazeera* (Qatar), and *Future TV* (Lebanon).

Content Internal to the USA That Focuses on the Outside World

Hardly any USA content focuses on the outside world. Newspapers tend to be the medium with the most foreign content. Big-city newspapers—especially the prestige press identified in Chapter 9—regularly cover foreign news; small-town newspapers may have a one-page column that lists headlines and one- or two-paragraph stories on a few countries around the world. But on radio and television, content focuses mostly on the USA. Occasionally, a reality program—such as *Survivor*—will take place in a foreign, usually exotic country. Sometimes a film will show scenes in a foreign country. Many cable-television travel programs focus on leisure destinations, many of which are to the south or in the Caribbean. Some radio news (particularly NPR) and some television news cover events in foreign countries if the events have implications for the USA. But in most cases, these are USA shows with USA actors and presenters.

MEDIA EXPORTS FROM THE USA

Newspaper Exports from the USA

A couple of USA newspapers are fairly easy to find in many parts of the world, including European countries, border towns and big cities in Canada, a few border cities in México, and some big cities across Asia and South America. These newspapers are *USA Today* and geographical editions of the *Wall Street Journal.* In addition, the *International Herald-Tribune,* carrying mainly *New York Times* stories, is widely available in Europe.

Radio Exports from the USA

USA radio forms are widely exported across the world. Domestic USA radio is easy to find in México and in Canada along their borders. Commercial USA radio station programming is also commonly heard on radio stations in the Caribbean islands. On a larger scale, US International Broadcasting Services—funded by the USA government—airs radio programs in countries around the world that are adjacent to other countries considered to be oppressive. The overall purpose of the US International Broadcasting Services is to advance USA ideals of democracy and freedom. The services include *Voice of America* (originally aimed at Nazi Germany), Radio Free Europe (originally aimed at Poland, Czechoslovakia, Albania, Hungary, Romania, and Bulgaria), Radio Liberty (originally aimed at the Soviet Union), Radio Marti (aimed at Cuba), and Radio Free Asia (aimed at Burma, Cambodia, China, North Korea, Laos, and Tibet). In addition, another radio export is Armed Forces Radio and Television (AFRTS), which is broadcast to areas surrounding

USA military bases located in other countries. The radio content often consists of news, health programs, country music, and business news. Most of this content is obtained secondhand from other media sources including CNN and ABC. Outside of the regions mentioned, it is not easy to find terrestrial USA radio stations in other countries. However, the USA contemporary commercial-radio model—described earlier as consisting essentially of a narrow program format, fast-talking deejays, heavy advertising, and regular contests and prizes—has caught on in many countries across the world. In addition, USA pop songs are regularly heard on radio in Europe, Africa, South America, and, to a lesser extent, Asia.

Television Exports from the USA

USA television programs can be found in almost all parts of the world. The genres that can be seen regularly are many: films, westerns, sitcoms, dramas, crime mysteries, talk shows, cartoons, sports, music videos, and many more. The series that are exported cover the 1950s all the way through the current season. However, most of these genres are exported as series from a previous television season, or as episodes that have aired in the USA a few weeks earlier. In addition, as mentioned before, AFRTS broadcasts television programs to areas surrounding USA military bases located in other countries. Content typically includes cartoons, news, sports, talk shows, and reality programs usually obtained secondhand from USA commercial television networks. Also, it is important to note the tremendous worldwide reach of USA (primarily Hollywood) films, which are regularly shown in cinemas in big cities and midsize towns across the world. Typically, these films have been released in the USA three months to one year earlier.

MÉXICO'S MEDIA IMPORTS

Newspaper Imports into México

In most parts of México, it is difficult to find any foreign newspapers. A very limited selection of European and USA newspapers generally is found only at towns very close to airports, pricier hotels catering to foreign tourists, and in towns along the border to the USA. The foreign newspapers that may be found include the *Financial Times* and the *Times* from the UK, the *New York Times* from the USA, *Le Figaro* and *Le Monde* from France, and *El Pais* from Spain. In large cities such as México City, Guadalajara, and Monterrey, the English-language newspaper the *Herald*—the international edition of the *Miami Herald* based in the USA—can generally be found at newsstands. However, the vast majority of México has little or no access to foreign newspapers in hard-copy form. In some regional Mexican newspapers such as *El Sol,* comic strips from the USA (for example, Hagar the Horrible and Archie) are translated into Spanish. In terms of newswires, it is about as common to see the state-owned Notimex news agency attributed as it is to see AP, Reuters, and AFP attributed. Sometimes, these foreign newswires are attributed jointly with the Mexican Editorial Organization (OEM), as in the attribution OEM-AP. It is also somewhat common to see USA-based reporters and newspapers credited in stories. These stories typically are written for USA newspapers, and then translated into Spanish for Mexican national daily newspapers.

Radio Imports into México

There is a fair amount of imported radio content in México. On the northern border, radio content from USA stations is easy to pick up. Across the whole of México, the BBC World Service can be heard on some of the IMER (government-funded, public-service stations). But mostly, foreign radio content takes the form of foreign songs performed by musicians from Cuba, Argentina, Spain, the USA, and the UK. In particular, bilingual foreign musicians who have a Latino heritage receive a lot of airplay in México. In addition, sometimes deejays utter whole sentences in English. Along the southern border with Guatemala and Belize it is difficult to find imported radio except on the shortwave band.

Television Imports into México

Television imported into México from other countries is pervasive throughout the broadcast day (see Table 9.4). The vast majority of programming comes from the USA. In fact, at most times during the day, people surfing through terrestrial, cable, and satellite television channels will typically come across a USA-based program every second or third channel. Virtually all program genres from the USA can be seen on Mexican television, but the most prevalent ones include films, television westerns, dramas, detective stories, music videos, sports, news, and comedies. Some programs have Spanish dubbed over, but most of the programs are in English with Spanish subtitles. Many programs appear with USA branding, such as WB, Fox News, and CNN. Some programs are USA-based program formulas reproduced as Spanish language programs, such as CNN en Español and ESPN in Español. Also, television ads that run in the USA can be seen on Mexican television with Spanish dubbed in for portions of the commercial. In addition, hosts of programs will occasionally utter whole sentences in English. Television offerings in México also somewhat regularly include imported programs from Spanish-speaking countries. For example, news reports and football (soccer) matches from other Latin American countries are common, as is coverage of festivals in Spain.

In México, the typical listing of basic cable/satellite channels includes a very large number of foreign channels, mainly from the USA. Many of these channels carry Spanish-language versions of programs developed in the USA. These versions are distributed to all of Latin America: Examples include *TNT, Playboy TV, History Channel,* and *Fox Kids.* In addition, the typical channel listing usually includes *BBC World* from the UK, CCTV from China, *ART* (Arab Radio Television) from Saudi Arabia and Jordan, *RAI International* from Italy, and *TVC Sat* from Spain.

Content Internal to México That Focuses on the Outside World

A lot of Mexican media content focuses on the outside world, with special attention given to the USA. Newspapers, radio news, and television news all regularly contain stories reporting on politics and economics in the USA. Many stories have to do with USA–Mexican immigration policies covering Mexicans who are seeking to move to the USA, Mexicans who are currently working in the USA, and Mexicans illegally living in the USA. The medium with the most USA-oriented content tends to be television. Almost every television newscast contains a story about a political or economic issue involving the USA. Other countries and events commonly covered by Mexican media include: Catholic Church news from Rome, Italy; soccer (football) matches from Latin America and Europe; festivals from Spain; and breaking news from hot spots in the world such as the Israel–Palestine border.

MÉXICO'S MEDIA EXPORTS

Newspaper Exports from México

Mexican newspapers are not regularly found in other countries. Along the border to the USA, occasionally it is possible to find regional newspapers from México. Also, in some big cities in the USA where there are high concentrations of Mexican expatriates—Chicago, Los Angeles, Phoenix—it is possible to find limited copies of *El Universal*, *Reforma*, and *La Jornada*.

Radio Exports from México

Domestic Mexican radio is somewhat common in the USA along the border. However, the radio content that is mostly exported from México is music—mainly pop music and regional-format music (see Chapter 9), which can be heard on radio stations throughout Spanish-speaking countries and in Spanish-speaking communities in the USA.

Television Exports from México

Mexican television is not generally exported around the world. The one exception—and it is a big exception—is the telenovela. As discussed earlier, telenovelas are widely distributed across the world, even to continents and countries such as Russia and Ghana, in which Spanish is not the primary or even a secondary language. In many foreign countries Mexican telenovelas are typically translated into the primary language.

CHINA'S MEDIA IMPORTS

Newspaper Imports into China

In all Chinese cities it is difficult to find foreign newspapers at newsagents, roadside vendors, or convenience stores because of the government's control over foreign-imported information. Major foreign newspapers can be found at foreign food stores close to expatriate communities in eastern seaboard cities and international hotels where tourists and businesspeople frequent, as well as public libraries. International hotels will generally carry *USA Today* or the *Wall Street Journal* from the USA, the *Financial Times* from the UK, *Lianhe Zaobao* (United Morning Paper) from Singapore, *South China Morning Post* from Hong Kong, and *Daily Youmuri* from Japan, as well as international newspapers such as the *International Herald-Tribune* or the *Asian Wall Street Journal*. With the exception of newspapers from Singapore and Japan, most foreign newspapers are in English. However, the majority of the Chinese public has little or no access to foreign newspapers in hard-copy form. In terms of news wires, the state-owned Xinhua News Agency is almost always attributed, though *Cankao Xiaoxi,* which focuses specifically on reporting government policy, sometimes has AP, Reuters, and AFP attributed.

Radio Imports into China

There is little imported radio content in China, with the exception of programs transmitted on China International Radio's (CRI) domestic service. CRI's imported foreign content focuses mostly on English instruction programming and travel features, with some music as well as current-affairs programming. The USA government-funded *Voice of America* (*VOA*) also broadcasts foreign programming into China, to promote USA-style democracy to Chinese listeners. In addition, the *BBC*, *Radio France International*, Australia's *ABC*, and Germany's *Deutsche Welle* can be found on shortwave. Broadcasts from these services are generally in Chinese or English, or a mixture of both. In addition, musicians from the USA can very occasionally be heard on Chinese radio.

Television Imports into China

In China, viewers frequently see television programming from the USA, the UK, and from other Asian countries such as Japan, Korea, and Singapore. Many large international media companies (Viacom, News Corporation, and Time Warner) have established exchange-of-content agreements in which Western programming is supplied to China's television stations while Chinese programming produced by CCTV is broadcast on mainly cable television networks in the USA (such as *Spike TV*).

More foreign programming is found on cable and digital pay television channels than on terrestrial and satellite services. There are two dedicated CCTV channels broadcasting in foreign languages on terrestrial and satellite television: English-speaking *CCTV-9* is geared toward Chinese people in China learning English and seeking to know about foreign countries through the English language, as well as foreigners (expatriates, businesspeople, tourists) learning about China while in China. For example, programming on *CCTV-9* often includes feature stories and documentaries about China's modern development and historical past. Spanish- and French-speaking *CCTV-15* is similarly geared toward European visitors to China. Other foreign satellite channels can be viewed in international hotels or in designated expatriate buildings in major eastern seaboard cities such as Beijing, Shanghai, and Shenzhen via satellite dishes. Most foreign channels are from the USA, such as *CNN*, *HBO*, and *Star Movies*. Many genres of television imports from the USA are popular in China, including television series, movies, animation, and documentaries. Examples include cartoons such as *Wild Thornberrys* and *Catdog* and movies provided by HBO. CCTV has also entered into television program-exchange agreements with suppliers in ASEAN (Association of Southeast Asian Nations) countries. Distribution of the UK's *BBC World Service* was curtailed after News Corporation removed it from satellite-service provider Star TV to appease the Chinese government, which complained about the UK-based broadcaster's negative coverage of China's human-rights record.

Content Internal to China That Focuses on the Outside World

A significant portion of the content in China's media—newspapers, radio shows (including economic and political news and English-language instruction), and television programs—is focused on the outside world, with special emphasis given to the USA and Europe. National newspapers regularly cover international news and events. Smaller-city newspapers typically dedicate a particular section to foreign news. Television and radio typically focus on international economic and political news that involves China's relationship with the USA, Europe, and important regional neighbors such as Japan.

MEDIA EXPORTS FROM CHINA

Newspaper Exports from China

Chinese newspapers are difficult to find in other parts of the world because the language barrier creates limited international appeal. However, the Chinese government is supporting the production of its online, English-language, *China Daily* newspaper service as a way to bring information about China to the rest of the world.

Radio Exports from China

Domestic Chinese radio is easy to find in neighboring countries Korea and Vietnam, as well as special administrative zones in Hong Kong and Macao. China's domestic radio broadcasts are also easily heard across the straits in Taiwan. Internationally, CRI can be heard across the world. The English Service is considered an important division because it is the most effective and convenient way to teach the world about China. The English Service offers a mix of content, with the focus mainly on news but also including a variety of feature programming and music. Music programs such as "Easy FM," "Joy FM," "Hit FM," "X FM," and "Afternoon Concert" are broadcast both internationally and domestically. CRI also operates an online English-language service with programming covering news, travel, and culture. CRI is also used as a strategic propaganda tool to support China's efforts to counter Taiwan's claims for independence.

Television Exports from China

Chinese television programs can be found in Asia, the USA, Europe, Africa, and Australia, either via CCTV channels carried by satellite and cable television service providers, or via USA satellite and cable channels that carry Chinese programming. In the USA, the Echostar satellite network carries Hong Kong's *ATV Home* in Cantonese, and *PHNIX* (Phoenix North America Chinese Channel) in Putonghua, *CCTV-4* in Putonghua, *CCTV-9* in English, and several channels from Taiwan's *ETTV* in Putonghua. Typical television genres that are exported from China include: documentaries, Chinese opera, animation, news, films, and music videos. Chinese documentaries are especially competitive in international markets that reflect Chinese antiques and natural landscape. Animation is also another popular export genre. For example, China's television animation *Legend of Spirits* has been exported regionally to Japan, Taiwan, and Korea. MandoPop and CantoPop video music is also popular in Korea and Japan. CCTV also exports its *CCTV-4* news program—which is rebroadcast in a half-hour format—mostly to satellite and cable television services in other countries. In addition, viewers can see a live feed of *CCTV-4* news via the CCTV web site.

GHANA'S MEDIA IMPORTS

Newspaper Imports into Ghana

In all parts of Ghana, it is difficult to find any foreign newspapers. Indeed, in many parts of Ghana it is difficult to find domestic newspapers. Even along the borders it is difficult to find foreign newspapers. Occasionally, foreign newspapers can be found at newsstands or with roving street vendors along the borders of the French-speaking countries Côte D'Ivoire (the Ivory Coast), Burkina Faso, and Togo, because people living near the borders of Ghana and its neighboring countries tend to speak both French and English. Also, some newspapers from Nigeria (the closest English-speaking country) can be found in the capital city of Accra or the big city of Kumasi. But foreign newspaper consumption is very low, primarily because of the lack of roads suitable for heavy vehicle traffic, plus the relatively small population of tourists visiting Ghana. In terms of newswires, it is most common to see the GNA (the state-owned Ghana News Agency) attributed, but occasionally Reuters or Xinhua (from China) is attributed.

Radio Imports into Ghana

There is a lot of radio content imported into Ghana. Three stations inside Ghana in the capital of Accra have European-based ownership. Two of the stations—*BBC Radio* from the UK and *Radio France International* from France—are public-service stations funded by foreign governments. The third station is the commercial broadcaster *Sky Broadcasting* from the UK. In addition, it is common to hear radio stations from the three neighboring African countries along the borders. Also, there are many stations from all over the world coming into Ghana by shortwave, a commonly used method of accessing radio in Ghana. Plus, it is very common to hear music from other African nations (often Nigeria and South Africa), European countries (usually the UK), the USA, and the Caribbean (especially reggae music) on Ghanaian radio stations. And BBC World Service radio programs (mainly news and discussion programs) are often carried by Ghanaian commercial radio stations during portions of the broadcast day.

Television Imports into Ghana

It is very common in Ghana to see television imported from other countries (see Table 9.6). Often there is as much or more foreign-produced content on Ghanaian television than content produced in Ghana. The most common imports include cartoons, soap operas, dramas, and films from the USA; telenovelas from México; news from Germany's *Deutsche Welle* and from the UK's *BBC*; and films and music videos from Nigeria. Nigerian films comprise approximately 75 percent of content from other African countries. For most Ghanaian television stations, importing television content—especially heavily produced programs such as dramas and comedies—is much more cost-effective than creating the television content in Ghana with the available financial, technical, and human resources.

In Ghana, the typical listing of basic cable/satellite channels includes mostly foreign channels from a very broad range of countries (see Table 8.22). Because satellite and cable penetration are so low in Ghana, most people do not have access to these types of channels. However, the channels that are available represent channels from many countries across a broad selection of the world, though most are from the USA. Examples include *ESPN*,

National Geographic, and *Hallmark* (USA); *SABC* (South Africa); *Supersport* (Europe); *BBC Food* (UK); *Canal+* (France); *CCTV* (China); and *Rheema TV* (New Zealand). In addition to these channels, there are several news channels from other countries, including *CNN*, *CNBC*, and *Bloomberg* (USA); *BBC World* and *Sky News* (UK); *Deutsche Welle* (Germany); *CCTV* (China); and *SABC* (South Africa).

Content Internal to Ghana that Focuses on the Outside World

A significant portion of Ghanaian media content focuses on a broad spread of countries and regions of the outside world, including: Europe, the USA, the Caribbean, China, and other African countries. The focus on the outside world is provided both by content carried by Ghanaian media and by foreign radio stations located in Ghana. In general, television provides the most foreign content. But newspapers also devote a significant amount of their coverage to events in foreign countries.

GHANA'S MEDIA EXPORTS

Newspaper Exports from Ghana

Ghanaian newspapers are very difficult to find outside of Ghana. The *Ghanaian Times* and the *Daily Graphic* can be found in border towns of Togo and the Ivory Coast; a limited number of day-old copies of these newspapers can be found in Ghanaian communities in New York City and London. In 2004, the only newspaper posting a web site with news articles was the *Daily Graphic*.

Radio Exports from Ghana

Ghanaian radio generally does not get exported very far. Some domestic Ghanaian radio— Ghana Radio's *FM Radio*, as well as some commercial stations—spills over the borders into Togo, the Ivory Coast, and Burkina Faso. In addition, Ghana Radio's *Radio 1* and *Radio 2* can be heard on shortwave throughout West African countries. In addition, Ghanaian musicians and songs by Ghanaian groups can be heard on other radio stations in West Africa performing "African" music, which generally consists of multiple harmonies accompanying a variety of percussion instruments.

Television Exports from Ghana

Ghanaian television programs or television channels are rarely exported outside of Ghana. Some Ghanaian documentaries and talk shows can be seen on Nigerian television.

LEBANON'S MEDIA IMPORTS

Newspaper Imports into Lebanon

Foreign newspapers are widely available in bookshops, supermarkets, and at newsstands and kiosks. The most widely available foreign newspapers are Arabic newspapers, such as

Saudi Arabia's *al-Hayat* and *ash-Shark al-Awsat* (both of which are printed in Lebanon as special editions), as well as Egypt's *al-Ahram*. Also widely available are the foreign-language newspapers that are produced for Lebanese readers, including the English-language *Daily Star* and the French-language *l'Orient le Jour*. Specifically at newsstands, it is common to see the UK's *Guardian, Telegraph, Financial Times, Express,* and *Sun;* the USA's *USA Today* and *Wall Street Journal Europe;* France's *Le Monde* and *Le Figaro;* and a Middle East version of the *International Herald Tribune*. Almost all major European newspapers can be found in the leading bookstores of the capital, Beirut. In terms of newswires, it is very common to see AFP attributed and somewhat common to see AP, Reuters, and MENA (from Egypt) attributed.

Radio Imports into Lebanon

Because Lebanon is a small country, it is easy to receive radio signals from stations of neighboring countries—mainly Syria, Jordan, the occupied Palestinian territories, and Israel. Regional radio stations with powerful transmitters in Egypt, Saudi Arabia, and Iran are also received in Lebanon. Additionally, Lebanon readily receives radio broadcasting from Western countries, including the UK's BBC Arabic Service, France's *Radio Monte Carlo,* and the USA's *Radio Sawa* (one of the US International Broadcasting Services). On Lebanese radio, it is very common to hear English-language songs mainly from the UK and the USA, and French-language songs from France—at all times of the day. It is also common to hear Armenian music on radio stations across Lebanon. On commercial radio, it is common to hear the USA-based formula with fast-talking hosts cracking jokes, playing songs, and running contests for prizes.

Television Imports into Lebanon

Television programs are commonly imported and then aired by Lebanese television broadcasters. As indicated in Table 9.7, television programs are imported from other Arab countries, as well as the USA, France, and to lesser extent from the UK, México, Argentina, and Germany. Usually, foreign programs are aired on Lebanese television in the originating language with Arabic subtitles. An exception is Mexican and Argentinian telenovelas; Arabic voices are dubbed in by Lebanese actors.

Most imported television programs on Lebanese television are broadcast as a syndicated series that ran in the exporting country during the previous season. All the Lebanese television channels air imported programs at all hours of the day. Films from Egypt, the USA, and France are a constant during the late evening hours. Other commonly imported Egyptian, USA, and French program genres include sitcoms, dramas, and films. USA cartoons are also a popular feature on the morning programs of Lebanese television stations.

In Lebanon, the typical listing of basic cable/satellite channels includes a lot of channels based in the USA, Europe (particularly France and the UK), and almost all Arab satellite stations. Examples include the UK's *BBC*; multiple-country Francophone *TV5;* the USA's *CNN, MSNBC, National Geographic, Disney,* and *MTV;* Germany's *RTL;* and the pan-European *Euronews*.

Content Internal to Lebanon That Focuses on the Outside World

Much of the content in Lebanese newspapers, radio shows (especially radio news), and television programs (especially television news) focuses on subjects having to do with relations between Lebanon and the Arab world, particularly in regions of armed conflict such as Iraq and the Palestinian Territories. For example, on January 5, 2005, the front page of *as-Safir* had four news reports. Three of the reports covered news in the Arab world: an AP/AFP/Reuters story, "Abu Mazen Condemns the 'Zionist Enemy': A Massacre of Children in Ghaza"; a Reuters/AFP/AP story, "The Assassination of the Governor of Baghdad and the Death of 6 Americans: The Sunnis of Iraq Warn Against 'Splitting the People of the Same Country'"; and an *as-Safir*/Reuters/MENA/AP/AFP story, "Ardoghan: Turkey will fill the Vacuum in the Region; Ghul Urges Israel to Accept Syria's Offer." Much of the Arab-oriented coverage also focuses on Syria.

LEBANON'S MEDIA EXPORTS

Newspaper Exports from Lebanon

All over the Arab countries, particularly the countries of the Arab Gulf (Kuwait, United Arab Emirates [UAE], Saudi Arabia, Qatar, Oman, Bahrain, and Yemen) where there are sizable Lebanese communities, it is fairly easy to find most Lebanese newspapers including *an-Nahar, as-Safir, al-Anwar,* and the *Daily Star.* Lebanese newspapers are also widely circulated in Syria and Jordan. Usually at newsstands in major European and African cities, it is fairly easy to find the Lebanese newspapers *an-Nahar* and *as-Safir.* In addition, almost all of the Lebanese daily newspapers have web sites that can be viewed from anywhere in the world where there is internet access.

Radio Exports from Lebanon

Lebanese radio can be readily received in Syria, Israel, the Palestinian territories, and Jordan because all of these countries are geographically small. In addition, Lebanese expatriates all over the world can receive the official government radio station via shortwave. Outside of these situations, Lebanese radio is not generally exported.

Television Exports from Lebanon

It is common to see Lebanese television programs of all genres in countries of the Arab East (Bilad ash-Sham, Egypt, and Sudan) and in the Arab Gulf countries (Bahrain, Kuwait, Oman, Qatar, Saudi Arabia, UAE, and Yemen). The most popular Lebanese television genres are entertainment programs, including soap operas. The Lebanese comedy program *My Wife and I* had the highest viewership in Saudi Arabia during the 2004 spring season. In addition, it is common to see Lebanese television personalities as news presenters, producers, and managers in the Arab Gulf countries.

COMPARATIVE SUMMARY

This chapter compared media imports and exports across the eight countries. Media imports and exports are like the seeds of a tree because they carry content to places far away from the originating media system. Some seeds take root in other countries, while others perish. Countries are exocentric if they regularly import a lot of foreign media content. Countries are ethnocentric if they do not import very much foreign media content. Countries are worldcentric if they regularly import media from other countries as well as export media content to other countries.

Worldcentric countries in terms of newspaper imports and exports include France and the UK. In both countries, it is fairly easy to find foreign newspapers from a variety of countries. In addition, in many countries around the world it is fairly easy to find major UK and French newspapers. Ethnocentric countries include the USA, México, China, Ghana, and, to some extent, Sweden. Though newspapers from other Scandinavian countries can be found fairly easily in Sweden, newspapers from other regions of the world can be found, but not very easily, and not on a widespread basis. Foreign newspapers in the USA, México, and Ghana are very difficult to find in large part because of a perceived lack of demand by consumers. In México and particularly in Ghana, there are additional difficulties in transporting newspapers on available roads. In China, the government restricts the availability of foreign newspapers because of sensitivities about political news. Lebanon is the only exocentric country out of the eight because foreign newspapers are fairly easy to find, while Lebanese newspapers are difficult to find outside of the Arab world.

There are no worldcentric countries among the eight countries in terms of radio imports and exports. But several countries—France, Sweden, México, China, Ghana, and Lebanon—regularly air foreign music on domestic radio stations. The music is primarily English-language contemporary music from the USA, and to a lesser extent from the UK. Additionally, in Lebanon, French contemporary music and other genres of French music are aired. Sweden also tends to air programming from neighboring Scandinavian countries and sometimes from continental European countries (Germany, France) as well. The UK and the USA are mainly ethnocentric countries in terms of radio imports and exports. Though radio stations in the UK frequently air both contemporary pop songs and more classic pop songs from the USA, it is not common to hear radio programming from other countries, except along the southern coastline. Radio stations in the USA sometimes air primarily rock-oriented or pop-oriented music from the UK, or music with UK musicians. And Spanish-language music can be heard on radio in some Spanish-speaking communities in the USA. But the vast majority of programming on radio in the USA—especially considering how many radio stations there are—is predominantly from the USA.

Worldcentric countries in terms of television imports and exports include France and the UK, though the UK is more worldcentric than France. The UK imports a lot of television programming and television channels from countries all over the world, and also exports programs and channels to other countries all over the world. France imports television programs and television channels from countries all over the world, and exports programs primarily to countries where French is widely spoken. Exocentric countries include Sweden, México, China, Ghana, and Lebanon. Though México exports a lot of telenovelas around the world, other Mexican television programming is not commonly and widely exported. Ghana and

TABLE 11.1   Table Summarizing Media Imports/Exports across Eight Countries

	NEWSPAPERS	RADIO	TELEVISION	INTERNET
France	Worldcentric	Exocentric	Worldcentric	Worldcentric
Sweden	Ethnocentric	Exocentric	Exocentric	Worldcentric
The UK	Worldcentric	Exocentric	Worldcentric	Worldcentric
The USA	Ethnocentric	Ethnocentric	Ethnocentric	Worldcentric
México	Ethnocentric	Exocentric	Exocentric	Worldcentric
China	Ethnocentric	Exocentric	Ethnocentric	Ethnocentric
Ghana	Ethnocentric	Exocentric	Exocentric	Worldcentric
Lebanon	Exocentric	Exocentric	Exocentric	Ethnocentric

Tally:

> Worldcentric: France 3, UK 3, Sweden 1, USA 1, México 1, Ghana 1, China 0, Lebanon 0
> Exocentric: Lebanon 3, Sweden 2, México 2, Ghana 2, France 1, UK 1, China 1, USA 0
> Ethnocentric: USA 3, China 3, Sweden 1, México 1, Ghana 1, Lebanon 1, UK 0, France 0

Source: Robert McKenzie.

Lebanon are the most exocentric countries, as much of the programming aired by television stations at almost all hours of the day is filled with imports from a variety of other countries. Ethnocentric countries include the USA and China. Television broadcasters in these countries do not regularly air foreign programs, and cable and satellite television providers do not regularly include foreign-based programming in the basic subscription packages. However, as a footnote, television networks in the USA regularly purchase copyright licenses to reproduce the basic formula of a program that has aired in another country (usually the UK), but use American actors and adjust the scripts and sets to meet perceived tastes of a USA audience.

Worldcentric countries in terms of the internet include France, Sweden, the UK, México, and Ghana. These countries generally allow for any internet content to be accessed privately or in public. Ethnocentric countries include China and, to a lesser extent, Lebanon. Though it is possible in both of these countries to access any internet content originating from any other countries, there are restrictions in internet cafés that limit the ability to access foreign content. In both China and Lebanon, government is strongly involved in providing internet service, and in preventing sexually explicit content from being accessed in internet cafés. Such content mostly originates from Western countries, so the restrictions effectively curtail imported internet content. Additionally, in China, the government is involved in restricting internet content that contains foreign news.

Table 11.1 summarizes media imports and exports for each country using the descriptive terms of ethnocentrism, exocentrism, and worldcentrism, when applied to newspapers, radio, television, and the internet. To put it all into a snapshot, out of the eight countries compared in this book, France and the UK are the most worldcentric in terms of media imports and exports; Sweden, México, Ghana, and Lebanon are the most exocentric—that is, they import a lot of media content; and USA and China are the most ethnocentric—that is, they import the least media content.

CHAPTER 12

MEDIA AUDIENCES

PRIMER QUESTIONS

1. What are your newspaper reading habits? Which newspapers do you usually read? At what time(s) of the day do you usually read newspapers? Where do you usually read newspapers? How much time do you usually spend reading newspapers on an average day?

2. What are your radio listening habits? Which radio stations or formats do you usually listen to? At what time(s) of the day do you usually listen to radio? How much time do you spend listening to radio on an average day?

3. What are your television viewing habits? Which television channels or television shows do you usually watch? At what time(s) of the day do you usually watch television? How much time do you usually spend watching television on an average day?

4. What are your internet habits? Which web sites do you usually visit? At what time(s) of the day do you usually access the internet? How much time do you usually spend on the internet on an average day?

5. Which medium do you interact with the most during an average day—newspapers, radio, television, or the internet?

Every time you read a newspaper, listen to a radio program, watch a television show, or surf the internet, you are joining together with tens, hundreds, thousands, perhaps even millions of people into an "audience" for the given media content. Though your individual habits of media use are unique to your own particular lifestyle and interests, researchers compile certain aspects of the way you and others interact with media—such as the average of how many hours of television you watch each day—into giant databases describing media audiences. Therefore, a **media audience** is actually an artificial construct that describes only the common denominators of individuals interacting with selected media.

In Chapter 3, a media audience was likened to the people who pass by a tree. Similarly, an audience of people living in a particular country represents passersby for a media system. A person who passes by a tree will be able to reach some of its leaves easily but will have to exert extra effort to reach other leaves. A person's access to, and indeed awareness of, all the tree's leaves depends on the directions in which the tree's feeder branches carry the leaves, and on the parts of the tree with which the person comes into contact. Similarly, media audiences can reach some but not all of the media content available in a media system, depending on where the content is carried, and where the audience comes into contact with the media system during daily routines. Content that is distributed through points of contact within an audience member's daily routines is easily reachable—for example, a newsagent that the audience member passes by on the way to work, a radio receiver in an audience member's car, a television set in an audience member's kitchen, or a web site saved as a bookmark on an audience member's computer at home. In contrast, content that is delivered through available media outlets but is censored or is too expensive or is offered at an inconvenient time, is unreachable even though an audience member may know it exists. And content that exists but is not delivered by any of the media outlets within an audience member's daily routines is not only unreachable but also may be unknown.

A RHETORICAL PERSPECTIVE
ON MEDIA AUDIENCES

As Roger D. Wimmer and Joseph R. Dominick explain in *Mass Media Research,* a number of private and public organizations with vested interests compile databases on media audiences. In countries with a prevailing libertarian philosophy for media systems, commercial firms usually compile most of the databases on media audiences. These firms sell the data to media organizations and advertisers, and release a small amount of data at no charge to the government and the public. In countries with a prevailing social responsibility philosophy for media systems, government-related agencies and commercial firms usually compile databases on media audiences. The government-sponsored data is often made available to the public for free, and is used by the government to study public behaviors and attitudes, to monitor and set public policy, to formulate strategies for distributing media content through public-service media, and to assess whether content is meeting educational or cultural goals. Also media organizations themselves compile databases about their own audiences, which are used in conjunction with databases purchased from commercial audience research firms, to formulate strategies for distributing media content—such as the outlet to be used for distribution (e.g., a cable channel versus a broadcast channel), the time slot in which to schedule the content, and what prices to charge for advertisements.

The majority of audience data that is complied is **quantitative**—that is, numerical information measuring people's habits related to media use. Usually, these numbers revolve around percentages of men versus women, as well as percentages of age brackets that have accessed particular media content. However, as Thomas Lindlof explains in *Natural Audiences* (1987), quantitative approaches to studying media audiences are often devoid of "situational contexts" that help to explain how media are encountered. Situational contexts are better characterized by **qualitative** data—that is, descriptive information about an audience's surroundings and culture that influence their interactions with media content, as well as how they think and feel as a result of the interactions.

In this chapter, a rhetorical perspective is used to combine both quantitative and qualitative information for comparing situations of media audiences across the eight countries. Combining both quantitative and qualitative information renders more interesting and more complete comparisons of media audiences across different countries, because—as described in Chapters 1 and 3—a rhetorical perspective constructs reasonable interpretations of how people are invited to feel, think, and behave in relation to the media that are available and the culture of the country in which they live. The rhetorical perspective in this chapter draws on the discussions from previous chapters to help create situational contexts providing reasonable explanations for the interactions of audiences with available media in each country.

SOURCE CITATIONS FOR STATISTICAL DATA

Sources of statistical information in this chapter are cited here to avoid cluttering the subsequent comparisons of information. For information on newspaper audiences, the primary source was *World Press Trends* (2003, 2002). For information on radio and television audiences, the primary sources included government-related regulators and public-service broadcasters listed in the preface of this book. For information on internet audiences, the primary sources included the following: InternetWorldStats (www.internetworldstats.com), Nielsen NetRatings (www.nielsen-netratings.com), Nordicom (www.nordicom.gu.se/mediastatistics_index.html), the European Interactive Advertising Association's (EIAA) *2003 Media Consumption Study* (www.eiaa.net/), Arbitron (www. arbitron.com), the Pew Internet and American Life Project (www.pewinternet.org), China Internet Network Information Center (CNNIC) (www.cnnic.net.cn/en/index), the U.S. Embassy in México, BuddeComm (www.budde.com.au), and "Global Diffusion of the Internet IV: The Internet in Ghana" (2004), by William Foster, Seymour Goodman, Eric Osiakwan, and Adam Bernstein. For information on newspaper, radio, and television specifically audiences in Ghana, a primary source was a study by Jonathan Temin and Daniel A. Smith published in the journal *African Affairs*, titled "Media Matters: Evaluating the Role of the Media in Ghana's 2000 Elections" (2002). For information on television and internet audiences in Lebanon, the primary sources were the Lebanese research group Information International and Internet Traders International (www.lebindex.com/index.html), respectively.

INTERNET AUDIENCES

Throughout this book, the internet has been identified as a medium that has shaken up previous paradigms of media distribution. The internet is not restricted by country borders, and, indeed, is hardly restricted by any kind of geographic limitations. Nor is the internet widely restricted by government regulation. Rather, the internet is mostly restricted by how audiences use it.

One dimension of worldwide internet use involves the most frequently used languages. As Table 12.1 shows, English was by far the most frequently used language on the internet in 2004, at 35.9 percent of total use. The next most frequently used language was Chinese, at 13.2 percent of total use. Spanish is the fifth-most-used language on the internet, at 6.7 percent of total use; and French is sixth at 4.4 percent of total use. Another dimension involves internet use across regions of the world. As Table 12.2 shows, Asia had the most internet users (31.7 percent of the world's internet users) in 2004, followed by Europe at 28.4 percent, followed closely by North America at 27.3 percent. Other regions of the world were far behind these three regions in percentages of users of the internet.

A third dimension involves countries with the greatest internet penetration. As Table 12.3 shows, in 2004 Sweden had the highest internet penetration, at 74.6 percent of the country's population; next were Hong Kong (72.5 percent) and the USA (68.8 percent).

TABLE 12.1   Top 10 Languages Used on the Internet

LANGUAGE	PERCENTAGE OF PEOPLE USING LANGUAGE
1. English	35.9%
2. Chinese	13.2%
3. Japanese	8.3%
4. German	6.8%
5. Spanish	6.7%
6. French	4.4%
7. Korean	3.8%
8. Italian	3.6%
9. Portuguese	2.9%
10. Dutch	1.7%

Source: Internet World Stats (www.internetworldstats.com).

TABLE 12.2   Percentage of Internet Users out of World Users Across Regions and Continents

REGION/CONTINENT	PERCENTAGES
Asia	31.7%
Europe	28.4%
North America	27.3%
Latin America/Caribbean	6.9%
Middle East	2.1%
Oceania/Australia	1.9%
Africa	1.6%

Source: Internet World Stats (www.internetworldstats.com).

TABLE 12.3   Top 10 Countries with Highest Internet Penetration

COUNTRY	PERCENTAGE OF INTERNET PENETRATION
1. Sweden	74.6%
2. Hong Kong	72.5%
3. USA	68.8%
4. Iceland	66.6%
5. Netherlands	66.5%
6. Australia	65.9%
7. Canada	64.2%
8. Switzerland	63.5%
9. Denmark	62.5%
10. South Korea	62.4%

Source: Internet World Stats (www.internetworldstats.com).

TABLE 12.4   Top 10 Countries with Highest Numbers of Internet Users

COUNTRY	NUMBER OF INTERNET USERS
1. USA	201,661,159
2. China	87,000,000
3. Japan	66,763,838
4. Germany	47,182,668
5. UK	34,874,469
6. South Korea	30,670,000
7. Italy	28,610,000
8. France	24,352,522
9. Canada	20,450,000
10. Brazil	19,311,854

Source: Internet World Stats (www.internetworldstats.com).

Aside from Sweden and the USA, none of the other countries discussed in this book were in the top ten in terms of internet penetration.

A fourth dimension involves countries with the largest number of internet users. As Table 12.4 shows, of the top ten countries with the largest number of internet users in 2004, the USA had the most internet users—more than double the users of the next closest country, China. The high use of the internet in the USA is probably a result of a combination of wide accessibility of the internet in the home, a predominance of English-language web sites, and a large population. In terms of other countries compared in this book, the UK had the fifth-largest number of internet users, and France had the eighth-largest number of internet users.

A significant activity on the internet involves searching for pornographic content. As reported by John Arlidge in a March 3, 2002, article on the *Guardian*'s web site, "The Dirty Secret That Drives New Technology: It's Porn," it is estimated there are over 80,000 adult web sites on the internet, and the two most popular word searches on the web are "sex" and "porn." According to *Web Search: Public Searching of the Web* (2004) by Amanda Spink and Bernard J. Jansen, adult web site searches constitute somewhere between 5 and 20 percent of all searches. Historically, pornography has been a central force not only in users searching for specific content, but also in driving major technological developments of the internet—particularly in the downloading of photographs and video. Now we turn to comparing audience uses of the internet as well as other media in the eight countries.

MEDIA AUDIENCES IN FRANCE

Newspaper Readers in France

In earlier chapters, we learned that newspapers are not as widely read in France as they are in the other seven countries, in part because readers in France prefer magazines to newspapers. Another reason is because newspapers—especially national newspapers—are formal, and contain elevated language that is not intended for a general-interest readership. We also learned that the largest circulating newspaper is the regional daily *Ouest France*.

Within this situational context, newspapers in France reach 31.4 percent of the population on a daily basis, and reach more men (33.2 percent) than women (29.8 percent). The age bracket that reads newspapers the most is forty-five to fifty-nine, at 25.3 percent of total readership. The next closest age bracket reading newspapers is sixty-five and older, at 24 percent of readership. In 2002, the average length of time per day that readers spent reading newspapers was thirty-one and a half minutes. Most people who read newspapers scatter their reading times between the hours of 1000 (10:00 AM) and 1700 (5:00 PM).

In France it is somewhat common to observe people reading newspapers in public places. Occasionally, people can be seen reading newspapers on trains, in parks, or at a *bureau du tabac* and at indoor/outdoor brasseries (cafés).

Radio Listeners in France

In France, the average adult listens to private, commercial radio approximately three hours per day, and to public, commercial radio approximately two and a half hours per day. Most radio listening in France is done in vehicles as people commute to and from work. A significant portion of radio listening also occurs in the home, but not so much in places of business. In France, radio listening peaks during two times. By far, most radio listeners—about 60 percent—listen to radio during morning peak time from 0600 (6:00 AM) to 0900 (9:00 AM). Afternoon peak time is from 1700 (5:00 PM) to 2000 (8:00 PM).

In earlier chapters, we learned that there are five national Radio France public-service networks and a multitude of commercial radio stations and networks. Listeners who scan across the FM band will come across private radio broadcasts at about a three to one ratio to Radio France (public-service) broadcasts. Within this situational context, typically about two-thirds of radio listening in France is to private radio, whereas about a third of listening is to public-service radio. Radio listeners in France are constantly exposed to advertising since both the public-service and the private-radio broadcasters carry advertising. In general, younger people tend to listen to private pop stations. The majority of pop songs are French, though USA and UK songs are also frequently heard. In general, older listeners listen to the Radio France network *France Inter,* as well as private stations, while seniors will typically listen to *France Bleu.*

Television Viewers in France

Adults view television an average of three and a half hours per day. Most television viewing in France is during "peak time," which is 0800 (6:00 PM)–2300 (11:00 PM).

As we learned earlier, though satellite and cable penetration in France is fairly low, the typical multichannel listings contain a fairly wide selection of channels from European countries and especially from the USA. We also learned that three of the six terrestrial television channels are public-service channels, while three are private television channels. However, despite the even split, the private broadcaster *TF1* (general interest) is typically viewed by about twice as many people as the second-most-viewed channel, the public broadcaster *France 2.* Regardless of the channel being watched, television viewers in France are exposed to a lot of educational programming (e.g., documentaries, serious programs, quiz shows), entertainment programs (often with an emphasis on culture), and films and comedies from the USA. Television viewers in France are also regularly exposed to advertising as all television channels carry it.

Internet Users in France

In France, about one-third of people online used the internet every day in 2004. The most frequent activity of people using the internet was sending and receiving email. About 55 percent of people online were connected to the internet between two and three hours per day. Most people used the internet between the hours of 1900 (7:00 PM) and 2300 (11:00 PM).

In terms of content, internet users in France accessed three major categories of web sites in 2004. Tables 12.5–12.7 list: the top ten web brands, the top ten online news and information destinations, and the top ten online entertainment destinations.

Table 12.5 shows that most people in France visited web sites of commercial companies. Of these top brands visited, users spent the most time visiting MSN and Wanado (a brand of France Télécom, a company in which the French government owns a majority of shares).

Table 12.6 shows Pages-Jaunes ("Yellow Pages") as the site most visited by users seeking news and information (users spend the third-most amount of time there). This information suggests that there is a large need by internet users in France to locate addresses and phone numbers of other people. The table also shows that users frequently visited news-related channels from portal and search-engine destinations. The table also shows a predominance of newspaper-based web sites being visited by users seeking news and information.

Table 12.7 shows that several visually oriented media sites (television, video, film) were frequently visited by internet users in France when searching for entertainment content. The table also shows that both the private television broadcaster *TF1* and the public-service broadcasting group France Televisions were popular sites.

MEDIA AUDIENCES IN SWEDEN

Newspaper Readers in Sweden

In earlier chapters, we learned that in Sweden most people have access at press bureaus primarily to newspapers from Sweden and from other Scandinavian countries. We also

TABLE 12.5   Top 10 Web Brands Visited by Internet Users in France

BRAND	PENETRATION	AVERAGE TIME PER PERSON (HOURS:MINUTES:SECONDS)
1. Microsoft	62.51%	0:50:54
2. MSN	58.47%	2:27:15
3. Google	57.35%	0:30:17
4. Wanado	54.98%	1:00:11
5. Free	49.66%	0:28:51
6. Yahoo!	34.49%	0:59:43
7. Voila	34.14%	0:18:19
8. Pages-Jaunes	31.8%	0:17:01
9. Lycos Europe	29.92%	0:23:54
10. Tiscali	28.46%	0:18:22

Source: Nielsen/NetRatings (September, 2004).

TABLE 12.6   Top 10 Online News and Information Destinations Visited by Internet Users in France

BRAND	PENETRATION	AVERAGE TIME PER HOUR (HOURS:MINUTES:SECONDS)
1. Pages-Jaunes	31.8%	0:17:01
2. Yahoo! News	6.79%	0:17:24
3. Meteo France	6%	0:05:14
4. Le Journal du Net	5.84%	0:04:09
5. Groupe Express-Expansion	5.41%	0:05:05
6. Nouvelobs.com	5.39%	0:08:07
7. Wanado News	5.26%	0:06:04
8. Le Monde	4.45%	0:22:53
9. Google News	4.26%	0:13:34
10. Wanado Yellow Pages	4.1%	0:00:39

Source: Nielsen/NetRatings (September, 2004).

TABLE 12.7   Top 10 Online Entertainment Destinations Visited by Internet Users in France

BRAND	PENETRATION	AVERAGE TIME PER PERSON (HOURS:MINUTES:SECONDS)
1. WindowsMedia	12.43%	0:05:58
2. TF1	12.06%	0:14:30
3. France Televisions	8.85%	0:08:44
4. Skyrock	8.1%	0:48:02
5. Allocine	7.97%	0:07:47
6. Universal Music	7.88%	0:08:33
7. Jeuxvideo.com	7.15%	0:22:25
8. Francaise des Jeux	6.93%	0:17:08
9. M6	6.83%	0:09:11
10. XPonsor	5.42%	0:01:44

Source: Nielsen/NetRatings (September, 2004).

learned that most Swedes, by far, obtain newspapers through home delivery. We also learned that people in Sweden often read a morning serious newspaper, and then an afternoon sensational tabloid. Within this context, newspapers in Sweden reach 88 percent of the population on a daily basis. Sweden is the only country among the eight countries where newspapers reach an equal proportion of men (88 percent) and women (88 percent). It is somewhat common to see people reading newspapers in public, particularly on trains. But since home deliveries account for 72 percent of sales, presumably most people read newspapers in the home.

Radio Listeners in Sweden

The average Swedish adult listens to radio approximately 2 hours and 36 minutes per day, mostly in vehicles as people commute to and from work. Radio listening peaks during morning and afternoon "drive times." However, a significant portion of radio listening also occurs in the home, especially in the early morning, as people get ready for the day.

In earlier chapters, we learned that there are seven Swedish Radio networks and that commercial radio is local/regional. Consequently, listeners who scan across the FM band will normally come across more public-service (SR) broadcasts than commercial radio broadcasts, at about a two to one ratio. Within this situational context, 50.7 percent of all radio listening is to the public-service stations, while 32.2 percent is to private commercial radio stations; the remaining 17.1 percent is to community stations. Accordingly, radio listeners in Sweden tend to have more limited exposure to advertising compared to other countries. In general, younger people listen to Swedish Radio's *P3* (contemporary music) or to commercial pop stations, during which they are exposed to a fairly equal mix of Scandinavian versus UK-based and USA-based songs. In general, older listeners listen to Swedish Radio's *P4* (local programming, news, activities, and culture).

Television Viewers in Sweden

In Sweden, the average adult views television for 2 hours and 25 minutes per day. Most television viewing in Sweden is during "prime time," which is 1800 (6:00 PM)–2300 (11:00 PM). Approximately 84 percent of the population in Sweden views television during 1900 (7:00 PM)–2200 (10:00 PM). In Sweden, most people watch television in the home. It is not very common to see television sets airing programming in public places.

As we learned earlier, Sweden has one of the widest selections of multichannel television listings from foreign countries, and television programs are often broadcast in foreign languages—most commonly English—while a black bar at the bottom of the television screen translates the programs into Swedish. We also learned that domestic television programming is primarily national in scope, and that of the three terrestrial channels, two are SVT noncommercial channels, and one (*TV4*) is a private commercial channel. This leads to a viewing pattern where 43 percent of audience viewing time is to SVT programs. The remaining percentage of viewing time is divided across the private commercial terrestrial broadcaster and private commercial multichannel broadcasters on cable and satellite. Regardless of the channel being watched, television viewers in Sweden are exposed to a lot of cultural and educational programming (e.g., documentaries, serious programs, quiz shows), entertainment programs (though often with a learning emphasis), and a variety of genres from the USA. Television viewers in Sweden have much less exposure to advertising than in other countries because it is more restricted in broadcast media content.

Internet Users in Sweden

In Sweden, about a third of people online used the internet every day in 2004. The most frequent activities included sending and receiving email, searching the web for information, and "running errands" (banking, paying bills, checking on prices of goods, etc.). On average, adults used the internet for seventy-two minutes per day.

TABLE 12.8   Top 10 Web Brands Visited by Internet Users in Sweden

BRAND	PENETRATION	TIME PER PERSON (HOURS:MINUTES:SECONDS)
1. MSN	61.59%	1:38:59
2. Microsoft	56.08%	1:38:59
3. Google	31.34%	0:27:13
4. FöreningsSparbanken	27.76%	0:14:54
5. Teila	27.68%	0:46:29
6. Aftonbladet	26.12%	0:25:54
7. Eniro	25.29%	0:42:02
8. Blocket	20.71%	0:11:15
9. Passagen	19.77%	1:00:54
10. LunarStorm	16.79%	0:08:32

Source: Nielsen/NetRatings (September, 2004).

In terms of content, internet users in Sweden commonly accessed three categories of web sites in 2004. Tables 12.8–12.10 list the top ten web brands, the top ten online news and information destinations, and the top ten online entertainment destinations.

Table 12.8 shows that most people in Sweden were visiting web sites of commercial companies. Most of these sites provide databases of "serious" news, weather, and sports information. Of these top brands visited, users spent the most time visiting MSN and Microsoft.

Table 12.9 shows that four newspaper brands and one television brand (SVT) were popular with users seeking news and information. The table also shows that internet users in Sweden were spending by far the most time online at the newspaper-based website of *Aftonbladet*. The table does not show that portals and search engines were popular with users seeking news and information.

TABLE 12.9   Top 10 Online News and Information Destinations Visited by Internet Users in Sweden

BRAND	PENETRATION	TIME PER PERSON (HOURS:MINUTES:SECONDS)
1. Afonbladet	26.12%	0:42:02
2. Eniro	25.29%	0:11:15
3. Dagens Nyheter	13.61%	0:17:46
4. Expressen	10.82%	0:21:41
5. Gula Sidorna	7.41%	0:04:22
6. Susning Nu	6.08%	0:02:04
7. Wikipedia	3.7%	0:02:16
8. SVD	2.8%	0:08:23
9. Göteborgs-Posten	2.56%	0:16:58
10. SVT News	2.34%	0:00:40

Source: Nielsen/NetRatings (September, 2004).

TABLE 12.10   Top 10 Online Entertainment Destinations Visited by Internet Users in Sweden

BRAND	PENETRATION	TIME PER PERSON (HOURS:MINUTES:SECONDS)
1. TV4	15.85%	0:19:13
2. Aftonbladet Entertainment	10.01%	0:05:44
3. Sveriges Television	9.97%	0:11:51
4. Windowsmedia	8.97%	0:05:18
5. Svenska Spel	7.94%	0:35:27
6. BiljettDirekt Ticnet	5.8%	0:11:19
7. Sveriges Radio	5.73%	1:29:45
8. Blip.se	5.35%	1:38:33
9. CDON.Com	4.95%	0:12:19
10. Ginza.se	4.53%	0:09:23

Source: Nielsen/NetRatings (September, 2004).

Table 12.10 shows that several traditional mass media organizations—newspaper, television, and radio organizations—are frequently visited by internet users in Sweden when searching for entertainment. As a whole, these top-visited brands indicate that internet users in Sweden visit entertainment web sites that offer information on television programs, celebrities, and music.

MEDIA AUDIENCES IN THE UK

Newspaper Readers in the UK

In earlier chapters, we learned that people in the UK have access to national and local newspapers, as well as USA newspapers, at several newsagents in even the smallest of towns. Part of the explanation for why British people like to read newspapers is their affinity for reading in general, and part of the explanation is their interest in the use of words to dissect and analyze a subject (as discussed in Chapter 4). Consequently, newspaper readership is spread out across almost all times of the day. We also learned that sensationalized tabloids have a high profile within the selection of available newspapers, and that UK tabloids are some of the raciest newspapers in the world. These factors probably contribute to the tabloid the *Sun* being the most read newspaper in the UK—and particularly for men, the "page 3 girl" is a major factor.

Within this context, newspapers in the UK reach about 50 percent of the population on a daily basis. The age bracket that reads newspapers the most is sixty-five and older, which constitutes 19.8 percent of readership. But for all age brackets fifteen years and older, the percentages of people who read a newspaper are within a few points of each other. In other words, no one age group really stands out as reading newspapers more than the other age groups.

In the UK, it is very common to observe people reading newspapers in public places—in pubs, on benches in towns and at beaches and in parks, and especially on commuter trains. It is also very common to see people in the UK carrying around newspapers.

Radio Listeners in the UK

In the UK, the average adult listens to radio approximately three hours per day. Most radio listening in the UK is done in vehicles as people commute to and from work. In the UK, radio listening peaks during morning and afternoon drive times. However, a significant portion of radio listening also occurs at home and in places of business.

In earlier chapters, we learned that there are five national BBC radio networks, several BBC regional networks, three national commercial radio networks, and many local commercial radio stations. Listeners who scan across the FM band will come across about as many BBC radio broadcasts as commercial radio broadcasts. Within this situational context, typically just over half of all radio listening in the UK is to the BBC stations, while less than half of all radio listening is to the commercial stations. Thus, radio listeners in the UK tend to have more limited exposure to advertising compared to other countries. In general, younger people listen to the BBC's *Radio 1* (contemporary music) or to commercial pop stations. The majority of the pop songs are UK- or USA-based. In general, older listeners listen to the BBC's *Radio 3* (classical, jazz, drama, discussion) and *Radio 4* (news, current affairs, history, Parliament, gardening).

Television Viewers in the UK

The UK and Italy have the highest daily averages for television viewing in Europe. In the UK, the average adult views television for almost four hours per day. Most television viewing is during "peak time," which is 1730 (5:30 PM) to 2330 (11:30 PM). Approximately 44 percent of the population views television during peak time. Most people watch television in the home; often, children have a separate television from parents.

As we learned earlier, the UK has the highest satellite television penetration rate among the eight countries, and also has a wide selection of multichannel television listings from foreign countries. We also learned that domestic television programming is primarily national in scope, and that of the five terrestrial channels available, two are BBC noncommercial channels, and three are private commercial channels. This leads to a pattern of viewing where *BBC 1* (general interest) and *ITV* (regional) are virtually tied as the most-viewed television channels. Regardless of the channel being watched, television viewers in the UK tend to be exposed to a lot of educational programming (e.g., documentaries, serious programs, quiz shows), entertainment programs (though often with a learning emphasis), and programs from the USA. Television viewers in the UK are exposed to less advertising than in other countries.

In addition, television viewers in the UK can watch a fair amount of interactive programming. As described in Chapter 8, a wide assortment of teletext pages can be selected using a standard television remote control. In addition, satellite television viewers can press a button on the remote control to bring up interactive programming while watching programming on many of the channels. For example, viewers of *Sky News* or *BBC News 24* can bring up headlines of top stories and then bring up selected videos of individual news reports. Similarly, viewers of *Channel 4* can bring up individual clips and camera shots from the television program *Big Brother.*

Internet Users in the UK

About 40 percent of people online used the internet every day in 2004. The most frequent activity of people online was using the web to find product information. Almost 60 percent

TABLE 12.11   Top 10 Web Brands Visited by Internet Users in the UK

BRAND	PENETRATION	AVERAGE TIME PER PERSON (HOURS:MINUTES:SECONDS)
1. Microsoft	62.24%	0.32.09
2. MSN	61.65%	2:08:01
3. Google	54.2%	0:23:27
4. Yahoo!	40.43%	1:11:33
5. BBC	34.14%	0:38:26
6. eBay	32.94%	2:10:14
7. Wanado	23.62%	0:21:16
8. Amazon	20.67%	0:20:26
9. AOL	20.63%	4:38:46
10. Ask Jeeves	16.73%	0:12:19

Source: Nielsen/NetRatings (September, 2004).

of people online were connected to the internet for an average of two to three hours per day. Most people—about one-fourth—used the internet between the hours of 1900 (7:00 PM) and 2300 (11:00 PM).

In terms of content, internet users in the UK commonly accessed three categories of web sites in 2004. Tables 12.11–12.13 provide the top ten web brands, the top ten online news and information destinations, and the top ten online entertainment destinations.

Table 12.11 shows that most people in the UK were visiting web sites of commercial companies. However, the BBC ranked fifth out of the top web brands visited. Of these, top brands visited, users spent the most time visiting AOL and eBay.

Table 12.12 shows that two BBC channels, news-related channels from portals and search engines, and newspaper sites were popular with users seeking news and information, who spend the most time at BBC News and AOL News and Weather web sites.

Table 12.13 once again shows that the BBC is frequently visited by internet users in the UK, but this time in the context of entertainment searches. As a whole, the top-visited brands indicate that internet users prefer entertainment web sites that offer movies, music, and games.

MEDIA AUDIENCES IN THE USA

Newspaper Readers in the USA

In earlier chapters, we learned that most newspapers in the USA are big-city or local newspapers; that newspapers are usually delivered to the home or purchased in a convenience store; and that foreign newspapers are often very hard or even impossible to find. We also learned that only one national newspaper (*USA Today*) has national content and is available at virtually every newspaper vendor. This situational context plus two other factors lead to *USA Today* having the largest circulation. One factor is that *USA Today* is distributed for free in many hotels. The other factor is that *USA Today* is similar in form to television, which Americans have a great affinity for viewing (see the data on television viewing in the next section), compared to television viewing in most other countries.

TABLE 12.12   **Top 10 Online News and Information Destinations Visited by Users in the UK**

BRAND/CHANNEL	PENETRATION	TIME PER PERSON (HOURS:MINUTES:SECONDS)
1. BBC News	13%	0:25:55
2. BBC Weather	6.68%	0:05:24
3. AOL News and Weather	5.7%	0:27:59
4. YELL.com	5.66%	0:09:41
5. Yahoo! News	5.63%	0:17:42
6. About.com	5.12%	0:02:37
7. News Corporation Newspapers	4.98%	0:19:41
8. Weather Channel	4.95%	0:06:38
9. Guardian Unlimited	4.58%	0:08:03
10. Google News	3.76%	0:01:15

Source: Nielsen/NetRatings (September, 2004).

TABLE 12.13   **Top 10 Online Entertainment Destinations Visited by Users in the UK**

BRAND	PENETRATION	TIME PER PERSON (HOURS:MINUTES:SECONDS)
1. BBC	34.14%	0:38:26
2. Windowsmedia	12.73%	0:04:22
3. Gorilla Nation Media	7.71%	0:05:51
4. AOL Music	6.45%	0:12:57
5. Internet Movie Database	5.56%	0:09:41
6. The National Lottery	5.55%	0:17:57
7. Play.com	5.11%	0:16:37
8. BskyB	5.08%	0:10:03
9. UGO	4.69%	0:06:48
10. LAUNCH	4.36%	0:13:14

Source: Nielsen/NetRatings (September, 2004).

Within this situational context, newspapers in the USA reach 55 percent of the population on a daily basis, and newspapers reach more men (58 percent) than women (53 percent). People tend to read newspapers mainly in the morning before they go to work. The two groups that read newspapers the most are the forty-five to fifty-four age bracket, and the sixty-five and older bracket, each of which constitutes 21 percent of total readership. The age bracket of eighteen to twenty-four constitutes only 9 percent of newspaper readership. In other words, USA newspapers tend to be read more by older adults.

It is somewhat common to see people reading newspapers at breakfast-oriented restaurants, particularly diners, and to see men reading sports sections of newspapers in bars.

Radio Listeners in the USA

The average adult listens to radio approximately 2.85 hours per day. Most radio listening is done in vehicles as people commute to and from work; thus, radio listening peaks during morning and afternoon drive times. However, a significant portion of radio listening also occurs in the home and at work. In 2004, 21 percent of people twelve years and older listened to internet radio during an average month.

In earlier chapters, we learned that most radio stations are private and commercial, though noncommercial NPR radio is regularly found in big cities and in some suburbs and rural areas. Still, listeners who scan across the FM band will come across commercial radio broadcasts most of the time. Usually there will only be one or two frequencies during a scan of the FM band where an NPR broadcaster can be found, and sometimes one or two frequencies on the FM band occupied by a noncommercial university or college broadcaster. Within this situational context, the majority of radio listening in the USA is to commercial stations, though NPR-member stations have significant proportions of upper-income and university-educated listeners. Approximately only one out of nine radio listeners regularly listens to an NPR-member station. Thus, radio listeners generally have very high exposure to advertising. In general, younger people listen to pop (Top 40) radio stations, and in big cities to hip-hop or dance stations. Older listeners tend to listen to news/talk stations or oldies stations. Country-music stations generally have widespread listenership, especially in rural and suburban areas. Radio listeners in the USA hear music that is almost always USA-based.

Television Viewers in the USA

The USA has one of the highest daily averages for television viewing in the world: The average adult views television for four hours, eighteen minutes per day. But that statistic only reveals part of the pervasiveness of television viewing in the USA, because in the average home the television is actually turned on for more than seven hours a day. Most television viewing is during prime time, which is 1900 (7:00 PM) to 2300 (11:00 PM), when approximately 60 to 70 percent of the population is watching. Most people watch television in the home. Usually, several television sets are located in different rooms throughout a home. Often, children have their own televisions. In addition, as indicated in Chapter 8, it is very common to see people watching television in public places such as bars/restaurants, medical offices, universities, and business waiting lounges. Figure 12.1 depicts a typical scene in a bar in the USA, where patrons are surrounded by television sets. The photo captures five of the nine television sets in the bar, each of which shows a different television program.

As we surmised in earlier chapters, foreign content is hard to find on television in the USA. We also learned that commercials permeate most television programming. In prime time especially, commercials routinely add up to twelve minutes per half hour, which typically results in less than eighteen minutes per half hour for regular programming once the minutage for promotions is also subtracted. And many infomercials seen mainly in the morning are essentially thirty minutes of straight advertising. This situational context leads television viewers to be exposed to clipped American programs containing multiple and prolonged advertising breaks. Thus, television viewers who surf up and down television channels will consistently come across ads. During certain segments of a half-hour cycle, viewers will almost exclusively come across ads, regardless of the television channel.

FIGURE 12.1   *Multiple Television Sets in a Bar in the USA*
Source: Robert McKenzie.

The omnipresence of advertising also affects the regular television content that viewers see. Because advertising as a sole method of financing discourages programs that do not appeal to the largest possible audience or a niche audience with high disposable income, most television programs—even more serious programs such as news programs or talk programs—are designed to entertain rather than to educate or challenge viewers. Below are just a few examples that help to illustrate how the overwhelming prevalence of advertising affects the content of television in the USA.

- Prime time consists almost entirely of entertaining dramas, comedies, and films, at the expense of educational or cultural programs.
- Documentaries do not occupy a large portion of television listings; of the documentaries that are broadcast, most focus on celebrities rather than on regular people or on educational subjects.
- Characters in some television shows are purposely shown to be carrying shopping bags or drinking sodas with the labels for the brands prominently framed in the camera shots.

To extend the last point, television program content routinely incorporates advertising-based "consumer" values into the plot line. A potent example is the plotline for an episode of the children's cartoon series from Disney called *American Dragon: Jake Long* (a series about a boy who is "entrusted with mystical powers of the American Dragon"). On January 22, 2005, an episode called "Dragon Breath" was aired, in which the plot line revolved around Jake getting bad breath just before he was to go on a date with a girl to the school dance. As Jake passed through school hallways looking to ask girls out on a date, people ran away from him, the female janitor put a bucket over her head, and another girl fell over and hit her head—all because of Jake's stinky breath, which was eventually cured when his dog placed a necklace with a potion in it around Jake's neck.

The subject matter of bad breath is more than just an arbitrary plot line for a television cartoon. Potentially, ideas for plot lines in children's cartoon series can revolve around non-commercial values such as "getting along," "sharing with others," "overcoming a fear of the dark," and other, limitless themes addressing the basic plights of being a child. But bad breath is a likely choice for commercialized television content that constantly airs advertisements for consumer products such as mouthwash, gum, and breath mints. Usually, these advertisements imply that something is wrong with your hygiene—something that can be fixed by a product. By association, the subject matter of bad breath in a children's cartoon is similarly rampant with fears about smelling bad, being made fun of by other children, being rejected by a potential girlfriend (or a boyfriend), and so on. A bad breath plot line in a children's cartoon or in any television series is a good example of a typical consumer-oriented value that is endemic to commercialized television content financed exclusively by advertising revenue.

Internet Users in the USA

In the USA, about 53 percent of people online used the internet every day in 2004. The most frequent activity of people using the internet was communicating with family and friends, looking for maps and directions, and finding product and service information. Most people used the internet between 1600 (4:00 PM) and 2200 (10:00 PM).

In terms of content, internet users commonly accessed three categories of web sites in 2004. Tables 12.14– 12.16 list the top ten web brands, the top ten online news and information destinations, and the top ten online entertainment destinations.

Table 12.14 shows that most internet users visited web sites of commercial companies. Web-site portals and search engines dominate the brands visited—of these, internet users spent the most time visiting AOL and Yahoo!.

Table 12.15 shows that internet companies are the primary source of online news and information for internet users. Only one newspaper-based company—Gannet Newspapers—is

TABLE 12.14   Top 10 Web Brands Visited by Internet Users in the USA

BRAND	PENETRATION	AVERAGE TIME PER PERSON (HOURS:MINUTES:SECONDS)
1. Yahoo!	60.73%	2:47:18
2. MSN	60.66%	1:39:17
3. Microsoft	57.88%	0:39:46
4. AOL	49.24%	6:48:16
5. Google	42.36%	0:29:27
6. eBay	31.06%	1:44:57
7. MapQuest	21.31%	0:11:58
8. Amazon	20.44%	0:19:18
9. Weather Channel	20.35%	0:21:03
10. Real	20.14%	0:37:59

Source: Nielsen/NetRatings (September, 2004).

TABLE 12.15   Top 10 Online News and Information Destinations Visited by Internet Users in the USA

BRAND	PENETRATION	AVERAGE TIME PER PERSON (HOURS:MINUTES:SECONDS)
1. Weather Channel	20.35%	0:21:03
2. CNN	15.97%	0:41:01
3. MSNBC	14.66%	0:20:26
4. Yahoo! News	14.6%	0:34:12
5. About.com	13.34%	0:04:47
6. Yahoo! Get Local	12.91%	0:08:20
7. AOL News & Weather	12.01%	0:47:10
8. WeatherBug	10.15%	1:04:53
9. Infospace Directories and Resources	8.75%	0:10:41
10. Gannett Newspapers	8.07%	0:14:20

Source: Nielsen/NetRatings (September, 2004).

TABLE 12.16   Top 10 Online Entertainment Destinations Visited by Internet Users in the USA

BRAND	PENETRATION	AVERAGE TIME PER PERSON (HOURS:MINUTES:SECONDS)
1. WindowsMedia	16.33%	0:11:08
2. Gorilla Nation Media	10.58%	0:09:14
3. ESPN	9.95%	1:02:14
4. AOL Music	9.93%	0:16:38
5. LAUNCH	8.54%	0:22:13
6. MSN Entertainment	8.09%	0:15:11
7. Yahoo! Sports	7.97%	1:30:02
8. Intermix Media	7.6%	0:22:44
9. NFL Internet Network	7.49%	0:28:45
10. CBS	7.4%	0:12:05

Source: Nielsen/NetRatings (September, 2004).

listed in this table. In addition, cable television companies—*CNN* and *MSNBC*—were popular destinations for internet users. Internet users spent far more time at WeatherBug seeking news and information than at any other online news and information destination.

Table 12.16 shows three sports web sites in the top ten most visited online entertainment sites. In addition, two web destinations geared to business start-ups—Gorilla Nation Media, and Intermix Media—are frequently visited entertainment destinations. As a whole, these top-visited brands indicate that internet users in the USA visited entertainment web sites primarily covering business advice, music, films, and sports.

MEDIA AUDIENCES IN MÉXICO

Newspaper Readers in México

In earlier chapters, we learned that in México there are many newspapers available—nationals, regionals, and locals. We also learned that many newspapers in México are significantly financed by government advertising insertions. This situational context is partly behind why there is a lack of publicly available data on newspaper readership—because newspaper executives are reluctant to have readership figures exposed that may be perceived as too small, relative to the amount of government funding that is received. Another factor contributing to the lack of public available data on newspaper readership is México's status as a developing country. Within this context, specific statistical information is available for México City, but for the entire country of México is largely in the form of rough estimates.

In terms of newspaper audiences, approximately 20 percent of people read a newspaper on a daily basis (in México City, this figure is 32 percent). The average newspaper gets passed around to five readers. In México City, the average person reads a newspaper for twenty minutes per day. In México, peak times and typical situations for reading newspapers are quite loose, largely because the average workday begins at 1000 (10:00 AM) and ends at 1900 (7:00 PM) or 2000 (8:00 PM) for most people. Because there is usually a two-hour lunch beginning at 1400 (2:00 PM), there generally is a more leisurely pace to working on the job, which in turn leads to newspaper reading being scattered throughout the day. Accordingly, it is common for people in México to read newspapers before they go to work, during work, and then to a lesser extent, in the evening after work. It is not common to see people reading newspapers on public transportation—mainly because it is usually very crowded.

Radio Listeners in México

In México City, the average adult listens to radio for approximately 3 hours, 25 minutes per day. It is estimated that outside of the capital, the average adult listens to radio around two hours per day. Most radio listening in México City is done in vehicles as people commute to and from work or take taxis. In México City, about two-thirds of people listen to radio while they are at work. Across the country, a fair amount of radio listening occurs in public community areas within smaller (often indigenous) communities. In México, radio listening peaks during three loosely defined "drive times" during the morning, midday, and afternoon or evening. But as is apparent from this wording, the concept of drive time is in its infancy, so morning, afternoon, and evening drive times do not have widely accepted standardized time frames.

In earlier chapters, we learned that most radio stations are private, and that almost all stations—including the government-funded IMER stations—run advertisements. Within this situational context, listeners who scan across the FM band will come across commercial radio broadcasts almost all the time. In some but not all markets there will be one or two frequencies during a scan of the FM band on which a community (indigenous), public, or university broadcaster can be found. Thus, radio listeners in México have regular and high exposure to advertising. In general, younger people listen to contemporary music stations, whereas older people listen to talk-oriented and regional music stations. Radio listeners in México hear a lot of music that is USA-based.

Television Viewers in México

The average adult views television two and a half hours per day—much less than radio listening. Most television viewing in México is during prime time, which is 1900 (7:00 PM) to 2300 (11:00 PM). It is roughly estimated that as much as 75 percent of the population in México views television during prime time. Most people watch television in the home, but it is also somewhat common to observe portable black-and-white television sets being watched in public. One setting involves an attendant in a shop or a small streetside stall who is watching television while customers browse. Another setting involves people—often taxi drivers—who have temporarily parked their cars and are waiting for someone. While people are waiting, they watch a portable television in their vehicles. Television viewers in México tend to be exposed to a lot of comedies, cartoons, political news, tele-novelas, and many genres of programming from the USA.

Internet Users in México

About 14 million of people online use the internet every day. About 75 percent of internet users are between the ages of sixteen and twenty-five—most of them students. The most frequent activity of people using the internet is emailing, surfing, downloading music, and searching for information and news. The average internet user spends between one and two hours per session. Most people use the internet between 0800 (8:00 AM) and 2000 (8:00 PM), suggesting—as it does for audience uses of newspapers, radio, and television—that media audiences in México have patterns of media use that do not bunch into peak or prime times, and instead are spread out over the course of the day. In 2004, there were twice as many internet users as personal computers connected to the internet, suggesting that most people are accessing the internet in public places such as schools, work, libraries, and (mainly) internet cafés. In terms of content, the top web sites accessed by internet users in México are (in rank order) Tod.to.com, esmas.com, AOL, and terra.com. This information shows that news, sports, and entertainment web sites are the most visited, and also reveals that once again, AOL is one of the top web sites visited.

MEDIA AUDIENCES IN CHINA

Newspaper Readers in China

Throughout the earlier chapters, we learned that Chinese people are big newspaper readers, and that there are many newspaper choices—both national and locals—available at roadside newsagents. One main reason why Chinese people read newspapers is that newspapers are both convenient to find and relatively inexpensive. Within this situational context, newspapers in China reach 74.3 percent of the population on a daily basis.

Thus, in China it is common to see people reading newspapers in public—waiting for buses, sitting in parks, and especially on trains. It is also common to observe people in more rural areas stopping to read viewing frames (see Chapter 8).

Radio Listeners in China

The average adult listens to national and local radio just over one hour per day. Most radio listening occurs in the home, and in private vehicles and taxis. Within this context, radio in

China reaches 69 percent of the population on a daily basis, with twice as many radio listeners in rural areas than in urban areas. There are three peak times for radio listening: morning 0600 (6:00 AM)–0700 (7:00 AM), midday 1200 (12:00 PM)–1315 (1:15 PM), and evening 1900 (7:00 PM)–2100 (9:00 PM). Because so few people own cars (less than 1 percent of the population), the main peak period for radio listening is from 0600 (6:00 AM) to 0700 (7:00 AM)—before people begin their commute to work by bicycle, bus, subway, or walking.

In Chapter 6, we learned that there are over 1,000 radio stations that come under the control of the government regulator SARFT. Within this situational context, typically more than half the Chinese population listens to China National Radio. Commonly listened to national programs include Xinwen He Baozhi Zhaiyao (Newspaper Briefs), Quanguo Xinwen Lianbo (National News), and Xinwen Zongheng (News Across the World). In general, young listeners listen to local radio stations that feature pop music. Older listeners tend to listen to news and current affairs programming on China National Radio. Radio listeners in China are increasingly exposed to advertising since government-owned stations began running commercials.

Television Viewers in China

In 2002, the average Chinese adult viewed television just over two hours a day. Most television viewing in China occurs during the "golden period," which is 1900 (7:00 PM) to 2100 (9:00 PM). Often, children's viewing of cartoons and quiz shows is given priority in the afternoon. Adult viewing usually begins with news broadcasts at 1830 (6:30 PM) and continues through the golden period.

As we learned earlier, China has a high penetration of terrestrial television, and also a high number of city-run, multichannel television listings. We also learned that domestic television programming is national and city-based in scope, with the government operating fifteen Chinese Central Television (CCTV) national channels, by far the most of the eight countries. However, the city-run television channels tend to be the most widely viewed in China; CCTV channels mostly are viewed by people living in Beijing. In 2004, the most popular channels in each of the three main markets were local—not CCTV—channels. In general, television viewers in China are exposed to an equal balance of educational programming (mainly news, talk shows, and documentaries) and entertainment programs (mainly quiz shows and modern melody dramas). In addition, people in China are increasingly becoming exposed to interactive programming. This is a result of the hundred interactive digital pay television licenses issued in 2004 by the government regulator SARFT (see Chapter 8), which allow users to check stock quotes and access culturally appropriate videos on demand.

Internet Users in China

In China, 64 percent of people who are online use the internet every day. The most frequent activity of people online is to search for information. Users, who are predominantly male (59.3 percent) and aged 18–24 years (36 percent), are connected to the internet for an average of two hours per day. About half of all internet users are online between 2000 (8:00 PM) and 2200 (10:00 PM).

In terms of content, users commonly accessed the internet for different reasons. Tables 12.17–12.19 list the following information about internet use in China: the top ten primary goals for accessing the internet, the top ten services most frequently used on the internet, and the top ten reasons for acquiring information on the internet.

TABLE 12.17   Top 10 Goals for Accessing the Internet in China

GOAL	PERCENTAGE
1. Get information	42.3%
2. Entertainment	34.5%
3. Study	9.1%
4. Making friends	5.5%
5. Get free resources (email, personal homepage, downloadable resources)	2.7%
6. Communication (receive/send emails, short messages, faxes)	1.8%
7. Learning research	1.1%
8. Sentimental needs	0.9%
9. Business activities	0.4%
10. Stock trading	0.3%

Source: China Internet Network Information Center (CNNIC).

TABLE 12.18   Top 10 Services Most Frequently Used on the Internet in China

SERVICES	PERCENTAGE
Email	84.3%
Search engine	64.4%
News	62.1%
Web page information	47.8%
Online chatting	40.2%
Software downloading/uploading	38.2%
Bulletin Board Service/community forum	21.3%
Internet games	15.9%
Online purchasing	7.3%
Online education	5.8%

Source: China Internet Network Information Center (CNNIC).

TABLE 12.19   Top 10 Reasons for Acquiring Information on the Internet in China

REASONS	PERCENTAGE
1. News	67.8%
2. Computer hardware and software	46.2%
3. Entertainment	46.2%
4. Living services	40.6%
5. E-books	27.5%
6. Education	22.9%
7. Science and technology	18.9%
8. Social culture	18.7%
9. Sports	15.1%
10. Job hunting	14.9%

Source: China Internet Network Information Center (CNNIC).

FIGURE 12.2   *A Male Gaming at an Internet Café in China*
Source: Ian Weber.

Table 12.17 shows that people in China primarily access the internet to get information and to be entertained. Users also commonly access the internet to study and to make friends, but are less likely to use it for business or stock trading.

Table 12.18 shows that the internet is the most frequently used service, followed by search engines to find information, and then accessing news and web page information, and finally chatting online with friends. The largest increase occurred in the use of internet gaming services for entertainment, which corresponds with the second-ranked primary goal for accessing the internet.

Table 12.19 shows that news information is the most widely sought information on the internet. Also, accessing information on computer hardware and software as well as entertainment is a top reason why people use the internet. The prominence of entertainment in all three tables supports the rise of internet gaming in China, which was a favorite activity of approximately 10 million users in 2004. Figure 12.2 shows a person gaming at an internet café.

MEDIA AUDIENCES IN GHANA

Newspaper Readers in Ghana

In earlier chapters, we learned that in Ghana, the distribution of newspapers across the country is difficult because of poor road infrastructure and weak audience demand. As a result, many Ghanaians do not live within range of available newspapers (or television broadcasts), or have access only to the state newspaper, the *Daily Graphic* (and GBC television and radio). We also learned that the newspaper industry—especially the private newspaper sector—was largely in an infancy stage after the 2000 elections.

Within this situational context, statistical data on newspaper readership in Ghana is almost nonexistent. Many newspapers have a circulation of only around 3,000 to 5,000 copies. Almost all newspapers are published in English, but there is a 53 percent English illiteracy rate among the population, who therefore are unable to read most Ghanaian newspapers. Accordingly, it is not common to see people reading newspapers in public. However, it is somewhat common to observe Ghanaians reading "community" newspapers in local bars, and hotel employees reading hotel-purchased newspapers at the workplace. It is estimated that the average newspaper is passed around to a dozen or so people. Because many Ghanaians do not have the disposable income to justify newspaper purchases, it is also common to observe Ghanaians reading newspaper pages for free that are displayed on the outside of newsstands.

Radio Listeners in Ghana

In Ghana, there is little statistical information on radio listening. However, it is widely believed that radio is a much more integral medium to the lives of most Ghanaians than newspapers, television, and the internet, mainly because radio reaches people who do not have access to the other media, and because radio is well suited to communication in indigenous languages—especially those that cannot be written. What is known is that a little less than half of Ghanaians listen to radio news on a daily basis, but that about 95 percent of Ghanaian teenagers and adults listen to radio on a daily basis.

In large part because many areas do not have electricity, it is common to see people carrying a portable radio, or listening to one at the workplace or in the home. In addition, Ghanaians often listen to radio in groups at a house or a business of someone who owns a radio receiver.

In earlier chapters, we learned that radio stations in Ghana are extending their reach to rural areas and that shortwave radio plays a significant role in radio listening. We also learned that radio stations in Ghana include not only Ghanaian radio stations playing all kinds of music from all over the world, but also foreign radio stations from France, Germany, and the UK. And we learned that both private and the state-owned GBC radio network carry advertising. Within this situational context, listeners who scan across the FM band typically come across a wide variety of English-language and indigenous-language programming from Ghana and all over the world, and will regularly be exposed to advertising—though advertising minutage is comparatively low. Younger listeners tend to listen to Western pop music (mainly from the USA), whereas adults tend to listen to indigenous music and discussion programs focusing on politics, health, and social/psychological advice.

Television Viewers in Ghana

Statistics on television viewing are also sparse. However, in earlier chapters, we learned that much of the population does not own a television set, and that access to television programming is limited to areas surrounding major cities. Across many parts of the country, GTV is the only channel available, though other channels from Accra are extending their reach. What is known is that about 65 percent of Ghanaians watch television on a daily basis, and that—as mentioned in Chapter 8—television watching often occurs in groups.

Within this context, it is very common for Ghanaian friends and family to watch television at someone's house, and for Ghanaians in cities to watch television at bars.

Television viewers in Ghana tend to be exposed to a lot of discussion programs, music videos, television-church programs, and a range of entertainment programs from the USA, Nigeria, the UK, and Germany. Both the private stations and the state-owned *GTV* network carry advertising. Thus, television viewers are routinely exposed to foreign programs and advertising.

Internet Users in Ghana

There are few statistics available on internet use in Ghana. As we learned in Chapter 8, in 2004, internet penetration of homes was about 0.08 percent. In 2003, there were only about 300,000 internet users in Ghana. However, Ghana has one of the most active and growing populations of internet users in Africa, who gain access primarily in the country's 600 or so internet cafés. Though 90 percent of internet cafés are located in the Greater Accra region, they can also be found in small villages providing access with dial-up connections at very slow speeds. Internet cafés typically have occupancy rates of between 60 and 90 percent. Outside of internet cafés, Ghanaians often gain access to the internet through their friends and family—as is the case for newspapers, radio, and television. Also, about half of all users access the internet at universities.

Within this context, Ghanaians use the internet for several purposes, the most common of which appears to be sending and receiving emails. According to an article by Briony Hale on BBC News Online, "In Search of Profitable Connections," some reasons that Ghanaians send email include: communicating with people by circumventing an expensive and unreliable phone system, trying to find a way out of Ghana, and attempting to make a financial or business connection that will improve quality of life.

MEDIA AUDIENCES IN LEBANON

Newspaper Readers in Lebanon

In earlier chapters, we learned that newspapers are not widely read in Lebanon mainly because they focus on political news and are targeted at the political elite rather than the average citizen. Additionally, Lebanese newspapers are expensive relative to the average person's disposable income. As a result, people often pursue alternative methods to access and read newspapers for free, such as to read a borrowed newspaper. Accordingly, 55 percent of Lebanese newspaper readers purchase their own newspapers, whereas 44 percent borrow newspapers. Another method is to make an agreement with the newspaper delivery person to deliver the paper in the morning and then collect it the next day in return for a weekly or monthly fee.

Within this situational context, about 62 percent of newspaper readers read only one newspaper, 23 percent read two newspapers, 6.5 percent read three newspapers, and 8 percent read four or more newspapers. People in the fifteen to thirty-four age bracket have the highest percentage (64 percent) of newspaper readership. People in the thirty-five to fifty-four age bracket make up 30 percent of the share of newspaper readership. And people fifty-five years and older make up 6 percent of the share of newspaper readers. Overall, newspapers reach more men than women.

It is common to see people reading newspapers in cafés, restaurants, barbershops, and other public places. Most Lebanese people read newspapers at home, usually early in the morning before they leave for work. Many people who do not find time to read a newspaper before leaving for work do so as soon as they reach their workplace.

Radio Listeners in Lebanon

There are no published figures about adults listening to radio for an average amount of hours per day. Some radio stations conduct their own studies, but they keep most of the findings private. However, it is understood that most radio listening is during the morning and afternoon hours. There is no commonly used concept of drive time to describe peak listening. The majority of listeners (71 percent) tune to the radio from their homes, whereas 54 percent listen to radio in vehicles, and 21 percent hear radio in the workplace.

In earlier chapters, we learned that almost all radio stations in Lebanon are private. We also learned that there is a large presence of foreign cultures in Lebanon, and that Lebanese people often embrace the customs and symbols of foreign cultures. Within this situational context, most radio listening is to private radio stations playing Western music. Because all radio stations are commercial except the official station, most listeners are consistently exposed to advertising. In general, younger people listen to private pop stations. In Beirut, music is the top radio-listener preference (82 percent), followed by news (44 percent), religious program (13 percent), political programs (12 percent), and sports programs (8 percent). In Beirut, Arabic music is the favored type of music for 96 percent of listeners. However, 51 percent regularly listen to Western music, mainly because both Arabic and Western music are usually presented within the same program. Those who listen to Western (French, UK, USA) music tend to favor classical (52 percent), pop (21 percent), rock (14 percent), and jazz (10 percent).

Television Viewers in Lebanon

Television stations have wide national reach because television signals can cover the relatively small distances of the country, and because there are so many cable outlets. This leads to a situational context where television is regularly viewed in public places, as well as in the home. Figure 12.3 depicts a streetside vendor and patron watching television at a shop.

Approximately 65 percent of adults view television for two to four hours per day. About 82 percent of the population views television on a daily basis, while 96 percent watch television regularly but not daily. The majority of viewers (71 percent) watch television during evening hours, 12 percent watch during the afternoon, and 8 percent watch during the morning. In Lebanon, the time period during which most people watch television is referred to as prime time, and is from 1900 (7:00 PM) to 2200 (10:00 PM). The viewing habits of females and males are similar except that twice as many females (17 percent) watch television in the afternoon than males (8 percent), while about three times as many males (7 percent) than females (2.5 percent) watch television after 2300 (11:00 PM). Viewers who watch television the most tend to be in the age bracket forty-five years and older. Table 12.20 shows hours of television viewing by different age brackets in Lebanon.

FIGURE 12.3 *Streetside Vendor and Customer Watching Television in Lebanon*

Source: Nabil Dajani.

As we learned earlier, a lot of television programming consists of political news and entertainment programs. Within this situational context, news is the most-viewed genre, followed closely by Arabic soap operas, entertainment programs, and Arabic movies. English-language movies and political programs are viewed by less than 10 percent of the population. In terms of soap operas, Egyptian soaps are the most popular, followed by

TABLE 12.20   Number of Hours of Television Viewing by Age Brackets in Lebanon

	1 HOUR	2 HOURS	3–4 HOURS	6+ HOURS
15–24 years	16.4%	26.4%	20.9%	2.7%
25–34 years	14.7%	29.4%	33.1%	2.5%
35–44 years		26.8%	44.4%	2.8%
45–54 years		17%	46.2%	3.8%
55–64 years		21.4%	17.9%	10.7%
65+ years			33.4%	33.4%

Source: Information International, Lebanon.

1. Ragheb Alama	11. Campus Card
2. House of Music	12. Kryolan
3. Polaris	13. Nassar Office
4. Entertainment TV	14. Yabazaar
5. AUST	15. Dijila Group
6. Lebanese International University	16. AZ TEC
7. Aqua Treat	17. Thrifty Car Rental
8. Hummer	18. Marina Kharma
9. Jeep	19. EuroLibano
10. Concord Travel	

FIGURE 12.4   *Top 20 Web Sites Visited by Users Accessing the Web through Internet Traders International in Lebanon.*

Source: Internet Traders International, Lebanon; www.lebindex.com (2005).

Lebanese soaps, then Syrian soaps. All Lebanese television channels carry advertising; therefore, viewers are regularly exposed to advertisements.

Internet Users in Lebanon

In 2004, little statistical information was available on internet users in Lebanon, primarily because of its early stages of development, and because the small size of country had not yet warranted substantial marketing studies assessing internet use. It is thought that the internet is used mainly by teenagers and adults to chat online, to send and receive email, and to meet new friends (particularly outside of Lebanon). University students regularly access the internet for free news and to search for information related to classes.

In terms of content, Figure 12.4 lists the top twenty web sites visited in 2004 by users accessing the internet specifically through the internet service provider (ISP) Internet Traders International, in Lebanon.

This figure shows that the most frequently visited web site was for a pop-Arab-music singer. The figure also shows that several web sites visited relate to university life, including Lebanese International University, AUST, Campus Card, and Nassar Office, and that most of the frequently visited web sites through this particular ISP are in English.

COMPARATIVE SUMMARY

In this chapter, media audiences for newspapers, radio, television, and the internet were compared across the eight countries. The concept of a media audience is somewhat of an artificial construct that adds up individual patterns of media use into general statements that describe similarities of media use among a large group of people. Though this kind of information can be somewhat instructive in describing how large groups of people interact with different media in different countries, a more balanced perspective is to study how a person interacts with media within a given media system. Such a perspective is a rhetorical one, because it considers how a person is guided by the selection of media regularly surrounding that person, to be exposed only to certain kinds of content.

A media audience was likened to those who pass by a tree. Just as the tree presents leaves for passersby to see—some of which can be reached, whereas others cannot—a media system presents content to an audience. Content can be reached because it automatically comes into contact with the audience, whereas other content remains inaccessible to the audience, when it is too expensive or too hidden amongst all the other choices.

This section summarizes and compares the content with which audiences regularly come into contact, across the eight countries. In France, newspapers do not have the kind of widespread audiences that other media have, or that newspapers have in other countries. As indicated earlier in this book, French people appear to have a preference for magazines over newspapers. Part of the reason for this may be that French national newspapers are very formal and are mainly geared to an intellectual audience. In Sweden, reading newspapers appears to be integral to the daily lives of most people, since almost 90 percent of the adult population—evenly split between men and women—reads newspapers every day. The high readership might be an indication that because Sweden is a small country with a minority language, its people are inclined to read newspapers regularly to learn what is happening across the world, because world events have direct effects on Sweden. Or the high readership might indicate that Swedes simply enjoy newspapers as a form of communication. In the UK, newspapers reach about half the adult population on a daily basis. It is possible that this number represents contradicting audience preferences. On the one hand, newspapers are readily available at newsagents located in even the smallest of towns, and right next to or inside of train stations, where many people pass through on their way to work. Thus, newspapers are constantly within arm's reach in UK life. On the other hand, UK newspaper biases are strong: The tabloids' sensationalism is often sordid, and the broadsheets as well as the tabloids tend to have assertive political orientations. These strong biases may lead many people to avoid buying a newspaper. In the USA, small-town newspapers have wide readership among the general population, and big-city newspapers have wide readership among urban dwellers. This is perhaps because much of the population in the USA is dispersed across spacious suburbs with little access to corner newsagents, so residents often subscribe to a small-town newspaper because it can be delivered to the home every morning. In México, newspaper readership is low, despite a plethora of national, regional, and local newspapers made readily available through newsstands and street vendors. This is likely a function of Mexicans perceiving that their limited disposable income is better spent elsewhere, and perhaps the assumption that most newspaper stories will predictably be about crime and government corruption. In China, newspaper readership is very high, particularly for the tabloids. A major reason is that the government distributes newspapers to places where people travel in their daily routines. Perhaps tabloids have high readership because their entertainment content provides a welcome deviation from official government propaganda that is standard content in the broadsheets. In Ghana, newspaper readership is very low. One reason may be that it is difficult to get newspapers to Ghanaians in regions just outside cities. Another possibility is that virtually no newspapers are in indigenous languages, most of which do not have a written form. And a third reason is that newspapers are expensive to many Ghanaians, given their available disposable income. In Lebanon, newspapers probably have low readership because the content does not address the concerns of average citizens, and because most newspapers present content that largely reflects orientations of a sectarian group or financial backer of the newspaper.

In terms of radio, the following observations were made. Radio listening is relatively widespread in all countries, but is probably the highest in Ghana. The main reason that radio listening is high in Ghana is because of the remoteness of the population and the friendliness of radio to indigenous languages and culture. The main reason that radio listening is high in the Western countries is because of its accessibility in the car. In the European countries, listening to public-service radio is high, for two main reasons. One is because public-service broadcasters have multiple frequencies all across the FM radio band. Another factor is that the public-service broadcasters air contemporary music aimed at young people, in addition to the traditional classical music or news programming aimed at adults. In the case of China, listeners are limited by the available selection to only government-run radio—though commercialization is diversifying the content somewhat. In the case of the USA and Lebanon, listeners are invited to listen mostly to private, commercial radio, which dominates the selections.

Television viewing is roughly around the four-hour mark for all countries, but within this time range, is significantly higher in the USA than in the other countries. One reason for this is the prevalence of televisions in the home, and also in public places where people travel. Another reason is that there are many different channels to watch, whether a person is accessing television by cable, satellite, or terrestrial signal. Also, Americans generally are visual people who have an affinity for information they can see, rather than information they can read or hear. In the European countries, as was the case for radio, viewers are invited by the channel selection equally to watch private television or public television. In the UK and Sweden, this means that viewers are exposed to significantly less television advertising than in the other countries. In the USA, México, and Lebanon, viewers are invited to watch mostly private, commercial television. In China, viewers are invited to watch only government-run television.

Since the statistics on the internet that were presented were not the same for all the countries, it is difficult to standardize the comparisons. However, it can be speculated that for users in all countries, the most visited web sites for all countries revolve around search engines, portals, or email. Individually, the internet probably is more attractive as a tool for purchasing products for users in France, Sweden, the UK, the USA, and to a lesser extent, México, but is more attractive as a link to the outside world for users in China, Ghana, and Lebanon. Across all countries, the internet continues to advance English as an international language.

This now wraps up the discussion of the ninth and final element of a media system to be compared across the eight countries. Next, Chapter 13 concludes this book by proposing some of the larger meanings for the comparisons of media across the eight countries, and by offering speculations about media systems across the world.

CONCLUSION

PRIMER QUESTIONS

1. In general, which of the nine elements of a media system—cultural characteristics, philosophies, regulation, financing, accessibility, content, imports/exports, and audiences—do you think has the greatest overall impact on a media system?

2. What have you learned about the media system of the country in which you are living, compared with media systems of other countries?

3. What, in your view, are some of the most unique attributes of each media system of the eight countries that were compared?

4. What are some of the similarities across the media systems of the eight countries?

5. What are some of the major policy issues that this book has identified, which are put into practice in every country when a media system develops?

SUMMARY OF THE CHAPTERS

Many people may find the world to be too big and too full of diverse populations, languages, and cultures to be conceptualized with much clarity. With some 200 countries inhabited by some 6.5 billion people collectively speaking 7,000 languages, it is a formidable challenge to understand how they all come together into a definable entity we call the world. Part of the difficulty is that the average person really experiences only a very tiny portion of the world. As a result, much of what we learn about the countries of the world comes through interactions with media content. But the content that we read in newspapers, listen to on radio, watch on television, and surf on the internet is hardly a free-flowing bonanza encompassing all there is to read, hear, and watch. Quite the opposite: Media content in any country is uniquely shaped by a multitude of forces, only some of which are obvious. Furthermore, the ability to understand the world from multiple perspectives is critically connected to the variety of the media outlets and the resulting content that is delivered within the geographic area in which a person lives.

One of the strongest forces affecting media content is the climate of globalization enveloping the world. Globalization is primarily a business-initiated activity that is connecting companies, governments, and people across the world's countries—even countries that previously have had minimal contact with each other. The chief players in this business-initiated activity are the global media conglomerates, which increasingly are distributing products—only some of which are media products—outside of their domestic markets to foreign markets across the far reaches of the world. Some of the global media conglomerates—such as News Corporation, Viacom, NBC Universal, Bertelsmann, Disney, Time-Warner, and Sony—are so mammoth that their wide assortment of media technologies reach into millions of homes all across the world and deliver content on a daily basis. The content that is delivered by global media conglomerates is both standard—that is, the content has common features regardless of which country it is distributed to—and it is idiosyncratic, because it often gets tweaked to conform to regulations and audience interests that are perceived to be unique to a particular country or region.

When we study media as a system consisting of interrelated elements, we are able to see processes and influences on content that otherwise might not be very apparent. We are also able to see how two or more elements have a direct relationship with each other, and how these elements have greater impacts on the media system in some countries than in others. But most of all, we are able to gain a comprehensive overview of how a collection of elements—cultural characteristics, philosophies, regulation, financing, accessibility, and audiences—work together to produce different kinds of general content, news reporting content, and content that is imported or exported.

Conceptualizing a media system as a tree, wherein the parts of a tree match up with certain elements of a media system, helps us to clearly visualize what a media system looks like—especially those "underground" elements that are more difficult to see than the "aboveground" elements. Conceptualizing a media system as a tree brings about imagery that also helps us see how one part of a tree affects an adjacent part, which affects another adjacent part, and so on. Just as the soil feeds vital nutrients to the roots of a tree, cultural characteristics of a country have deep-seated and pronounced effects on the philosophies that emerge to define the purpose of a media system. Major philosophies include authoritarian, libertarian, communist, social responsibility, developmental, and democratic-participant. Philosophies for media systems are translated into media regulations, the most central of which are government or government-related regulations—though other important regulating influences are exerted also by citizen groups, advertisers, audiences, and media organizations. Just as a tree trunk provides a foundation for the branches that rise up into the air, regulation sets the foundational parameters for the ways in which media content is financed, leading to the accessibility of media in a given geographic area—that is, the newspapers, radio frequencies, television channels, and internet web sites that are available. Just as tree branches carry and form leaves into unique patterns, the accessibility of media delivers a unique selection of content to a particular geographic area. Just as some leaves stand out from the others, one type of content that draws heightened attention to itself is news reporting, which offers commentary on both the media system as well as the welfare of society in general. Just as the seeds of a tree carry the potential for content to sprout up in faraway locations, another type of content is that which is exported from a media system in one country, and then imported by media systems in other countries. And just as passersby can come into contact with a tree, audiences can interact with newspapers, radio, television, and the internet. The patterns and habits of the ways that audiences interact with media as they go about their daily routines are profoundly affected by the content that is available, as well as how easy and costly it is to access the content.

UNIQUE ATTRIBUTES OF EACH COUNTRY'S MEDIA SYSTEM

France's media system revolves around a marketplace in which the state is both a regulator of broadcast content and a competitor for broadcast audiences. The French government takes an active role in promoting culture as well as political pluralism in media content. France has an extensive global media reach through its association with former colonies and current territories. France is one of three countries (the others being China and Lebanon) in this book that have regulations setting quotas for how much foreign-language media can be imported, to preserve the stature of French culture and the French language. French media content in both broadcast media and newspapers often contains expressions of art and culture in keeping with a French penchant for beauty.

Sweden's media system revolves around a limited marketplace in which the government plays an active role in promoting opposing political viewpoints and protecting children, as well as limiting violence and maintaining open access to public records. Newspapers are funded to guarantee opposing political viewpoints, whereas Sweden has a limited commercial broadcast marketplace in which public-service radio and television are favorably positioned against private competition, and are financed to provide multiple outlets delivering Swedish cultural programming as well as programming for Finnish-speaking audiences. Because Swedish audiences live in a relatively small country, they are accustomed to regularly consuming imported as well as domestically produced English-language content. Following a societal outlook that the virtues of nature extend to human behavior, everyday Swedish media contain some of the most vivid depictions of nudity, sexuality, and the human body.

The UK's media system revolves around a marketplace in which the government has a strong presence in requiring both commercial and BBC television broadcasters to fulfill rigorous public-service obligations. In this marketplace, multiple BBC radio and television services are steadily positioned against strong commercial competition. The UK has an extensive global reach in the distribution of media content primarily because of an acclimation to the English language by populations in so many parts of the world, as well as the UK's continued relationships with Commonwealth countries and former colonial countries. Especially considering its size, the UK has perhaps the most sophisticated media system out of the eight countries—insofar as it hosts multiple newspaper, radio, television, and internet outlets; its content is widely distributed both domestically and internationally; and policies and regulations governing these outlets, plus detailed research on media audiences, are intricately developed and readily available to the public.

The USA's media system revolves around a robust commercial marketplace in which the government prefers to stay on the sidelines, letting competition have the first chance to set the rules. One area in which the government is actively involved in the marketplace is in restricting nudity and profanity. The reliance on market forces results in a media system that is almost entirely profit driven. As a result, the USA has far more advertising minutage present in radio and television content, and more advertising space in newspaper content, compared to the other countries. The pervasiveness of advertising that results in almost all media forms in the USA significantly shortens and speeds up the other content. The USA media system is the most prolific exporter of both media outlets and media content around the world. Contrarily, the USA does not import much media content from other countries. More typically, the USA imports formats of television shows from other countries, which are then produced domestically so the shows can be modified to suit the perceived tastes of USA audiences.

México's media system revolves around a marketplace in which the government has a strong presence in guaranteeing the dissemination of government information through newspaper, radio, and television content. The government guarantees this presence through licensing stipulations for radio and television broadcasters, and through paid insertions in newspapers. Though México's media system is well-developed, the country itself is in a developmental stage of attempting to address inadequacies in infrastructure, economy, societal welfare, and political democracy—while attempting to move beyond a legacy of government corruption and internal conflicts. Though México's media system operates in a primarily commercial marketplace, the federal government funds diversified content carried on IMER radio stations, whereas the state governments fund public-service content on public television stations.

China's media system revolves around a marketplace in which the government controls almost all operations of newspapers, radio stations, television stations, and internet service providers. The Chinese government is allowing an increasing commercialization of media content resulting in newspapers and broadcasters carrying more advertising. Chinese media are strictly prohibited from criticizing government policies, and from airing foreign content containing Western values deemed to be morally degrading. With the world's largest population, China presents the largest potential domestic media audience.

Ghana's fledgling media system revolves around a marketplace in which the government takes an active interest in guaranteeing that media have the right to free expression, including criticism of the government. Many of the government's regulatory guidelines are aimed at securing democracy, though regulators lack essential resources and enforcement powers to actively implement the regulations. Ghana's media marketplace was previously dominated by state-owned media, but is accommodating the growth of private media. Though both state-owned and private media accept advertising revenue, the lack of capital on the part of vendors as well as the lack of disposable income by the general population has hindered the growth of this method of financing.

Lebanon's media system revolves around a marketplace in which a weak government competes with religious sects and financial interests to regulate the media—a situation that largely results from the ten-year civil war. Both Lebanon's media system and the country as a whole are in a developing stage. In post-civil-war Lebanon, the private sector plays a more active role in the development of the country's media system than the government. However, two areas in which the government plays an active role in regulating media include restricting content that arouses religious or ethnic conflicts, and restricting sexually oriented content that offends traditional morals. Yet, in the context of the Middle East region, Lebanon has one of the most advanced and freest media systems. In Lebanon, there is an abundance of foreign-language content in newspapers, radio, television, and the internet—content that originates not only from Western countries (primarily France, the UK, and the USA), but also from within Lebanon.

FINAL THOUGHTS ABOUT "THE FOREST"
OF MEDIA SYSTEMS

This last section borrows from the tree metaphor one more time, to help us close this book with broader speculations about media systems across the world. As the heading of this section implies, media systems across the world are intertwined with each other in such a way as to produce something akin to a worldwide forest of media systems. In order for us to leave behind the individual observations about media systems that have been made, so that global speculations can be posed, this section addresses universal policy issues that have cut across the chapter discussions. Policy issues are essentially decisions about media operations that either have been deliberately made or have arisen as a result of a country's cultural inclinations or intended philosophies for a media system.

One issue that has reverberated throughout this book involves policy decisions about the extent to which a media system should offer private versus public media. It seems to be a near-universal policy across most countries that newspapers should operate primarily as private media. In contrast, policymaking in most countries regarding broadcast media seems to provide for more of a balance—although rarely an exactly equal balance—between private and public media. One common assumption behind such policymaking is that private broadcast media are thought to be less vulnerable to government influence and more responsive to consumer tastes. However, the idealism of this assumption is countered by observations throughout this book that while private media allow audience members to select content from a range of choices, that range is significantly limited by a number of economic and political factors. An alternate assumption behind such policymaking is that public media are thought to be less vulnerable to government influence and more responsive to the good of society as a whole. However, the idealism of this assumption is countered by the reality that audiences do not have much direct involvement in defining for public broadcasters what kinds of media content serve the good of society as a whole. Policymaking discussions in this area are also complicated by existing models that blur the distinctions between private versus public media—for example, as in the case where private media have public service requirements (such is the case in the UK and the USA), or where public media are permitted to air advertisements (as is the case in France and Ghana). Moreover, as the internet continues to proliferate in the delivery of content that has originated in newspapers and on radio and television, and in the delivery of content that originates on internet web sites, it remains to be seen whether government-related policymakers will implement public funding for the internet, along with regulations stipulating that the internet has to meet yet-to-be-defined standards of public service. In the final analysis, media systems that are dominated by private media will likely be missing certain dimensions of public good, whereas media systems that are dominated by public media will likely be missing certain dimensions of audience entertainment.

A second issue is news reporting as a product, public service, or propaganda. Because news is not a form of fiction like other genres of content, it serves as an authoritative factual description of the events it covers. But as Chapter 10 demonstrated, news reporting in every country embodies an outlook that is endemic to the particular country, and therefore provides a nationalistic tone that often reinforces the righteousness of the given country. Though news reporting in a particular country may be packaged as objective or truthful, in reality it cannot escape the context of the time period in which it is reported, nor the economic, social, and political landscape in which it functions. Depending on how news is positioned within a media system, the following shortcomings may result: News positioned as a product tends to downplay audience betterment because its primary goal is to deliver entertainment that will attract a sizable-enough audience; news positioned as a public service tends to downplay audience desires because its primary goal is to convey information that the audience should know; news positioned as propaganda tends to obscure audience tastes because its primary goal is to deliver interpretations that the government wants the audience to believe. None of these assessments of news is particularly pleasing to acknowledge. Nevertheless, the central point is a critical one—that news reporting serves larger economic and political motives requiring a critically thinking audience to continuously apply skepticism to the information that is delivered, with the understanding that news reporting is largely nationalistic and serves fundamentally to reinforce the integrity of the values of the originating country and the culture in which it is delivered.

A third issue is policy decisions on nudity, sexuality, and profanity. Though all of these concepts are about distinctly different subject matters, in policy discussions about media content they are often grouped together. It is truly amazing and confusing that in some countries nudity and sex between two adults in media content is perceived of as a natural phenomenon but in other countries is perceived of as a degradation of morals. Similarly, it is fascinating how in some countries certain words in media content are considered to be profane, yet in other countries the concept of profanity in any kind of discourse does not seem to exist—let alone the discourse of media content. Policymaking in these areas will continue to be framed by predominant perceptions of morality in the particular country, but will also be affected by the degree to which audiences discover how these subject matters are presented by media content from other countries.

And a fourth issue is policy decisions about violence. Similar to the subject discussed in the last paragraph, it is fascinating how violence in media content is presented so differently. One school of thought—generally followed by the European countries—is that violent content is most appropriate in news coverage because it realistically and appropriately shows the horrors of crime and war. This same school of thought tends to assume that showing violence in fiction-oriented media content has a more gratuitous prupose, and is therefore harmful to society. Another school of thought—generally followed by North American countries—is that violent content is better left to fictitious content, but that across most genres of content, violent content presented in a graphic way should be avoided. This school of thought assumes that showing violence in a close-up camera shot is needlessly offensive—or "gross," as it is sometimes called.

As this book draws to a close, hopefully in the future you will continue to seek to examine media systems of other countries around the world. If you do, perhaps you will decide that certain elements of media systems of other countries are basically very similar. Or perhaps you will decide that certain elements of media systems of other countries are basically very different. Either way, you will probably conclude that every media system has both liberating and constraining qualities. In the end, as a result of reading this book, you likely are persuaded that comparing media from around the world can free you from cultural myopia—that is, interpreting the world solely from the vantage point of the media system of the country in which you are living.

REFERENCES

14th Statistical Survey on the Internet Development in China. (2004, July). Beijing: China Internet Network Information Center (CNNIC).

Albarran, Alan B. (2002). *Management of Electronic Media*. Belmont, CA: Wadsworth/Thompson Learning.

Altschull, J. Herbert. (1984). *Agents of Power: The Role of the News Media in Human Affairs*. New York: Longman.

Arab Ad. (May 2004). Media—Revolution and Pitfalls in the Arab World, p. 6.

Arbitron. (2002). Radio on the Go. How México City Radio Reaches Consumers at Work and in Vehicles. Available at www.arbitron.com/downloadsMexicoPresROGEng.pdf.

Arlidge, John. (March 3, 2002). The Dirty Little Secret That Drives Technology: It's Porn. *Guardian*. Available at www.guardian.co.uk.

Bachman, Kate. (2002, September). Rock Jocks Not to Fade Away. *Mediaweek* 12 (35): 9–109.

Bagdikian, Ben H. (1990). *The Media Monopoly*, 3rd ed. Boston: Beacon.

Battah, Habib. (2004, March 26). Leading Satellite Networks 'Pull the Plug' on Illegal Cable Operators. *Daily Star*, p. 3.

Beech, Hannah. (2000, February 7). Beijing tries to build barriers. Retrieved on April 4, 2002, from www.time.com/time/asia/magazine/2000/0207/asiadotcom.regulation.html.

Brooklyn College. (1999). Chinese cultural studies: Philosophy and religion in China. Retrieved on October 12, 2003, from academic.brooklyn.cuny.edu/core9/phalsall/texts/chinrelg.html.

Browne, Donald R. (1999). *Electronic Media and Industrialized Nations*. Ames: Iowa State University Press.

Budde Comm. (2005). Available at www.buddee.com.au.

Cai, D. and Swartz, B. C. (2002). Perspectives toward the United States in selected newspapers of the People's Republic of China. *Spring 2002 Report for the US China Security Review Commission*.

Central Administration of Press and Publications of P. R. China. (1990). Bao Zhi Guan Li Zhan Xing Gui Ding [The temporary regulations on newspaper management]. Retrieved on April 15, 2004, from www.waterpubl.com.cn/info/InfoDetail.asp?id=358.

Central Administration of Press and Publications of P. R. China. (2003). Guan Yu Zhi Li Bao Kan Tan Pai Shi Shi Xi Ze [The regulations on newspaper subscriptions]. Retrieved on April 14, 2004, from www.china.org.cn/Chinese/zhuanti/baokan/432307.htm.

Centre for the Study of Intelligence. (1997). The Chinese media: More autonomous and diverse—within limits. Retrieved on February 14, 2004, from www.cia.csi/monograph/425050797/1.htm.

Chin, Y. C. (2003). China's regulatory policies on transnational television drama flow. *Media Development* 3.

China Internet Network Information Center. (2004). Available at www.cnnic.cn/en/index.

Co-Regulation of the Media in Europe. (2003). Strasbourg, France: European Audiovisual Observatory.

Collins, Richard, Garnham, Nicholas, and Locksley, Gareth. (1988). *The Economics of Television: The UK Case*. London: Sage.

Compaine, Benjamin M. (1979). *Who Owns the Media?* White Plains, NY: Harmony.

Dajani, Nabil. (1989). The Arab Media: Watchdog or Subservient. In *The Vigilant Press: A Collection of Case Studies, Reports and Papers on Mass Communication, No. 103*. Paris: United Nations Educational Scientific and Cultural Organization (UNESCO).

Dajani, Nabil. (1992). *Disoriented Media in a Fragmented Society: The Lebanese Experience*. Beirut, Lebanon: American University of Beirut Press.

Dajani, Nabil. (December 2003). Disparity between Public Interest and Money and Power (in Arabic). *al-Mustakbal al-Arabi*, no. 250.

Dajani, Nabil. (2001). Lebanese Television: Caught between Government and the Private Sector. In Atkins, Joe (Ed.), *Journalism as a Mission: Ethics and Purpose from an International Perspective*. Ames: Iowa State University Press.

de Beer, Arnold S. and Merrill, John C. (2004). *Global Journalism*. Boston: Allyn and Bacon.

Donald, S. H., Keane, M., and Yin, H. (2002). *Media in China: Consumption, Content, and Crisis*. London: RoutledgeCurzon.

Enzensberger, H. M. (1970). Constituents of a Theory of the Media. *New Left Review* 64: 13–36.

Evening News (May 13, 2004). "No Apology Says Anlo Afiadenyigba Chief," p. 1.

Fallows, James. (1996). *Breaking the News: How the Media Undermine American Democracy*. New York: Pantheon.

FCC Policy Statement. (April 6, 2001). Available at www.fcc.gov/eb/orders/2001/fcc01090.html.

Fletcher, Victoria. (2003, May 13). Package Holidays Lose Out to DIY Deals. *London Evening Standard*, p. 8.

Foss, Sonja K., Foss, Karen A., and Trapp, Robert. (1991). *Contemporary Perspectives on Rhetoric*. Prospect Heights, IL: Waveland.

Foster, William, Goodman, Seymour, Osiakwan, Eric, and Bernstein, Adam. (2004). Global Diffusion of the Internet IV: The Internet in Ghana. *Communications of the Association for Information Systems* 13(38): 1–47.

France. (2003). Melbourne, Australia: Lonely Planet.

Frederick, Howard H. (1993). *Global Communication and International Relations*. Belmont, CA: Wadsworth.

Gannon, Martin J. (2001). *Understanding Global Cultures*. Thousand Oaks, CA: Sage.

Garnham, Nicholas. (1990). *Capitalism and Communication*. London: Sage.

Gerbner, George, Mowlana, Hamid, and Nordenstreng, Kaarle (Eds.). (1993). *The Global Media Debate: Its Rise, Fall, and Renewal*. Norwood, NJ: Ablex.

363

Gershon, Richard A. (2001). *Telecommunications Management*. Mahwah, N.J: Lawrence Erlbaum.

Golding, Peter, and Harris, Phil (Ed.). (1997). *Beyond Cultural Imperialism*. London: Sage.

Gunter, Barrie. (1997). *Measuring Bias on Television*. Luton, UK: Luton University Press.

Hale, Briony. (2003, June 9). In Search of Profitable Connections, *BBC News Online*, available at http://news.bbc.co.uk/1/hi/business/2974418.stm.

Hayden, Anders, (2003). Europe's Work-Time Alternatives, pp. 204–205, *Take Back Your Time*, by John de Graaf (ed.). San Francisco: Berrett-Kohler Publishers.

Hegel, Georg Wilhelm Friederich. (1956). *The Philosophy of History*. Trans. Jay Sibree. New York: Dover.

Hegel, G. W. F. *The Philosophy of Right*, Trans. T. M. Knox. New York: Oxford University Press, 1967. Translation of: *Grundlinen der Philosophie des Rechts*.

Henley, Jon. (2004, March 6). Gloves Come Off in a Very French Row over Defence of the Language. *Guardian*, p. 3.

Herman, Edward S. and Chomsky, Noam. (1988). *Manufacturing Consent*. New York: Pantheon.

Hester, Al. (1990). The Collection and Flow of World News. In John C. Merrill (Ed.), *Global Journalism: A Survey of International Communication,* 2nd ed. New York: Longman.

Hester, Al. (1973, Winter). Theoretical Considerations in Predicting Volume and Direction of International Information Flow. *Gazette* 19: 239–247.

Hilliard, Robert L. and Keith, Michael. (1996). *Global Broadcasting Systems*. Boston: Focal.

Hocking, William Ernest. (1947). *Freedom of the Press, a Framework of Principle. A Report from the Commission on Freedom of the Press*. Chicago: University of Chicago Press.

Hofstede, Geert. (2001). *Culture's Consequences: Comparing Values, Behaviors, Institutions, and Organizations Across Nations*. Thousand Oaks, CA: Sage.

Hofstede, Gert Han, Pedersen, Paul B., and Hofstede, Geert. (2002). *Exploring Culture: Exercises, Stories and Synthetic Cultures*. Yarmouth, ME: Intercultural.

Hutchins Report on Commission on Freedom of the Press. (1947). *A Free and Responsible Press*. Chicago: The University of Chicago Press.

Infinity Broadcasting Corporation of Pennsylvania, 2FCC Rccl2705, 1987, available at www.fcc.gov/eb/Orders/2004/DA-04-387A/html.

Information International, Lebanon. (2004). http://www.information-international.com/sri.php.

InternetWorldStats. (2004, October 23). Available at www.internetworldstats.com.

Internet-World-Stats. (2003). www.internetworldstats.com.

Jensen, Klaus Bruhn. (1987, Winter). News as Ideology: Economic Statistics and Political Ritual in Television Network News. *Journal of Communication*, 8–27.

Jiang, Y. P. (2002). Zhong Guo Wang Luo Mei Ti Xian Zhuang Fen Xi He Zhan Wang [The analysis of online media in China]. Retrieved on April 15, 2004, from www.cddc.net/shownews.asp? newsid=1997.

Kamalipour, Yahya R. (2002). *Global Communication*. Belmont, CA: Wadsworth.

Kamalipour, Yahya R., and Snow, Nancy. (1999). *Images of the U.S. Around the World*. Albany: State University of New York Press.

Kamalipour, Yahya R. (2004). *War, Media, and Propaganda: A Global Perspective*. Lanham, MD: Rowman and Littlefield.

Knightley, Philip. (2003, April 2). The Battle for Our Hearts and Minds. *Guardian*.

Krippendorff, Klaus. (1980). *Content Analysis: An Introduction to Its Methodology*. Beverly Hills, CA: Sage.

Kuhn, Raymond. (1995). *The Media in France*. Cornwall, UK: T. J. Press.

Lambeth, Edmund B. (1995). In John C. Merrill (Ed.), *Global Journalism: A Survey of International Communication,* 2nd ed. New York: Longman.

Lee, C. C. (2003). *Chinese Media, Global Contexts*. London: RoutledgeCurzon.

Lerner, Daniel. (1958). *The Passing of Traditional Society: Modernizing the Middle East*. Glencoe, IL: Free Press.

Leow, Jason. (2004, April 10). China's media shake-up. *Straits Times*, p. A2.

Liddle, Rod (May 7, 2003). Sod off, madge. *The Guardian*. G2, p. 5.

Lindlof, Thomas R. (1987). *Natural Audiences: Qualitative Research of Media Uses and Effects*. Norwood, NJ: Ablex.

Liu, Song-shi. (2003). War on corruption catches journalists in crossfire. Retrieved on May 21, 2004, from www.atimes.com/.

Locke, John. (1894, originally published 1689). *An Essay Concerning Human Understanding*. Oxford, England: Clarendon.

Locke, John. (1993, originally published 1698). *Two Treatises of Government*. London: J. M. Dent.

Lonely Planet. (2003). Available at http://www.lonelyplanet.com/destinations/europe/sweden.

Machiavelli, Niccolo. (1992, originally published 1515). *The Prince*. Trans. W. K. Marriot. London: Everyman's Library.

Marx, Karl. (1967, originally published 1848). *The Communist Manifesto*. Harmondsworth, UK: Penguin.

MacBride, Sean, et al. (1980). *Many Voices, One World*. London: Kogan Page.

McKenzie, Robert. (2002). Contradictions in U.S. Law on Obscenity and Indecency in Broadcasting: A Bleeping Critique. *Feedback* 43(3): 28–34.

McKenzie, Robert. (1999). Images of the U.S. as Perceived by U.S. Students in France. In Yahya R. Kamalipour (Ed.), *Images of the U.S. Around the World*. Albany: State University of New York Press.

McLuhan, Marshall and Powers, Bruce (contributor). (1992). *The Global Village: Transformations in World Life and Media in the 21st Century*. Oxford: Oxford University Press.

McLuhan, Marshall. (1964). *Understanding Media*. New York: McGraw-Hill.

McPhail, Thomas L. (2002). *Global Communication: Theories, Stakeholders, and Trends*. Boston: Allyn and Bacon.

McQuail, Denis and Siune, Karen (Eds.). (1986). *New Media Politics: Comparative Perspectives in Western Europe*. London: Sage.

Medhurst, Martin J. and Benson, Thomas W. (Eds.) (1984). *Rhetorical Dimensions of Media: A Critical Casebook*. Dubuque, IA: Kendall/Hunt.

Meng, J. (2003). Shen Du Tou Shi: Da Zheng He Zhong De Zhong Guo Dian Shi Ye [China's TV in the process of a great integration]. Retrieved on April 15, 2004, from http://cjr.zjol.com.cn/gb/node2/node26108/node30205/node194994/node195002/userobject15ai1926375.html.

Merrit, Davis "Buzz." (1998). *Public Journalism and Public Life.* Mahwah, NJ: Lawrence Erlbaum.

Meyer, Philip (1987). *Ethical Journalism.* New York: Longman.

Mill, John Stuart. (1982). *On Liberty.* Harmondsworth, UK: Penguin.

Miller v. California. (1973). 413 U.S. 15, 24.

Min, D. H. (2002). Zhong Guo Wang Luo Mei Ti Fa Zhan Bian Nian (1995–2001) [The development history of China's online media (1995–2001)]. Retrieved on April 15, 2004, from http://it.sohu.com/37/67/article204646737.shtml.

Ministry of Information Industry. (2000). Hu Lian Wang Xin Xi Fu Wu Guan Li Ban Fa [The administration rules on the Internet content providers]. Retrieved on April 15, 2004, from www.mii.gov.cn/mii/hyzw/hygl/hlwxx.htm.

Mohammadi, Ali. (1997). *International Communication and Globalization.* London: Sage.

Moran, Albert. (1998). *Copycat Television: Globalisation, Program Formats and Cultural Identity.* Luton, UK: University of Luton Press.

Mowlana, Hamid. (1996). *Global Communication in Transition: The End of Diversity?* Thousand Oaks, CA: Sage.

Musa, Mohammed. (1997). From Optimism to Reality. In Golding, Peter and Harris, Phil (Eds.). *Beyond Cultural Imperialism.* London: Sage.

Nerone, John C. (Ed.). (1995). *Last Rights: Revisiting Four Theories of the Press.* Urbana: University of Illinois Press.

Nielsen NetRatings. (2004). Available at www.nielsennetratings.com.

Official Airline Guide. (2003). Data provided by Danielle Molder, Sales and Marketing Development Director.

Paradise, James, F. (2003). *Making Sense of China's New Media Environment.* Hong Kong: CMM Intelligence.

Pew Internet and American Life Project. (2004). Available at www.pewinternet.org.

Pierce, David. (May 13, 2004). Taxes: All Agree Something Has to Change. *Pocono Record* p. A1–A2.

Plato. (1975). *The Laws.* Trans. Trevor J. Saunders. London: Penguin.

Plato. (1974). *The Republic.* Translated by G. M. A Grube. Indianapolis, IN: Hackett Publishing Company.

Plato. (360 BC). *The Statesman.* Translated by Benjamin Jowerl. *In the Dialogues of Plato,* London: Oxford University Press.

Portilla, Jorge. (1984). *Fenomenologia del Relajo.* Mexico City: Crea.

Quainoo, Samuel E. (Ed.). (2004). *Africa Through Ghanaian Lenses.* Binghamton, NY: Vestal International.

Quarterly Report on Informal Consumer Inquiries and Complaints Released. (2003, November 20). Washington, DC: Federal Communications Commission.

Raboy, Marc (Ed.). (2002). *Global Media Policy in the New Millennium.* Luton, UK: University of Luton Press.

Radio Times. (April 2, 2003). p. 87.

Reporters without Borders. (2003). Study reported at www.peacehall.com/news/gb/english/2003/11/200311220239.shtml.

Rivers, William L., Schramm, Wilbur, and Christians, Clifford G. (1980). *Responsibility in Mass Communications.* New York: Harper and Row.

Rosen, Jay. (1996). *Getting the Connections Right: Public Journalism and the Troubles in the Press.* New York: Twentieth Century Fund.

Rosen, Jay and Merritt, Davis, Jr. (1994). *Public Journalism: Theory and Practice.* Dayton, OH: Kettering Foundation.

Rosen, Jay and Taylor, Paul. (1992). *The New News v. The Old News.* New York: Twentieth Century Fund.

Rostow, Walt Whitman. (1971). *The Stages of Economic Growth: A Non-Communist Manifesto.* Cambridge: Cambridge University Press.

Scandinavian Europe. (2003). Victoria, Australia: Lonely Planet.

Schiller, Herbert I. (1996). *Culture Inc.* New York: Oxford University Press.

Schiller, Herbert I. (1976). *Communication and Cultural Domination.* New York: International Arts and Science Press.

Schramm, W. (1994). *Mass Media and National Development.* Stanford, CA: Stanford University Press.

Seib, Philip. (2002). *The Global Journalist.* Oxford, UK: Rowman and Littlefield.

Siebert, Frederick S., Theodore Peterson, and Wilbur Schramm. (1963). *Four Theories of the Press.* Urbana: University of Illinois Press.

Silvia, Tony. (2001). *Global News: Perspectives on the Information Age.* Ames: Iowa State University Press.

Sinofile.net. (2003). *Commercially-oriented Newspapers Facing Challenges in the Market.* Retrieved on 10 November, from www.sinofile.net/Saiweng/swsite.nsf/FullStory?readform &BFDC0BFB3C18B54F48256D5C002752D8.

Smith, Adam. (1991, originally published 1776). *The Wealth of Nations.* London: Everyman's Library.

Spink, Amanda and Jansen, Bernard J. (2004). *Web Search: Public Searching of the Web.* New York: Springer.

State Administration of Radio, Film and Television. (1997). Guang Bo Dian Shi Guan Li Tiao Li [The administration rules on radio and television]. Retrieved on April 15, 2004, from www.waterpubl.com.cn/info/InfoDetail.asp?id=358.

State Administration of Radio, Film and Television. (2003). Guan Yu Cu Jin Guang Bo Ying Shi Chan Ye Fa Zhan De Yi Jian [The approaches of encouraging the development of radio, television, and films]. Retrieved on April 10, 2004, from www.sarft.gov.cn/manange/publishfile/21/1568.html.

State Administration of Radio, Film and Television. (2003). Guang Bo Dian Shi Guang Gao Bo Fang Guan Li Zhan Xing Ban Fa [The temporary regulations on advertisements on radio and television]. Retrieved on March 22, 2004, from www.sarft.gov.cn/manage/publishfile/20/1006.html.

State Council of P. R. China. (2001). Chu Ban Guan Li Tiao Li [The administration rules on publication]. Retrieved on April 15, 2004, from http://press.gapp.gov.cn/web/baokcb/2001-12-12?3248.htm.

Stevenson, Robert L. (1994). *Global Communication in the Twenty-First Century.* New York: Longman.

Su, Z. W. and Ding, J. J. (2003). *Asian Communication & Media Studies* (Ya Zhou Chuan Mei Yan Jiu). Beijing: Beijing Broadcasting Institute Press.

Tai Chi Academy. (2003). Introduction to Chinese medicine. Retrieved on October 12, 2003, from www.taijichinesemedicine.com/TCM2.htm.

Tehranian, Majid. (1999). *Global Communication and World Politics*. Boulder, CO: Lynne Rienner.

Temin, Jonathan and Smith, Daniel A. (2002). Media Matters: Evaluating the Role of the Media in Ghana's 2000 Elections. *African Affairs* 101: 585–605.

Travel Industry Association of America. (2002). Available at www.tia.org/Press/pressrec.asp? Item=242.

Tunstall, Jeremy. (1977). *The Media Are American*. New York: Columbia University Press.

United Kingdom English for the American Novice. (1995). Available at www.hps.com/~tpg/ukdict/ ukdict-8.html

University of Virginia Geospatial and Statistical Data Center. (1998). *United States Historical Census Data Browser*. ONLINE. University of Virginia. Available: http://fisher.lib.virginia.edu/census/ [July 15, 2003].

Volkmer, Ingrid. (1999). *News in the Global Sphere: A Study of CNN and Its Impact on Global Communication*. Luton, UK: University of Luton Press.

Wagner, Thomas. (2003, June 22). Associated Press Story. *Pocono Record*, p. A8.

Wang, Yi Lian Mei. (2003, 24 September). MTV Quan Qiu Yin Yue Tai. *NetEase.com*. Retrieved on March 28, 2004, from http://corp.163.com/corpnews/editor/030924/030924_1545.html.

Weber, Ian. (2003). Civic participation in China? Reinventing authoritarian control in interactive online news. A paper presented to the Digital News, Social Change and Globalization conference in Hong Kong SAR, December 11–12, 2003.

Weber, Ian. (2004). Digital broadcasting in China: Issues, challenges and opportunities. *New Media & Society* [Forthcoming].

Weber, Ian and Lu, J. (2004, March). Handing over China's internet to the corporations. *International Institute for Asian Studies Newsletter* 33(9).

Weber, Ian. (2003). Localizing the global: Successful strategies for selling television programs to China. *Gazette* 65(3): 273–290.

Weber, Ian. (2002a). Reconfiguring the control and propaganda modalities: A case study of Shanghai's television industry. *Journal of Contemporary China* 11(30): 53–75.

Weber, Ian. (2002b). Shanghai Baby: Negotiating youth self-identity in urban China. *Social Identities: Journal for the Study of Race, Nation and Culture* 8(2): 347–368.

Weber, Ian. (2001). Shanghai youth's strategic mobilization of individualistic values: Constructing cultural identity in the age of spiritual civilization. *Intercultural Communication Studies* 10(2): 23–46.

Weber, Ian, Chang, M., and Liu, X. (2004). Comparing media shaping of digital television in China and Britain: A content analysis. *Asian Communication Media Forum*.

Wimmer, Roger D. and Dominick, Joseph R. (2003). *Mass Media Research: An Introduction*. Belmont, CA: Wadsworth.

World Book Encyclopedia. (2003). Chicago: Worldbook.

World Factbook. (2004, 2003, 2002). Available at www.cia.gov/cia/publications/factbook/geos/ us.html#People.

World Press Trends. (2003, 2002). Paris: The World Association of Newspapers.

World Tourism Organization. (2002). *World Tourism in 2002: Better Than Expected*. Available at www.world-tourism.org/newsroom.

World Tourism Organization. (2002). *Tourism Highlights 2002*. Available at www.world-tourism.org.

Yu, G. M. (2001). Wo Guo Chuan Mei Ye Fa Zhan De Guan Jian He Wen Ti [The keys and problems in the development of media industry in China]. Retrieved on April 14, 2004, from http://cjr.zjol.com.cn/gb/node2/node26108/node30205/node177211/user.

INDEX